The False Cause

The False Cause

Fraud, Fabrication, and White Supremacy in Confederate Memory

ADAM H. DOMBY

University of Virginia Press

CHARLOTTESVILLE AND LONDON

University of Virginia Press
© 2020 by the Rector and Visitors of the University of Virginia
All rights reserved
Printed in the United States of America on acid-free paper

First published 2020

9 8 7 6 5 4 3 2 1

Library of Congress Cataloging-in-Publication Data

Names: Domby, Adam H., author.
Title: The false cause : fraud, fabrication, and white supremacy in Confederate memory /
    Adam H. Domby.
Description: Charlottesville : The University of Virginia Press, 2020. | Includes bibliographi-
    cal references and index.
Identifiers: LCCN 2019024406 (print) | LCCN 2019024407 (ebook) |
    ISBN 9780813943763 (hardcover) | ISBN 9780813943770 (epub)
Subjects: LCSH: Soldiers' monuments—Moral and ethical aspects—Southern States. | White
    supremacy movements—United States—History. | United States—History—Civil War,
    1861–1865—Monuments—Moral and ethical aspects. | United States—Race relations—
    History—19th century. | United States—Race relations—
    History—20th century. | United States—Historiography.
Classification: LCC E645 .D66 2020 (print) | LCC E645 (ebook) | DDC 320.56/909—dc23
LC record available at https://lccn.loc.gov/2019024406
LC ebook record available at https://lccn.loc.gov/2019024407

Cover art: Confederate Soldiers' & Sailors' Monument, Libby Hill Park, Richmond, VA, 1894
(Shutterstock.com/Felix Lipov)

For Matthew and Eli

Contents

The False Cause

Introduction

On August 20, 2018, the night before classes began at the University of North Carolina at Chapel Hill (UNC), hundreds of protesters gathered in front of a 105-year-old Confederate monument nicknamed "Silent Sam" to demand its removal. Four large banners masked the statue from view. One called "for a world without white supremacy," while another emblazoned with "Not One More" listed victims of racial violence. A small number of counterprotesters, some of whom had ties to neo-Nazi and other white supremacist organizations, scuffled with the activists.

Though the rally was nominally in support of history graduate student Maya Little, who in April protested the monument by pouring paint and blood on it, organizers had another purpose, unbeknownst to most. A few of the leaders had planned ahead, using the large banners blocking Silent Sam to hide their preparations to topple the statue. A rope was attached to the monument, and around 9:30 p.m., students pulled—and down came Sam. Ripped from his place of prominence at the entrance to campus, the bronze man was placed in storage as university administrators wrung their hands. The ensuing debates around what to do with the fallen monument ultimately led to the resignation of UNC's chancellor and the removal of the statue's base in January 2019. While the statue's ultimate fate remains undecided as of February 2019, it is clear that the local community does not want the monument returned.[1]

This distaste for the monument did not form overnight. In 2003, when UNC professor Gerald Horne called for Sam to be pulled down, the university dismissed the idea out of hand. But the next fifteen years saw a shift, and between August 2017 and December 2018, at least nineteen UNC departments passed resolutions calling for the removal of the statue. Faculty in numerous departments signed public letters supporting protesters. The governor, the mayor of Chapel Hill, and eventually—due to pressure from protesters—even the UNC chancellor called for removal of the monument. This shift in opinion was extraordinary: In 2012, activists had asked for contextualization of the statue, worrying that a request for removal would be too extreme to garner serious consideration. Protesters six years later rejected contextualization out of hand.[2] What changed?

Several factors led Chapel Hill residents to connect Confederate monuments with white supremacy. Foremost, the national conversation about such symbols changed after white supremacists' terrorist attacks in Charleston and Charlottesville in 2015 and 2017, respectively. By 2018, many Americans had realized there were deep connections between Confederate monuments and white supremacy—connections that went beyond the causes of the Civil War. This was not a new discovery to historians—but the scholarly consensus on the topic reached the public in fresh ways. While the murder of black churchgoers in Charleston focused attention on Confederate symbols, the events in Charlottesville, where neo-Nazis and other hate groups gathered in support of a monument to Robert E. Lee, centered attention specifically on monuments and how they drew white supremacists. Most Chapel Hill residents disliked having a magnet that attracted Nazis to their community, no matter what it stood for.

But the groundwork for tearing down Silent Sam had been laid even earlier. In 2011, two events changed the debate locally. The first was the formation of the Real Silent Sam Coalition, a group of activist students and community members who felt that UNC needed to address its problematic racial history. These activists and the cohort that followed them would educate the public about the ties between white supremacy and Confederate monuments. The second was the publicization of the original dedication speech given by Confederate veteran Julian Carr. Published in a *Daily Tar Heel* letter to the editor, excerpts from the address provided activists with a powerful talking point to counter claims that the monument had nothing to do with race. Carr's own words, discussed more fully in this book's first two chapters, not only explicitly tied the monument to celebrating white supremacy but also lauded racial violence, including the speaker's horse-whipping of an unnamed African American woman "until her skirt hung in shreds."[3]

When I first published Carr's words in the *Daily Tar Heel* in 2011, I had hoped to teach a few people about the Jim Crow South. I did not realize how activists and other scholars would use the speech to shift the debate around the monument. Activists publicized the speech and disseminated additional historical research to educate the public through op-eds, protest signs, poetry readings, and speeches. By 2017, almost every news article published about the monument quoted the racist dedication speech. For anyone following the story, it has become impossible to deny that the monument had at least some ties to white supremacy without willfully ignoring evidence. As public opinion shifted, the monument's location in Chapel Hill became untenable. Sam ceased to represent the values of the community.

Though some decried removing Silent Sam as "sanitizing history" or "erasing the past," the actual narrative of the past that Sam was designed to propagate was never accurate in the first place. The statue was supposed to teach future generations a whitewashed past that covered distasteful facts with fabricated memories. Indeed, Carr's speech was not just racist but also filled with deceit. A false past, premised in part upon exaggerations, fraud, and invented stories, provided ideological support for white supremacy during the Jim Crow era.

This book examines the connections between lies, historical memory, and white supremacy. The collective historical memory propagated by Carr and other Confederate veterans—called the "Lost Cause" narrative—celebrated the Confederacy and its soldiers despite their defeat on the battlefield. Aspects of this narrative, championed by Confederate veterans and their heirs, remain widely accepted today. This book details how white supremacy, fraud, and fabricated memories have fundamentally shaped how Americans, especially white southerners, recalled the past. Lies and falsehoods influenced American understandings of the cause of the war, the military prowess of Confederate soldiers, the level of dissent across the Civil War South, the frequency and causes of desertion, the nature of slavery, and the role of racism in American history. Moreover, at the turn of the twentieth century, a Lost Cause narrative celebrating white supremacy became a crucial rhetorical tool for white North Carolinians in their efforts to justify segregation, disenfranchisement, and racial discrimination. As one historian has argued, this narrative "provided a foundation on which southerners built the Jim Crow system."[4] The devastating interplay of white supremacy and false memories of the past during the late nineteenth and early twentieth centuries is the focus of this book. The invented narratives propagated during the Jim Crow era not only continue to exist but still serve to perpetuate racial inequality.

There is a difference between how historians and the public understand the past. For the purposes of this book, "History—what trained historians do—is a reasoned reconstruction of the past rooted in research."[5] When scholars turn their attention to the ways in which the public recalls and commemorates the past, however, they are studying historical memory. Personal memories of the Civil War were written down, disseminated, and molded into coherent narratives. Americans who had not fought, even those not yet born, thus learned a collective memory of the past—an understanding of how we got where we are. The construction of a collective historical memory involves forgetting inconvenient elements of the past and creating a coherent narrative out of anecdotes, interpretations, and storylines in order to give meaning to events. Of course, no two individuals view the past in exactly the same manner. Still, certain tropes, themes, beliefs, and even some anecdotes are pervasive, if not hegemonic, within the various understandings of the past that individuals within any given group hold.

Historians often envision Civil War memory as a set of competing master narratives or interpretations held by different groups of Americans. David Blight identified three narratives in his influential *Race and Reunion,* though other scholars sometimes use four. The narratives that arose after the war can be roughly categorized as (1) the Lost Cause, (2) Emancipationist Memory, (3) the Unionist Cause, and (4) southern Unionist Memory. These narratives, which often contradicted and countered each other, tended to be promoted, respectively, by former Confederates, African Americans, northern whites, and southern white anti-Confederate dissenters. With few exceptions, the Unionist memory largely died off and has often been overlooked by scholars.[6] Though this book focuses on the Lost Cause memory, specifically the one crafted in North Carolina during the early twentieth century, white Unionist and African American countermemories also play significant roles in the story.

Few aspects of any of these narratives were actually universally held within any given group; each version of the past was colored by local and regional variations. Among Lost Cause proponents, for example, there were competing narratives over which state was most loyal to the Confederacy. North Carolina—like all the former Confederate states—had its own version of the Lost Cause, defined by its unique postwar politics and wartime experience.

But even in the face of local particularities, several central tenets of the Lost Cause were embraced by many, if not most, white southerners in the century after the Civil War. First, the Confederacy's cause was noble and just, and the war was fundamentally about states' rights, not slavery. Second, slavery was benevolent and slaves content in their station, so much so that the Civil War and Reconstruction upset a natural racial hierarchy. Third, Confederates were among the greatest soldiers in history, and they were only defeated due to the Union's superior manpower and resources. These tenets led to the conclusion that instead of being remembered as traitors, Confederates should be recalled as heroic defenders of American principles. This memory of the past offered a useful tool for politicians wanting to justify and defend white supremacy in the Jim Crow South.

In North Carolina, the primary focus of this book, white supremacist politicians "needed" the Lost Cause perhaps more than in any other state.

Historians of memory rarely focus on North Carolina, yet Democrats in the state had the greatest need for a unifying narrative to attract white voters, and the state had the most to forget about the war.[7] North Carolina's Confederate reputation was one that did not always shine. It was the second-to-last state to secede, having voted against secession in a popular referendum on February 28, 1861. Only the firing on Fort Sumter, Lincoln's call for volunteers, and the secession of Virginia (which left North Carolina isolated) prompted the state's legislature to secede. The actual population never endorsed secession; in fact, many North Carolinians actively opposed the Confederacy.[8] Indeed, North Carolinians were reluctant to enlist in the Confederate army and the state had more conscripts and draft exemptions than any other. While not necessarily a sign of anti-Confederate sentiment, an estimated twenty-four thousand North Carolinians deserted from Confederate units during the course of the war, more deserters than from any other state. Additionally, an estimated ten thousand white and five thousand black North Carolinians enlisted in the United States military.[9]

For much of the war, North Carolina was peripheral to the main campaigns. In 1862, Union forces invaded the state from the coast, but that front remained a sideshow to the conflict in Virginia. The Union presence along the coast provided an escape route for fugitive slaves and white dissenters, and both African American and white Unionists aided the US army. Deserters and draft dodgers forced the Confederate high command to send frontline troops to suppress dissent in the Piedmont, while Unionist sentiment led to intracommunity strife in the mountains. In the final months of the war, as the Confederacy collapsed, more of the state experienced Union invasion. Fort Fisher, one of the last strategically important coastal forts held by Confederates, fell to a Union assault in January 1865. In March, William Tecumseh Sherman's troops entered the state from the south, while George Stoneman's cavalry invaded from the west, his troops advancing as far east as Winston-Salem before the war ended. By late April, when in the largest surrender of the war Johnston capitulated to Sherman near Durham, Confederates controlled only a fragment of the state.[10] North Carolina's lack of key battlefields and poor military performance meant former Confederates in the state had much to paper over with fabricated memories.

If Confederates struggled to unite the North Carolina home front during the war, white Democratic control of North Carolina was also weaker in the late nineteenth century than in many other southern states. North Carolina's biracial Republican Party had more white supporters than that of any other state in the former Confederacy, threatening the hegemonic control of white supremacists. Indeed, while most southern state governments remained securely in white Democratic hands for over fifty years after Reconstruction, North Carolina's biracial Fusion movement returned Republicans and African Americans to positions of power as part of a winning coalition in the 1890s before a series of white supremacist campaigns of terror, race riots, intimidation, cheating, and unapologetic appeals to racism returned Democrats to power. To ensure no further threats to white political control, Democrats amended the Reconstruction-era constitution in 1900 to functionally disenfranchise nearly all African Americans in the state. Disenfranchisement alone was not enough, however, and was accompanied by efforts to attract white support. Due to the long-standing division among white North Carolinians, a fabricated collective memory in which the state's whites had always been united by race became central to the rise of Jim Crow in North Carolina and its maintenance during the first half of the twentieth century.[11] This false history obscured a tradition of biracial cooperation in an effort to keep whites and blacks from reuniting politically. Jim Crow leaders used appeals to white racial solidarity to trump the reality of shared economic interest that cut across the color line.

How we believe the past played out is crucially connected to our identities, which in turn drives how we act in the future. As historian Fitzhugh Brundage argues, "Cultural remembering forges identity, justifies privilege, and sustains cultural norms," and memory is "the product of intentional creation" to achieve specific ends.[12] The identity of white southerners in the postwar South—which "justified segregation and disenfranchisement"—was heavily based on a narrative of the past.[13] Other historians have shown that terrible crimes against humanity can be committed by "unifying" a group "around what is effectively a false or skewed version of their history." For the Jim Crow South, the Lost Cause served as part of what one historian calls "a carefully fabricated version of southern history" that justified racial discrimination.[14] The ties between memory and white supremacy have proven impossible to ignore because, since its inception, the Lost Cause's "very existence depended upon dehumanizing a group of people."[15]

The Lost Cause vision of the past was selective and used for racist ends, and large parts of it were also false. While neither history nor memory can ever be entirely objective, memory, unlike history, is not bound by facts, sources, or evidence. The gap between what actually happened and what society recalls is often a vast chasm. Additionally, memory, both historical and individual, evolves and is not reliant upon research as much as it is upon culture and the needs of the present. C. Vann Woodward pointed out in 1951 that "one of the most significant inventions of the New South was the 'Old South,'" referring to how remembrances of the antebellum and Civil War eras were constructed and used to sustain the postwar South's society and culture.[16] By 1900, much of what white southerners, especially former Confederates, recalled about the Civil War era went beyond "selective remembrance" and entered the realm of "pure fabrication."[17] The Lost Cause narrative, in short, relied upon numerous falsehoods large and small.

The Lost Cause's most obvious lie is its account of the war's causes. Historians have shown that by the early twentieth century, Confederate memory proponents reframed the war as a conflict over states' rights instead of slavery. After the war, southern whites replaced a slaveholders' republic with "a newly revised, newly remembered Confederacy—a Confederacy that pretended to have fought a heroic struggle not for slavery but for liberty, defined as the right of states to self-determination."[18] This allowed Confederates to be recalled not as traitors but as noble patriots fighting to defend a set of American principles that survived the war, despite defeat on the battlefield. With the overturn of Reconstruction and a myth that the war had been over states' rights, the Confederate war effort appeared to not have been in vain. Indeed, the Lost Cause narrative required losing the war's actual cause from the story so that former Confederates could claim a victory.

In addition to a new gallant cause, this narrative required a legacy of valiant military deeds. The Lost Cause presented Confederate soldiers as the greatest in human history, warriors who only lost the war due to the overwhelming resources of the North. While many Confederate soldiers fought well, those who failed to be fully committed to the Confederate cause still needed to be recalled as volunteers fighting to the last. A military record that was anything less than stellar would not serve the needs of Confederate veterans during the Jim Crow era. In "fabricating a history" white men "elevated their own deeds during the war and their efforts to redeem the South afterward."[19] As such, Confederate mythmakers excised the memory of southern dissenters, Unionists, deserters, draft dodgers, and even ambivalent southerners from their retelling of the war.

Loyal whites were crucial, but the Lost Cause also depended on a memory of faithful slaves and a benevolent vision of the "peculiar institution." Former Confederates did not want slavery recalled as the brutal, extractive system premised upon violence that, in fact, it was. By depicting the antebellum era as idyllic, race problems in the Jim Crow South could be attributed to emancipation, Reconstruction, or supposed northern interference. In essence, Confederate memory makers argued, segregation and disenfranchisement sought to return the world to its proper order, and the racial violence of the turn-of-the-century South was caused not by virulent racism but by misguided efforts to provide African Americans an equality they neither desired nor deserved.[20]

The construction of a coherent Lost Cause narrative was not always a deliberate process. At times, it was an organic one built on minor exaggerations and fabrications woven into daily life. Some stories were created to serve a specific purpose for an individual, often for monetary gain; others, to garner social capital; and others still to aid in political mobilization. Some individuals rewrote their wartime experiences to obtain pensions, frequently committing fraud. Politicians improved their war records to attract voters. In their efforts to craft a usable past, memory makers created, at times out of thin air, stories that served contemporary needs. These tales did not just reflect what was expected by the dominant storylines of the war; they contributed to the creation of a master narrative. While historians have addressed the larger inaccuracies of the Lost Cause's main tenets—for instance, the centrality of slavery to secession—they have spent less time uncovering a network of smaller fabrications that underpinned the larger Lost Cause myths about the South.

It should surprise no one that people lied and groups recalled the past inaccurately. Historical memory is constructed from selective remembering, targeted focus, exaggeration, and, this book argues, outright lies. From the Cardiff Giant to the Virginia Dare Stones, American history is full of attempts to fabricate the past, often in pursuit of money or fame. Hoaxes can play upon existing aspects of ideology and identity by manipulating expectations, and thus lies can tell historians a great deal about culture.[21] French scholar Pierre Nora explained that memory "only accommodates those facts that suit it," but he might have added that memory can make up false details that suit it as well.[22] The Lost Cause, like all collective memories, involved aspects of the past being "willfully recalled and deliberately forgotten."[23] But in addition to lies of omission, outright fraud and the creation of events and entire people out of thin air played a role in the formation of the Lost Cause. These lies helped shape understandings of the past that affected Americans' identities. From the men who committed pension fraud to the leading Confederate veterans who rewrote the reasons for the war in monument dedication speeches, North Carolina's Lost Cause provides an excellent example of the role of fabrication, as opposed to mere selective forgetting, in historical memory, demonstrating the terrible impact lies have on a society.

While some might object to the use of the word *lie*, as it implies intent to deceive (in which case *falsehood* and *fabrication* still remain appropriate words), I use the term where there was clear intent when these fabrications were created. These lies were often passed on and repeated by others who may not have realized the truth or simply did not care. A combination of purposeful lying, unquestioningly accepting tales that fit into an expected or useful framework, and unknowingly spreading falsehoods contributed to the strength of the Lost Cause.

Often, those propagating fictions should have known better. Many of these tall tales and inaccurate interpretations were called out by observers, both white and black. As Ethan Kytle and Blain Roberts have pointed out, during Reconstruction the Lost Cause "functioned as a countermemory, rather than as a master narrative."[24] Only in time did the Lost Cause become the dominant narrative in the South, at least among whites, and take on near-hegemonic power. There were alternative understandings of the past against which people could "fact check" the Lost Cause, and to imply otherwise ignores African American memories of the war that still survive. The time and effort that Confederate mythmakers spent defending the Lost Cause not only highlight that they were aware that other narratives existed but also indicate that alternative memories posed a danger to their interests.

While some of the stories were clearly fictitious when created, other cases are less clear-cut. As such, I often use terms that do not imply intent, in order to distinguish moments of fabrication that were unintended or careless as opposed to deliberate. Nonetheless, some of these untruths only appear unknowingly false if observed in a vacuum. When examined as a whole, it becomes clear that the frequent repetition of fictions as facts was not a series of isolated mistakes but instead a pattern of falsehoods reflecting leading ex-Confederates' indifference to historical accuracy, if not a general mendacity.

A less provocative term than *lie* might obscure the purposeful creation and use of these constructions, and thereby render them innocuous. As media commentators of the early twenty-first century have argued, calling a factually incorrect declaration a "misstatement" because we lack conclusive proof of the speaker's intent is itself a form of misrepresentation. *Misstatement* superficially appears to be a "neutral word," but it actually implies a lack of intent that may, in fact, exist.[25] Indeed, assuming the best in people is no less an assumption than presuming the worst. This book operates from the belief that by focusing on what was fabricated, a historian can zero in on those aspects of the past that needed covering over—those parts of the past where the truth was the most problematic and thus worthy of study.

Of course, less important than if a specific tale was a lie, a mistake, or even factual is how these stories were appropriated for political ends. The exact truth of any one anecdote is almost incidental to how those memories were used to uphold racial hierarchies. Scholars know that "to expunge the real and implant a false past is a common despotic ruse."[26] Indeed, the Lost Cause helped maintain undemocratic one-party control of the South by providing a historical narrative that justified violence and oppression and fostered a white identity. Fabricated tales provide us a lens through which to understand how memory and white supremacy functioned in tandem. The Lost Cause is crucial to understanding the Jim Crow era, as well as modern white supremacist ideology, because it provided "crucial ideological ballast for white supremacy by rooting the contemporary racial hierarchy in a seemingly ordained historical narrative."[27] A twisted memory of united political action by southern whites also helped fashion a political identity that called on white southerners to vote a specific way. In mobilizing whites politically through appeals to the past, the Lost Cause served as a form of "history as identity politics."[28]

Lies also expressed power in the segregated Jim Crow South. Masha Gessen has pointed out that "lying to assert power" functions as an authoritarian tool to undermine democracy. At times, both those fabricating pasts and their audiences likely recognized that the truth was being stretched, but the fact that one could get away with lying demonstrated who was in charge and who was not. In this way, even when recognized as false, lies about the Civil War could still reinforce white supremacy.[29]

This book is not simply a collection of debunked falsehoods. Rather, it is a meditation on how fabricated historical memories have been and continue to be used to justify white supremacy. The book uses many small anecdotes and yarns to analyze the formation of memory. Each tale contributed to the creation of fictional narratives, which in turn upheld the inaccurate interpretations of the past that make up the Lost Cause. Construction of this false past upheld the biggest lie of all: that whites were a superior race. Indeed, I chose the title *The False Cause* in part because of the Lost Cause's ties to ideologies of white supremacy, which I view as pernicious.

The Lost Cause served not only to assuage the masculinity of white southern men—although it did do that too—it was used as a political tool to unite southern whites politically, threaten African American political activism, and justify Jim Crow. The fraud and fabrication that formed the foundation of the Lost Cause were central to the perpetuation of racism and racist power structures across the Jim Crow South. For example, recollections of superior white southern valor helped justify white supremacy. Similarly, the myth that nearly all whites supporting the Confederacy helped rally southern whites to vote based on their racial identity. A memory of paternalistic slavery and images of loyal slaves created a fictional past that showed how accepting racial hierarchies would lead to prosperity. A belief that all racial strife originated because of northern intervention in southern politics encouraged white southerners to oppose federal authorities' attempts to end disenfranchisement, lynching, segregation, and other forms of oppression. Southern politicians used the Lost Cause as a tool to cement white supremacy.

There was more to the Lost Cause than lies and white supremacy. Other factors contributed to its formation, including the trauma of a destructive war, gender relations, and battlefield events. This work, however, focuses on the ties among lies, memory, and white supremacy. These mutually reinforcing elements remained dependent upon each other. The politics, identity, and ideology of white supremacy dictated the shape of Lost Cause memory in the early twentieth-century South almost as much the war itself did. From campaigning on appeals to a shared history to offering veterans' pensions in exchange for votes, white supremacy and racial politics suffused the Lost Cause and vice versa. The manner in which the Lost Cause held up white supremacy evolved, but it remained premised upon the lies that proliferated during the Jim Crow era. Over 150 years after the Civil War, many of these fabricated stories and ideologies still pervade Americans' understandings of the past and continue to influence American politics.

Although alive in popular memory, many Lost Cause fabrications have been largely excised from recent academic histories. All reputable historians of the twenty-first century reject the claim that slavery had little to do with the war, and slavery is now understood as an exploitive system premised on violence and terror. Few academics ever accepted the relatively recent "black Confederates" myth.[30]

Other aspects of the Lost Cause, however, remain visible in recent histories, in part due to the continued acceptance of fabrications. An expectation of superior Confederate valor, loyalty, and military ability remain a feature of numerous military histories, while desertion and dissent are still often ignored. Some elements of the Lost Cause have occasionally seen a slight resurgence. While, by the turn of the twenty-first century, scholars largely rejected the racist understandings of Reconstruction promulgated in the early twentieth century, some aspects of the racist early twentieth-century historical narratives promulgated by William Dunning and his students have begun reappearing in subtler neo-Dunning interpretations of the past.[31] Most obviously, specific anecdotes of questionable origins still make appearances in otherwise excellent history books.

Despite the generally positive direction in which academic history is trending, all too often, professional historians still dismiss Lost Cause advocates, flaggers, and neo-Confederates as absurd and laughable, unworthy of their time. Yet, to untrained readers, a modern variation of the Lost Cause narrative, complete with tens of thousands of black Confederates and noble soldiers fighting for limited government, may not appear inaccurate. As academics become less and less trusted and as a majority of one political party's membership thinks higher education harms the country, it is not enough simply to dismiss "fake history."[32] To many Americans, the Lost Cause interpretation of the past has as much, if not more, weight than what historians write; indeed, a majority still struggle to identify the cause of the Civil War. While digitization and the internet allow anyone to do extensive historical research, they also allow anyone to publish stories about the past, and Americans struggle to determine which sources are reliable. Historians cannot dismiss neo-Confederates as internet trolls because their version of the past is finding its way into textbooks in Virginia, academic standards in Texas, and the minds of our students.[33] This book thus seeks to engage at times directly with what Kenneth Noe pointedly called an "underground Civil War bibliography" of nonacademic writings about the Confederacy. Though "real historians disdain" these neo-Confederate works, given their prevalence in modern America, professional historians need to engage neo-Confederate arguments and treat them critically.[34]

Historians, however, must go beyond debunking bogus anecdotes and busting Lost Cause myths. Fact checking is not enough when addressing lies that undermined democracy. I seek to also reveal what purpose these lies served, how larger false narratives formed from them, and the way these fabrications continue to influence American society.[35] This book goes beyond exposing previously undetected frauds—although it does expose numerous deceptions heretofore unnoticed. Instead, deconstructing falsehoods provides insight into how the Lost Cause narrative was created in the first place: with fraud, fabrications, and white supremacy. Conflicts over how we understand, commemorate, and remember the past are not merely academic. In February 2019, Chapel Hill activists erected a marker honoring the woman Julian Carr bragged about beating during the dedication of UNC's Confederate monument. It was promptly stolen by neo-Confederates, who were clearly not motivated by a desire to teach all history.[36] The fights over the nation's commemorative landscape mirror contemporaneous battles for control of the political landscape. These battles are ongoing, they are passionately fought, and they matter.

1

Rewriting the Past in Stone

Monuments, North Carolina Politics,
and Jim Crow, 1890–1929

In July 1913, a large crowd gathered on the University of North Carolina (UNC) campus to witness the unveiling of a new monument to the school's Confederate veterans. It was a momentous event with an estimated crowd of around one thousand people. The monument, which was the product of a joint effort by the United Daughters of the Confederacy (UDC) and the university, featured a decidedly young-looking soldier, representing a student heading off to war. The organizers spared no expense, spending the hefty sum of $7,500 to commission Canadian sculptor John A. Wilson to construct the monument. In fact, it had taken years for the UDC and the president of the university, Francis Venable, to raise the money, largely from alumni donations; in the end, it still took a loan from the university to secure the full amount to pay for the statue. Although inclement weather forced the speeches inside, the unveiling was a festive occasion, complete with flags and bunting, made more so by coinciding with Class Day as part of the university's graduation ceremonies.[1]

In time, the statue would be known as "Silent Sam" and become a national news story, but in 1913, it had no nickname. Indeed, the origins of the nickname are unclear. One story goes that Sam was unable to shoot because his belt lacked a cartridge case. In another version, he was completely silent because he only shoots when a virgin walks by. The truth is, he had no cartridge belt because the Canadian sculptor who cast Sam was unfamiliar with mid-nineteenth-century weaponry. In fact, he was never meant to be silent, and those who organized, funded, and dedicated the monument would be horrified at the thought that future generations would see Sam as a pacifist. Speeches given at the unveiling made explicit what the monument celebrated and what message Sam was meant to impart to the public: it was intended to remind viewers that those students who fought for the Confederacy were heroes of the white race. Indeed, the monument was meant, at least in part, to be an enduring testament to the success of white supremacy.

The speakers that day were a who's who of the North Carolina elite. After an opening rendition of "Dixie," Henry A. London—who, as a UNC student, had entered the Confederate army in 1865—spoke first. Although he was there to introduce the keynote speaker, North Carolina governor Locke Craig, London was himself a prominent figure in the monument-building movement and Democratic politics. He and industrialist Julian Shakespeare Carr, the other Confederate veteran speaking that day, already knew each other, likely from college. They were two of the leading Confederate veterans in the state; with London as his adjutant general, Carr commanded the state division of the United Confederate Veterans (UCV), the largest Confederate veterans' organization. They were longtime political allies in Democratic politics as well.[2] London, who served as a state senator and ran a newspaper in Pittsboro, had been a messenger and aide for General Bryan Grimes in 1865, claiming to have carried the order to lay down arms to General William Cox's troops at Appomattox. Later, he wrote extensively about the war, including a history of his unit, as well as giving numerous speeches at monument unveilings.[3] Indeed, the unveiling ceremony at UNC mimicked most dedications between 1902 and 1926, the peak of Confederate monument building in civic spaces across North Carolina.

London's wife, Bettie Jackson London, a prolific fund-raiser and a leading member of the UDC, also gave an address that day. Apart from the presence of Confederate veterans themselves, white women played a key role in the creation of the monuments, helping to preserve and promote a narrative of the past that celebrated Confederate soldiers. Karen Cox demonstrated in her groundbreaking work that after the UDC's founding in 1894, the organization took increased leadership in advancing a Lost Cause version of the past and in so doing played a crucial role "in shaping the social and political culture of the New South." Other historians have expanded on Cox's work to examine how white women played central roles as guardians of Confederate memory and in spreading the gospel of the Lost Cause. The UDC and earlier women's groups spent decades working to ensure that a narrative sympathetic to the Confederacy was retold and passed on. Indeed, women were largely responsible for the erection of these monuments.[4] As the largest woman's association dedicated to promoting a Lost Cause narrative of the war and erecting monuments, the UDC has had an outsized role in how we remember the past. In the case of UNC's monument, Bettie London led the fund-raising campaign for the monument. Although Governor Craig gave the keynote oration, women participated at multiple central moments of the unveiling ceremony: Mary Hicks Williams, president of the North Carolina division of the UDC, gave

Unveiling of the Confederate monument at the University of North Carolina, June 2, 1913. (Courtesy of the North Carolina Postcard Collection, North Carolina Collection Photographic Archives, Wilson Library, UNC-Chapel Hill)

a short address, while Bettie London presented the monument to President Venable, and a group of women did the actual unveiling.[5]

As white women "founded the Confederate tradition," they did so with the veterans' thanks and aid. Veterans served as "living monuments" alongside those in bronze and granite, and the survivors' presence and words gave extra authenticity to the monuments. Ultimately, they provided members of the UDC legitimacy in their role as guardians of the past.[6] No dedication was complete without a Daughter presenting the monument to a veteran with his grateful acceptance. In creating a narrative that made Confederate veterans heroic, white women were partners with veterans in protecting white southern masculinity.

At UNC, the last speaker of the day was Julian Carr, who, dressed in a military uniform, provided the "Thanks of the Student Veterans."[7] While white women exerted influence and power in their fund-raising and political activism, much of the raw material for their narrative of the war—especially those parts about battlefield heroics—came from the veterans themselves. Carr's role as a veteran recounting war stories was not just about thanking the UDC but also about passing on tales of white men fighting valiantly to protect the very women who now guarded their memory. As scholars have pointed out, it was often "elite white men who wrote the books that articulated the Lost Cause," which women then popularized.[8] Confederate veterans entrusted southern white women with epic war stories to pass on to future generations, the topic of the next chapter.

The present chapter examines how leading politicians and white elites employed a fabricated past, including numerous lies and falsehoods, to celebrate and justify white supremacy around the turn of the twentieth century. In North Carolina, a series of increasingly vicious white suprem-acist campaigns run by Democrats in the 1890s culminated in 1900 with their takeover of the state government, the disenfranchisement of most African Americans, and the institution of one-party rule. Shortly thereaf-ter, Confederate monuments increasingly began appearing in front of city halls, courthouses, and other public buildings. The correlation between the erection of such monuments and the success of the Democratic Party's white supremacy campaigns was not coincidental. In 1868, after battlefield defeat and the subsequent political and social gains made by black North Carolinians, former Confederates had little to celebrate. By 1901, however, Reconstruction had been overturned and African Americans largely disen-franchised. Many former Confederates in North Carolina felt they had won a victory for the cause of white rule and finally "corrected" some of the war's most disagreeable consequences.

Between 1890 and 1924, former-Confederates-turned-Democratic-leaders repeated the same basic historical narratives, littered with myth and exagger-ation, at political and commemorative events. Though this narrative evolved over time—and new details were added—some core tenants of the Lost Cause had already formed in the decades after the war. Among the many fabrica-tions repeated were that slavery was benevolent and beneficial, that Recon-struction—the era after the Civil War in which the South was reintegrated into the Union—was a period of corrupt rule driven by northern interfer-ence, and that there had existed a united white South, unanimously devoted to the Confederacy, during the war. This solid white South had supposedly remained committed to the cause of white supremacy ever since. Most sig-nificantly, by fabricating a history in which the Confederacy fought not for slavery but for states' rights, Confederate mythmakers could claim a victory instead of a defeat. Combined with their victory in politics, this Lost Cause remembrance provided ex-Confederates a means to celebrate white suprem-acy through the presentation of Confederate soldiers as an epitome of white masculinity. These myths, partially premised upon lies, exaggerations, and spin, were directly tied to the 1890s campaigns for white supremacy in North Carolina and the subsequent erection of Confederate monuments.

These monuments and the narratives they evoked undermined parts of the war's outcome by justifying and defending white hegemonic control of southern politics. While all historical narratives distort reality, the narrative that former Confederates propagated was not only especially egregious in its inclusion of overtly false aspects but was also specifically crafted in ways that allowed it to be used to uphold white supremacy. What makes the Lost Cause so relevant to contemporary history is not that it was heavily based on fabricated stories but that it shaped the twentieth century. The speeches and lives of the speakers at UNC in July 1913 clearly show how Confederate monuments, white supremacy, Jim Crow, and a distorted memory of the past were tied together. Far from "playing a limited role in modern southern culture," as some historians argue, the proponents of the Lost Cause helped construct Jim Crow in North Carolina with both fabricated narratives and the physical colonization of public space in the early twentieth century, which in turn laid the foundation for all that has followed.[9]

Memories evolve. Today, when those wishing to preserve Confederate monuments say that these statues bear no connection to white supremacy, they are rejecting what many of those central to their erection had hoped future generations would learn from stone and bronze. Despite the frequent denunciation of overt white supremacist rhetoric, the narrative that neo-Confederate and other Confederate apologists promote is a direct descendent of the Lost Cause narrative that Confederate veterans created. Ironically, exaggerations, narrative arcs, tales, and falsehoods similar or identical to those that ex-Confederates used to justify white supremacy in 1913 are now used by monument supporters to try to detangle the Confederacy from accusations of racism. Moreover, despite assertions, many of which are no doubt sincere, by those who wished to maintain Silent Sam in a place of honor on UNC's campus that the statute has "nothing to do with racism," the narrative of history they advocate provides an explanation of the past that still helps reinforce and justify discrimination within American society.[10] While the explicitness and self-awareness of the ties between celebrating the Confederacy and upholding white supremacy have changed, the connections—as well as many of the false anecdotes—remain in popular understandings of the war.

A native of Chapel Hill and UNC student, young Julian Carr joined the Confederate army in late 1864, serving during the last few months of the conflict. He made his fortune after the war with tobacco before diversifying into cotton mills. Though largely forgotten by the turn of the twenty-first century except as the namesake of the town of Carrboro, he was a giant in his time. An economic, political, and philanthropic leader, he served on the board of trustees for UNC and as chairman of the state's Democratic Party. Like many white Southerners of his generation and ideological bent, Carr's life was marked with seeming contradictions. A staunch racist, he nonetheless protected his mixed-race half-brother and donated funds to both white and black educational institutions.[11]

Despite his seeming kindness toward African Americans through donations and vocal assertions that he was their friend, Carr was a devoted white supremacist and member of the Ku Klux Klan.[12] A leading donor and architect of North Carolina's white supremacist politics in the Jim Crow era, Carr actively worked to segregate society and maintain a racial hierarchy. In the 1880s, he was already funding a newspaper for Randolph Shotwell, who had been pardoned by President Grant after being convicted for his leadership in North Carolina's Ku Klux Klan. When Shotwell died, Carr essentially gave the paper to Josephus Daniels, later funding the purchase of additional newspapers for him, including the state's paper of record, the *News and Observer*. With Carr's backing, Daniels became a leading Democratic newspaperman, using the press to push white supremacist policies and politics before eventually becoming secretary of the navy.[13] In 1900, Carr bragged that he had already spent $10,000 "in legitimate campaign expenses to carry white supremacy."[14] He supported white supremacy not only through his political activities and donations but also in the way he rewrote the past.

Carr's public persona, as demonstrated in speeches, electoral campaigns, and philanthropy, heavily revolved around being a former Confederate soldier. He was known as "General Carr" because of his role as a leading Confederate veteran, not because of his wartime rank of private. In 1886, Carr helped found a forerunner of the UCV, the North Carolina Confederate Veterans Association, which worked to fund the state's home for old soldiers. Elected to head the North Carolina Division of the UCV in 1899, he served in that role until 1915, when members promoted him to command the organization's Department of the Army of Northern Virginia. In 1921 and 1922, the UCV's members elected him to lead all ex-Confederates, making him the most senior Confederate veteran in the country.[15] Being a former Confederate was part of Carr's self-identity in death as well as in life. His modest gravestone remembers him as "General Julian S. Carr" alongside dates of birth and death. On his footstone is inscribed simply, "He was a Confederate Soldier." A second marker reading, "J. S. Carr, CSA," ensures that visitors have no doubt about where his wartime sympathies lay.[16]

As the head of state and national veterans' organizations, Carr was one of the leading North Carolinians involved in commemorating the Confederacy. His election over twenty times to various leadership roles implies that the narrative he promoted was widely accepted by other veterans. Though I return to Carr frequently, I could have used any number of other white North Carolinians to find comparable quotes and make the same arguments, but one cannot understand how North Carolina's Lost Cause memory was crafted and functioned without addressing him. Due to his influence and for narrative drive, this book frequently uses Carr as a window into both how North Carolina's Confederate veterans understood the past and how white supremacists fabricated a useful memory of the war.

Carr was proud to give the dedication speech at his alma mater's monument dedication in June 1913, and he made clear to the audience what purpose he believed the monument served. After reiterating that North Carolina had provided thousands of soldiers and that southern women had been steadfastly loyal to the Confederacy, Carr explained a key lesson that he felt this monument would impart to future classes:

> The present generation, I am persuaded, scarcely takes note of what the Confederate soldier meant to the welfare of the Anglo Saxon race during the four years immediately succeeding the war, when the facts are, their courage and steadfastness saved the very life of the Anglo Saxon race in the South—when the "bottom rail was on top" all over the Southern states—and to-day, as a consequence, the purist strain of the Anglo Saxon is to be found in the 13 Southern States—Praise God.[17]

Gently chastising a younger generation that had been spared civil conflict, Carr reminded those in attendance that the superiority of whites needed to be carefully attended to, even in 1913. At the same time, Carr was claiming a kind of victory for Confederate soldiers, one that revolved around preserving a status quo in which white people remained on top politically, socially, and economically. For Carr, this was a monument as much to white southerners' victory over Reconstruction, when white conservatives retook control of the state government, as it was to the defeated soldiers of the actual war. Indeed, Jim Crow–era Confederate monuments were as intimately tied to the memory of Reconstruction as they were to remembrances of the Civil War. One scholar has found that out of thirty Confederate monument dedication speeches sampled, thirteen explicitly celebrated the overturning of Reconstruction.[18] These were victory monuments.

Fifty years after the war, Carr remained convinced of the Confederacy's righteousness and that whites' continued racial superiority had been demonstrated in the overturning of Reconstruction. In fact, he was so proud of the part he played in subduing African Americans that he asked the audience to humor him as he shared his part in the reassertion of white supremacy, announcing:

One hundred yards from where we stand, less than ninety days perhaps after my return from Appomattox, I horse-whipped a negro wench, until her skirts hung in shreds, because upon the streets of this quiet village she had publicly insulted and maligned a Southern lady, and then rushed for protection to these University buildings where was stationed 100 Federal soldiers. I performed the pleasing duty in the immediate presence of the entire garrison, and for thirty nights afterwards slept with a double-barreled shotgun under my head.[19]

For Carr, the Ku Klux Klan, vigilante justice, and the repression of blacks was a continuation of the war, one that was justified by the cause of preserving white supremacy.[20]

While Carr's address sparked intense controversy after its rediscovery in 2011, ultimately resulting in the monument's toppling by protestors in 2018, it did not seem remarkable or extraordinary when the speech was delivered, receiving far less attention in local newspapers than the governor's keynote. Reporters likely failed to mention his celebration of white supremacy and violence because although Carr's language at UNC was more direct than usual, the sentiments he expressed were common in speeches given at monument dedications across the state. Many former Confederates sought to celebrate the postwar success of white supremacy with monuments. For instance, in 1929, a monument dedicated at the thirty-ninth UCV's reunion in Charlotte, North Carolina, included an inscription praising Confederate veterans because, by "accepting the arbitrament of the war, they preserved the Anglo-Saxon civilization of the South and became master builders in a re-united country."[21] Carr's views about these monuments were mainstream among white southern elites; he was, after all, the head of the UCV and a major political figure in North Carolina. That same week, US vice president Thomas Marshall's UNC commencement address similarly discussed how the "'Anglo Saxon' race . . . had elevated the standard of civilization."[22] Similar racial language can also be found in the rhetoric of the 1920s Ku Klux Klan, as well as the speeches given by leading members of the UDC and UCV, and by southern Democratic politicians around the turn of the century.[23] Rhetoric was linked to action. Governor Locke Craig, who spoke alongside Carr at the UNC memorial dedication, had been one of the formulators of North Carolina's grandfather clause, which effectively disenfranchised African Americans.[24]

The creation of Confederate monuments was thus part of a larger project to celebrate the success of white supremacy, remind the public of the proper order of things, maintain white racial unity, and cement white control in the South's politics and upon the landscape. It is true that these

monuments were also meant by some to sincerely honor Confederate soldiers, as their modern defenders so often assert. It is important to realize,
however, that not only do monuments frequently have multiple overlap-
ping meanings but honoring Confederate soldiers also served as a means
of celebrating the success of white supremacy.

Carr and others recognized that a diverse cast of white heroes could help
instill certain ideological values and racial pride in future generations. In
1901, Carr thus called for "the great Anglo Saxon race" to erect a memorial
to Sir Walter Raleigh in the Englishman's namesake city. Carr saw North
Carolina as "the cradle of Anglo-Saxon civilization and the birthplace of liberty in America," and celebrating Raleigh was yet another way to recognize
white superiority. In 1907, when a monument to Worth Bagley, the only
US naval officer killed in the Spanish American War, was dedicated at the
North Carolina capitol, one speaker "declared amid cheers that only in the
south today is to be found the pure vein of the grand old Anglo-Saxon Race,
by which this government was founded." The fact that an African American seaman died alongside Bagley was forgotten.[25] Monuments to Confederate soldiers were therefore only the most prominent and common of a
variety of markers erected during the early twentieth century to celebrate
white supremacy and to exert hegemonic control over the landscape, just as
it had already been exerted on politics.

Given that those who placed Confederate monuments upon the landscape
while openly connecting them to celebrating white supremacy were often
leading political figures, it should come as no surprise that the appearance of these monuments correlated to an upturn in the success of white
supremacy as a political ideology. While today Confederate monuments are
seen across the South in front of nearly every courthouse, only in the early
twentieth century, after Jim Crow was firmly in place, were most North Carolina markers erected.

Indeed, there was little chance of Confederate monuments being placed in
front of North Carolina's courthouses in the 1860s and '70s. In the aftermath
of the war and the failure of Presidential Reconstruction, a biracial coalition
of Republicans—which included African Americans, white wartime dissenters, and even some former Confederates—had taken control of the state in
1868. They soon founded a statewide public-school system and instituted
numerous legal reforms necessary in the aftermath of emancipation. Accusations of corruption, political violence, cheating, intimidation, and appeals
to white supremacy, however, contributed to the eventual return of North
Carolina's conservatives. Though the state legislature fell to the Democrats in
1870, the Republicans "remained competitive and continually challenged the

Democratic Party" throughout the nineteenth century. Indeed, they maintained control of the governor's office until 1876 and then only lost to Democrats by a thin margin.[26] Even in 1886, Republicans won nearly 47 percent
of the state house seats, and only gerrymandering and other undemocratic
forms of "'judicious' cheating" kept Republicans from greater success.[27]

While Reconstruction's end is often thought of as the last time Republicans controlled southern states during the nineteenth century, a "Solid
South" that overwhelmingly went Democratic did not exist in North Carolina in the late nineteenth century. Indeed, North Carolina continued to
send black Republican congressmen to Washington until 1901. Additionally, North Carolina and Virginia both experienced periods where Democrats lost control of state governments. Virginia witnessed the Readjuster
coalition taking power from 1879–83, while in North Carolina, a coalition
formed between Populists and Republicans retook control of the state in
the 1890s. After eighteen years out of power, Republicans had a resurgence
before disenfranchisement ended their ability to get out the black vote.[28]

In 1894, the so-called biracial fusion of Populists and Republicans took
control of the North Carolina legislature; two years later, the Fusionists won
the governor's mansion. The success of the Fusionism was short lived, however. In 1898, the Democrats retook the legislature through appeals to white
supremacy and the violent suppression of African American voters. Immediately after the election, Wilmington experienced a deadly race riot that
resulted in a coup of the Republican-led city government. Two years later,
in 1900, Democrats won the governorship as they had during the 1870s,
through hook, crook, intimidation, violence, and the mobilization of voters
along racial lines. This reassertion of Democratic control was devastating to
the long-term political aspirations of both Republicans and African Americans. As part of their white supremacist political campaigns, Democrats successfully campaigned for a state constitutional amendment to disenfranchise
African Americans with a grandfather clause, which functionally required a
rigged literacy test for African Americans but not for illiterate whites. They
also created numerous other obstacles to African American voting, including
poll taxes. Dependent as it was on a biracial coalition, Fusionism could not
survive the violence by hostile Democrats when combined with legal disenfranchisement. After 1900, North Carolina would be under one-party control
until after the successes of the civil rights movement in the 1950s and 60s.
Not until the 1970s and Nixon's "southern strategy" appealing to white racial
resentment would a Republican be North Carolina's governor, and then
largely due to party realignment.[29]

In North Carolina, the fall of the Fusion movement ushered in the
state's Confederate monument boom.[30] After the turn of the century, towns

increasingly began putting up Confederate monuments in public spaces. Historians have noted that in many southern states, the surge of monument construction took place "from the late 1880s through the 1910s." But this rush of monument building and the move from cemeteries to public squares actually came later to North Carolina, owing to its unique political history.[31] Not until 1892, for example, did a single North Carolina county courthouse get a Confederate monument in front of it; only two other monuments were unveiled in public squares during the 1890s. During the term of Fusion governor Daniel Russell (1896–1900), four Confederate monuments were dedicated in the state, two of which were in cemeteries. But from 1902 to 1910, after Fusionism ended, at least twenty-four monuments went up in public squares, town commons, or courthouse yards. A similar number were dedicated in the following decade. Beginning around 1920, the designs began to shift away from statues of common soldiers in town squares toward historic locations themselves being marked. After the start of the Great Depression, monuments tended to be smaller and lack statuary, likely due to greater economic constrains. In short, the peak monument-building period for the common soldier monuments seen across North Carolina's public squares was from 1902 to 1926.[32]

These first twentieth-century monuments were different than earlier memorials. In the aftermath of the war, the Lost Cause narrative served many purposes. For example, it assuaged concerns about white masculinity in light of surrender and emancipation. It also helped those grieving loved ones mourn their loss; throughout the 1870s and '80s, Ladies' Memorial Associations interred Confederate soldiers and erected a small number of monuments, primarily in cemeteries as memorials to the dead. The transition from cemetery to public square paralleled a changing purpose of these monuments as they increasingly served as celebratory markers instead of sober memorials.

The Lost Cause narrative was not new in the 1890s. Indeed, Richmond journalist Edward Pollard published *The Lost Cause,* which laid out many of the central tenants of the narrative with which the book shared its name, in 1866. The last decade of the nineteenth century, however, did see major developments in how white southerners commemorated the war. In 1889, the UCV was founded, and five years later, it was joined by the UDC, which would supplant the Ladies' Memorial Associations as guardians of the Lost Cause. The UCV and UDC, often working in tandem, would become two of the most important driving forces in how white southerners would recall and commemorate the Confederacy in the early twentieth century.[33]

Not all white southerners supported erecting Confederate monuments. During the Fusion era, most of the state's Republicans and Populist officials actively opposed their erection. Despite this resistance, one of the few Confederate monuments to go up during the Fusion era was at the state's capitol building. Authorized by the Democrat-controlled legislature in 1892, the monument was short the final funds needed three years later, so a bill to appropriate the money was put before the legislature. While every Democrat in the statehouse supported the bill, only 35 percent of Republicans and 33.5 percent of Populists voted for it.[34] Although the bill passed, the vote would be used against those who opposed the appropriation as a means of portraying white Republicans and Populists as enemies of white supremacy.

Even before most were erected, Confederate monuments were already tied to racial politics. Five years after the appropriation passed, during the 1900 electoral campaign, the Democratic Party–controlled *Durham Sun* heavily criticized William Gaston Vickers for his vote against providing funds for the capitol's Confederate monument. Calling attention to the candidate's opposition, the paper asked readers what veterans would think of "a man voting against a measure to honor the memory of our fallen braves? A man who will turn his back on the loved and lost, and now running with a gang, opposed to white supremacy, and the Constitutional Amendment [to disenfranchise African Americans]?" Newspapers also contrasted Republicans' votes on Confederate monuments with an 1895 vote to adjourn to honor the memory of recently deceased African American orator Frederick Douglass. Democrats further claimed that Fusionists had failed to adjourn on the birthdays of Robert E. Lee and George Washington. Despite the fact that the House had actually observed Lee's birthday (Washington's occurred on a weekend), accusations that this "insult to the patriotism, intelligence and virtue of the white people" demonstrated "negro domination" of the legislature were effective. Democrats stoked racial fears with mendacious tales of black rapists and exaggerations about the extent of black officeholding and power. These Democratic appeals to white supremacy, alongside voter suppression efforts, worked: Vickers lost the election.[35] Two years later, Julian Carr rolled out the old complaint about honoring Douglass in an article he wrote explaining why Confederate veterans would not abandon the Democratic Party.[36]

Votes on Confederate monuments were a lose-lose proposition for many Fusionists. Dependent not just on black voters but also on white constituents, including some former Confederates, members of the Fusion coalition could not vote on such a bill without angering someone. In an effort to avoid controversy, some representatives simply abstained from voting. Some white Republicans and Populists appear to have supported the Confederate monument as a convenient way to inoculate themselves against accusations of betraying their race or of supporting "negro domination." Democrats recognized this fact and also lambasted those Republicans who supported the monument bill in 1895, saying they only did it to "try and stave off the odium" of having voted to honor Douglass.[37] Multiple senators changed their stance during the contentious debate, and one even changed his vote during the final roll call, dramatically providing funding for the controversial monument by a single vote.[38]

For Democrats, the decision-making process was much simpler. In 1900, to be called a white supremacist was not an insult for a North Carolina Democrat. Rather, it was a requirement for election. Democrats headlined their printed slates with the motto "For White Supremacy," as Democratic "white supremacy clubs" popped up around the state to mobilize voters. That year, "General" Carr ran for Senate on a platform that "the White man shall rule the land or die," promising to disenfranchise African Americans and liberalize pension laws.[39] Newspapers noted that all four Democratic Senate candidates were committed to "the ever-winning issue, white supremacy."[40] Carr and one of his opponents, Alfred Waddell—a leader of the Wilmington race riot—were not only both prominent white supremacists and leading Democrats but also two of the most well-known Confederate boosters in North Carolina. As did countless other Democratic politicians, both men used their Civil War service as evidence of their bona fides on the issue of white supremacy. Although neither Waddell nor Carr would win the nomination in 1900, white supremacy nonetheless reigned supreme. The victor, the uniquely named Furnifold McLendel Simmons, had also been a key organizer of the white supremacy campaigns of the 1890s; he went on to serve as senator for the next thirty years.

In many ways, Waddell had a stronger claim than Carr as an advocate for white supremacy. Carr was widely known as a moderate on racial issues among North Carolina Democrats. In 1912, W. E. B. Du Bois would even call Carr a friend to Durham's African American population.[41] Carr did not oppose the economic advancement of African Americans and seems to have viewed it as good for business. Indeed, the Carr family appears to have used African American laborers to undercut white wages in cotton mills. While Carr gave loans to black businesses—likely netting himself a profit—his relationships with African Americans always carried a paternalistic and unequal power dynamic.[42] Despite his willingness to support African American uplift, Carr remained a firm believer in segregation, racial hierarchy, and white supremacy. Being a racial moderate in 1900 meant Carr did not openly call for violence against African Americans, as some other prominent former Confederates did. Nonetheless, as evidenced by his braggadocious storytelling, Carr was clearly not above using violence if he felt African Americans were out of place and always blamed them for any bloodshed.

While some historians have defended Carr as a racial moderate with "relatively good" relations with African Americans, pointing out his philanthropy and loans as signs of "Carr's efforts on behalf of blacks," his charity came with a catch.[43] In 1898, Carr published an open letter he penned as the chairman of the Durham County Democratic Executive Committee to set the record straight. Responding to allegations he was too friendly with African Americans, Carr assured voters he was fully committed to white supremacy, explaining, "I have done so much to elevate the negro, and in trying to help him help himself, that I have oftentimes been criticized. . . . So I repeat I am a friend of the negro in his place, but mind you, HE MUST BE IN HIS PLACE." This last bit was crucial. Carr would aid African Americans, especially when he could profit from it, but he made clear that "I am for my color first, last, and all the time, and it is best for the negro that I should be so, because it is an admitted fact, that the negro is not capable or competent for self-government." Carr declared that his friendship and aid were always conditional, stating to the public, "While I enjoy their respect and confidence not one of them for his right arm would presume to forget a negro's place in my presence." Carr's benevolence was dependent on the recipients' acceptance of an inferior social and political status. African Americans came to him because they knew he was generous and that by being respectful and acting subservient, they might garner material rewards. Even Carr, however, recognized that there were limits, stating, "Hundreds of them bring their troubles to me for advice, except about election times; then, they never consult nor advise with me."[44]

Carr's opposition to African Americans' political involvement was not necessarily contradictory with his philanthropy; in fact, white supremacy can be understood as central to his donations. In a capitalistic society, money is a form of power. Philanthropy, paternalism, and patronage provided a means to control African Americans. So long as black education, business, and community institutions were reliant on Carr's paternalism to overcome inadequate state funding, leading African Americans dared not openly oppose Carr and had to temper their criticisms of Jim Crow. Such philanthropy also gave white southern donors and politicians the ability to influence curriculum. While many white supremacists opposed black education because they saw literacy as encouraging political involvement, historian of education James Anderson argues that donors like Carr believed they could educate "blacks to accept or internalize the idea that white southerners had some legitimate right to rule over them." Du Bois and others lavished praise on Carr because continued donations were dependent on continued acclaim. The very gifts that Carr's modern defenders cite as proof of his benevolence can therefore be seen as the tools that he used for racial control.[45]

Carr's record on race is mixed at best. He appears even less moderate when considered on the wider spectrum that includes white and black Republicans and Populists who opposed disenfranchisement. Still, he was more moderate on race issues than many of his fellow Democrats. After all, Carr's paternalism aimed at controlling African Americans with minimal violence.

Waddell, by contrast, actively and openly called for racial violence. Though a moderate during Reconstruction, after Waddell's career stagnated, he found the road to political recovery through appeals to white supremacy. Waddell helped lead the 1898 Wilmington race riot, which overthrew the elected biracial government in that city. The riot resulted in the death of somewhere between nine and three hundred African Americans, depending on which accounts are to be believed. During the 1900 campaign, Locke Craig celebrated Waddell's role in the riot, as it "had removed the last obstacle which lay before the avalanche of white supremacy."[46] Two years after leading a coup, Waddell ensured that another putsch of a democratically elected government would be unnecessary by effectively ending democracy, at least for African Americans. In a speech given the day before the 1900 canvas, he told his followers, "Go to the polls tomorrow, and if you find the negro out voting, tell him to leave the polls and if he refuses, kill him, shoot him down in his tracks. We shall win tomorrow if we have to do it with guns." Waddell had no qualms about killing, declaring that whites would "throw enough dead bodies in the Cape Fear [River] to choke up its passage to the sea."[47] His white followers did as instructed and restricted access to the ballot, ensuring Democratic control of the state government for decades to come. Carr and Waddell are just two examples of the many Confederate veterans and leading Confederate memory makers who ran for office that year. Locke Craig and Henry London, the other speakers at UNC's monument dedication, were both elected to the state legislature in 1900 on similar platforms. In sum, those who oversaw the solidification of white rule in North Carolina in 1898 and 1900 later helped cement their ideology on the landscape with Confederate memorials.

The biracial nature of Fusionism convinced Democratic leaders not only that African Americans must be driven from the polls but also that strategies must be developed to attract more whites to the Democratic fold and to convince them that African American disenfranchisement was in their best interest. A sense of shared history served as one of the means by which Democrats sought to unite white voters behind their party banner. Hence, fond remembrance of the overthrow of Reconstruction, the return and maintenance of white-only rule, and the commemoration of the Confederacy were tied together for the monument makers of the early twentieth-century South. Historian K. Stephen Prince argues that "a white supremacist rewriting of Reconstruction was an indispensable corollary to the rise of Jim Crow." Indeed, remembering Reconstruction as a time of corruption, black and carpetbagger misrule, and vigilante justice was critical to justifying white supremacy to the rest of the nation, and in particular, to southern whites.[48]

Monument men like Carr wanted to instill in whites a racial identity based on a shared historical memory. Creating a narrative in which whites had an unbroken history of consensus and united political action was part of that process. This memory of whites acting together during the antebellum period, in support of the Confederacy, and then during Reconstruction was meant to inspire whites to vote with their race. North Carolina's leaders, whom political scientist V. O. Key Jr., characterized as a "progressive plutocracy," used history to maintain power. As scholars have pointed out, "A well-crafted historical paradigm inoculated children against interpretations dangerous to the aristocratic class," and so, through historical narratives, "southern whites absorbed a veneration for the Confederate Cause, an intense resistance to black civil rights, and a deferential spirit toward their proper leaders."[49] Fusionism's success threatened white supremacy not only due to the number of votes it garnered but also because it promoted a different historical narrative than the one trumpeted by Confederate veterans like Carr. Indeed, some Fusionists reportedly called Confederates "traitors" who should have been disenfranchised, a viewpoint that Democratic newspapers played up to attract veterans to their side.[50] Similarly, Populism rebelled against "oligarchy and privilege, and therefore, by its very character, it was hostile to the Lost Cause tradition," not to mention in its acceptance of biracial political coalitions.[51]

The fabrication that Carr and others engaged in went beyond the selective focus, emphasis, and forgetting necessary in the creation of any historical narratives. Instead, they actively created elements, anecdotes, and facts that were demonstrably false. As part of an effort to use historical narratives to help build a racial identity that called upon whites to vote for Democrats, Carr and London erased the memory of white Republicanism in the South and created a myth of a solid white South that had not previously existed. For example, in a 1900 campaign speech, Henry London implied there had only been a "few thousand white Republicans" in North Carolina until the 1896 election, when Populists broke from the Democratic Party and joined the Republicans on a Fusion ticket.[52] On his way to winning a state Senate seat, London deployed a fabricated memory of the past in which nearly all southern whites had united behind the Democratic banner since the Civil

War. The reality was that before 1900, the white South was not nearly as solid as he claimed. Only with the massive decrease in voter turnout after 1900 did North Carolina become a solidly Democratic state.[53]

Looking at the 1867 election makes clear that former Confederates were making up a past. Back-of-the-envelope math reveals that in fact, many white southerners voted for Republicans. In 1867, Republicans supported the drafting of a new state constitution, while Conservatives largely opposed it. Given that 93,006 people voted for the constitutional convention and only 72,932 African Americans were registered, an absolute minimum of 20,074 whites voted for the convention, thus supporting the state's Republican-led Reconstruction efforts. An examination of county-level results increases that minimum number to 22,808 whites favoring the convention.[54] General Edward Canby, in charge of North Carolina at the time, estimated that 31,284 whites voted for a convention and 32,961 against; the majority of those opposed to the convention abstained from voting in an effort to delegitimize the election. Canby's numbers seem more than reasonable, as they were based on an estimate that only 11,210 registered African Americans (about 15 percent) failed to vote.[55] Contrary to Democratic assertions, white Republicans in North Carolina were not new in the 1890s. Indeed, one scholar has found that North Carolina's Republican Party had "the highest rate of white members among Southern Republican parties: as much as 30 percent white," a fact that leading Democratic political strategists, including London, surely understood.[56]

That a politician lied about the past is no surprise, but the way these falsehoods were used in white supremacist campaigns is important to understanding North Carolina's politics. A myth of a Solid South where whites voted en bloc apprised whites that voting Democratic was the norm for people like them. The fragility of white unity in North Carolina meant that historical narratives that encouraged whites to vote Democratic served an even more important purpose than in states where whites more reliably voted along racial lines. Claims that only a few whites voted Republican also facilitated the false belief that voting Republican would lead to "negro domination" of the government, despite the relatively small number of black Republicans who actually held office.[57]

Democratic politicians were not alone in rejecting the biracial nature of Reconstruction government in North Carolina. At the turn of the century, historians also denied the existence of local white support for Reconstruction. UNC history professor Joseph Grégoire de Roulhac Hamilton declared, "It is a known fact that [Canby's] figures could not be correct" regarding white support. In reality, Canby's estimates seem conservative, given the confirmed white support for the convention in some areas. Indeed, in twenty-one counties across the Piedmont and the Appalachian region, at least 40 percent of *registered white* voters supported the convention.[58] Despite being a historian, Hamilton, who likely attended the dedication of UNC's Confederate monument, bought into the Lost Cause narrative of Reconstruction and thus believed there had been a Solid South where almost every "native white" had supported the Confederacy and opposed Reconstruction.[59] Hamilton pushed a white supremacist narrative of Reconstruction in his historical writings, just as Carr and London did in their speeches. A protégé of William Dunning, the foremost historian of Reconstruction at the time, Hamilton was part of a group of historians, now known as the Dunning school, who helped legitimate the Lost Cause's narrative about the past. Their interpretation of history was premised on a belief in white supremacy and remained the dominant historical interpretation for decades.[60]

Monument dedications and political addresses employed the same rhetoric about the past to mobilize support and cultivate a racial identity—what Benedict Anderson would call an "imagined community"—in which individuals saw themselves as sharing characteristics and interests with the other members of a group.[61] By encouraging white southerners to see themselves as white first and white supremacy as a benefit to them, Democrats sought to mobilize voters. Depicting Reconstruction as a time when corrupt northerners manipulated blacks into oppressing whites helped create a shared identity that vindicated disenfranchisement. During a 1900 campaign speech, for instance, Henry London appealed to white unity by describing "the times in North Carolina under negro and carpet-bag rule; [and] the relief that Democrats gave by their county government law, by which the county and town governments were kept in the hands of the white people." Depicting the white supremacy campaigns of the 1890s as the heirs of the violent "Redemption" campaigns of the 1860s and '70s that ended Reconstruction, London declared that "the campaign of 1900 is to make white supremacy permanent" by forever overturning one major outcome of the war: African American enfranchisement.[62]

The Lost Cause narrative of Reconstruction was crucial to justifying disenfranchisement and stoking fears of "Negro domination."[63] In a speech to a Democratic convention at the end of the nineteenth century, Carr likewise invoked fears of Reconstruction to push for African American disenfranchisement, warning, "Already we are threatened with terrible visions of these calamitous and disreputable times, and the ghosts of '68 and '70 are stalking around in the land."[64] White vigilante groups active during the 1898 and 1900 elections even wore red shirts as a uniform, visually harkening back to similar red-wearing militants who violently helped overturn Reconstruction in South Carolina in 1876.[65]

The ties between white supremacy and the Lost Cause were not limited to celebrating Reconstruction's violent overthrow. Alongside this jubilant memory of postwar racial triumph was a constant assertion that slavery had been benevolent and slaves content. In reality, branding, whipping, permanent separation of children from their parents, and the sale of sex slaves were all commonplace in the antebellum South. Running away, murder, revolt, and other forms of resistance occurred throughout the era of chattel slavery. Yet, in various venues, Carr declared that "slavery at the South was the gentlest and most beneficent servitude mankind has ever known."[66] Erasing the reality of slavery as a brutal system of exploitation dependent upon torture, the threat of violence, and violence itself provided part of a historical reason for voting Democratic. At both political rallies and Confederate commemorations, Carr routinely recalled how slaves and masters had been friends, and only the interference of northerners had created problems between races. Speaking to a civic club in Southern Pines, Carr argued that although "the negroes had behaved most faithfully to their masters during the war," after the conflict, the "Freedman's Bureau sought to make the negroes irritated against the whites, and here they succeeded in inflaming them into bitterness."[67] Mobilizing this Lost Cause memory of the past to overturn black political gains, Carr argued that through disenfranchisement race relations would be restored to normal, benefiting both whites and blacks.[68]

The belief that white northerners caused racial tensions in the South was joined by the assertion that African Americans had never actually asked for the ballot or freedom. Carr and other Democrats actively obscured the wartime reality that by 1864, nearly 400,000 men, women, and children had already escaped slavery and reached freedom behind Union lines, and almost 180,000 African Americans, many of them former slaves, fought in the United States Army during the war.[69] In a typical 1900 campaign speech, Carr promised that disenfranchisement would help return the tumultuous race relations of the time to the alleged harmony of the antebellum era. Instead of the threat of disenfranchisement or racial violence harming race relations, Carr declared that it had been "the great crime" of the North "vesting eight millions of ignorant vicious colored people with the franchise" that caused all of North Carolina's problems. Making the tie between history and modern politics explicit, Carr assured his audience that "it was never too late to correct a mistake."[70] This narrative of the past could be mobilized to oppose outside intervention in southern politics at the same time that it helped unite white southerners desiring both racial privilege and peace in their communities behind an ideology of white supremacy.

Disenfranchising African Americans also provided a sense of victory to Confederate veterans, marking an overturn of at least some of Appomattox's results. Indeed, Carr attempted to rewrite the war's outcome and erase black agency by asserting that the North had given the franchise to African Americans vindictively, "in the vain hope of humiliating that proud civilization which they had been unable to conquer in war."[71] As one leading southern studies scholar has pointed out, "The 'Lost Cause' ethos not only defended secession and glorified the society that white southerners had gone to war to preserve, but actually transformed their tragic military defeat into a tremendous moral triumph."[72] But to truly convert defeat into victory would require retroactively changing what the war was fought over.

In 1861, there was general agreement among white southerners that slavery was the root cause of secession and the Civil War. As Charles Dew points out, "The secessionist of 1860–61 certainly talked much more openly about slavery than present day neo-Confederates seem willing to do."[73] Lincoln summed up the cause of the war in his second inaugural address thusly: "These slaves constituted a peculiar and powerful interest. All knew that this interest was somehow the cause of the war."[74] While the issues that drove the South to secession were complex, they all related "somehow" to slavery. The expansion of slavery into the territories, difficulty maintaining a balance between slave and free states in Congress, the Fugitive Slave Act, the demand for a federal slave code, John Brown's raid, the circulation of abolitionist literature, and the election of an anti-slavery Republican as president were all key causes of the war. The Mississippi Secession Convention made clear its dispute with the Union when it began its list of complaints with the statement "Our position is thoroughly identified with the institution of slavery—the greatest material interest of the world."[75]

Despite the war's cause being clear in 1860, by the early twentieth century, many former Confederates downplayed or denied the Confederacy's link to slavery. Hardly a twentieth-century invention, this distancing of the Confederate cause from slavery began as soon as the war ended. As Caroline Janney and others have persuasively argued, by the 1880s, former Confederates were increasingly denying "that their quest for independence had been anything other than a constitutional struggle to protect state rights."[76] By the first decades of the twentieth century, the denial of slavery as the driving cause of the war had become enshrined in white southern memory.

Here lay one of the most crucial falsehoods that Carr and other former Confederates used in their rewriting of the past to specific political ends. In his public addresses, when discussing the causes as the war, Carr usually avoided mentioning slavery or denied its role in the conflict. For example, at

UNC's monument dedication, he declared that Confederate soldiers fought "from a high and holy sense of duty . . . for their childhood homes, their firesides, the honor of their ancestors, their loved ones, their own native land." In his typical fashion Carr asserted that southerners should "be grateful that our struggle" had kept "alive the grand principle of local self-government and State sovereignty," and that this principle protected America from despotism.[77] It is worth considering Carr's logic for a moment. If the Confederacy had been fighting for states' rights, then why had the victors not destroyed states' rights when they won? Since states retained many rights, the Confederacy had somehow persevered and protected what they fought for, despite defeat on the battlefield. In remembering the war as a conflict about a constitutional principle that had survived, victory was fashioned out of defeat. Because the Supreme Court had continually held that states individually controlled many matters, Carr celebrated the survival of states' rights, declaring in one speech that "Lee accomplished what he fought for, and more than could have been accomplished had he been victorious."[78]

In many ways, the monuments dedicated in the early twentieth century were not memorials for mourning but rather victory celebrations. In 1905, at the dedication of a monument in Statesville, North Carolina, for instance, W. D. Turner actually rejected the term "Lost Cause" because he claimed the Confederacy had not lost. Instead, he argued, "There was no surrender on the 9th of April 1865, but a compromise," a statement that would have confused both Grant and Lee. Indeed, he continued, "The North won the Union and abolition; the South won the constitution for the Union, the rights of the people and State sovereignty." The monument's simple west-facing inscription—"Defenders of State Sovereignty"—furthered this version of the past.[79]

There is little to suggest that Carr and other Confederate veterans distanced themselves from the cause of slavery primarily because they feared public admonition over the morality of the peculiar institution. As noted above, many former Confederates, including Carr, depicted slavery as a civilizing influence that benefited the enslaved. In denying that slavery caused the war, former Confederates were not espousing equality but were rather converting historical losers into memory's victors.[80] Even at a speech at Bennett Place, where Confederate general Joe Johnston literally surrendered his army, Carr concluded his speech by declaring, "WE LOST BUT WE WON," a statement that hinged on the war's purpose not being the preservation of a now extinct institution. Not surprisingly, Carr celebrated at Bennett Place how well Confederates fought "in the face of adverse public sentiment abroad engendered by the insidious propaganda that we were fighting to perpetuate human slavery."[81]

Although neo-Confederates today often separate slavery from the causes of the conflict to skirt accusations of white supremacy, such a claim in 1913 instead reinforced racist ideologies. Historians have shown that "slavery and race were not interchangeable." Denying slavery as the cause in the early twentieth century allowed former Confederates to claim a victory for white supremacy even as they defended slavery as a benevolent institution. Indeed, this denial corresponded with increased celebrations of white supremacy's success.[82] In his famous 1861 "cornerstone speech," Alexander Hamilton Stephens, vice president of the Confederacy, connected white supremacy to the founding of the Confederacy when he stated, "Our new government is founded upon exactly the opposite idea" from the founding fathers' belief in the "equality of races." He continued, "Its foundations are laid, its corner-stone rests, upon the great truth that the negro is not equal to the white man; that slavery subordination to the superior race is his natural and normal condition." Years later, as part of an essay entitled "Slavery Not the Cause of the War," Virginia Judge George Christian claimed that Stephens had not been discussing the *cause* of the conflict; rather, Stephens had simply asserted "'the great truth that the negro is not the equal of the white man,' and isn't this fact recognized as true to-day in every part of this land?"[83] Christian was hardly arguing that the Confederacy had been in favor of racial equality.

These claims of southern victories for states' rights and state sovereignty were critical to defending contemporary efforts to disenfranchise African Americans with arguments that voting was a state and not a federal issue. In essence, Turner's claim that the war ended in a "compromise" conceded that the Thirteenth Amendment abolishing slavery had been passed while conveniently forgetting the Fourteenth and Fifteenth Amendments, which protected the civil rights of African American and enlarged federal powers. Ratified in 1868 and 1870, the Fourteenth, which provided equal protection under the law regardless of race, and the Fifteenth, which protected African Americans' right to vote, were two of the most important legal outcomes of the war. By championing the principle of states retaining sovereignty over local issues, white southerners provided a legal defense of their disenfranchising African Americans. The Lost Cause has often served as a "call to arms" for white southerners to provide "united resistance to federal intrusion into state affairs."[84] It is no coincidence that those opposed to the civil rights movement in the 1950s and '60s frequently argued that federal intervention was illegal, as the matters at hand were state issues. Today, those seeking to limit the federal government's efforts to protect both civil and voting rights still often focus on the importance of states' rights while downplaying how the Fourteenth and Fifteenth Amendments expanded federal jurisdiction.

Rewriting the cause of the war also helped ensure that what might otherwise be recalled as treason was instead remembered as patriotism. The Republican politicians who called former Confederates traitors in 1900 were not alone. Indeed, in 1928, W. E. B. Du Bois wrote that he felt Robert E. Lee should be thought of as "a traitor and a rebel—not indeed to his country, but to humanity and humanity's God."[85] In the Lost Cause retelling, however, instead of betraying the Constitution to preserve slavery, the Confederacy had paradoxically preserved the Constitution by seceding from it. In arguing that its cause was to defend the Constitution, the Confederacy became not only victorious but also righteous and legal. This effort to transform what might just as easily be recalled as traitorous rebels into American patriots in the memory of white southerners has been remarkably successful. Indeed, as scholars have noted, Confederate soldiers have become American soldiers in the eyes of many Americans. The same cannot be said of others who fought against the United States. Loyalists during the American Revolution are rarely treated as American heroes. The Sioux during the Dakota War, and the Cheyenne and Arapaho from the Colorado War, all contemporaneous with the Confederacy's rebellion, are similarly rarely remembered as *American* heroes.[86]

This phenomenon, as well as defenses of secession's legality, still empower those wishing to celebrate Confederates as heroes and patriots. Defenses of secession's legality allow a distinction to be drawn between Confederate soldiers and others who rebelled, such as enslaved people, without recognizing any double standard. The Lost Cause's claims that secession was legal and that the preservation of the Constitution was the Confederacy's aim—alongside stories of honorable conduct in battle—allow some white southerners to celebrate Confederate soldiers as American heroes fighting for freedom while simultaneously viewing figures like Denmark Vesey, John Brown, and Nat Turner as murderers who broke the law. Alternatively, both slave revolts and the Confederacy could be seen as breaking the law by taking up arms against the state, demonstrating a willingness to kill for their "freedom." The crucial difference between rebel groups in this alternative interpretation was that one wanted to free the enslaved from the horrors of slavery, while the other fought to maintain the privilege of holding people in bondage.[87] Alongside a rewriting of the cause, claiming that secession was legal or actually in defense of the Constitution has often been used to put a veneer of respectability on what otherwise might be seen as a racist double standard in how Americans remember rebels.

Paradoxically, rewriting the cause of the war to marginalize slavery helped former Confederates continue advocating for white supremacy by recasting southern white men as victorious American heroes. Denying slavery as a cause of the war facilitated sectional reconciliation, as it allowed southern white men to cultivate a heroic image of themselves. This denial was also used to shape a new political order and social hierarchy in which African Americans were severely disadvantaged. Rewriting the cause of the war was part of an active effort to proclaim victory morally and in memory, if not on the battlefield, and ultimately, to uphold a system of racial segregation and prejudice. Combined with white southerners' victories over Reconstruction and Fusionism, changing the war's cause provided rhetorical vindication to former Confederates that they had been correct about white supremacy all along.[88]

In both political speeches and Confederate commemorations, the Lost Cause narrative was used to justify not only legal disenfranchisement of African Americans but also the historical and contemporary racial violence necessary to achieve and maintain white political supremacy. In the eyes of both the "moderate" Carr and the more extreme Waddell, the Ku Klux Klan were a force for good aimed at reestablishing the peaceful antebellum race relations that northern intervention had ruined. A belief in formerly faithful slaves, the misrule of Reconstruction, and an ideology of white supremacy thus justified the violence that brought about "Redemption" and maintained Jim Crow. A past in which African Americans had become, "under the influence of the Freedman's Bureau, in many sections, a menace to social order" provided an opening for a heroic Klan to ride in and return society to its "natural" order.[89] In one speech, Carr celebrated how whites had fought with the following goal in mind: "The Anglo Saxon civilization for which the South was famous was now in peril of being subverted, and anarchy was swiftly approaching. To check it, an organization known as the invisible empire commonly called 'The Kuklux,' was adopted by many whites where the conditions were the worst; and it exerted power through terrorizing evil doers. They interfered only with those who were seeking to commit crimes against society."[90] Thus, in his Lost Cause retelling, the Klan became a stabilizing force reasserting peace and the proper order instead of a cause of strife. African Americans were not the victims of white southern violence but rather of unscrupulous carpetbaggers in Carr's description of the past.

The justification of Klan violence, which aimed at uniting white southerners behind Jim Crow policies, went beyond political campaigns. Led by the UDC, white women were central to teaching a heroic narrative of racial violence to future generations. In 1913, for instance, just a few months after Silent Sam was erected, the UDC's national convention "unanimously endorsed" Mrs. S. E. F. Rose's forthcoming book, *The Ku Klux Klan or Invisible Empire,* and "pledged to endeavor to secure its adoption" in classes and placement in libraries. The Sons of Confederate Veterans (SCV) passed a similar resolution the next year. The book's dedication declared that its purpose was to "inspire [southern youth] with respect and admiration for the Confederate soldiers who were the real Ku Klux, and whose deeds of courage and valor, have never been surpassed, and rarely equaled, in the annals of history." Rose portrayed the Klan as a "remarkable organization, whose services were of untold value to the South" and spoke of how it formed for the "purpose of protecting the homes and women of the South." The book, an expansion on an earlier pamphlet sold as a fund-raising tool for a monument at Jefferson Davis's Mississippi home, recounted a Lost Cause version of a Reconstruction full of carpetbaggers who were stopped because "many brave heroes—the Confederate Soldier—who endured all the hardships of those four terrible years of war, were still left to protect, with their last drop of blood, their beloved southland."[91] Reconstruction could not be separated from the war in the minds of Rose and Carr, as both saw the racial violence of former Confederates as crucial to the white South's success.

This heroic narrative celebrating racial violence functioned best if slavery were remembered in a positive fashion, lest violence seem unproductive or unwarranted. For this reason, the UDC and other organizations not only pushed the Lost Cause as correct but also attempted to censure counternarratives. In Kentucky, the UDC successfully lobbied for a law banning a theatrical version of *Uncle Tom's Cabin* and "any play that is based upon antagonisms alleged formerly to exist, between master and slave, or that excites race prejudice." The hypocrisy of the final clause of the sentence coming from a group celebrating the Klan, the blatant unconstitutionality, and the denial of alternative narratives were all symptomatic of the racism and political stakes that drove this retelling of the past.[92]

Perhaps even more significant were efforts to control secondary education. In 1919, the UDC commissioned Mildred Lewis Rutherford to create a pamphlet—*A Measuring Rod to Test Text Books, and Reference Books in Schools, Colleges and Libraries*—to provide curriculum guidelines for southern schools. The UDC encouraged schools to only adopt books that passed their standards, requesting that libraries stamp all books that failed with the tag "Unjust to the South."[93] Among the requirements was that texts had to state, "The War Between The States Was Not Fought to Hold the Slaves," and "Slaves Were Not Ill-Treated In the South." The UCV and SCV created a committee of five veterans and five sons of veterans to endorse the standards, among them Carr.[94] In 1920, in an expanded version of *A Measuring Rod* entitled *Truths of History: A Fair, Unbiased, Impartial, Unprejudiced and Conscientious Study of History,* Rutherford asserted that the "South is the negro's friend," and that any racial strife in the South was caused by "incendiary literature" from the North. "All that the South asks is to be let alone in her management of the negro, so that the friendly relations may occur," wrote Rutherford.[95] These educational standards explicitly aimed to instill an ideology of white supremacy in future generations by teaching children that racial violence was a product of northern interference that would disappear if African Americans just resumed their proper place.

The positive depiction of Klan violence also justified Reconstruction violence's ideological descendent, Jim Crow–era lynching. From 1877 to 1950, over four thousand African Americans were lynched in the South. These horrific murders were used to terrorize black communities, keep African Americans from political activism, and uphold the Jim Crow racial order. By shifting the blame for the South's racial strife to outsiders manipulating previously content African Americans into making uppity demands, lynching in the present could be justified as a necessary evil correcting the greater threat of racial equality.[96] While decrying lynching as awful, Carr stated that he was unwilling to denounce it until African Americans stopped raping white women. He was playing on a common trope, as lynching victims were frequently accused of sexual misdeeds. During a speech to an African American audience, Carr declared, "Mob law tends to anarchy; assault upon helpless women is worse than anarchy." Blaming the victims of racial violence is not a new phenomenon. Carr similarly asserted that African Americans bore the blame for lynching, and "the question of the future of the Southern negro is one that must be deferred for settlement until we have restored safety and a feeling of security to the humblest woman in the poorest cabin in the remotest corner of the most thinly settled portion of the South." Carr openly demanded that African Americans "must say one word in denunciation of lynching where they utter ninety nine in condemnation of the crime which has evolved lynch law."[97] There was no need for equality, as in Carr's eyes, white women's purity and feelings of safety mattered more than black lives.

Carr frequently defended lynching with the myth of loyal, happy slaves during antebellum times. In another speech (also likely to a black audience), he declared that during the war, "our Southern womanhood was not only safe in the keeping of the black race, but they were actually guarded and protected by them." The problem that led to lynching, in Carr's account, was that "no finer type of the colored man is to be found than the type of black man—all too scarce now, that was raised and trained by southern masters and mistresses."[98] As Tara McPherson has pointed out, tales of happy slaves "functioned as a kind of escape scenario, simultaneously underwriting and disavowing . . . fierce lynching campaigns, insisting on a more perfect past, where paternalistic race relations ensured the good behavior of loyal servants."[99] Without slavery to keep African Americans in line, Carr felt that other means had to be used. He and other Lost Cause advocates constructed a narrative of the past stretching from slavery to the present that provided an insidious rationalization for violence against African Americans.

The Lost Cause narrative was useful for uniting whites, but Carr did not stop at trying to sell his version of history to whites in the South and to critics in the North. He wanted a memory of the past to convince southern blacks that behaving and remaining subservient was in their best interests, wielding historical narrative not as a uniting tool but as a threat. Likely invited to speak in large part because of his philanthropy, Carr spoke at historically black Biddle University's graduation in 1911. The industrialist told the African American graduates that denying that slaves and masters had friendly relationships was not only ahistorical but dangerous; he told students that he "would warn you for your own success in life in the land where you must dwell, for your own happiness, if not for your own safety, that you put from out your hearts the feelings of bitterness, which you might cultivate to your own hurt by believing the fiction of fanaticism." The threat toward African Americans that they accept his version of the past and be happy about it or else was explicit. Carr then claimed slavery had Christianized and civilized Africans, and faithful slaves, who cared for their white families even after emancipation, should serve as appropriate role models to African Americans. He even went so far as to argue that the enfranchisement of blacks by northerners evidenced southern whites' success at civilizing "a race of near barbarians," which may have created some cognitive dissidence, given his stance on black enfranchisement.[100]

Carr's demand that his historical narrative be accepted was part of a larger threat. He called upon African Americans to stop appealing to northerners for money "on the ground of the negro's ill-treatment" in the South. Rather, Carr argued, "The Southern white man is the negroe's best friend," and "there is no negro who has lived on this soil *and behaved himself* who has not his white friends upon whom he can call in an emergency."[101] The implication was clear: friendship—and protection from white friends—was contingent on southern blacks' subservience and complacency. Dependent on his donations, university administrators could not make a scene or object to Carr's rhetoric. Everyone in the room likely recognized that Carr was being less than honest about the past, but in telling an obvious lie that no one could publicly contradict, Carr expressed his power, reminding his audience who controlled things in North Carolina.

Carr refused to accept that African Americans might have legitimate political aspirations of their own, telling one assembly, "It is only when you have been prevailed upon to further the political ambitions of a part of the white men of North Carolina, in the late nineties, that peaceful relations of the races here have been temporarily broken." In presenting Fusion coalition successes as a product of northern carpetbaggers cynically manipulating black voters and not of the desires of both black and white North Carolinians, Carr even argued that black North Carolinians benefited from the state's violent return to white Democratic control. In Carr's telling, Fusionism was a second Reconstruction, complete with the same ending and the same cause: outside meddling in southern politics leading to racial violence and the eventual reassertion of white supremacy. Carr's historical narrative served as both an implicit and explicit threat that should people of color try to exert political influence again in the future, they could expect to meet violence once again.[102]

Although the Lost Cause was pervasive in the early twentieth-century South, it was not universal. Historians often overlook African American memories of the Civil War, but African American counternarratives provided some of the most significant opposition to the Lost Cause. A reporter for the Baltimore *Afro-American,* for example, contradicted the message that Confederate veterans were crafting at reunions and monument dedications, attempting to remind readers of a countermemory characterized by an immoral and vanquished cause. Reporting on the UCV's 1929 reunion in Charlotte, at which the veterans dedicated a monument celebrating Anglo-Saxon civilization's victory over Reconstruction, the author recounted how speakers in front of "four thousand senile veterans of the Confederate army" had made "utterances" that "indicate that they have entered their second childhood." Sarcastically portraying veterans rewriting their past as an issue of dotage instead of propaganda, the *Afro-American* reporter objected to multiple claims, including that "slavery was not the cause of the war" and that Confederate "victory was essentially a victory of the spirit." After detailing how preserving slavery was central to the war, the writer argued that if "the war was fought to determine whether a state may secede from the union and whether slavery was to remain a legalized institution," then "the rebels lost on both counts." In fact, the author pointed out that the Confederates had actually been "whipped." While the article was contemptuous and sarcastic in tone, the issue was pressing and deadly serious. The rewriting of the past to make heroes was dangerous because, as the journalist wrote, "the lost cause was not only lost but misguided and God-forsaken. It admits of no sentimental gloss."[103]

African Americans and their allies had resisted many elements of the Lost Cause narrative since the Civil War. Many black Americans recalled a war fought for freedom and understood slavery as a "cruel system." Emancipation Day, a holiday on which southern blacks celebrated the end of slavery, vividly displays this alternative remembrance of that past. In their version, "When the last army of the Confederacy was surrendered by Johns[t]on to Sherman—there was not a colored man in all the South who did not shout with joy," as one Emancipation Day speaker told his audience in 1870. Instead of slavery as a school for civilization, African Americans argued that the South's peculiar institution had "forced" ignorance upon them.[104] And just as the Lost Cause justified the desires of white supremacists, the counternarrative provided an argument for African American rights. If ignorance was pushed upon African Americans, then why should they be penalized and lose rights for the crimes of whites? Celebrations of the Thirteenth, Fourteenth, and Fifteenth Amendments contrasted strongly with the Lost Cause's continued obsession over states' rights. Annual Emancipation Day celebrations frequently included resolutions against mob violence and protests against disenfranchisement.[105]

Still, African Americans had to be careful how they pushed back against the glorification of the Confederacy. Especially after disenfranchisement, the threat of violence influenced African American celebrations and public remembrances. Direct attacks on the Lost Cause could lead to reprisals. For example, in 1901, African Americans in Mildred, North Carolina, celebrated Lee's surrender. White newspaper reports of the celebration across the state included "a little advice" that African Americans "let General Lee and his surrender alone." While Emancipation Day gatherings would be tolerated, celebrations that demeaned Lee would be met with threats. "Too many people here staked their all on the Lost Cause to view with complacency glorification over the downfall of their great chieftain," one newspaper warned.[106] That same year, a similar plan "to give thanks to God for the surrender of Gen. Robert E. Lee" was abandoned when organizers were informed that such an event was "untimely and objected to" by their white "friends."[107] The danger of pushing back too hard led some African American speakers to temper their retelling of the past or even to repeat parts of the Lost Cause to avoid angering their white neighbors.[108]

The idea that there were no other historical narratives for white southerners to learn is a mistaken assumption. In addition to the presence of African Americans' countermemories, some prominent former Confederates disagreed with the rewriting of the past. Confederate colonel John

Singleton Mosby, the famous "Gray Ghost" who befuddled Union commanders in northern Virginia and Maryland, did not accept any pretense
about slavery's role in the war. In 1907, Mosby read Judge Christian's essay
"Slavery Not the Cause of the War," discussed above. In his work, a typical
Lost Cause essay, Christian not only denied that slavery caused the war
but also asserted that because northern merchants had owned most slave
ships, the North was responsible for slavery.[109] In a letter to a friend, Mosby
complained that this was historical revisionism, as "the South went to
war on account of Slavery. South Carolina went to war—as she said in her
Secession proclamation—because slavery wd. not be secure under Lincoln.
South Carolina ought to know what was the cause for her seceding."[110]

Even as Mosby admitted slavery's role in the war, he distanced himself
from any lingering questions about slavery's morality, writing, "I am not
ashamed of having fought on the side of slavery—a soldier fights for his
country—right or wrong—he is not responsible for the political merits of
the cause he fights in. The South was my country."[111] Although acknowledging that the war was caused by slavery, the former guerrilla denied any
personal responsibility for trying to uphold the institution, much like some
modern-day Confederate celebrators disconnect monuments and flags
from the war's racial roots by arguing that these symbols only honor the
soldiers and not the cause. Mosby's position about the war's cause, however, was less popular among white southerners, and denials that the Confederacy was founded to protect slavery continued in politics and public
memory, as it does even today. In 2017, Virginia state senator Dick Black,
representing part of the very region where Mosby fought, asserted, "None
of those [Confederate] soldiers fought to defend slavery." Two years earlier, at UNC, one of the organizers of a neo-Confederate protest to "Defend
Silent Sam's Honor" inaccurately claimed that Confederate soldiers had
opposed "'overbearing government, taxes' and the taking of their land," as
well as "Northern Oppression," but had not fought for slavery.[112]

Carr was not deaf to other narratives—after all, he constantly assailed
them as inaccurate. But when he and other veterans denied that slavery
caused the war, on some level they knew better. Indeed, Carr was not above
shifting his narrative when circumstances called for it. In his Southern Pines
address, he even admitted that "the underlying cause of the disagreement
was the institution of African slavery."[113] Sometimes, as in 1899 while speaking to an African American audience, he skimmed over the topic and downplayed its importance, saying, "This is not the time and place to discuss the
causes of the war for Southern Independence, growing out the divergence
of civilization, and sectional interests in tariffs, navigation laws, rights in
slave property, and the like, with legislation believed to be favoritism for

one section, and oppression for the other."[114] These admissions stand in stark contrast to other speeches where Carr declared, "It is heralded that the northern cause was the cause of liberty and the southern cause the cause of slavery. In seeming that is true; in reality the absolute reverse of it is true," or as he told a group of Union veterans in Detroit, the South did not "appeal to arms to maintain slavery."[115] Clearly, Carr catered his historical interpretation to his audiences. It is ironic that in those speeches where Carr openly admitted that slavery caused the war, it was usually to highlight how loyal slaves had remained. By acknowledging the stakes of the war for African Americans, Carr made the faithfulness of slaves all the more impressive.

The whitewashing of history and fabricating of past events has had lasting impacts on southern society. Stories that African Americans were happy except when outsiders interfered appeared yet again in the civil rights era, when southern segregationists claimed that African Americans were content until "outside agitators" intervened.[116] Even today, politicians and opponents of local protests often inaccurately claim that the majority of protestors are outsiders to the community as a means of delegitimize them. In the twenty-first century, members of neo-Confederate groups frequently use the term "carpetbagger" online to refer to white liberals and historians who openly challenge the Lost Cause, regardless of their geographic origins. Often, these comments are accompanied by assertions that liberals do not really care about African Americans and only want to stir up racial resentment to achieve political goals. Liberals are the real racists, in the rhetoric of the neo-Confederates, because there would be no racism if northern radicals would just stop talking about it. In this manner, the same erasure of black agency and denial of local tensions that Carr preached remains alive today. This does not just occur on the political fringes. This pretense of outside agitators appeared in an email the UNC chancellor sent to students before a 2017 protest calling for Silent Sam's removal.[117]

Though less popular than it was in 1913, even the Lost Cause's heroization of racial violence still survives. In 2017, Georgia legislator Tommy Benton, who claimed the Ku Klux Klan "made a lot of people straighten up" and "was not so much a racist thing but a vigilante thing to keep law and order," was named to a state study committee on civics education![118] He was eventually removed, but only after he sent a mailer to fellow lawmakers denying that slavery caused the Civil War.[119] Benton's views were not confined to the state legislature: he taught history in Georgia schools for thirty years before being elected to office.[120]

While Benton is an extreme case, Ethan Kytle and Blain Roberts have pointed out that "though tempting, portraying southern proponents of

whitewashed memory of slavery as outliers is mistaken."[121] Indeed, polling
data make clear that the Lost Cause remains very much alive. In 2011, a
Pew Research poll found that 48 percent of Americans believed the Civil
War was "mainly about states' rights," while only 38 percent viewed slavery
as the main cause. Nine percent viewed the two issues as equally at fault
for the war. In other surveys, southerners and whites have been found to
misidentify the cause of the war even more frequently, but Pew's survey
found that even 39 percent of African Americans believed that slavery was
not what brought about the conflict.[122] Clearly, many Americans, even those
who do not celebrate the Confederacy, believe certain false aspects of the
Lost Cause narrative to be historically accurate, likely due to its enshrine-
ment in school textbooks, prominent monuments, and popular culture.

The Lost Cause continues to shape American politics as well, especially
on the right. There is a strong correlation between historical and political
viewpoints, with self-identified conservatives far less likely to view slavery
as the cause of the war. A 2015 McClatch-Marrist poll, using a different
methodology than Pew, found that only 47 percent of those identifying as
"Conservative" or "very Conservative" viewed slavery as "the main reason
for the Civil War," while an equal proportion disagreed. A striking difference is seen among self-identified liberals, 67 percent of whom identified
slavery as the primary cause of the war. Moderates fell in the middle, with
55 percent correctly identifying the conflict's root.[123] Today, those espousing
a Lost Cause narrative find that a whitewashed version of history allows
them to ignore the central role of race and racism in shaping American
history, culture, and society. Indeed, the polarization of politics witnessed
in the early twenty-first century is reflective not just of policy differences
but also of fundamental disagreements about the nature of past events.[124]

The modern white power movement, including neo-Nazis, white nationalists, the Klan, and other "alt-Right" groups, did not assimilate Confederate
symbols. Rather, the white power movement was created, both literally and
symbolically, out of the Confederate movement. Modern-day flaggers and
fans of the Confederacy wishing to disassociate their symbols from overt
white supremacists, neo-Nazis, and segregationists often fail to recognize
the roots of the modern white supremacy movement. While it is true that
the Confederate flag took on greater importance and renewed connections
to racism thanks to segregationists during the civil rights movement, Confederate symbols were already intimately tied to white supremacy. Indeed,
long before veterans linked white supremacy and Jim Crow to celebrating the Confederacy in the early twentieth century, the Confederate flag
already carried a racist connotation, and time has only added more layers of

connections. For instance, during the violent 1876 campaign to "redeem" South Carolina from Republicans, C. Irvine Walker, future commander of the UCV, led the Charleston Rifle Club under a Confederate battle flag as they attempted to keep African Americans from voting with armed patrols and a campaign of terrorism.[125]

Today, some of those devoted to celebrating the Confederacy recall the past in a manner even less historically accurate than Carr did during the Jim Crow era. In 2017, one SCV member told a reporter at North Carolina's state fair, "Those men that fought for the Confederate States were honorable men. They were our ancestors, they were not racists."[126] Herein lies the problem: one does not preclude the other. Many of the men and women who erected the Jim Crow–era Confederate monuments that now dot the southern landscape did so to preserve a belief that they felt the Confederacy had shared: all men were not created equal.

A split has occurred in how neo-Confederates understand the war. While some Lost Cause believers do not recognize the ties between the historical narrative they espouse and white supremacy, others remain avowedly white supremacists, white nationalists, or white separatists. Confederate monuments have become a central gathering place for neo-Nazis in the twenty-first century. Both the avowedly racist and those who deny racism are direct descendants of Carr's narration.

The Lost Cause's foundation of lies facilitated the modern disassociation of symbols from their historical meanings. To provide historical support for Jim Crow–era ideologies of white supremacy required not just a twisting of timelines but also the fabrication of a multitude of myths and lies, including that slavery was benevolent and Reconstruction a failure caused by northern interference. Between 1865 and 1900, the fact that the Confederacy was founded to preserve slavery was largely replaced in white southern memories with a new cause as a means of claiming victory. Since then, the Lost Cause has evolved further to the point that even the monuments' creators' intentions to celebrate white supremacy have been forgotten and replaced with arguments that the Confederacy had no connections to racism. Denials of slavery's connection to the war serve a new purpose: to separate the Confederacy from accusations of racism. As overt white supremacy became increasingly socially unacceptable, a new form of the Lost Cause evolved without as many obvious ties to white supremacy, providing one more fabrication of the past for historians to untangle.

2

Inventing Confederates

Creating Heroes to Maintain White Supremacy, 1900–1951

Addressing the crowd at the University of North Carolina's Confederate monument dedication in 1913, Mary Hicks Williams, president of the North Carolina Division of the United Daughters of the Confederacy (UDC), celebrated the "over 700 monuments" the organization had already put up across the South. This was more, she claimed, than had been erected to any other "single cause." These monuments had a purpose, and Williams knew it, declaring, "Poor is the country that boasts no heroes, but beggared is the people who having them, forget."[1] Monuments, she recognized, helped people remember historical figures as heroes, and heroes were part of a process that ensured a specific memory of the war was passed on to future generations.

Monuments were not the only thing needed to propagate the Lost Cause narrative. As discussed in the first chapter, a remembrance of the past that recalled the triumph of white supremacy and Confederate veterans was crucial to both white supremacist political campaigns and to the erection of monuments. For that, the UDC and the Confederate veterans also needed stories of heroes and their valorous deeds to justify the statuary. After all, they needed someone to honor as well as something worth celebrating.

Consider, then, the 1913 dedication speech Julian Carr gave at the University of North Carolina (UNC). It began like most of his addresses about the Civil War by reveling in the glory of the Confederate soldier. He announced, "No nobler young men ever lived; no braver soldiers ever answered the bugle call nor marched under a battle flag," before comparing Confederates to other legendary soldiers. Led by "the world's greatest hero, Robert E. Lee," said Carr with clear hyperbole, "the Spartan lived again in the Confederate Student Uniform. . . . Leonidas clad in the Confederate Students Uniform, arose from the dead to fight under its folds again for his country."[2] Though obviously exaggerated, Carr's version lives on today in history books, both popular and academic—precisely as Carr would have wanted. In an undated speech fragment, Carr laid out what historians should remember about the Confederate soldier. After comparing Confederate military feats to Austerlitz and Thermopylae, he declared, "In fact, the historian of the 20th century that does not do justice to the skill and bravery of the Confederate Army is an unmitigated fraud."[3] Fortunately, I am writing on that topic in the twenty-first century.

In addition to rewriting why the war happened and the nature of southern racial relations, Lost Cause boosters rewrote the conduct of the Confederate army and state. As one scholar has noted, the Lost Cause myth required tales of "heroism against great odds" and not "defeats, desertions, and dissent."[4] The veterans rewriting the past thus needed stories of widespread volunteerism and battlefield valor. Stories of a united population that supported the Confederacy served a similar purpose to the perception encouraged by Democrats in the 1890s that nearly all whites united against Republicans during Reconstruction. The fact that large numbers of whites opposed the Confederacy undermined an imagined history of whites uniting, and it raised awkward questions about how devoted North Carolinians had been to the Confederacy.

Tales of battlefield heroics and volunteerism were also used to demonstrate the superiority of whites. As part of their effort to reconcile the Confederacy's defeat with arguments of white supremacy—after all, how could the greatest soldiers have lost?—North Carolina's veterans claimed to have contributed the most and best troops of any state. Unfortunately for them, North Carolina's wartime history was not as impressive as the veterans wanted to believe. While many North Carolinians fought well, the state's desertion rate, opposition to secession, widespread Unionism, and resistance to conscription undermined claims that there were "no braver soldiers" than those from the Old North State.

Julian Carr, Henry London, and other speakers at Confederate commemorative events in the early twentieth century needed heroic North Carolinians devoted to the Confederacy to celebrate, so to a considerable extent, they created them. These mythmakers ignored their own war records and created stories and even soldiers out of thin air to justify white rule in the South. In doing so, they created fissures within the Confederate memorialization movement across state lines, provided an opening for fake veterans, and left a narrative of the war that still pervades how Americans remember the war. Even today, some historians are influenced by the Lost Cause depiction of exemplary battlefield valor and volunteerism.

Confederate memory makers often recalled the war as one that all white southerners unanimously wanted and supported, creating a solid white South during the war in memory, if not reality. Accordingly, those who erected UNC's monument wanted the school's students remembered as fully supporting the Confederacy. Speakers at the dedication who portrayed the students as unwaveringly devoted to the Confederacy aimed to create heroes of white supremacy that future students might emulate. For example, Governor Locke Craig's keynote address contributed to a myth of widespread, enthusiastic support for the Confederacy by glorifying the way that "these boys were not drafted, the authorities of the University tried to keep them here," pushing a narrative of volunteerism that covered over those who were less enthusiastic about fighting.[5]

While some students and graduates were indeed among the most devoted to the Confederate cause, others were far from enthusiastic about the war. UNC alumnus James Pettigrew, of Gettysburg fame, rushed off and joined the Confederacy right away, stormed Castle Pinckney in Charleston harbor in 1860, and remained a devoted Confederate until his death.[6] Other UNC students, however, had been active opponents of secession. While John Wesley Halliburton, along with a few other students, flirted with Unionism before he was convinced to go with his state, George H. Williamson, a student at UNC at the start of the war, joined the United States Navy.[7] Older graduates also fought for the Union. Colonel Junius Brutus Wheeler, who attended UNC from 1849 to 1851, served as a professor of engineering at West Point throughout the war. Perhaps the university's most notable former student who fought against the Confederacy was Major General Francis Preston Blair Jr., whose father helped found the Republican Party.[8] While most UNC graduates did not join the United States military, many students and alumni wished to avoid Confederate service, and contrary to Craig's assertion, many were, in fact, conscripted.

Indeed, at least two of the dedication speakers knew firsthand that Craig's claims were inaccurate. Henry London, who introduced Governor Craig, and whose wife led the fund-raising campaign to erect the monument, had been among the students who failed to rush off to war. Instead, he had enjoyed his time in college, smoking, drinking, dancing, and carousing, as well as usually attending class.[9] Far from volunteering, as a junior in February 1864, London watched as "a half dozen" underclassman liable for conscription were rounded up and marched off to be enrolled. A week later, in a letter to his sister, London wrote, "Tell Pa not to be afraid of their taking me, as Gov [David] Swain [president of UNC] says there is no danger" of upperclassmen losing their exemption from conscription. Reflecting on the situation, he told his sister, "I would not care much if they did [conscript me], as I hate the idea of skulking, as it were, out of the army, when my Country needs my services so much, but yet when an exemption is proffered a man, he can scarcely be blamed for taking it."[10] When rumors of imminent conscription reached campus in October, London wrote in his diary that while he himself was "perfectly indifferent" as long as he got to serve with his brother, other students were more emotive. As the college administrators lobbied to keep the upperclassmen in school, London recorded how the senior class awaited word of whether they would have to go to war "with fear and trembling . . . some hoping, and others giving up [in] despair."[11] Indeed, London avoided service until he could no longer put it off, being conscripted near the end of 1864.

Was London aware of the irony in his own plea as he introduced the governor that "forever may the monument remain as an object lesson to teach all future generations that duty is the sublimest word in the English language," or had he come to remember his own past as he wanted others to recall it?[12] What went on in his mind and whether he had actually forgotten how he avoided service remains unclear, but the claim that all UNC students went eagerly off to war would be repeated in future years. Even the monument's inscription recounting that the soldiers answered "the call of their country" overlooked those who were dragged to the battlefield by conscription officers. Lost Cause advocates, however, attempted to erase from the narrative any sign of southern white ambivalence toward the Confederacy.

Carr, the only other veteran on stage, also knew that many students refrained from volunteering, as he had himself been conscripted. Though he had turned eighteen in October 1863, he waited to go to war until the next year, when he could no longer put it off. While his biographers and profilers later claimed that he had volunteered, evidence from the period indicates otherwise. Even once he officially entered service, Carr did not rush off to fight. Instead, he managed to get detailed to work as a clerk for the conscription bureau. Until at least September 1864, Carr focused instead on getting others to fight.[13] He was likely nineteen by the time he saw battle, despite that fact that he could have volunteered two years earlier. That men exaggerated their military service is no surprise—this occurs after every war—but these exaggerations served specific purposes related to white supremacy, allowing the Confederate soldier to be recalled as the pinnacle of manhood.

The extent of Confederate volunteerism has been overstated in historiography as well as in the public imagination. Even some historians still seem to assume that Confederate soldiers or even most white southerners were nearly unanimously devoted to the cause and unbreakable until the end. One recent book calls Lincoln's belief in southern dissenters "a delusion."[14] While Lincoln was wrong about the extent, organization, and strength of Unionism, recent historiography shows that many southerners opposed

Confederate authorities. It is worth noting that West Virginia seceded from Virginia, *white* southerners contributed 100,000 men to the US Army, and over 200,000 African Americans, the majority from the South, also served in the US military.[15]

The speakers at UNC in 1913 were not just fabricating volunteerism, however—they literally created Confederate soldiers who had never existed. Reporting on the monument's dedication, Henry London's newspaper, the *Chatham Record,* detailed how "no other institution of learning, either North or South, sent so many soldiers into the army during the War between the States as did the University of North Carolina."[16] London's claim demonstrates how rapidly fabrications evolved. At the dedication just a few days earlier, Carr had actually said that no university *except the University of Virginia* contributed so many Confederate soldiers.[17] London may have misheard, but regardless, Carr's numbers were questionable to begin with. In the two weeks leading up to the dedication, Carr and university president Francis Venable corresponded about how many students had served and what ranks they achieved.[18] Like the proverbial fish, the numbers kept growing. In a May 28 letter, Venable admitted to Carr that he had no "exact or satisfactory data," but he felt "it is nearer 1000 than [the] 500" privates Carr had estimated in an earlier correspondence, concluding, "I think it would be safe to say about 1000 privates." A 1901 study from which Carr based his initial estimates had claimed that 1,062 UNC graduates served, but by the time he was in front of a crowd, Carr claimed 1,800 UNC-affiliated enlistees of various ranks in his speech.[19] The numbers were clearly made up—indeed, one scholar estimates that were only 1,592 living UNC alumni at the time of the war.[20] As can be seen in the accompanying table, over the course of a few letters, the two men made up over seven hundred soldiers, including three major generals. They also fabricated casualties, nearly doubling the number of UNC dead. By exaggerating the numbers, Carr made North Carolina appear more devoted to the Confederacy and hence less responsible for defeat.

In the aftermath of the war, debates arose over who was at fault for the Confederacy's loss. In an effort to lay the blame for defeat elsewhere, many veterans argued that their state's troops had been the most loyal, devoted, and courageous. These debates, which on the surface seem petty and unimportant, betray larger concerns. As the Lost Cause narrative was crafted, there was not always a solid Confederate version of the past, but the importance of portraying Confederate soldiers as heroic and noble was paramount for southern whites to lay claim to the right of local self-government without African American participation.

The truth was that North Carolina's Confederate record was questionable at best. Secession came late, large sections of the state had a reputation

TABLE 1. The number of UNC students claimed at each rank in various sources

Rank	Kemp Battle's study (1901)	Carr's estimate (May 27, 1913)	Venable's adjustments (May 28, 1913)	Carr's speech (June 2, 1913)
Lt. Gen.	1	1	1	1
Maj. Gen.	1	1	4*	4
Brig. Gen.	13	13	13	13
Col.	50	50	71*	71
Lt. Col.	28	28	39*	30
Majors	40	40	65*	65
Adjutants	46	46	46	46
Surgeons	71	71	71	71
Captains	254	254	254	254
Lt.	155	155	161*	161
Noncommissioned	38	38	38	38
Privates	365	500*	1,000*	1,000
Calculated total from above	1,062	1,197*	1,763*	1,754
Total claimed	1,062	1,500*	N/A	1,800*
Total dead	312	500*	N/A	500 or 600*
Total number from classes of 1850–62	842	842	N/A	842
Calculated total from classes other than 1850–62	220	658	N/A	958

Note: Asterisks indicate when inflation occurred.

for Unionism, and numerous regions had required frontline troops to suppress dissent during the war. North Carolina also had more exemptions from the draft than most states, and both the state's supreme court and governor had hampered Confederate conscription efforts. With a poor war record, the highest desertion rate, a history of large numbers of white Republicans, and the recent success of the Fusionists in the 1890s, at the turn of the twentieth century, no group needed the Lost Cause narrative of superior military ability more than North Carolina's Democratic Party.[21]

In 1901, North Carolina's state government produced a five-volume set, *Histories of the Several Regiments and Battalions from North Carolina, in the Great War 1861–'65*, in which the authors, including London, pushed a narrative of superior North Carolina bravery. The books came with engraved covers stating, "First at Bethel / Farthest to the Front at Gettysburg / And Chickamauga / Last at Appomattox," which by the early twentieth century had become a mantra of North Carolina's accomplishments repeated by those enamored with its variation of the Lost Cause. North Carolinians claimed to have provided the troops who died first at the Battle at Bethel, advanced farthest at Gettysburg and Chickamauga, and fired the last volley at Appomattox. So central was this to remembrance of North Carolina as the most accomplished Confederate state that Julian Carr repeatedly declared in speeches at both Confederate celebrations and Democratic campaign rallies that on every monument in North Carolina "should be carved First at Bethel—Foremost at Gettysburg, Farthest at Chickamauga—Last at Appomattox."[22]

Efforts to create a memory of North Carolina as the most loyal state with the most and best Confederate soldiers created fractures between states. In 1913, Carr was not breaking new ground when he said at UNC's monument dedication, "And I dare to affirm this day, that if every State of the South had done what North Carolina did without a murmur, always faithful to its duty whatever the groans of the victims, there never would have been an Appomattox . . . and the political geography of America would have been re-written."[23] A debate over which state was most loyal to the Confederacy was already well established, and Virginians, who also wanted to claim that they were not at fault for defeat, had long objected to statements like Carr's touting North Carolina as the most loyal.

Judge George Christian of Virginia took offense at North Carolina's claims and published a report complaining that these boasts "proclaim the fact that the troops furnished by her were better, and therefore, did better . . . than those from any other State."[24] Christian's report, titled "North Carolina and Virginia in the Civil War," focused on a variety of claims North Carolinians made about their state's heroics. He began by objecting to assertions that North Carolina provided more troops than Virginia, as this "necessarily implies that North Carolina was more loyal to the Confederate cause than Virginia."[25] Even in 1903, Judge Christian could understand a basic principle of historical memory: collective memories evolve. Questioning each of North Carolinians' claimed achievements, he noted contemptuously that North Carolina's claims had started as "First at Bethel, Last at Appomattox," while Gettysburg and then Chickamauga were added later. Then again, Christian was a great reviser of history himself. He produced the report on

the causes of the war to which John Singleton Mosby had objected for denying slavery's role in the conflict. Other historical articles he wrote laid the
blame for Andersonville on the Union, declared that the North started the
war, and contrasted Union and Confederate actions to show that Confederates fought more gallantly.[26] While Confederate veterans south of Virginia
agreed with many of Christian's reports, Henry London and others felt that
his complaints about North Carolina besmirched the state's reputation.

Thus, the North Carolina Literary and Historical Association formed a
committee of seven veterans to write a book refuting the Virginian. London
provided a chapter titled "Last at Appomattox," while other prominent veterans wrote chapters on North Carolina being "First at Bethel," "Farthest at
Gettysburg," and "Farthest at Chickamauga," as well as one on the number
of troops the state furnished. In 1904, the essays were published as *Five
Points in the Record of North Carolina in the Great War of 1861–65*. At the
top of the cover page, the North Carolina motto, *Esse Quam Videri*—To be
rather than to seem—prefaced their argument that regardless of appearances, North Carolina had contributed more than other states. Perhaps the
reverse, *Videri Quam Esse*, would have been more appropriate.[27] Even the
book's claim as to the number of North Carolina troops, 125,000, is suspect
but remains commonly accepted by historians.[28]

On July 3, 1863, after the largest artillery barrage ever up to that point, dis-
gruntled Confederate general James Longstreet, not wishing to give the
order, simply nodded to his subordinate's request for permission to charge.
Three Confederate divisions under the command of Isaac Trimble, James
Pettigrew, and George Pickett streamed out from under the cover of the
trees to march across an open field in central Pennsylvania toward the center of the Union's line. This was, of course, the famed Pickett's Charge.
Overly romanticized in literature, art, and film, the third day of the Battle
of Gettysburg was anything but romantic.[29] Minié balls, shells, canister, and
grapeshot poured into the Confederate charge. There was nothing enjoy-
able about one's head being blown to pieces by a screaming hunk of metal
or an arm being ripped to shreds by shrapnel. The ultimately futile charge
resulted in a Confederate retreat after causalities in excess of 50 percent.
Ordered to regroup his division, Pickett famously remarked, "General Lee, I
have no division now." Four days later, a soldier walking the battlefield still
could not avoid the "smell of putrified blood."[30] According to legend, memory, and popular histories, the disastrous charge on July 3, 1863, was "the
high-water mark of the Confederacy." It was, many white southerners felt,
the deepest into Union territory the South ever went; after that point, the
South lost the initiative and fought a defensive war for the next two years.

A fight over who fought better at Pickett's Charge and, by extension, who bore responsibility for its failure started early. Pickett's own report was so damning that Lee had it destroyed, so historians do not know exactly what it said. Some commentators blamed Pettigrew, and rumors spread quickly regarding the cowardice of North Carolina troops.[31] Within weeks of the battle, Virginia newspapers reported that Pettigrew's men had retreated first, leaving "Pickett left alone" to be annihilated without support.[32] North Carolina newspapers objected to such depictions of Pettigrew's troops, which impinged on the honor of "North Carolina, whose blood has been shed upon every field, whose deeds have proudly illustrated the heroism and chivalry of the South, and whose people from Buncombe to the sea have been the soul of loyalty, devotion and patriotism."[33] This debate did not end after Appomattox.

Nearly fifty years after the charge, as he spoke to the crowd gathered on UNC's campus in June 1913, Governor Locke Craig noted that "nothing more heroic was ever done in war" than that charge across a Pennsylvania field, and that North Carolina's troops had been "equal to the Spartans at Thermopylae." Craig's recounting emphasized the heroic, erasing anyone who behaved less courageously than those who made it to the Union lines, and ignored the giant tactical mistake that in retrospect Pickett's Charge clearly was. Painting all North Carolina soldiers with one brush, Craig told his audience that their state deserved the lion's share of credit, adding, "History should write Pettigrew and Pickett's charge. They both led it. North Carolina was the farthest and foremost."[34] One of the preeminent battlefield historians of the Civil War, Earl Hess, points out that Pickett's Charge "has come to symbolize the Confederate War Effort itself."[35] Because of this symbolism, the charge's increased importance in postwar debates over memory continued long after the last veteran died; a monument to North Carolina's claim that they went farthest was even erected at Gettysburg in 1986.[36]

By 1913, "farthest at Gettysburg" had already become a rallying cry for North Carolinians defending their state's Confederate record. But who went farthest? On the surface, to a military historian, the debate borders on the absurd. Veterans, however, used it as a means of measuring Confederate devotion without considering how differences in terrain, starting point, exposure to artillery, and enemy troop quality might have impacted the battle. What "farthest" even meant was never clearly demarcated, and so Virginians and North Carolinians created definitions that suited their needs. Judge Christian carefully defined it as who had "penetrated the enemy's works farthest," an honor that belonged to Virginians.[37] North Carolinians demarcated *farthest* as who made it farther east; because the Union line bent backward where Pettigrew's men attacked, this definition allowed North Carolina to claim the title despite having never penetrated Union lines.[38]

Even were a definition agreed upon, the reality of what actually occurred at Gettysburg is unknowable. Indeed, firsthand accounts often shed little light about how far two units marched in comparison to each other. Contradicting reports—the result of a desire for glory, an impetus to excuse mistakes, and the fog of war—make many details of the battle hard to discern. Each soldier only saw fragments of the action and remembered even less, and as time passed, recollections became less reliable.[39] As with every battle, the smoke of fabrication obscures scholars' views as much as the fog of war did those of the soldiers who witnessed the battle. One veteran told John Bachelder, an early historian of the battle, that he faced "a herculean task to separate the truth from the falsehood in the multitude of reports that have rained down on you since 1863."[40] David Buehler, vice president of the Gettysburg Battlefield Memorial Association, heard many "preposterous and absurd claims" at the countless monument dedications he attended. He attributed these inaccuracies to a combination of factors: "partially because the members of each command saw only what transpired in its immediate front, and then again, the recollections of what did occur are frequently colored by camp-fire stories, until fact and fancy become intermingled."[41] These fabrications were not always purposeful. In an effort to make sense of a traumatic experience, veterans incorporated stories they heard from others, even if they themselves did not witness a specific event. Some tales, however, were just lies. Fifty years after the war, Pickett's own wife apparently fabricated letters from her husband to make him look better.[42]

These debates focusing on who was most valiant served to erase some aspects of the battle entirely. Pettigrew's troops served to stand for North Carolinians and Pickett's for Virginians. Ironically, Pettigrew's poorest-performing troops were from Virginia. Large numbers of the 22nd Virginia did not even charge, and many of Pettigrew's Virginians who did start never made it past the Emmittsburg road, being turned back by an inferior force of 150 Ohio infantrymen. Because of loyalty to their home state, however, Virginia's veterans tended to overlook or obscure the failures of Pettigrew's Virginian troops.[43] Indeed, Christian's rebuttal of North Carolina's claims pointed out that the 55th North Carolina and "Brockenbrough's [brigade] *were the first troops to give way,*" neglecting to mention that Brockenbrough's troops consisted of three Virginia regiments and one Virginia battalion.[44] In refuting the arguments Virginians made, North Carolinians also rarely focused on Pettigrew's Virginians—who, after all, were commanded by a North Carolinian—and instead focused on examples of Tar Heel bravery.[45] Neither side of this debate had any desire to slander other Confederate soldiers, thus making the entire Confederacy seem less impressive; they just wanted to be seen as the most heroic themselves.

This focus on finding examples of bravery, real or fabricated, led veterans to invent imaginative ways to spin even the most damning of facts in a positive light. In 1901, in the third edition of his pamphlet *Pickett or Pettigrew? North Carolina at Gettysburg,* W. R. Bond actually tried to paint disorganized fleeing (instead of an organized retreat) by North Carolinians as evidence of the soldiers' devotion to the Confederacy. Bond argued that Pettigrew's men "felt that to surrender when there was a reasonable hope of escape was very little better than desertion," while Pickett's Virginians "were not quite as extreme as this."[46] Hence, Bond explained, Pettigrew's men fled pell-mell to the rear to avoid capture, while Pickett's men surrendered to save their lives.

The attempt to deny that North Carolinians surrendered in large numbers was not based on reality. Plenty of North Carolinians and other Confederates surrendered at the Battle of Gettysburg. Indeed, the Union captured at least twice the number that were killed.[47] Casualties for the charge have been estimated at around 1,123 killed and 3,750 captured, and Pettigrew's men may have actually provided more prisoners than Pickett's.[48] With the exception of battles involving African American troops, battlefield surrender was common. Indeed, surrender happened more frequently in the Civil War than in any other American conflict. Approximately 462,634 Confederate soldiers surrendered at some point in the conflict, including at Appomattox and other large-scale surrenders.[49]

In fairness, if Confederates felt they were honor-bound to continue fighting, then surrender might have seemed a quick way of returning to battle. Up until Gettysburg, the Dix-Hill Cartel, which provided for the exchanging of prisoners, had largely worked to quickly return men from both sides to combat. Indeed, for many Confederates, not surrendering seemed to increase the likelihood of dying needlessly, while giving up ensured they could continue fighting after being exchanged. David Silkenat has shown that "rather than engage in close-quarters or hand-to-hand combat with the enemy, which would have resulted in heavy casualties, soldiers on both sides concluded that when enemy soldiers came in such close contact, surrender was the inevitable result." In later battles, after the end of the Dix-Hill Cartel, some soldiers became more reluctant to surrender. This is not to say that many soldiers did not fight valiantly but rather to show that in 1863, surrender was not yet viewed as an end to one's military service. As a matter of survival, Silkenat argues, "the frequency of Confederate surrenders during Pickett's Charge indicates that many rebel soldiers went into the assault believing that allowing themselves to be taken prisoner was preferable to assaulting an ensconced Union Line." Indeed, Silkenat's research implies that a willingness to surrender may have contributed to the failure of the charge.[50]

When Henry London finally went to war in 1865, his elite social status likely helped ensure he was made a courier. Indeed, it was this fortuitous assignment that led to his moment of fame.[51] On April 9, 1865, London carried the cease-fire order to General William Cox's brigade. Cox's North Carolinians reportedly received the order to cease firing last. This event became the root of the postwar claim that North Carolina fired the last volley at Appomattox, and London used his part to launch himself into the upper ranks of the Lost Cause boosters. As former Confederates from North Carolina and Virginia engaged in a long dispute over which state contributed more to the Confederacy, London's story became key evidence of North Carolina's devotion to the cause. In his frequent speeches at Confederate monument dedications and memorial days, London often spoke of his role in the Army of Northern Virginia's final moments.[52]

If "farthest at Gettysburg" seems like a pointless argument, claims about who fired last at Appomattox seem almost ridiculous. Why did George Christian and other Virginians care who fired the last volley and object to North Carolina's claim?[53] After all, Virginians could have interpreted North Carolina's claim that they were "Last at Appomattox" as a sign that London was the least competent messenger. Or, if one were to take a less snarky and more sympathetic view—and what is likely the historically accurate explanation—they might have simply noted that the North Carolinians were on the extreme right of the Confederate army, meaning London had the farthest of any courier to carry the surrender order. Put simply, who fired last mattered because North Carolina was rewriting its past at the expense of Virginia's. Just as they were doing when they claimed they had marshaled more forces per capita and suffered more causalities than other states, North Carolinians were showing that they had done everything they could to achieve victory. Implicitly and explicitly, this meant that other states did not contribute as much as they could have.

To Christian, if North Carolinians only stopped fighting and surrendered because Lee and the rest of the army forced them to, then Virginians might be perceived as at fault for defeat. Indeed, London even claimed that Bryan Grimes, the North Carolina commander to whom London brought the fateful message, considered warning his men that surrender was eminent so they might try to escape and then join Johnston's army in North Carolina. Only the intervention of General John Gordon of Georgia kept Grimes from acting. Gordon supposedly asked the North Carolinian melodramatically if he was going "to desert the army and tarnish his honor as a soldier, and added that it would be a reflection on General Lee and an indelible disgrace to him (Grimes) if he, an officer of high rank, should escape while a flag of truce was pending." Whether true or not, London's telling of the surrender told audiences that honor alone forced Grimes and his North Carolinians to surrender, and that "so horrible to General Grimes was the idea of surrendering" that he considered deserting.[54] His reluctance to surrender demonstrated North Carolina's loyalty to the Confederacy, displacing blame toward the Union's overwhelming numbers and, perhaps inadvertently, on Lee, a Virginian.[55]

A reputation tarnished by surrender, desertion, retreat, cowardice, and defeat all contradicted the claims of Carr and others that they had been the greatest soldiers since Thermopylae, so in writing accounts of the battle, they erased everything negative. That old soldiers exaggerated their conduct in war is hardly surprising or unique, but they erased their failings not just because they wanted to be remembered fondly by their grandchildren. The stakes were far greater. Debates over which state was most loyal, contributed more troops, fired last at Appomattox, or went farthest at Gettysburg were not just contemporaneous to white supremacy campaigns across the South—they were *connected*. These debates were largely driven by individuals involved in Democratic politics because both the individuals and Lost Cause narrative were closely tied to white supremacist politics.

A heroic narrative about Confederate soldiers was crucial both to justify white political control achieved through undemocratic means and to unite southern whites behind the Democratic Party. In a 1900 campaign speech arguing for a literacy requirement for voters that included a grandfather clause exempting whites, future North Carolina governor Charles Aycock declared that whites had already earned the ballot over the generations because the "Anglo-Saxon race is the all conquering race intended by God to be the rulers of the world." To prove this, Aycock rhetorically asked an audience, "Who were the men that carried the banner of the Confederacy farthest North at Gettysburg?" The answer he provided them: "White men, every one of them." Indeed, in defeat, Aycock argued, whites had earned the right to rule the South because "the superiority of the white man" had been shown by their deeds at Gettysburg.[56]

While he declared that whites had already earned their vote, Aycock claimed that the same could not be said for African Americans. Justifying the literacy requirement for black North Carolinians to vote, he told the audience that because "the Negro can't get [suffrage] from inheritance, therefore we say he must get it by education."[57] If white North Carolinians fought poorly, then the entire premise that whites alone deserved to rule might became suspect, so Aycock, Carr, and others turned a literal defeat into a rhetorical victory. Similarly, if black North Carolinians had fought well, then they would have earned the ballot as well. In the Lost Cause version of history that Carr and Aycock imparted, the role of black Union troops was forgotten because actions that proved black manhood were unacceptable. Indeed, Carr told a black audience, "The freedom of the negro race was given to him, after a bloody struggle between white men, in which the negro had little part."[58] As discussed in the previous chapter, myths of loyal slaves and corrupt Reconstruction were used to justify disenfranchisement and racial violence. Tales of black soldiers challenged claims that slaves had been loyal and never wanted freedom until white northerners interfered and created racial strife in the South.[59]

At political rallies in the early twentieth century, Gettysburg was often used as a contrast to African Americans' supposed inability to govern. In July 1900, at a speech given to one of the state's "white supremacy clubs" that sprang up during that year's campaign, Charles F. Warren laid out this argument in a typical form. He claimed that Gettysburg, where North Carolinians, "by the winnows of dead at the furthest point," marked the "zenith" of the Confederacy, proved the nobility of white men, while the misrule of Reconstruction showed that "the negro must not, shall not, rule this land."[60] It seems notable that veterans from Virginia and North Carolina disagreed the most over the history of the war. North Carolina with Fusionism and Virginia with the Readjuster movement were the two states where Democrats had the hardest time uniting whites under the banner of white supremacy after Reconstruction.

Even children who witnessed the election of 1900 picked up on how Gettysburg and the memory of the Lost Cause were being used to justify white supremacy and the disenfranchisement of African Americans. For example, Mary Belle Gary's 1901 grade school graduation paper on "the spirit of liberty that characterizes North Carolinians" compared the success of the white supremacy campaign a year earlier to both the success of the Ku Klux Klan and the valor shown when "true to [North Carolina's] character, North Carolina troops went farthest up the slopes of Gettysburg and made the last charge at Appomattox." She concluded her graduation speech by celebrating the election of 1900, where North Carolinians and their "love of liberty . . . wrested North Carolina's government from the Fusionists and established White Supremacy forever."[61]

Maintaining a historical narrative centered on Anglo-Saxon achievements encompassed more than just the Civil War. The memory of North Carolinians as central at Gettysburg and Appomattox was part of a larger attempt to recollect key "Anglo-Saxon" accomplishments as centered on North Carolinians. The state had its own founding narrative that looked away from Massachusetts, Pennsylvania, and Virginia and instead centered the story of "Civilization" in America on North Carolina. The Roanoke colony's Virginia Dare was recalled as the "first child of Anglo-Saxon blood" born in the United States.[62] Though Dare was often portrayed as a grown woman, there is no evidence that she survived to adulthood—and hence, white North Carolinians were not descendants of hers. Claims were also made throughout the nineteenth and twentieth centuries that a "Mecklenburg Declaration of Independence" signed in 1775 (a year before the actual Declaration of Independence) meant North Carolina declared independence first, before Jefferson ever wrote his famous words. Of course, the document was most likely fraudulent, as no record existed of it before 1819.[63]

Beginning in the late 1880s, a group of Greensboro residents began working to commemorate the Battle of Guilford Courthouse as a "mecca of Patriotism" that celebrated North Carolina's crucial role in the Revolution. In addition to monuments about the actual battle, the Guilford Battleground Company erected memorials to North Carolina generals who had died before the battle even occurred. The company aimed to make North Carolina central to the American Revolution and in 1901 even erected a monument on their Guilford County park to a 1771 skirmish from an earlier conflict that occurred in Alamance County, claiming it was "the first battle of the Revolutionary War." Further linking two distinct conflicts, the monument conflated two individuals who bore the same name. Much as with the claims of an earlier declaration of independence, reality was less important than celebrating North Carolina's leadership. A monument to the Battle of Kings Mountain, which by then was known to have occurred in South Carolina, was similarly dedicated at Guilford. North Carolinians claimed the victory as theirs because at the time of the battle, there was confusion as to within which colony Kings Mountain was located. The Alamance monument was eventually relocated to the actual site of the prerevolutionary skirmish, while the monuments to generals who never set foot on the battlefield and the Kings Mountain marker were all removed by the National Park Service in 1937.[64]

Exaggerating battlefield valor and the extent of volunteerism were not the only historically inaccurate aspects of how Confederate veterans wanted themselves remembered. Perhaps no aspect of the state's reputation caused more hand-wringing among North Carolina's Confederate memory makers than its high rate of desertion.[65] During the war, numerous commanders noted that North Carolinians had a tendency to be less reliable. Robert E.

Lee even complained about the state's desertion rate, which was the highest within the Confederacy.[66] Historian Joseph Glatthaar argues that the increased rates of Virginians and North Carolinians taking "French leave" from Lee's army likely had to do with opportunity. It was, after all, far easier for a North Carolinian to get home from Virginia that it would be for a Texan.[67] In addition to a legacy of desertion, the state had an attendant reputation for anti-Confederate dissent.[68] Captain Thomas Hunter, briefly in charge of the defenses of Roanoke Island, found eastern North Carolinians so disloyal that he felt "the maintenance of this position possible only so long as it is defended by troops from another State or from a more loyal part of North Carolina."[69] Lost Cause advocates made a concerted effort to deny dissent and desertion, or barring that, to display them as signs of courage and devotion.

Like erasing white Republicans from accounts of Reconstruction, ignoring or even denying that dissent existed served to help create unified, loyal Confederates in the minds of white southerners. In 1905, at the unveiling of the Forsyth Confederate Memorial in Winston-Salem, Alfred Waddell, who led the Wilmington coup in 1898 and had run against Carr in 1900, told the crowd that "it was the morale of the Confederate Army and the Confederate people that made them forever famous."[70] That Forsyth County had voted against secession and been home to numerous bands of deserters and dissenters was forgotten. The fact that the county had resorted to a draft because it could not fill its enlistment quotas in March 1862 (a month before the start of conscription) was similarly erased.[71]

Other Lost Cause boosters tried to make a place for individuals with Unionist politics by making the state's devotion to the Confederacy all the more remarkable. In a speech two years earlier, Julian Carr openly admitted that "Forsyth was a Union County" that opposed secession before explaining that even the most loyal Union man came over to the Confederacy in 1861 once the war began. "The people of Forsythe County were typical of the state at large in that their loyalty to the Union, strained at length to the breaking point, re-acted from Lincoln's call for troops to 'suppress the rebellion,' to an embrace of the 'Lost Cause,'" declared Carr.[72] Not only did his narrative help separate the state's secession from slavery, but it also ignored the hundreds of deserters, recusant conscripts, Unionists, and other dissenters from the region who never came over to the Confederate cause.

North Carolina boosters often denied that North Carolina had high desertion rates. In *Pickett or Pettigrew? North Carolina at Gettysburg,* W. R. Bond not only claimed that North Carolinians retreated to avoid surrender at Gettysburg but also contested the rates of desertion for the state. Bond's pamphlet, one of many publications to which Christian and other Virginians had objected, claimed that "with the exception of South Carolina probably no State in the Confederacy had so few soldiers 'absent without leave' as North Carolina," but that "owing to unfortunate surroundings neither the head of the army nor the administration ever realized this fact."[73] What exactly those surroundings were that misled Lee remained unclear.

Bond even argued that those who deserted were actually the most loyal Confederates. He claimed that desertions "never occurred" in summer but only in winter: "When the men had time to think of their families, hundreds of whom were suffering for the necessities of life, did the longing desire to see them and minister to ther [sic] wants overcome every other sentiment, and dozens of them would steal away."[74] In reality, desertion increased after Chancellorsville and Gettysburg.[75] Bond was neither the first nor last defender of the Confederacy to present desertion as a noble act to protect one's family. A fundamental aspect of the Lost Cause narrative and the artificial memory of a unified white South was ensuring that deserters were not remembered as dissenters or cowards. Indeed, by presenting deserters as going home to protect their families, these deserters could be lauded as the epitome of white manhood. But while some clearly did desert for the sake of their families, not all deserters did, and the veterans pushing this narrative often did so to unite southern whites politically. And they succeeded, as this view of Confederate desertion has been reiterated by numerous historians.[76]

One of the easiest ways to keep deserters from being seen as disloyal was to co-opt their story into legends of superior manhood and devotion. Confederate memory makers presented family responsibilities as an acceptable reason to desert. The story of artilleryman Edward Cooper was a favorite to tell at dedications and other Confederate celebrations. Julian Carr frequently ended his speeches with Cooper's wartime experiences. The tale begins with Cooper receiving the following heartbreaking letter from his wife in 1863:

> My dear Edward;—I have always been proud of you, and since your connection with the Confederate Army, I have been prouder of you than ever before. I would not have you do anything wrong for the world; but, before God, Edward, unless you come home, we must die! Last night, I was aroused by little Eddie crying. I called and said "What's the matter, Eddie?" And he said, "Oh mama, I am so hungry!" And Lucy, Edward, your darling Lucy, she never complains, but she is growing thinner and thinner every day. And before God, Edward, unless you come home, we must all die. (Signed) Your Mary[77]

Cooper, a loyal Confederate, immediately and repeatedly asked his commanding officer for a furlough, but his requests were rejected. Of course, as a father, he had no choice. Loyal to the Confederacy but fearful for his family, Cooper deserted and went home, a classic example of divided loyalties. Upon his arrival, Mary hugged him and whispered, "I am so glad that you got your furlough." Apparently, she sensed something was wrong, and, realizing with horror that her husband had deserted, cried, "Oh Edward, Edward, go back! Go back! Let me and the children go down to the grave, but oh, for heaven's sake, save the honor of your name." And so Edward returned to his unit to face his court-martial willingly. Carr explained to audiences that the court-martial had no choice but to sentence Cooper to death, though it pained all five judges to do so, even to the point of tears. Luckily, the great hero of the Confederacy, Robert E. Lee, pardoned poor Edward.[78]

Cooper's story did not end there. He returned to his unit, but during the next battle was mortally wounded. Though his whole unit had been killed or fled, the dying artilleryman continued to fight. Spotting the general who had sentenced him to die, Cooper called out, "General, tell me, I have one shot left, have I saved the honor of Mary and Lucy?" Edward Cooper, hero of the Confederacy, then fired one last round before "the husband of Mary and the father of Lucy sank by his gun to rise no more."[79] Cooper was the perfect hero for Confederate memory makers: a private, a nonslaveholder, loyal to the Confederacy, pardoned by the great Lee, who died heroically defending honor and his family.

Cooper's tale supported the Lost Cause mythology in a multitude of ways. His dying for Mary glossed over the causes of the war, presenting Confederates as fighting to protect their families. Lee provided a classic southern aristocratic gentleman, saving the soldier from death. Most importantly, the story presented an acceptable reason to have deserted while remaining loyal, as Cooper only fled to protect his suffering family. By recognizing and embracing the complexities and hard choices many deserters had actually been forced to make, the Lost Cause valorized deserters without requiring a disavowal of their devotion to the Confederacy. As discussed in the next chapter, over time, an alternative countermemory of principled desertion by Unionists was replaced with desertion from a sense of familial responsibility. Edward Cooper's story, told over and over, contributed to this forging of the myth of the loyal deserter.

There was only one problem with the story: Edward Cooper was a fabrication. Though historians still cite his letter as authentic, no contemporary record of the court-martial, pardon, or man exists. He was not real. While some historians might point to the destruction of Confederate archives as an explanation, a deeper look at the story and how it changed over time makes clear that it was meant as a parable at best, but more likely was just a lie.

The story and Cooper's trial and death sentence bear little semblance to wartime reality. First and foremost, there was never a requirement to sentence deserters to death; courts-martial had broad leeway to consider extenuating circumstances, and indeed, the vast majority of deserters received lesser sentences.[80] In fact, courts were careful to avoid sentencing men to death just because an example was needed.[81] The majority of captured deserters were returned to duty and never even tried, and of those tried and convicted, most were never executed.[82] Only 6 percent of Confederate courts-martial resulted in death sentences, most of which were never carried out. Studies show that despite 1,342 North Carolina deserters being returned to service in just the four months from December 1863 to March 1864, there were only 160 to 170 actual executions of North Carolina troops throughout the entire war. This small number arose out of 450 death sentences and 3,200 courts-martial.[83] A case like Cooper's would almost certainly have resulted in some minor punishment by his commanding officer—likely the docking of pay—and would be unlikely to go to trial. Additionally, because Cooper returned, had he been court-martialed, the appropriate charge would have been being the lesser crime of being absent without leave, not desertion. Executing men who returned on their own made little sense for an army chronically short of manpower. The death sentence, however, added a heroic moment for Robert E. Lee to be seen as the perfect soldier and southern gentleman. Ironically, Lee actually felt that the army was too lenient on deserters and argued for more executions to maintain order.[84]

Where, then, did the story originate? The first version of it appears in 1874 at a political gathering in Tuscumbia, Alabama.[85] Told by ex-Confederate general Cullen Battle, who claimed to have been the president of the court-martial, the story proliferated in newspapers across the country, reaching San Francisco by October.[86] In the years that followed, newspapers periodically reprinted it. Like a game of telephone, details changed, shifted, and were created.[87] Shortly before his death in 1904, the head of the United Confederate Veterans (UCV), John B. Gordon, appears to have added a new twist to the story by claiming that the officers of Cooper's unit raised money for the poor man's family.[88] By 1910, when the UCV publication *Confederate Veteran* republished the story (not for the first time), the story had changed so that the officer who told the story was Armistead Long, head of artillery for the Confederate army, and Cooper's death now occurred at Cold Harbor in 1864.[89] Adding new fictions on top of old lies, Long reportedly recounted this story at a dedication for the cornerstone of the Lee statue on

Monument Avenue in Richmond twenty years earlier, despite there being no contemporary evidence that Long was even at the dedication.[90]

As the story periodically reappeared, it was frequently used for new purposes. In 1914, a minister left off Cooper's subsequent death and utilized the story as an example of how God can pardon men. Numerous papers across the country republished the sermon, once again spreading the legend of Cooper, which now had Lee standing in for God.[91] That same year, the story was recycled by former Confederate general D. H. Hill at the dedication of North Carolina's Monument to Confederate Women to focus on how Mary made Edward return to his unit. What had been a story of the divided loyalties men faced now became a story that emphasized Confederate women's unbreakable devotion to the Confederacy.[92] Hill was not breaking new ground; in advocating for the monument's construction, Carr had already used the Cooper story in a similar manner.[93]

Just as details were gained, some were also lost. In 1890, the *News and Observer* (Raleigh) reported that Edward Cooper had recently died in New York, and the story of his supposed court-martial was again recounted.[94] Four days later, the paper retracted the story after a New Berne paper noted that Cooper supposedly died on the battlefield. Thus, in investigating its mistake, the *News and Observer* in 1890 finally recognized the fraud that so many future authors would not, announcing, "We gather . . . that the story is a fiction." The paper went one step further in attempting to debunk the tale by pointing out that "so far as we know there was never in North Carolina such a case of threatened starvation."[95] Unfortunately, historians missed this article.

Historians of desertion should have known better, but the letter was too compelling and reinforced a generally accepted understanding that many deserters left because of family suffering. Over twenty modern history books cite the story of Edward Cooper, demonstrating how the Lost Cause still pervades the historiography. In many cases, a reliance on faulty secondary literature is responsible for the story's proliferation. Mary's letter has been frequently quoted and republished without all the unbelievable details surrounding it. Because of this decontextualization, numerous well-known historians apparently never saw the parts of Cooper's story that indicated that the letter was inauthentic. Mary Cooper's letter appeared vetted and presented them with a poetic example of desertion for nonideological reasons. In other cases, however, historians should have known better.[96]

Perhaps it is time to put the Cooper tale to rest, with the hope that future historians of desertion will not use it to argue that deserters left to protect their families. There is certainly plenty of evidence that desertion was spurred by concerns for those at home, though little so eloquent or pathetic. How many more fabricated stories derived from postwar sources still fill our history books? The sad truth is, historians do not know. No scholar of desertion has previously questioned the obvious holes in the Cooper story. As historians we need to ask ourselves how we use sources created after the war and how they have influenced our expectations. This is especially true for historians of dissent, desertion, and Confederate nationalism. Dissent and desertion remain understudied topics, but numerous community studies and micro-histories have already shown that unwavering support for the Confederacy was not nearly as ubiquitous as some scholars would like to believe. Many Confederate deserters may indeed have felt deep personal devotion to the Confederacy, but the stories that have engrained such an image of heroism into the American imagination are not always based on reality. Stories like Cooper's have led many southern whites—and a few historians—to accept a flat and unnuanced depiction of life in the Confederacy.[97]

Why were fabricated tales like that of the humble and loyal Cooper such important stories for Carr and other Confederate mythmakers? Because so much of the historical justification for disenfranchisement and white rule in North Carolina was based on narratives about Confederate nobility and valor, these lies mattered. Disloyal or cowardly deserters threatened the constant claims that "Anglo-Saxon valor reached its most perfect development" at Gettysburg and that Confederate conduct had demonstrated the superiority of the white race so central to political rhetoric at the turn of the twentieth century.[98] Turning desertion into a sign of racial superiority, and holding Mary Cooper up as an example of the superiority of white women, served to help justify Jim Crow.

Leading monument builders in North Carolina repeated tall tales and exaggerated their dubious military records, both to champion white supremacy and to boost their political prospects. In 1900, when Carr ran for the US Senate, his war record became a point of contention. In their effort to raise enthusiasm for their candidate, some of Carr's supporters exaggerated his service. A pamphlet produced and circulated around Asheville asked voters, "What is Mr. Simmons' [Carr's opponent] one year of service in the comfortable office in Raleigh during the campaigns of 1898 and 1900 to Jule Carr's three years in the trenches in the dark days of 1862, 1863, and 1864?" Carr's wartime record and Simmons's role in later violent, racist political campaigns were both touted as credentials to be the state's flag bearer for white supremacy, but Carr's was vastly exaggerated, as he had not entered service until 1864. Carr's own role in this embellishment remains unknown, but it led to numerous articles attacking and defending his war record. Some articles claimed that Carr had served honorably as a

"General" Julian Shakespeare Carr in his Confederate veteran's uniform. During the war Carr served as a private. (Courtesy of the Julian Shakespeare Carr Papers, Duke University Archives, David M. Rubenstein Rare Book and Manuscript Library, Duke University)

messenger but not in battle, while others claimed he fought valiantly.[99] The truth remains unclear, but the exaggerated claim about Carr's lengthy service would be repeated: in 1921, a profile in a Raleigh newspaper claimed that Carr had volunteered at sixteen.[100] While they may not have always explicitly lied about their war records, men like Carr and London presented their military service in such a way as to achieve political goals and gain social capital. Carr wore a Confederate general's uniform to provide a military flair he had never earned as a soldier, his rank having been granted by the UCV. In their retelling of events, veterans often made their rudimentary, and even reluctant, service into something noble, all while repeating war stories that they should have known were suspect.

While these former Confederates turned politicians were hardly the first or the last politicians to exaggerate military service, the manner in which Carr and other ex-Confederates used their service to push a policy of white supremacy makes them stand out. Carr's long history of using Confederate military valor to celebrate white manhood makes clear that he was trying through his exaggerations to be not just a war hero but specifically a hero of white supremacy. Indeed, the pamphlet with the questionable claims compared his military service to his opponent's political efforts for white supremacy, not to claim that his opponent was a coward and Carr courageous. The fabrications were designed to show that Carr—who was concerned he might be seen as too moderate on racial issues—was equal to his challengers in his devotion and contributions to white supremacy. In response, Furnifold Simmons, one of Carr's opponents in the 1900 campaign, had veterans write letters to newspapers declaring their support for him despite his lack of military service, as he was too young to have served. One wrote, "For the last ten years of his life [Simmons] has been fighting for the old Confederate and his children the battles of Anglo-Saxon against negroism harder than any man in this state."[101] Confederate service or some other role in supporting white supremacy had become a prerequisite for Democratic politicians of that generation, leading Carr to exaggerate.

While not all monument builders had poor military records, much about the actual military service of North Carolina's leading Confederate veterans still remains unexplored. London and Carr were not the only Confederate boosters whose military records might have given voters pause. When Carr joined his unit, the 3rd North Carolina Cavalry, in late 1864, the unit was hardly steeped in glory. They had not been at Gettysburg, Antietam, or any of the major Virginia battles before Petersburg. Instead, they spent much of the war on picket duty in eastern North Carolina, guarding bridges and railroads with occasional minor raids. Even a veteran of the 3rd who wrote a regimental history self-consciously noted that "there is an infinity of duties besides the actual shock of pitched battle" when describing the unit's service.[102] Alfred Waddell served in the same unit, and his war record also had little worthy of note. Much of Waddell's wartime experience was actually spent in the hospital, as he was a sickly fellow. Forced to resign, he received a medical discharge due to "chronic gastritis complicated by hepatic derangement."[103] None of this is to say the 3rd North Carolina Cavalry was filled with cowards, but only that the unit did not have as many opportunities to prove itself. Additionally, while these leading proponents of North Carolina monuments had war records that were less notable than those of many other veterans, they represent only a small sample. While it is tempting to think that Carr, London, and Waddell's commitment to celebrating the Confederacy arose from a sense of overcompensation, this would be overly simplistic. Their devotion to white supremacy—and perhaps a bit of personal ambition—appear to have driven their fabrications far more than any insecurity.

Of all those political figures apparently fabricating a personal history for political ends in North Carolina, Charles F. Warren's was among the most tenuous. A Democratic politician who helped raise funds for monuments, he also joined Carr in giving speeches before the North Carolina

Literary and Historical Association.[104] Born in 1852, Warren had been too young to serve in the Confederacy, but that did not stop him from donning the Lost Cause's mantle for political ends. Warren played up his time as a student at Washington College (soon to be Washington and Lee), where he claimed to have studied under the great Robert E. Lee himself. One of the stories Warren appears to have spread was that among the papers found on Lee's desk upon his death were Warren's own exams.[105] The problem with this narrative was that Lee never actually taught classes, and although he attended examinations, the ex-Confederate leader died early in Warren's second year of attendance. In fact, Lee died in October, having fallen ill September 28, 1870, less than two weeks after classes began, so his desk would have been unlikely to contain any examinations.[106] Yet this claim of studying under Lee helped Warren's political pursuits and shaped how he was remembered. A decade after his death, a memorialist recalled that Warren "would have made a magnificent soldier," had he not been born too late, for "no man ever lived who knew less the sensation of fear." His lack of fear, the speaker posited, may have come "from his association with the greatest war captain of all time, during the days he sat at the feet of Robert E. Lee."[107] The ties between white supremacy and Confederate memory were clear, and Warren recognized that anyone running under a white supremacist banner would benefit from connections to the Confederacy's premier hero.

The fabrication of history did not go unnoticed by outside observers. The *Richmond Planet,* a black newspaper, ridiculed those erecting the city's Robert E. Lee monument, saying, "The men who talk most about the valor of Lee and the blood of the brave Confederate dead are those who never smelt powder or engaged in battle. Most of them were at the table, either on top or under it, when the war was going on."[108] It was not just African Americans who pushed back against tales that Confederates were superior soldiers. In 1916, at a Confederate celebration in Lexington, Virginia, the son of a Union soldier challenged Carr's assertion that the Confederate army "was superior because it was composed of the best blood of the South, while the [Union army] was largely made up of mercenary soldiers."[109] Carr's obsession with the racial purity of the Confederate army was once again indicative of his continued use of Confederate memory to uphold white supremacy.

Leading white supremacists, Democratic politicians, and those erecting monuments were not the only ones fabricating stories of military valor. William Marvel has shown that the last twelve "Confederate veterans" to die were all fake. In fact, the last Confederate reunion had no real veterans. Too young to have actually fought, many of the "last Confederates" had added a few years to their age in the 1920s and '30s to garner a pension or local fame. When they then outlived the actual last Johnny Reb and Billy Yank, they continued their lies to avoid being exposed as frauds. Social and real capital were both up for grabs; the men received pensions, free medical care, and even a place to stay at Confederate homes. They played the role they were expected to and retold stories that fit the mold of the well-established Lost Cause, and in exchange they were cared for. Many of these last surviving fraudulent Confederates claimed to have been in the Junior Reserves or to have enlisted in the last days of the war, thus explaining their longevity and lack of records, but as seen in the next chapter, pension fraud and lying about one's service record were prevalent long before the 1940s and '50s. For each of these impersonators who lived to be in their nineties while claiming to be well over one hundred, there were surely many others who died early enough that their claims never came under serious scrutiny.[110]

Long after these men had been shown to be fraudulent, fans of the Confederacy continued to present them as honorable and noble veterans. In 1986, when Jay Hoar published an uncritical "epic prose elegy" to the last surviving Confederate veterans, he devoted an entire chapter to those Confederates who died after 1951, all of whom were clearly fake. Many of the other "Old Reb Standouts" he details in the book are also frauds. The evidence was there for Hoar to see; he even discussed challenges to some of these men's legitimacy. Despite this, he included in his list of last Confederates two men who supposedly died when over 130 years old, including one who claimed to be the son of President James Monroe. Unwilling to consider or not caring that this might be fraud, Hoar treated his remarkable and unsubstantiated parentage, Confederate service, and age of 133 as factual![111] Had the claims been true, the modern-day Methuselah would have been the oldest recorded person ever by over a decade.[112] The men fit the expectations of the Lost Cause, and a desire to keep a connection to what by then was being recalled as the noblest cause and most heroic of soldiers led people to accept questionable claims.

A disinterest in finding the truth is often as important as lying in the creation of false collective memories. In 1910, former Confederate guerrilla John Singleton Mosby, never one to romanticize the Confederacy, explained why he rarely attended reunions. "There are too many frauds," Mosby told a reporter. "If I had as many men as they now say there were with me, I could have driven Grant out of Virginia. . . . Every time they have a reunion there are some one hundred or more who register as Mosby's men, and they are looked on as heroes, I bet a lot of them have been born since the war began."[113] He may have been right. Because veterans, the UDC, and historians had spent decades portraying Confederates as superhuman, many people were more willing to accept these elderly men as legitimate.

A newspaper recounting the interview with Mosby accurately noted, "We think so highly of our Confederate veterans that the very suggestion that there are frauds among them is painful."[114]

Monuments and tales of heroic Confederates helped create a memory of a perfect soldier above reproach that these frauds played upon. As Governor Craig gave his address at UNC in 1913, he celebrated all the young Confederates who fought, stating, "In that great day there was the democracy of manhood. Every good soldier was an aristocrat and every brave man was enlisted in the order of royal knighthood. They were all thrilled by the pulsation of heroic youth. By their devotion to a cause, by the duties and the honor of a soldier, they were all lifted to a finer manhood."[115] Craig's depiction, and others like it, contributed to the construction of a memory of Confederate soldiers who were as stoic and ubiquitous as the monuments themselves. The act of being a Confederate soldier became evidence of a man's personal qualities. The proliferation of noble stories, many of them based on complete fabrications, not only helped uphold the Lost Cause and white supremacy but also created a presumption that there was no need to check the credentials of an ex-Confederate's service because all Confederates were great soldiers and none deserted. This widespread belief in the honorable service of nearly all white southern men opened the door for pension fraud.

In retrospect, the fact that it took the United States just four years to crush a rebellion that spanned nearly half a continent seems remarkably quick.[116] It took time to bring the North's demographic and industrial superiority to bear. Although the US military grew to outnumber the Confederacy's, the US Army numbered just 16,367 in December 1860.[117] Efforts to expand the military were hampered by a variety of factors, including incompetence, corruption, logistics, and an untrained citizenry. During the American Revolution, George Washington's Continental army, facing an enemy with more resources and experience, fought for eight years and won. In modern times, ISIS, Al-Qaida, and the Taliban, facing aircraft carriers, precision bombs, drones, and the most capable professional army on earth, have all lasted far longer than the Confederacy. While perhaps not a fair comparison—the Revolution occurred before armies massively expanded in scale during the nineteenth century, and modern insurgents have embraced asymmetrical strategies designed to protract conflicts—the idea that the Confederacy was somehow more successful than reasonably expected may partially originate from a distorted view of the Confederate soldier. The reality is that the Confederate army was ultimately strategically unsuccessful and had problems with desertion.

Military historians have at times inadvertently served to reinforce the Lost Cause narrative. As critics have noted, battlefield narration, or guns and bugles history, often "serves to commemorate, if not celebrate, the Confederate cause and to lend it credibility if not legitimacy" by never engaging the larger issues of the war. Bruce Collins argues that "the strongest contemporary image of the Confederacy remains its fighting prowess," which has even been strengthened by historians studying the common soldier. Because some newer military history "treats the fighting men of both sides as equal . . . the study of military history both smooths, even almost romanticizes, the image of the Confederacy and strengthens the view of the conflagration as indeed a 'brother's war.'"[118]

Recently, historians have started being more critical in their analysis of the martial ability of Confederate soldiers. Joseph Glatthaar's *General Lee's Army*, for example, uses statistics to examine desertion, resistance toward conscription, and discipline problems arising from southern culture, as well as noting Confederate volunteers' attachment to slavery.[119] But historians attempting to temper the dominant image of Confederate soldiers are clearly fighting against well-engrained assumptions. Earl Hess's award-winning *Civil War Infantry Tactics* presents as an almost surprising revelation that "in many ways the Union army was qualitatively better than the Confederate army."[120] This should hardly seem groundbreaking, given the outcome of the war, yet Hess, Glatthaar, and other scholars leading this reassessment of the Confederate military are working against an expectation of Confederate superiority that remains among military historians.

Though scholars have pointed out that "the historical records simply do not bear out the idealized picture of the Confederate common soldier," some historians continue to propagate an overly simplistic view of Confederate soldiers as a singular courageous group instead of a diverse group that included deserters, cowards, courageous individuals, and men just trying to survive.[121] In what is perhaps a display of just how influential Confederate veterans were, a recent operational history of the war repeatedly compared the Confederacy to Sparta.[122] The unspoken implications about military skill in this comparison are hard to miss, and even the word choice parallels Carr's and Craig's. Passages like "no other soldiers in American history could match the commitment of both the Union and Confederate rank and file" are not just purple prose. This modern use of superlatives when discussing "exceptionally hardy" Civil War soldiers not only does a disservice to American soldiers from other wars but also paints them as a unified group without individual character traits. [123]

While reputable scholars no longer argue that slavery had no role in the coming of the war, the Lost Cause's portrayal of the military abilities of Confederate soldiers has remained in mainstream historical interpretations. It makes sense that aspects of the Lost Cause continue to influence our understanding of the past. The stories Carr and others told in memoirs, speeches, and regimental histories were used by previous generations of historians to write their master narratives of the war. The works of Shelby Foote, Douglass Southall Freeman, and others who took in the Lost Cause as children were often the first books about the Civil War that future scholars read. Because the Lost Cause framework influenced the narrative with which many historians begin, it is hardly surprising that courageous Confederates still appear. Even those historians of the war who do not directly use or cite questionable sources and accounts and only use wartime documents to re-create the past cannot help but be influenced by the Lost Cause; suspect sources helped create much of the foundational narrative off of which modern historians are working. Because of their success in shaping our starting narrative, those who crafted the Lost Cause continue to hold an undeserved influence on how historians study the war. We begin our studies with an older framing in our minds, so all too often, we find what we expect. When filling in narrative gaps of otherwise original research, historians have a tendency to fall back on the old narratives they first learned. Some authors—especially those focused on other elements of the conflict—may not realize how depicting the past with a courageous, unwavering white South supporting the Confederacy is as central to the Lost Cause as denying that slavery caused the conflict.

Even today, suspect sources such as unit histories are often uncritically used by historians. One historian deemed old regimental histories "unmitigated trash—the worst example of municipal chauvinism; used more often for self-promotion or [the] glorification of ancestors."[124] Despite this, some scholars still seem to believe that veterans writing after the war "self-consciously strove for accuracy."[125] In reality, a new generation of scholars has shown that these narratives were not written to pass on uncritical analysis to future generations but rather to ensure that the writers' own units were remembered "free of anything embarrassing, unmanly, or dishonorable and that would endure for generations heroically." Postwar myth creation was a massive undertaking, as "both Confederate and Union soldiers filled volumes, noting the particular role their unit played in the war, downplaying failures and dissension, and highlighting sacrifice and camaraderie, while paying little attention to the war's larger context. The higher the casualties, the more proudly heroic the regiment's claim."[126]

While true for northern units as well, these problems were exacerbated in Confederate regimental histories by the fact that they actually lost. Henry London's history of the 32nd North Carolina recounts how "the failure of the expedition against Newbern," in which the unit participated, "was through no fault of" that regiment. Indeed, the entire history is largely an uncritical explanation of how the Confederacy failed despite the 32nd displaying "courage and conduct . . . unsurpassed in the annals of war." Discussing the unit's first commander, London claimed that the men "implicitly obeyed his orders and had entire confidence in him, and in the midst of battle were under perfect control."[127] That in 1862 this commander reported problems with his men deserting (presumably against his orders) went unmentioned in London's exaggerated account.[128]

Accounts of battlefield heroics frequently display a continued joy in recounting Confederate courage. In one of his final pieces, the late Wiley Sword contended that "for sheer drama, for military pageantry, for a bold demonstration of the essence of Southern spirit, and perhaps even as the ultimate example of the valor of the American fighting man, the vicious encounter at Franklin . . . seems without parallel."[129] This celebration of white masculinity was not new. Sword's version of events echoed that of Julian Carr, who declared in various speeches, "Franklin! Eternal monument of undying devotion, of courage without a parallel, for all future time thy name shall stand for Confederate Prowess," and "the charge of the Light Brigade fades into insignificance by the side of the charge of the Confederate soldiers at Franklin, Tenn."[130] Another way of looking at the Battle of Franklin is to see it as the dumbest, most useless slaughter in American history, when thousands of southerners died for no reason, in a foolish attack, for a cause they had already lost. While it took incredible courage on the part of the men, not every Confederate soldier at Franklin fought with such foolhardy bravery.

To be clear, most military historians are not neo-Confederates actively trying to support the Lost Cause; in fact, many include critical analysis that undermines aspects of that narrative. Sword's books *Courage under Fire: Profiles in Bravery from the Battlefields of the Civil War* and *The Confederacy's Last Hurrah: Spring Hill, Franklin, and Nashville* were both criticized by neo-Confederates for not being kind enough to John Bell Hood. Though Sword retained a strong admiration for the bravery of Confederate soldiers, as a historian, he remained capable of a critical assessment of Hood and the unnecessary slaughter at Franklin. His assertion that Hood's memoirs written after the war might be anything less than 100 percent true led the Hood Historical Society to publish a paid notice in *Civil War News* accusing Sword of "the Desecration of a Confederate Hero."[131] The Hood Historical Society, focused on celebrating ancestors, remained incapable of critical analysis. Even those historians undermining aspects of the myth of superior Confederate military ability have frequently maintained a reverence for the Confederate soldier. Examining the poor discipline of Confederate soldiers in 1959, historian David Donald argued that "the [white] Southerner made an admirable fighting man but a poor soldier."[132]

Historians are not necessarily coming to their conclusions solely because of the Lost Cause, either. This book makes no pretense of being a military history. Many Confederates were likely competent soldiers. That being said, given how falsehoods and exaggerations clearly influenced the master narrative from which scholars are starting, historians need to reconsider the Confederate soldier with historical memory in mind. In a controversial 2014 article, Gary Gallagher and Kathryn Meier called for scholars to return to studying the military history of the conflict. Indeed, this study of memory leads me to a similar conclusion. An examination of the manner in which the Lost Cause influenced our expectations about the Confederate military, including unit cohesion, desertion, Confederate nationalism, battlefield performance, and the tactical ability and performance of Confederate generals and soldiers, seems warranted.[133] As a starting point, desertion's critical impact on the Confederate war effort is still often ignored, and its extent still remains to be satisfactorily measured.[134]

Critiquing some poorly executed memory studies, Earl Hess argued in 2014 that "understanding the real battlefield of 1861–65 is essential to understanding everything else about the Civil War."[135] The same can be said in reverse. Integration of diverse types of scholarship goes in many directions. To understand the real battlefield requires us to understand the memory of the war as well. It may be true that the "Confederate people demonstrated robust devotion to their slave-based republic . . . and sacrificed more than any segment of white society in United States history," as some scholars suggest, but the reason so many Americans—including a few historians—view the Confederacy in this manner is at least partially due to postwar fabrications meant to uphold white supremacy.[136]

3

The Loyal Deserters

Confederate Pension Fraud in Civil War Memory, 1901–1940

On the last day of 1923, David Pinkney Yokley applied for a pension based on his service in the 48th North Carolina over sixty years earlier. When the eighty-one-year-old Yokley applied, 9,135 North Carolinians were already receiving pensions, including some 750 who had been added to the pension list in the past year. By that point, the total number of veterans receiving pensions was dropping; over 1,500 pensioners had died the previous year.[1] Designed to recognize the state's debt to "the deserving veterans and widows of ex-Confederate Veterans," these pensions were intended for Confederate soldiers who had served faithfully, and efforts were initially made to keep deserters off the roll.[2] These efforts were short-lived and highly ineffective. By the time Yokley applied, pensions for deserters had proliferated, and examples of pension fraud could likely have been found in every county across the state. These former deserters presented themselves as loyal Confederates and were often recalled as such in both life and death.

Among those who received a pension from the state of North Carolina for which he was not technically eligible was David Yokley. Conscripted in August 1862, Yokley had deserted just a month later with his brother, Charles Jefferson Yokley, and their uncle, Joseph Yokley. In 1864, the Home Guard captured one of the Yokley brothers. As a Confederate squad escorted their prisoners "tied with their hands behind them" along a plank road connecting Salem and High Point, around a dozen armed dissenters ambushed the rebel soldiers and freed the prisoners. Whether as captive or rescuer, David Yokley almost certainly participated in this mission—it was, after all, led by his father. Other rescuers included neighbors and at least one of Yokley's other brothers. David and his uncle left the county shortly after and fled to the safety of Union lines.[3]

Though in theory ineligible due to his desertion—not to mention lack of service—David Yokley claimed to have been a loyal Confederate, and he received a pension for three years until his death in 1926. For sixty dollars a year, Yokley erased his past.[4] Even if men like Yokley did not believe their own lies, the Confederate pensions like those he and other former anti-Confederate dissenters received helped strengthen the Lost Cause as the primary means of understanding the war among white southerners. As historian John Inscoe notes, within the "belief system" of the Lost Cause, "there was no room for divided loyalties, for internal dissent, or for guerrilla warfare," and so dissent had to be expunged from memory.[5] Pensions helped. And so, although David Yokley had been listed in a newspaper as a deserter within five weeks of being conscripted, his obituary sixty-four years later remembered him as "a brave old Confederate soldier."[6]

After taking up arms against the Confederacy and fleeing to Indiana, one might expect David Yokley to vocally oppose efforts to celebrate the Confederacy.[7] Indeed, he even appears to have dabbled, at least a little, in Republican politics.[8] Despite his wartime experiences, however, Yokley does not appear to have been especially tied to the Union. His second marriage—to a sixteen-year-old, born a decade after the war—endured until his death. What Yokley told his young bride of the war remains unknown; however, he may have failed to mention his wartime resistance. In her 1930 application for a widow's pension based on his Confederate service, she answered the question "Was your late husband a deserter?" with a one-word answer: "No." The application was denied only because her age—fifty-five instead of the minimum sixty—made the young widow ineligible.[9]

Yokley and his wife were hardly the only insincere family members when it came to pension applications. His uncle Joseph's widow, Cordelia Yokley, received a pension from 1924 until her death in 1927 for her late husband's entire month of loyal Confederate service before he deserted and escaped to Union lines. Unlike David's wife, Cordelia definitely knew her husband's status as a deserter, having married him in 1864 while he was on the lam and shortly before he fled north.[10]

Understanding the role of money in shaping the Lost Cause is critical for historians of memory, as well as for any scholar using pension files. The Yokley family and other North Carolinians actively helped erase the memory of their wartime dissent in part due to pensions, as well as the social capital being a Confederate veteran brought. In turn, pensions helped buttress a southern racial hierarchy through both the erasure of dissent and by presenting pensioners as white heroes to celebrate. Pensions helped unite southern whites politically along racial lines by ensuring that wartime enmities and memories of divided communities were not passed on to future generations. Today, dissent, desertion, and intracommunity conflict are largely forgotten, even by some scholars of the Civil War. This was not always the case, but money helped make it so.

Marita Sturken remarks about the Vietnam War that "remembering is in itself a form of forgetting," and the creation of the Lost Cause was no different.[11] Pensions, war claims, and other means of monetizing wartime experience served as driving forces in the creation of postwar memory, including a Lost Cause myth that presented a Solid South where support for the Confederacy was nearly unanimous. This myth was strengthened around the turn of the twentieth century, as pensions served as a form of welfare, a tool for political power, and a crafter of memory. Pensions and other rewards open to former Confederates helped create a memory of an idealized solid Confederacy by discouraging dissenters from speaking out against the Lost Cause. During the early twentieth century, some former deserters who had previously proclaimed themselves Unionists began supporting a narrative that celebrated Confederate veterans. Many rewrote their own pasts to appear as if they had been staunch Confederates when in fact they had deserted or even taken up arms against Confederate authorities. While the specific fabrications recounted in each pension application were not necessarily widely circulated, "pensioner" was a public identity that carried with it an official stamp of legitimacy and numerous expectations about their service. Pensioners had been certified by the state as devoted Confederates deserving of honor, and they would be remembered as such, often presumed to have fit the stereotypical depiction of Confederate soldiers discussed in chapter 2.

Confederate pension applications help reveal how white southern memories of the war changed over the years. That the Yokley family came to remember themselves as Confederates and embraced the Lost Cause is indicative of a failure of a counternarrative celebrating anti-Confederate dissent. In examining the Lost Cause in Kentucky, Anne Marshall has shown how "Union memory . . . became too closely associated with emancipation and African American progress for white Unionists to accept it as their own."[12] While racist sensibilities pushed former dissenters away from an emancipationist memory that celebrated the death of slavery, there were also pull factors that drew people to the Lost Cause instead of maintaining a white Unionist memory distinct from African Americans' recollections of the war. A countermemory of anti-Confederate dissent formed in the immediate aftermath of the war but in the long term proved weaker than the Lost Cause. In the end, the monetary and social capital available to former Confederate soldiers encouraged people to forget events that contradicted the glorious narrative provided by the Lost Cause, which in turn served to reinforce white supremacist power structures in North Carolina.

Though the pensions were initially reserved for those seriously injured during the war and for war widows, North Carolina liberalized its pension laws to expand eligibility at the turn of the twentieth century. Before 1900, only about forty-five hundred veterans and widows had applied for pensions due the strict disability requirements. Beginning in 1901, the number of applications increased with the expansion of eligibility from just the grievously wounded to include any of "the brave old soldiers [who] were no longer able to plough as they had been" due to age, infirmity, or disability.[13] The more lenient standards created an influx of applications. In the forty years after eligibility was opened up, thirty-five thousand pension applications were filed with the state.[14] Although old age could now be the cause of infirmity instead of a war wound, Confederate service and financial need remained key requirements. North Carolina pension administrators only occasionally investigated attempts to defraud the state, however, a topic that scholars have heretofore overlooked.

Technically, the 1901 law that expanded pension eligibility banned deserters from receiving pensions, but some veterans actually saw this blanket ban as a flaw in the law. In a 1901 letter to a Greensboro newspaper about who should be entitled to pensions and membership in the United Confederate Veterans (UCV), Thomas Rhodes argued that some deserters were better than others. Rhodes felt that those who deserted to the Union were distinct from those who "violated their furloughs by remaining at home over time for starving wives and children."[15] He argued that the latter category, which included himself, should not be penalized because they had deserted to help their families as opposed to betraying their country. Many former Confederates agreed, and by the turn of the century, this was already a standard means of dividing deserters into two classes: loyal Confederates who "laid down their arms out of an overpowering sense of duty to their families at home" and those who "turned their guns on their former comrades."[16] This ignored the fact that deserters at home were actually more likely to point guns at their former comrades than those who deserted to the Union. As with the fabricated story of Edward Cooper, the public and even some historians latched onto this heroic depiction of desertion.[17] No one individual singularly invented this vision of desertion for family as the norm, but pensions contributed to the myth's solidification in collective memory.

Moreover, in the early twentieth century, there was a general understanding that deserters in the last days of the war were a distinct class. One county board even discussed whether those who went home after the March 1865 Battle of Bentonville had really deserted. The board decided that those men should be eligible for pensions, despite Robert Hoke, who had commanded a division at Bentonville, insisting they were deserters.[18] Hoke aside, most people seem to have agreed that leaving in the final days of the Confederacy was not really deserting, and the former

Confederate division commander's opinion had little impact on how pensions were issued.

In 1903, the legislature agreed that not all deserters were equal, amending the law such that "no soldier who was honorably discharged or who was in service at the surrender shall be considered a deserter, even though he may have deserted at some time during the war."[19] Befitting North Carolina's reputation for absenteeism, going absent without leave (AWOL) was no longer grounds for losing a pension. This new definition of desertion made it easier for individuals who previously might have been labeled dissenters to get pensions by claiming they had returned.

The legislature's amending of the pension law in 1903 had important legal ramifications, changing the legal standard that officials used.[20] Whether an applicant had been with his unit, at a prisoner of war camp, in a hospital, or on a legitimate furlough became the crucial legal test for applications. The new rules, however, essentially allowed deserters to claim that they had returned in the event that they were accused of desertion. For instance, George Dull of Forsyth County initially had his pension application rejected because he claimed that he had been on his way back to his unit when Lee surrendered. His unit's records show that he was captured at Gettysburg, exchanged in March 1864, and then went AWOL. Whatever the truth of the matter, Dull made the mistake of telling the board that he had been away from his unit at the war's end. Had he not mentioned it, he would have gotten his pension. In 1917, when he reapplied, Dull neglected to mention his absence, and this time, his pension was approved.[21] Dull's questionable case aside, this adjusted standard made some sense. Many of those who went AWOL may have been taking French leave, intending to return to the front eventually.

But intent was not actually important to the new standard. Susan Younts answered the question "Was your late husband a deserter?" with the cagey answer "Not at [the] close of the war." When her answer raised suspicions, she successfully argued that her husband had been arrested by the Home Guard and returned to the Army of Northern Virginia before Appomattox. Though there were no wartime documents to support her claim, she provided an affidavit from a neighbor as evidence.[22] In 1909, Michael Swain's widow admitted on her application that her husband died in Castle Thunder while being held for desertion, yet she received a pension.[23] Had they applied in 1901 or 1902, Younts, Swain, and Dull might have been denied, had anyone investigated. The new standard, however, allowed individuals of questionable commitment to be remembered as committed Confederates.

Efforts to cull pension lists of deserters were rarely effective. In 1901, newspapers across the state reported that a wartime list of deserters from western North Carolina had been found and that at least twenty men listed were already drawing pensions.[24] Some newspapers claimed that fifty deserters with pensions had been identified.[25] When further investigation revealed two deserters living in the old soldiers' home, outrage ensued. Newspapers published local pension lists so that undeserving frauds might be spotted.[26] Instructions were sent out to county pension boards to investigate each claim carefully.[27] A new system of county advisory boards was established to try to detect ineligible applicants, but it did little to stop deserters from applying and receiving pensions.[28]

Estimates of how many pensions were undeserved ranged as high as 20 percent, and these estimates may not have been too far off.[29] At least 17 percent of approved soldiers' applications in Davidson County for 1901 (eighteen individuals) should not have been eligible based on the stricter standard. Similar oversights can be found in the widows' applications, as at least eight out of the eighty-six Davidson County widows receiving pensions that year should have been ineligible. By 1909, 10.7 percent of Davidson County residents receiving pensions (twenty-nine individuals) would have been otherwise ineligible without the 1903 law change. Another twenty-one pensioners (7.8 percent of the 1909 list) should still have been ineligible due to poor service records, even under the more lenient standards. A decade later, the percentages remained similar.[30]

Comparing wartime records with pension lists makes clear that how deserters were treated in practice did not change due to this scandal. At least 15 percent of all twentieth-century applicants in Davidson County should have been ineligible due to their service record in 1901. Out of 618 application files, at least 45 were for soldiers who went AWOL but returned to their units before the surrender, and those applicants were eligible for pensions after the 1903 changes to the law. Another fifty (or 8 percent of all Davidson County files) should have been denied, even with the more lenient standards. Ineligibility due to their service record, however, rarely stopped former deserters or their widows from getting pensions. Of those fifty applications that should have always been rejected, at least forty-six were eventually approved for pensions, while two were denied for insufficient disability.[31] This is a far higher rate of fraud than is found today in any American welfare, unemployment, or food assistance programs.[32]

Little was done in most localities to stop fraud. In 1902, Davidson County's new advisory board of veterans discovered only one deserter, Thomas Smith, whose pension had been approved the year before. In other words, the new advisory committee detected less than 4 percent of ineligible pensioners. Other counties found similarly small numbers.[33] By 1904, Smith's widow was receiving a pension for his service, presumably as the new rules propagated in 1903 made her eligible.[34] In a few places, primarily in the western portion of the state, more concerted efforts were made to cull deserters from the rolls. As part of the 1901 statewide effort to find desert- ers, at least ten Yancey County pensioners were removed from the rolls. These men accounted for 12 percent of all Yancey County veterans receiving pensions at the time. But the 1903 standards made it much harder to keep even the least deserving deserter off the rolls, and by 1906, all but one had begun receiving a pension again.[35] Similarly, in 1909, all of the surviving pensioners in Davidson County who undeservedly slipped by the board in 1901 were still receiving their pensions, and additional deserters had joined them. In one extreme case, R. G. Gordon deserted the same month he was conscripted, yet his pension application was approved in 1907.[36] Unless they made the mistake of outing themselves, like Dull and Younts, investi- gations of ineligible claimants were unlikely to occur. Deserters remained on the books in most communities, thus ensuring that few reminders of desertion survived.

The efforts undertaken in 1901 and 1902 appear to be the last major attempt (if we can call it that) to clear deserters systematically from the pen- sion lists. As part of the reworking of the pension system in 1903, the advi- sory board was combined with the county pension board, decreasing the number of people examining each application.[37] Rarely did anyone object to their neighbors receiving a pension. Exactly why so few neighbors objected is unclear, but some North Carolinians believed that fear of retaliation con- tributed to the silence.[38] The fact that efforts to inform on former deserters usually fell on deaf ears may also have contributed to a general reticence to point fingers. As time passed, younger neighbors had little knowledge of desertion, having not witnessed the war. Additionally, having learned growing up that all Confederates fought heroically, they had little reason to suspect fraud.

Even when someone spoke up, keeping deserters off the pension rolls proved nearly impossible. For example, after being conscripted in 1864, Thomas E. Johnson of Wilkes County deserted to the enemy within months of joining his company—one report stated that he stayed only a single night. Arriving at Union lines, he promptly took the oath and spent the rest of the war in Cincinnati. He received a North Carolina pension begin- ning in 1901, and not until 1912 did anyone object to it. Then, after over a decade of payments, Johnson made the mistake of telling his neighbor and fellow pensioner about his less than stellar record. Ironically, and perhaps a testament to how many deserters received pensions, the pensioner who reported Johnson's admission was himself a former deserter. Though John- son briefly lost his pension, it was reinstated within a year.[39]

Fraud was hard to detect, so unless someone openly contradicted the expectations that Confederates had fought in a devoted manner, there was little chance of detection. As the muster rolls from the war were not easily accessible to investigators, detection was largely based on the memories of members of county pension boards or community informants. Members of the local pension boards often lacked any personal knowledge as to who from their county had deserted. From 1908 to 1936, for example, the six men who sat on the Davidson County Pension Board had not served with most of the applicants. Two had served in Company I of the 14th North Carolina, one in the Junior Reserves, and two in units recruited from other states. The final member was the son of a deceased veteran.[40] In 1909, only 7 out of 163 Davidson pensioners had served in Company I of the 14th North Carolina, and even deserters from that regiment had their applications approved.[41]

When the pension bureau checked available records, it rarely helped. In the 1880s, North Carolina commissioned John Wheeler Moore to publish a roster of North Carolina's Confederate troops. Moore gained access to the muster rolls in Washington, DC, which would later be used to create the Compiled Service Records that historians and genealogists now use to check a soldier's service record.[42] But authorities rarely checked Moore's *Roster of North Carolina Troops,* and then only to determine whether someone had enlisted.[43] While Moore noted who was captured, killed, and wounded, he failed to note desertion.[44] This striking oversight is indicative of the overarching purpose of Moore's *Roster* as a form of commemoration and celebration rather than as a means to detect fraud. Hence, most deserters were listed in Moore's book as noble Confederate soldiers even if they spent most of the war hiding in the woods.

Even when individuals were missing from the *Roster,* applicants still received pensions. Elizabeth Black's late husband never appeared in the records of the 14th North Carolina. When she applied in 1921 for a pension based on his service record, the Davidson County clerk included an affidavit that her husband's "name does not appear on the roster, but he drew a pension as having been a member of Co. B. 14th Regiment, which I presume was correct."[45] Whether Black served or not, this was enough for the pension to be approved.

Desertion was low on the priority list of most pension officials. Far more applicants were rejected for other reasons, such as insufficient disability or not being poor enough, than were even investigated for their service record. Insufficient disability was the most common reason for rejection and remained the most pressing issue for most pension review boards. Indeed, in September 1901, at the same time that counties were supposed to be checking for deserters, the State Pension Board announced it would accept only those who were "totally or three-fourths or greater disabled" because they had too many applicants for the money appropriated. The state board rejected more applications from Davidson County than they accepted that year because of this decision. The urgent focus on disability further distracted from the short-lived efforts to find deserters.[46]

Most of those applications rejected due to a problem with an applicant's service records involved men who had served in the Home Guard or on a work detail but had never enlisted in Confederate service. These individuals all outed themselves as ineligible on their applications. Bizarrely, when the state amended the law in 1903 to allow AWOL soldiers to receive pensions, Home Guard service was removed as a pensionable service. Thus the men who had hunted deserters were made ineligible for pensions just as those deserters they had captured became eligible. Pension lists from that year show that numerous men lost their pension when the Home Guard ceased counting as service.[47] John Chappell of Surry County saw his application rejected because he had been in the Home Guard, even though he claimed to have been disabled when a deserter shot him in the leg.[48] Ironically, the deserter who shot him would have had an easier time getting a pension than Chappell.

Sitting down in 1915 to write about his experiences for the local chapter of the United Daughters of the Confederacy (UDC), Daniel Eaker recounted the most exciting moments of his war. He told of how he was nearly captured at Gaines Mill but escaped as Union soldiers fired at him, and how he witnessed a woman running across the battlefield carrying her child. He wrote of seeing Stonewall Jackson being carried away after being shot by his own men at Chancellorsville; Eaker reported he fought on the next day and "helped capture 20 Federal soldiers" with the assistance of only nine other Confederates. He was a regular Confederate war hero, but his fighting ended with his capture at the Battle of Falling Waters. The veteran remained a prisoner until paroled at the end of the war, or so he told the UDC, which published his account in a local newspaper.[49]

Despite Eaker's assertions to the women who requested his account that "I am glad that I responded to my Country's call and was a Confederate soldier," and that he remained in prison "until I was paroled," wartime and postwar records tell another story.[50] Captured in July 1863, Eaker took an oath of allegiance to the United States of America and volunteered to join the Union army in January of the next year. Using different doctors and officials from neighboring counties to notarize the official documents so as not to be detected, he had applied for pensions on the basis of both his

Confederate and Union service. The more lucrative federal pension was never received, as he had failed to actually muster into the US Army—not to mention his disqualifying service in the Confederate army. Eaker had experienced more luck closer to home. In 1901, Eaker's application with North Carolina was initially approved, but then it came out that he had been a deserter.[51]

Still, Eaker would be remembered as a Confederate. Within a year, he was added back to the pension lists.[52] In the years to come, he continued to appeal his Union pension application, even as he received a Confederate pension from North Carolina and lied to local women about his devotion to the Confederacy. On his death, the county paid for his burial as a Confederate veteran, and in 1930, his family received a Confederate gravestone from the US government.[53] Tasked with preserving the noble history of the Confederacy, the UDC collected the stories of veterans but rarely stopped to question their accuracy. Eaker is just one example of how those who lied to get pensions helped write the memory of the war. Even those who never wrote a narrative of their experiences still helped enshrine a specific narrative about Confederate soldiers.

Elkanah Wall, for example, also lied. After volunteering in 1861, Wall deserted to the Union in October 1863 and signed an oath of allegiance in 1864, promising not to take up arms again and to spend the rest of the war in Philadelphia. Yet forty-five years later, he asserted that he had been wounded fighting near Richmond in 1864. No record exists of him returning to his unit, so it seems most likely that he lied on his pension application and not on his 1863 oath. No one objected to his pension application, perhaps because they had forgotten his desertion, or perhaps because the pension system had become a necessary means of caring for the indigent elderly. After all, Wall was no longer capable of farming.[54] The immediate purpose of lies was often not for some greater rewriting of history. Many applicants perjured themselves to get pensions not out of a desire to be recalled heroically, or even out of avarice, but out of need.

Scholar Elna Green argues that Florida's pension system served as an early "Confederate welfare system." North Carolina's operated similarly, thus lionizing the Confederacy while also providing for the aged and infirm.[55] In an era before federal welfare and a national social safety net, care for the poor and indignant was left to individual counties. In 1892 and 1894, respectively, Forsyth County spent $3,075.58 and $4,400.77 aiding the "outside poor," supporting the county home for the aged and infirm, and providing coffins for deceased paupers. Thus the monetary inducements for pension boards to ignore fraud were not necessarily directly connected with a desire to create a heroic memory of the Confederacy.[56]

Because the pension system acted as an early statewide welfare system, county boards were incentivized to approve pensions for disabled citizens for which the county would otherwise be responsible.[57] For example, Jesse Wall, another member of Elkanah's unit and likely his family, appears to have had no issues getting his pension despite deserting in 1863. Though his name was published in the local paper as a new pensioner, no one objected. On his application, Jesse noted his inability to "make support for myself and wife."[58]

This use of the pension system to take care of the elderly was not accidental. Pension laws were designed to keep counties from having to support indigent veterans. In addition to service, eligibility was equally based on need. Per the 1903 pension act, pensioners had to have an accumulated wealth of less than $500.[59] Denials because of a person's wealth appear more frequently than rejections for unsatisfactory war records. Many North Carolinians saw the pension system as first and foremost about providing for the aged. Elderly former Home Guard members, those who had served on work details, and even people who had hired substitutes all continued to inquire about pensions for their service in the 1920s despite being ineligible.[60] As the veterans grew older and grayer, concern about service eligibility decreased, and the focus shifted to ensuring that the needy elderly did not suffer.

In short, someone had to pay for indigent former deserters or they would die. With the increasing costs associated with caring for the aging veteran population, no wonder a county pension board might overlook a little wartime desertion. Jesse Wall was not alone in his need for support one way or the other. John Chappell's 1932 rejection, due to the fact that he only served on the Home Guard, meant that Surry County residents would have to continue to support him through "donations from the county and private individuals," as they had the preceding few years.[61] Forsyth County's Zadock Stafford, who had deserted after just three months of service, noted in his approved pension application that he was unable to work due to paralysis. The approval ensured that the county would not have to pay for his upkeep.[62] By December 1911, pensions were funneling over $8,000 into Forsyth County for the care of the elderly. While not all pensioners would necessarily otherwise land in the county poorhouse, some former county-supported paupers from the 1890s received pensions after 1900, directly saving the county money.[63]

Pensions facilitated a specific memory of the war being passed on to future generations by ensuring that being known as a loyal Confederate carried both social and economic rewards. Overlooking fraud facilitated the forgetting of desertion and dissent. The leniency and lack of investigations allowed those who otherwise might have presented themselves as wartime dissenters to be welcomed into the pantheon of Confederate heroes.

Consider the case of Davidson County resident Henry Newby. On February 18, 1864, Newby deserted to a Union gunboat off Wilmington and was brought to Fortress Monroe. There, he signed an oath of allegiance to the United States and was released to spend the rest of the war in Pennsylvania. Yet five decades later, the seventy-three-year-old veteran claimed he had received wounds to his foot and heel in 1863, an injury of which no wartime record exists. His obituary recognizing him as one of the last veterans in Thomasville, North Carolina, made no mention of his desertion. Indeed, in the years before his death, he had regularly attended Confederate reunions as well, where apparently no one awkwardly mentioned his acquittal in an 1863 court-martial or subsequent flight to the enemy.[64]

Newby's pension not only provided a monetary reason to hide his desertion but also provided an identity that carried valuable social capital. These pensions both provided needed cash to impoverished veterans and legitimized them as respectable members of society. Even the poorest veteran was still respected, and at annual reunions, both local and national, veterans were feted by members of the community. Newby, for example, attended reunions in Richmond and Washington, DC.[65]

Widows' pensions could also help erase the dissent from the historical record while providing women with both monetary and social capital. After his capture in 1864, John Meredith requested that he be allowed to take the oath of allegiance, as he had "always been a Union Man." The Confederate conscript claimed to be able to "substantiate his loyalty by persons residing" in the North. His request to take the oath and go to Indiana was approved on March 17, 1865. Unfortunately for Meredith, the wheels of bureaucracy took too long; he had died twelve days earlier in Elmira Prison. How sincere his protestations of loyalty were remains unknown, but they were surely not mentioned, if they were even known, back in North Carolina when his widow, Cynthia, successful applied for a pension in 1901.[66]

Former deserters exploited the dual focuses of celebrating the Confederacy and providing for the aged to slip through the cracks. The administrators facilitated this in the pension bureau's later years by allowing elderly individuals, unable to take care of themselves and suffering memory loss in their dotage, to receive pensions if neighbors vouched that they had served, even if they did not know in which unit or when. No one could recall what unit Louisa Grubb's husband had been in, but four veterans testified he had enlisted early in the war. Her pension was granted even though her husband had been dropped from the 15th North Carolina's rolls in April 1863 for deserting to the enemy. Louisa's pension was granted, likely in no small part because a stroke left her unable to care for herself.[67] Other widows received pensions with the wrong unit listed.[68] One applicant was approved without any unit listed, as he was no longer able to speak.[69] In general, pension boards cared about the finances and disability of applicants more than about the accuracy of a soldier's service record.

Sometimes individuals who were only babies during the war got pensions. Aaron Cockerham, the third to last "Confederate Veteran" to die in North Carolina, claimed to have been born in 1847, but records from his three marriages, his death certificate, seven different censuses, and his gravestone all make clear he was born in October 1859, indicating a fraudulently acquired pension. When he successfully applied for a pension in 1930, however, he noted that he was "incapable of making his support for his family."[70] Allowing fraudulent pensions not only saved counties money but also fabricated a false past.

It seems that no one really wanted to find fraud. County pension boards, Confederate mythmakers, North Carolina politicians, and deserters all had incentives to overlook desertion. Pensioners wanted money, county officials wanted to keep from having to support indigent community members, and those wanting to celebrate the Confederacy had little desire to admit that the Confederate army included massive numbers of deserters or that not all white southerners supported the cause. Politicians also saw pensions as a form of patronage and political spoils that they wielded to gain votes in their home districts. North Carolina's Democratic politicians often opposed federal pensions for Union service while supporting Confederate pensions, clearly indicating who they perceived as their supporters.[71]

Just like the contemporaneous monuments going up across the South, pensions were linked to white supremacist ideology. Besides the extremely small number of exceptions discussed in the next chapter, North Carolina's pensions for Civil War service were exclusively issued to white citizens, meaning that they served as a form of welfare only available to whites. This fit solidly into a worldview where whites deserved more than African Americans. Pensions, however, were more than just welfare for aging whites— they reinforced white supremacy through both patronage and a narrative of white unity and heroism.

The liberalization of Confederate pensions was tied directly to white supremacist political campaigns. Indeed, it was no coincidence that Julian Carr and other members of the Democratic Party led the effort to make pensions more accessible. At the turn of the century, pensions for ex-Confederates helped cement the Lost Cause as the dominant collective memory among white southerners and served as a tool to secure Democrats near hegemonic control of the state. As historians have pointed out, it makes sense that the largest expansion of Virginia's pension program came in the same period "often associated with the rise of the Lost Cause movement." Pensions "allowed white Conservative Democratic leaders to celebrate Confederate veterans" at the same time they were instituting Jim Crow.[72] As Democratic politicians cited the heroics of Confederates at Gettysburg to justify disenfranchisement and white rule, pensioners provided living examples across the state to hold up as evidence of white supremacy.[73]

Turn-of-the-century calls for the expansion of pension eligibility were part of the anti-Fusionists white supremacy campaigns of the 1890s and 1900s.[74] Attempts to disenfranchise African Americans and promises of Confederate pensions were two sides of the same coin. Democratic candidates' promises to liberalize pensions served to attract white support, reward racial loyalty, and create white heroes. Campaign literature frequently connected support for white supremacy and support for Confederate veterans.[75] The defeat of the Fusion coalition and the beginning of one-party rule in North Carolina in 1901 was marked by the swearing in of white supremacist Charles Aycock as governor and Democrats rewarding the support of veterans by fulfilling their campaign promises regarding pension eligibility. Once authorized, pension officials often ruled on applications in a manner to garner votes for the Democratic Party.

Politics and personal antipathies often played a role in whether a deserter's pension application was approved. For instance, David Teague's pension was unsuccessfully challenged when someone claimed he had deserted. The bureaucrats in Raleigh recognized that fifty years after the war, people were often mistaken or "may have some personal grudge" that led them to lie. Indeed, the auditor noted that "we have so many cases of this kind to come up that experience has taught us to 'go slow' in accusing an Ex-Confederate soldier of having been a deserter unless we can substantiate the charge."[76] Teague was lucky. While pension officials were apparently overly cautious about personal disagreements leading to accusations of fraud, many were less concerned about politics corrupting the system. E. D. Smith of Yadkin County claimed his neighbor accused him of desertion in retaliation for his failure to pay a debt or because he did not vote Democratic, leading to his pension's subsequent suspension.[77] Similarly, Jesse Stegall of Forsyth County felt "his faithful service to the Democratic Party" had made him enemies in his Republican-leaning community.[78] If true, Stegall was in an uncommon situation, as Confederate pensions were usually used by Democrats and not Republicans to gain support. In reality, Stegall was likely trying to make his case by appealing to state-level officials who were Democrats, knowing that pensions were being used to reward political allies.

Politics and patronage played a major role in the administration of pensions, serving as a means of maintaining white hegemony in North Carolina. Democrats used pensions as a political stick as well as a carrot in their efforts to garner white votes. In Randolph County, James Fields, who had voted Republican, promised officials contritely that he and his son would always vote Democratic in the future if they reinstated his revoked pension. On October 24, 1912, a local Democratic leader, A. N. Bulla, wrote the state auditor to request the veteran's reinstatement, as "I do feel like he should have his pension if he does the right thing now." In response to Bulla's assertion that "if you will write me a letter so that I can show him that you will get him reinstated, both he and his son will give us a full ticket," the state auditor replied the very same day, promising to have Fields's pension restored. Someone in the auditor's office wrote on the letter, "Look this up & put his name on!!"[79] The decision was clearly driven by the forthcoming election; the fact that he was one of a number of pensioners dropped from the pension list in 1909, allegedly either for being too wealthy or for desertion, appears to have made no difference in the auditor's deliberations.[80]

The Fields case was part of a long-standing effort in Randolph County to only provide pensions to Democrats. Indeed, reinstating Fields's pension was the conclusion of a minor scandal that erupted in September 1910 when the *Randolph Bulletin* published allegations that party membership determined who got pensions. Democratic- and Republican-allied newspapers had published competing accounts of why Fields lost his pension. Fields was accused at various times of never having enlisted, of having been a deserter, and of not being sufficiently disabled.[81] In fairness, his war record was not stellar. Fields had been under arrest since the day after his muster, and he was later court-martialed and sentenced to hard labor for desertion.[82] The correspondence between officials makes clear, however, that Fields's voting record was what really concerned them.

Democrats in Randolph County were not alone. In neighboring Forsyth County, a veteran complained in a local newspaper in 1902 about his denied pension. Because he went AWOL for a week before being captured and returned to duty, the veteran was technically ineligible for another year. However, he believed his denial could be attributed to his admission that he was a Republican, writing, "Had I told them I was a Democrat I would have got a pension, as other Democratic deserters did." Why the board was even asking him about his party affiliations was never addressed. Ironically, the old veteran believed that a Democratic deserter was at fault for the whole affair. His characterization of the Forsyth pension board seems more accurate than Stegall's, as the county's pension board actually included a Democrat who had deserted to the enemy in the last months of the war.[83]

Another reason his application may have drawn the ire of a board composed of Confederate veterans was that he vocally announced that he had opposed the war, writing, "Like a large majority of the conscripts, I was forced into the war against my will."[84] Indeed, pointing out that not all whites supported the Confederacy was a political act as much as an act of historical interpretation in 1902. His open statements that he had been disloyal undermined the myths of the Lost Cause that Confederate pensions and politicians were actively shaping. Silence regarding desertion was not a problem, but flaunting that the South had been divided and discussing being forcibly conscripted was unacceptable to some Democratic officials by the early 1900s. His challenging a vision of the South where whites had unanimously supported the Confederacy was likely his greatest sin.

Indeed, opposing the Lost Cause's narrative of volunteerism and devotion—and hence undermining white supremacy—was the quickest way to have a pension application denied. One of David Yokley's cousins presents a striking example of an attempt to garner an undeserved pension that also provides a cautionary lesson for scholars using pension applications. The copy of Jacob Yokley's pension application found online is misleading. The application clearly has "approved" written across the front of it, which might lead a historian or genealogist to believe that Jacob had been a devoted Confederate and received a pension. Jacob's case, however, was one of those rare instances in which an investigation actually occurred. The results of these investigations do not appear in the digitized pension application file, instead appearing in a separate collection of correspondence held in the state archives. Scholars of the Civil War should remember that the complexities of wartime loyalties are rarely reflected accurately in the often incomplete administrative records made by the pension bureau.

In his application, Jacob swore he had been in the 70th North Carolina State Troops (1st Junior Reserves) beginning in 1864. Closer investigation reveals that Jacob had never served at all—he was actually a recusant conscript who took up arms against the Confederate Home Guard. Jacob attempted to twist, or indeed rewrite, the past to create an economically useful narrative. In a testament to how lackadaisically pension boards were looking for fraud, Jacob's application was initially approved. His pension was only revoked after neighbors challenged his eligibility before he received his first check.[85]

What undid Jacob Yokley, as opposed to so many of his relatives and neighbors—besides never having served—was that he was a braggart. Shortly after submitting his application in 1925, Jacob boasted to his neighbors about how he "drew a gun on the home guard" when they tried to capture him.[86] Jacob apparently took great pride in his ability to avoid capture, bragging that "he was too sharp for the home guard," but ultimately, he was not too sharp for the pension board.[87]

As with the Forsyth County Republican whose application was rejected, Jacob's blatant refusal even to pretend he had been loyal to the South was as unacceptable as his actual lack of service. His vocally undermining the Lost Cause with tales of resistance could not be overlooked. Had he kept quiet, Jacob likely would have received his pension without issue, as Aaron Cockerham and others who never served did.[88] Instead, tasked to investigate the case, the local pension board, likely embarrassed at having approved his application in the first place, informed state officials that Jacob had admitted to them not only that he had failed to serve but also that he had hidden by wearing "women's clothes."[89] Jacob's open admissions contradicted the accepted narrative of the Lost Cause in just too many ways. His critics' attempt to emasculate him with accusations of crossdressing served to reassert the masculinity of loyal Confederates. While this may have happened— indeed, deserters occasionally disguised themselves as women to avoid Home Guard patrols—it also functioned to separate Jacob from the masculine, honorable Confederate hero pensioners were supposed to represent.[90]

What made Jacob's case stand out was that he got caught. Pension boards were not completely oblivious to ineligible claimants slipping through, but their leniency was obvious to the many applicants who tried to take advantage of it. Like Daniel Eaker, Delila Hill applied for pensions from both the federal government and the state government. Both were denied. It seems likely that the fact that her husband had not only been arrested as a deserter from the 21st North Carolina but had also then joined the Union army after being captured in 1864 may explain why the local board rejected her application. For Hill's Confederate pension application to be approved would have required the signature of the same Davidson County Superior Court clerk who had previously notarized documents for her federal pension application.[91] Still, the fact that Hill even applied is a testament to how pension boards were perceived, and had she lived long enough to reapply, she would likely have been approved. In another brazen example, James J. Young deserted from *both* armies yet still applied for a pension from both the Union and Confederacy.[92] Though he was eligible for neither, his Confederate pension application was approved by the same county board that rejected Hill's. Others in similar situations also applied for multiple pensions.[93]

At least on the surface, North Carolina's Democrats opposed any pension for Confederate deserters who joined the Union army. In 1902, objections to these "galvanized Yankees" receiving federal pensions flourished across the state, when North Carolina senator Jeter Pritchard, a Republican, proposed a bill in Washington authorizing pensions for former Confederate soldiers who had joined the US Army during the war. Though this would have brought federal dollars into the state at a time when federal pensions were transferring wealth out of the South, many former Confederates found this unacceptable. The state division of the UCV passed a resolution denouncing the bill because it "rewards treachery and perfidy by giving to Confederate deserters for fighting against their former flag and comrades." Some commentators denied that North Carolina would receive much money, although others estimated it would bring $5 million annually into the South. Senator Pritchard, a Republican, lost his reelection campaign that year, in part due to his opposition to Confederate pensions while supporting pensions for galvanized Yankees.[94] The widespread disenfranchisement of African Americans also helped seal his defeat. Democrats used the politics of pensions as a wedge issue, and in doing so, they made clear what sort of service they felt should be seen as heroic in North Carolina.

Like Jacob Yokley, galvanized Yankees challenged the Lost Cause. The existence of Confederates who switched sides was even harder to explain away than desertion. As discussed in the previous chapter, desertion could be explained by the demands of family. Joining the Union army, though, undermined the myth of the heroic and unwavering loyal Confederate soldier. Thus, while there were extensive efforts to highlight politicians' opposition to galvanized Yankees being rewarded for their Union service, attempts to stop deserters were so weak that even galvanized Yankees like Eaker and Young could slip through the cracks. In effect, pensions encouraged them to forget their Union service, at least publicly.

Most Confederate pensioners were not lying about their service record, and the ineligible pensioners discussed here represent a minority of applications. That minority, however, indicates a willingness to overlook desertion. Even after 1927, when the federal government completed the Compiled Service Records that detail the military careers of each soldier, North Carolina only rarely wrote to Washington to learn about a soldier's service. Unless they already had questions, the word of a few neighbors was enough to approve a pension. It seems that the myth of the Solid South was strong enough by 1920 that many white North Carolinians accepted that most white southerners would never have deserted or dissented, and if they did desert, they must have had good reason. Investigations, then, were simply unlikely to yield results in the minds of those enculturated with the Lost Cause.

Pension fraud was not limited to North Carolina, nor was the state's failure to stop it exceptional. In 1906, Georgia's pension commissioner, J. W. Lindsay, noted in his annual report that there was "considerable fraud in the pension rolls which under the present laws it is practically impossible to detect." Lindsay stated that he had examined War Department records and determined that some applicants who claimed to have been captured had actually been deserters. He lacked authority, however, to do anything about these deserters receiving pensions. The next year, he complained again that grand juries "are still very lax" in their duties of detecting fraud. He would make a similar complaint in 1909, but despite his repeated requests for more authority, county grand juries would remain "the only check" on fraud in the state.[95] Few Georgians seem to have taken Lindsay's concerns seriously.

Part of the problem is that there was an expectation, encouraged by the narratives that Confederate veterans and Democratic politicians pushed, that veterans were noble and honest. In South Carolina, a minor scandal ensued after ex-Confederate general Irvine Walker declared in 1911 that there "ought not to be more than 2,000 soldier pensioners" despite the previous year's rolls listing 4,886. In reply, the state's comptroller general called the accusation "reckless" while asserting that as "the administration of pension laws . . . is entrusted to ex-Confederate soldiers" and "the Confederate soldiers can be trusted to conduct the interests of their comrades," the public need not worry about fraud. A. S. Salley Jr., secretary of the state's historical commission, similarly declared that he doubted fraud was common, insisting that doubting the claims of old soldiers would lead to "gross historical mistakes and myths will be perpetuated." A newspaper reporting on the issue noted that Salley's "faith in [the] honor of Gallant Confederate soldiers" led him to dismiss accusations of pension fraud.[96]

The Lost Cause narrative had been extremely successful at creating an expectation of honesty for elderly veterans across the South. When considering John Singleton Mosby's contention that many self-proclaimed veterans at reunions were fakes, one reporter had noted that "the very suggestion that there are frauds among them is painful." The reporter only reluctantly concluded, "It would be safe to wager a dollar against a doughnut that if Mosby's men were pensionable the pension agents could find a thousand of them out of the original eight hundred."[97]

In April 1865 shots rang out along the northern border of Davidson County, North Carolina, as a detail of Michigan cavalrymen traded rounds with a Confederate skirmish line. Sent to find horses to replace their exhausted mounts, the Michiganders had found themselves cut off from their unit's encampment. Seeking a way around the Confederate forces, the men asked a passing farmer for directions. The farmer found himself in a position to contribute directly to the Union cause for the first time since the war began—a service he gladly provided, having long suffered under Confederate governance. He directed the soldiers on how to bypass the enemy position, but as no good deed goes unpunished, the Union troopers commandeered the helpful man's horse and "fired at the Confederate soldiers several times" before riding off. Whether the shots hit their marks remains unknown, but anyone who died did so needlessly; though word had not yet reached North Carolina, Robert E. Lee had surrendered the day before.[98]

Thus, as the Confederacy took its last breath, the US Army finally arrived in Davidson County. The war, of course, had been there for much longer. Since 1861, Confederate loyalists had fought an "inner war" in the Piedmont of North Carolina against anti-Confederate dissenters. Characterized by robberies, arsons, death threats, and bushwhacking, violence steadily increased over the course of the war. Local citizens, including the farmer who had helped the troops, covertly fed deserters and hid escaped Union prisoners, while bands of deserters, recusant conscripts (the nineteenth-century equivalent to draft dodgers), and other dissenters openly resisted Confederate authority. In 1863, a regiment of Confederate regulars sent to suppress resistance had scoured the woods in northern Davidson County, hunting for deserters.[99] Over the course of two months, the unit helped capture at least three thousand deserters, while others died resisting. In March 1865, Lee dispatched a battalion of sharpshooters from his already-strained Army of Northern Virginia, again to suppress dissension. The unit, consisting of local men, summarily executed five dissenters in Forsyth County to the north, then sent fifty more captives back to the front lines.[100]

The helpful farmer, Samuel D. Yokley—the father of the same David Yokley who received a pension despite deserting after one month of service—would belatedly be reimbursed for his horse after submitting a claim to the Southern Claims Commission. The commission, created in 1871, allowed loyal southerners to receive compensation for property that federal forces commandeered for the war effort. Commissioners examined written testimonies as well as wartime documents to determine whether a claimant had really remained loyal to the Union throughout the entire war, a key condition for compensation.[101] The federal government set the standard for loyalty extremely high, and any aid given to the Confederacy, even if the alternative had been death or bodily harm, could result in rejection. Fortunately for the Yokley family, the federal government approved Samuel Yokley's claim in 1878, and he entered the history books as a certified Unionist. Within a generation, however, members of the family would largely reject their Unionist identity and portray themselves as staunch Confederates.

The embrace of the Lost Cause by former dissenters was neither preordained nor inevitable. In the immediate aftermath of the war, numerous reasons existed to maintain the memory of dissent and create a cohesive Unionist identity. The Southern Claims Commission, bitterness over wartime mistreatment, and political fights pitting former Confederates against the Republican Party all encouraged the creation of a Unionist identity. This identity, premised upon tales of principled Unionism, flourished during the 1870s in the North Carolina Piedmont.[102]

During the 1860s and '70s, powerful external forces encouraged dissenters to remember their opposition to the Confederacy as a product of patriotism. Though stronger Unionist sentiment had developed out of resentment toward the Confederacy, the patriotism and uncompromising support for the Union expressed in Southern Claims Commission claims was partially a product of the legal standards for proving loyalty. The commission's enabling legislation ensured that claimants framed their resistance around their love of the Union when testifying. Because the government defined true Unionist resistance as being a product of patriotism, claimants' answers stressed rigid political allegiances. Even the standardized list of questions for claimants highlighted specific motivations and actions. Encouraged by newspapers, politics, and pecuniary interests, a narrative of uncompromising Unionism, principled dissent, and patriotism became the standard means for describing dissenters' resistance during Reconstruction.

Yet this once widespread countermemory of dissent largely disappeared by the mid-twentieth century. The Yokley family's history is suggestive as to why a robust Unionist counternarrative to the Lost Cause failed to take permanent root in the Piedmont. The complexity of wartime dissent hampered efforts to create a lasting shared memory of opposing the Confederacy. Basing an identity on a myth of uncompromising principle required extreme massaging of individual memories for many dissenters. By contrast, the Lost Cause and memories of a Solid South proved a powerful narrative for contemporary needs. In this context, it was frequently easier to forget the myriad reasons for dissent than to remember their complexities. Ultimately, however, the collective amnesia that North Carolinians like the Yokley family experienced was not solely a product of former Confederates chiefly writing their history; rather, former dissenters actively contributed to the erasure of dissent from the dominant narratives of the Civil War.[103]

Neither the most transparent opportunist nor most self-effacing claimant, Samuel Yokley provides a window into the motives, means, and memories of dissent during the postbellum era. At first glance, one might expect Yokley to have been a secessionist from the start of the war. Already a prosperous famer in 1860, the forty-five-year-old owned multiple farms and held stock in the North Carolina Railroad. He was invested in the South's peculiar institution as the owner of fourteen enslaved people.[104]

Nevertheless, Yokley, a prewar Whig, vocally opposed secession because he correctly believed that it would result in the end of slavery. Thus his family belonged to that substantial portion of the Piedmont's population that remained unconvinced of the need for a new nation.

His opinion of the Confederacy only diminished over time, exacerbated by his wartime experience.[105] First, Confederate loyalists threatened to burn his farm "because [his] boys would not fight for the Confederacy and [he] protected them." In addition to these threats of arson, Confederate troops also arrested Yokley three times. In the fall of 1863, for example, Captain John Gilmer of the 21st North Carolina arrested Yokley in an attempt to force his sons to return to service. Yokley, who was lightly dressed, later recalled how the Confederates "would not allow me to go home after my coat." Following a cold night under arrest at a local school, Yokley refused to go any farther. According to Yokley, the twenty-two-year-old captain "ordered a portion of his men to shoot me; they immediately surrounded me and presented their guns at me." Yokley called his bluff, telling the brash young officer, "If you kill me you will only have one old man out of the way." After a few moments, the officer and his men marched off, leaving Yokley alone in the school. He was lucky; the 21st North Carolina killed a number of dissenters during their sweep of the Piedmont for deserters. Yokley's experiences clearly intensified his allegiance to the Union. As this case suggests, however, conscription and the subsequent Confederate harassment of recusant conscripts, deserters, and their families may have created more "Union men" than any other act of the Confederate government, including secession.[106]

Samuel Yokley testified using the language of patriotism, but close examination of his testimony reveals that family and self-interest were at least as important to his resistance. Yokley's third arrest resulted in a revealing conversation regarding the roots of his resistance. After a night in the Forsyth County courthouse "without anything to eat," he was dragged before an enrolling officer, who announced his intent to enroll one of the farmer's younger sons. Yokley declared that his son "did not belong to the Confederate service [as] he was 16 years of age" and threatened to "spend the last dollar, the last nigger & the last horse before they should have him." As Yokley made clear to the officer, protection of his family was central to his resistance. Upon learning that Yokley owned slaves, the enrollment officer asked the farmer why he failed to support the Confederacy. Yokley indignantly replied "that I had lived under the Government of the United States; & it's Constitution & Government had always protected me and my property."[107] His resistance thus appears to have largely evolved not from blind patriotism but rather from a strategic consideration of what would best serve his family.

Although Yokley would give anything for his son's safety, he was less willing to give his last dollar, slave, or horse to the Union. In fact, the day after the federal cavalrymen took his horse, Yokley attempted to protest to the unit's commander and retrieve his animal, but the troops left the area before he reached their encampment.[108] Still, the constant harassment and mistreatment he had suffered at the hands of Confederate authorities ensured that by 1865, Yokley identified more strongly with the Union than the Confederacy. Ideology and loyalty are always fluid, and there were limits to the Yokleys' love of the flag as well as tangible reasons for their allegiance to the Union. For Samuel Yokley, his wartime political loyalties remained first and foremost about protecting his sons and secondly preserving his property.

A sense of patriotism almost certainly helped motivate the Yokleys' opposition to the Confederacy, but self-interest determined the manner of dissent and level of resistance. Unlike some dissenters who attacked the farms of secessionists and Home Guard officers to intimidate them, the Yokleys sought to avoid conflict.[109] For most of the war, the Yokleys' resistance consisted of avoiding service and helping others do the same. The family never attacked the Confederate war effort directly by cutting a rail line, burning a bridge, or attacking a supply wagon. That changed in 1864, however, when the Home Guard captured one of Yokley's sons and the others took up arms. The goal of their raid on Confederate authorities was not to bring about the fall of the Confederacy, though the perpetrators eagerly awaited its demise. Rather, the Yokleys went to rescue their kin.[110] Dissenters like the Yokleys often avoided conflict with Confederates, only taking up arms to protect themselves and their family members.

A narrative of uncompromising Unionism ignored the complexity of dissent and failed to adequately contain the wartime reality many dissenters experienced. When Andrew Yokley, Samuel's brother, submitted a claim to the Southern Claims Commission, he declared, "I did all that I could for the cause. I kept out of the army." Keeping out of the army was apparently about all Andrew Yokley felt he could do, as he first hired a substitute and then hauled wood for the railroad so as to be exempt from conscription. Only when that exemption became too costly did Yokley join his nephews hiding in the woods. Even his reasons for joining the anti-Confederate secret society, the Heroes of America, seems passive and self-defensive in nature. He later recalled how the Piedmont-wide organization "was a protection for Union men, there was nothing bad or murderous about it." Serving on a detail hauling wood for the Confederate railroads or paying for a substitute had in no way been antithetical to joining the Heroes of America. The Heroes never actively attacked the Confederate war effort as a guerrilla organization, and many members of the Heroes likely opposed conscription more than the Confederacy itself.[111] Andrew's contention that not fighting and helping others on the run proved his loyalty was unconvincing to the commissioners, who felt that he should have taken to the woods earlier.

Dissenters' experiences resisting the Confederacy were as varied as their motivations. Unlike former Confederate soldiers who shared memories of battle and fighting for the Lost Cause, dissenters had trouble fashioning an analogous shared experience. Members of the Yokley family, for example, dissented and avoided military service in a variety of ways. During the first year of the war, many families like the Yokleys, less supportive of the Confederacy, went about their lives with relatively few major disruptions. The advent of conscription in 1862, however, often pushed even the most ambivalent citizen into taking a stand on the war. Too old to serve himself, Samuel Yokley watched as the Confederacy conscripted two of his six sons, as well as his younger brother. As already noted, all three deserted and returned home to hide in the woods. In the latter part of the war, a fourth son became a recusant conscript, joining his brothers in the woods. Another of Samuel's sons, who had left home for Missouri before the war, fought in the US Army. The Yokley family, then, included deserters, recusant conscripts, detailed workers, and a Union volunteer. All of these individuals considered themselves and each other "Union men," and their community largely agreed during and after the war.[112]

Local definitions within the South of what made someone a Unionist varied greatly from the federal government's standard. Though the government required unwavering conviction, the actual claimants throughout the 1870s insisted that dissenters of all sorts were actually Unionists. While the government deemed Andrew Yokley disloyal, denying his claim, Samuel Yokley considered his brother to be a Union man, asking Andrew to testify as a witness for his own successful claim. Indeed, previously denied claimants frequently provided testimony for their neighbors' approved claims and vice versa. Mapping the social networks of individuals identified as Unionists within the claims records shows that approved claimants considered many of their neighbors, even those with denied claims, to have been true Union men.[113]

North Carolina's postwar Unionist identity was built with unstable foundations. A dependency on patriotic motivations and divided communities instead of shared experiences created inherent weaknesses within white Unionist memory. This memory was premised on maintaining divisions within the white community. By contrast, the Lost Cause depended on racial divisions being maintained. Indeed, almost all southern whites were welcome to share in the glories of the Lost Cause, while to be a white Unionist required uncompromising devotion to the flag and persecution by other white southerners. According to the Lost Cause narrative, most white dissenters had not even dissented; deserters left to provide for their family, work details provided important material support for a fight against overwhelming odds, and even fighting for the Union still proved one's manhood.[114] Recusant conscripts and galvanized Yankees remained the only categories that failed to have a place in the Lost Cause narrative, and these could be overlooked by simply ignoring them. In the end, a white Unionist memory failed to sustain a usable counternarrative to the Lost Cause. Thus, the Yokleys embraced Unionist or Confederate identities when convenient and when it paid. The family's history implies that attempts to use a narrative of dissent based on Unionism to create a postwar identity for political organization may have been inherently weaker than Democratic appeals to white supremacy and monetary spoils.

Jeffrey Vogel has argued that federal pensions were a "key political issue through which Northerners and Southerners negotiated the terms of reconciliation."[115] In a similar way, state pensions in North Carolina helped bring about reunion within divided southern communities. In turning former Unionists into ex-Confederates, pensions helped ensure that wartime enmities between white southerners were not passed on to future generations by motivating dissenters to forget (at least publicly) their anti-Confederate experiences. In essence, pensions helped heal communities that had been divided by war by helping to create a memory of a Solid South where "white southerner" was analogous to "Confederate." But there was a cost to reconciliation and this healing of divisions: alternative identities, political allegiances, and historical narratives that had previously rationalized supporting a biracial Republican Party were all sacrificed.

Pensions served those devoted to white supremacy by venerating Confederate service, rewarding racial solidarity, and creating heroes of white supremacy as well as a memory of a Solid South. As many historians have pointed out, the resurgence in Confederate memory from 1890 to 1920—demonstrated by both the erection of Confederate monuments and the issuing of pensions—corresponded to the rise of Jim Crow. Increasingly, Confederate memory worked to unite whites along racial lines celebrating the honor and bravery of the white race; pensions for nearly any veteran allowed every old man to be remembered heroically. In the context of these developments, Unionist memory simply failed to remain useful. Dependent upon a memory of division and persecution, thus dividing neighbors and even families, an anti-Confederate identity ceased to serve present needs. As the number of former dissenters decreased due to death and emigration, Democratic politicians, too young to have fought, presumably became more politically acceptable than their ex-Confederate predecessors for whom dissenters had refused to vote. With the end of the Southern Claims Commission and the introduction of Confederate pensions, even the earlier monetary incentives to celebrate dissent were replaced by new motivations to proclaim a Confederate affiliation.[116] Thus, in the early twentieth century, family replaced principle as the profitable explanation for desertion. The monetary incentives as well as the social capital being a veteran brought were more powerful than a memory of dissent.

Dissenters were not passive in the creation of an amnesia of dissent. Pensions encouraged the forgetting of dissent even among those who spent the war challenging Confederate authority, yet the pensioners had to apply. The same desire or need for money that had led dissenters to see dollar signs in staunch devotion to Union with the Southern Claims Commission now made some "forget" their past devotion to the Stars and Stripes. Thus former dissenters who had first shaped a Unionist identity into a political allegiance during Reconstruction actively participated in the erasure of dissent from popular memory after the turn of the century.

The Yokley family was not unique—other Davidson County deserters transformed themselves in the public eye from anti-Confederate dissenters to Unionists and then to Confederates in less than a generation. In 1866, when asking Union forces to retrieve his property taken by the Home Guard members who had hunted him as a deserter, Burgess L. Gallimore portrayed himself as "loyal."[117] Yet when he applied for a Confederate pension in 1914, he failed to mention his loyalty to the Union, his two desertions, or his eventual defection to Union forces. Instead, his pension would come to be seen as a badge of loyalty and devotion to the Confederacy. When he died in 1921, the local newspaper remembered Gallimore as a "highly respected Veteran." Other deserters were similarly remembered in obituaries.[118] Their embrace of the Lost Cause ensured that Confederate service became a key piece of how these men were remembered.

Whereas recalling desertion as an act of loyalty to the Union could pay financial dividends in the 1870s, Confederate pensions provided widespread monetary and social incentives to forget desertion in the early twentieth century. John Crouch is among the most surprising of Davidson County pensioners. Crouch and his brother Augustin were drafted into the 48th North Carolina in 1862. In May of the next year, after both had received wounds, they deserted and returned home. They were arrested and returned to Virginia, where Augustin was executed in January 1864. John deserted to Union lines shortly thereafter, took the oath of allegiance, and spent the rest of the war in Philadelphia. His subsequent leadership in the Moravian Church did not keep him from requesting a pension that he should not have been eligible to receive.[119] Crouch's revising of his personal past for a pension may have been part of a broader rewriting of the past by his family. His brother's gravestone inaccurately proclaims Augustin as a volunteer and makes no mention of execution, though it does note that he "died near Orange Co. VA."[120] The fact that even conscripts and deserters with the weakest of war records could be recalled as devoted volunteers helped fabricate a memory of a Solid South where all whites supported the Confederacy.

The memory of Samuel Yokley's oldest son, Andrew, presents a striking example of the family's anti-Confederate roots being forgotten. Andrew J. Yokley had moved west in 1860. He entered federal service in 1862 and was killed in an ambush by Confederate guerrillas while carrying dispatches in Arkansas two years later. The family had not known of his enlistment or death in US service until after the war, as they were unable to communicate across the lines. Still, Samuel Yokley eventually collected his son's back pay, and in 1884, his wife applied for her son's pension, at which time loyalty to the Union still paid. In her pension application, she proclaimed that her family had been "loyal to the union through the war."[121] The pension was initially denied, and it took six years' worth of correspondence and additional evidence to finally start receiving twelve dollars a month. However, the monetary incentive to remember Andrew's service and sacrifice disappeared with his mother's death in 1904.

Today, the Yokley family apparently has no memory of how their ancestor fought against the Confederacy. By 1982, an amateur genealogist tracing the family's heritage believed that Andrew died "of a pistol wound reportedly inflicted by Jesse James while working with the Pony express." The Pony Express ceased operation in 1861, years before Andrew actually died and while Jesse James was barely fourteen. Instead of celebrating Andrew's devotion to the Union and his military service within the US Army, the family created a heroic story that entirely disconnected his death from the war.[122]

The creation and ultimate failure of Unionist counternarratives remains an under-studied topic, but it has the potential to change our understanding of the war. Scholars still occasionally use the term "South" interchangeably with the Confederacy and "southerner" with Confederate supporter, ignoring a substantial portion of the population, white and black, that played a crucial role in both the war and in Reconstruction. Some southern whites and many African Americans contested the rise of the Lost Cause myth with their own countermemories. Seen vividly in the Southern Claims Commission records and Reconstruction-era election campaigns, the myth of the Solid South did not take hold immediately after Appomattox. It had to be created. In the decades that followed, communities remained divided. Wartime loyalties and memories of the war helped shape a disordered society, and many southerners, black and white, refused to be labeled as supporters of the Confederacy in the immediate aftermath of the war.

As historians increasingly look at the history of Unionism, desertion, and dissent, studies of historical memory present a unique opportunity to understand the nature of dissent. Examining these southerners' memories of the war not only provides insight into why Unionism was forgotten but also displays the complexity of competing wartime loyalties. Indeed, the ease with which the Yokleys forgot old loyalties forces us to question how constituent dissent was to both the family's postwar and wartime identities. If nothing else, the prevalence of pension fraud should demonstrate that North Carolina's pension records can be a risky proposition for scholars wanting to know about the actual conflict.

Ignoring pension fraud and celebrating pensioners as model citizens helped impart the Lost Cause to future generations in a subtler way than monuments and speeches. In a cyclic manner, pension fraud served to reinforce the Lost Cause narrative by creating a memory of near unanimous and unflagging support for the Confederacy. This in turn provided fertile ground for swindlers by removing an expectation that there were deserters who might apply for pensions. Like tales of heroics at Gettysburg, pension fraud helped transform ex-Confederates from failed rebels who might be considered traitors into patriotic white American heroes. Pension fraud played a minor part of the Lost Cause's creation, but the amnesia of dissent it facilitated was necessary to create a memory of a solid white South full of heroic gray-clad soldiers, unwavering in their support for the Confederacy. As the next generation came of age, its members saw pensioners as evidence of a past full of heroic Confederates, without deserters or dissent. In this way, fraud helped provide a mythic past that white southerners could celebrate and use to justify their political hegemony.

4

Playing the Faithful Slave

Pensions for Ex-Slaves and Free People of Color,
1905–1951

The CSS *Curlew* sank quickly. A shell crashed through the deck of the side-wheel steamer and continued downward, puncturing her hull. Her crew drove her toward shore in a desperate attempt to ground her before she sank. They managed to run her aground directly in front of the Confederacy's Fort Forrest, a seven-gun floating battery consisting of a set of barges anchored along the shore. The *Curlew* had entered the battle intending to support Fort Forrest and nearby Fort Bartow as they attempted to repulse the US Navy and Army from landing on Roanoke Island. Instead, the *Curlew* ended up masking the Confederate battery and taking its seven cannon out of the fight as well. Both the ship and the battery were eventually burned to prevent their capture.

In an 1883 account of the battle, the captain of the CSS *Beaufort* remembered that the *Curlew*'s Captain Thomas "Tornado" Hunter had found himself pantless at the end of the intense battle. How he received his nickname is not entirely clear, but the *Beaufort*'s captain claimed that Hunter was "very excitable," citing his wardrobe malfunction as one example. Indeed, the underdressed commander reportedly could not offer an explanation for how his pants blew off.[1]

The Battle of Roanoke Island was a minor battle rarely recalled today, but it provides an excellent example of how narratives can be crafted. What a historian stresses in his or her narrative changes interpretations. Some scholars might see Hunter as a brilliant commander attempting to save his ship to fight another day. One might even dismiss the story about the missing pants as a postwar joke, as even the *Beaufort*'s captain recalled Hunter as a gallant officer. While it is plausible that the story was made up, perhaps there was a kernel of truth in this account of a captain who cannot even manage to keep his pants on during battle.

An alternate interpretation of the sinking of the *Curlew* is that Hunter's command was incompetent. This retelling replaces "Tornado" Hunter's gallantry with a brash, disorganized captain. A single "shot or shell" went through the ship's hull. Unable to deal with a single hole, the "very excitable" Hunter fled the battle, shouting incoherently to nearby ships, perhaps in a near panic.[2] His overreaction resulted in his taking both the ship and Fort Forrest out of the action prematurely. Indeed, considering that Hunter beached his ship so close that the Confederate forces could not burn the *Curlew* for fear that it would ignite the wooden base of the fort, perhaps Hunter was lucky not to have crashed into the fort instead. This alternate retelling of the story is likely unfair to Hunter. In truth, the ship was probably sinking quickly; archeological investigations indicate that the ship's inferior construction meant that a single round drove out an entire hull plate.[3] Still, Hunter's decision to come so close to Fort Forrest remains questionable.

Whatever the truth, somehow, the loss of the *Curlew* became a heroic event in postwar retellings instead of an example of Confederate naval incompetence. Just as historians can craft divergent narratives using different emphasis and order, various memories of the past are constructed by selective remembrance and by stressing particular aspects of the past.

The *Curlew* provides a second example of historical "spin" that borders on outright fabrication. During the Battle of Roanoke Island, the *Curlew*'s pilot, Eli Williamson, had his right arm broken by the shattered wheel of the ship.[4] Like many civilian sailors, Williamson was pressed into service, and like other veterans, he received a pension from the state of North Carolina as an elderly man. Nothing in Williamson's story seems surprising except for one major fact: Williamson was not white.

Williamson was a free person of color when the war started. As a black man who was not enslaved, the pilot occupied a liminal space, neither enslaved nor citizen. In 1905 Williamson became one of the first African Americans to receive a Civil War pension from the state of North Carolina. Though likely the earliest such pensioner, he would not be the last.[5] In the twenty years following Williamson's pension, the North Carolina General Assembly granted a small number of pensions to individual African Americans with private bills.[6] Then, in 1927, two and a half decades after liberalizing pension eligibility for veterans, the state authorized the pension bureau to begin formally accepting applications from African Americans for a new type of pension. These "Class B" pensions were not for soldiers but for free people of color and ex-slaves who had worked during the war as body servants or laborers, often building fortifications for the Confederacy. Williamson, as one of the first nonwhite North Carolinians to get a pension, was rare, as he actually qualified under the original pension act for his impressed service within the Confederate navy. He was also unique from the other pensioners this chapter discusses in that his labor was on a ship.

Williamson was a pathbreaker in presenting himself as a happy and obedient black man in order to gain a pension and other material rewards. Upon his death in 1915, he was remembered in North Carolina newspapers as "a follower of the Southern Confederacy," but was his loyalty sincere? Some local whites accepted him as such. A year earlier, a local newspaper claimed that "he still remained loyal to the South till the end of the war."[7] At first glance, it appears that a true "black Confederate" soldier—a black Confederate volunteer—might have been discovered. Indeed, Williamson has been cited as such by neo-Confederate writers.[8] Digging deeper, however, reveals a different story.

Though he portrayed himself as a loyal Confederate to white southerners when he was an elderly man, Williamson had not always claimed to support the Confederacy. Like Samuel Yokley in the previous chapter, Williamson also submitted a claim with the Southern Claims Commission, in his case for a horse and cart taken by Union raiders in July 1863. The claims commission determined whether southerners who claimed they remained loyal during the war deserved reimbursement for property taken by Union troops. One of Williamson's witnesses, Benjamin Weston, recalled in his 1874 supporting testimony that Williamson, "like all his race, was loyal to the government of the United States."[9] The claim was approved with almost no investigation, as a decade after the war, the commissioners could not yet imagine black Confederates.

Despite his earlier claim of loyalty to the Union, Williamson's work as a pilot was presented as evidence of loyalty to the Confederacy in the early twentieth century. In 1914, the *Albemarle Observer* printed an appeal to white North Carolinians for donations to support the elderly Williamson. By then in his nineties and having moved to Washington, DC—which meant he lost his state pension—Williamson and his white advocates presented the former pilot as a "faithful old darkey" who remained on the *Curlew* due to his loyalty to the Confederacy. George Withy, a white ship captain who authored the appeal for donations, pointed out that "after the Battle of Roanoke Island this old darkey could have gone over to the Federals in the capacity of Pilot" but did not, "preferring to remain loyal to his friends and the South." Not surprisingly, the article did not dwell on the fact that Williamson avoided returning to the Confederate navy after his arm healed. How many North Carolinians sent contributions is unknown. Williamson, however, was playing a role that other free people of color and former enslaved people used to advance economically and socially: that of the loyal black southerner.[10]

White southerners saw a use for an individual like Williamson in their defense of segregation and white supremacy and crafted a memory of the pilot accordingly. After his death, the white southern press erased any hint that his service might have been involuntary. In 1915, multiple southern newspapers republished his Washington, DC, obituary, but they all tellingly left out one line from the original: "The Confederates kept a strict guard over Williamson until the close of the war."[11] Recounting Williamson as serving only under duress would have undermined claims of widespread black loyalty to the Confederacy. Indeed, Williamson's obituary in the *Albemarle Observer* even claimed that "he remained loyal to the South and received a small pension from his state, and in the end was given an honorable discharge from the Confederate States navy."[12]

Williamson was not a volunteer and never received a discharge. He was almost certainly impressed along with the *Curlew*, a civilian steam ship on which he had served as chief pilot before the war, ferrying passengers between Edenton, Hertford, Elizabeth City, and Nags Head. Williamson's familiarity with both Albemarle Sound and the ship meant that he remained on board as a skilled pilot after the Confederacy transformed the civilian transport into a gunboat. If any emotion kept Williamson on board willingly, it was likely his attachment to the ship; in the 1850s, he had named his daughter Curlew.[13]

Examining how he navigated a world where his skin tone put him at a material disadvantage might lead us to think that Williamson had no loyalties at all. Previously overlooked evidence makes it clear that he had little sympathy for the Confederacy. Though both Williamson and white southerners presented him as a loyal Confederate when convenient, Williamson's family recalled him differently. His daughter Seabird, also named after a ship he piloted, later recalled that "although working for the Confederacy, he helped many Union soldiers, and some Confederate general remarked, 'If it hadn't been for the damn pilot, we'd have won the war.'"[14] While it seems doubtful that any general said such a thing, hyperbole aside, the oral tradition within the family of undermining the Confederacy raises questions about Williamson's wartime conduct. Indeed, it is tempting to imagine that Williamson might still have been steering the *Curlew* when it inauspiciously grounded in front of a Confederate battery taking those additional guns out of action. Sadly, whether he stayed at his post after his arm was broken during the battle remains unknown.

Whatever the truth about Williamson, pensions for people of color forced to work for the Confederacy have been used since their issuance to buttress the Lost Cause and ideologies of white supremacy. In the late twentieth and early twenty-first centuries, Class B pension applications for former slaves and free people of color began to be cited as proof that there were "black Confederate" soldiers serving alongside their masters.

Presenting Confederates as racial progressives who accepted black soldiers as equals, this modern misinterpretation claims that black Confederates "prove" white southerners were not racist because their slaves fought alongside them. The depiction of the Confederacy as some sort of post-racial utopia where happy slaves took up arms in defense of their homes and were treated as equals to their white counterparts is simply not based on reality. While there may have been some African Americans in the South who identified with the Confederacy in some manner for a variety of socioeconomic, psychological, and personal reasons, the numbers were clearly smaller than some neo-Confederates would like to believe, and Eli Williamson was not among them.

The goal of this chapter is not to disprove every example of an African American helping the Confederacy. War and humans are complex, and so were the relations between southerners. I merely aim to shine light on how narratives were crafted, what purpose these narratives served, and what pensions actually represented at the time they were issued. In doing so, however, I discovered no evidence of "black Confederates" serving alongside white soldiers. Quite the opposite: like other historians, I discovered ample evidence that Confederate soldiers, leaders, and official policy opposed the introduction of black soldiers and that black Confederates are a creation of the late twentieth century. As discussed in this chapter and the next, I found that examples of African Americans cited to show black southerners supporting the Confederacy frequently reveal the opposite: enslaved southerners yearned to be free but occasionally presented themselves as loyal slaves retroactively. Neither black nor white North Carolinians of the Civil War generation believed there had been black Confederate troops during the conflict.

Like Confederate soldiers who accepted African American laborers but rejected the prospect of black soldiers, the white southerners who designed the pension system wanted it clear that ex-slave pensions were not equal to those for white veterans. In fact, Class B pensioners and stories about faithful slaves were cited as proof that a racial hierarchy had existed peacefully before and should continue to endure. As historians have pointed out, during the early twentieth century, "memories of loyal, faithful slaves would serve as a model for the 'proper' postwar racial order in the age of Jim Crow, disenfranchisement, and lynching." Stories about the benevolence of slavery were used to argue that whites should be in charge, races were unequal, and that even many slaves had agreed with the principles of white supremacy. In the early twentieth century, tales of loyal slaves aided white southerners in defending segregation and inequality by blaming racial strife on northern interference.[15]

Despite the seemingly contradictory nature of these two interpretations, the modern myth of black Confederate soldiers emerged from the older fabrications and misrepresentations of happy slaves. Indeed, accounts of thousands of black Confederates defending the South are "best understood as extensions of the loyal slave narrative."[16] As representations of simple-minded blacks who were loyal to their masters failed to fit in a world that increasingly rejected the overt rhetoric of white supremacy, these tales evolved to defend the memory of the Confederacy in new ways. What began as a celebration of slaves' loyalty to their masters became a memory of slaves devoted to the Confederacy before evolving into myths about slaves actively fighting for the Confederacy. These shifts took place over decades, but the introduction of Class B pensions was a crucial step in this evolution.

In many ways, these pensions were part of symbiotic relationships premised on individuals fashioning new narratives of their own pasts. Both the recipients of these pensions and the white politicians who issued them gained something from the monetary exchange. For African Americans, pensions provided money, social standing, and access to perks usually reserved for whites. For white North Carolinians, pensions gave them an example to which they could point of what a good African American looked like, a powerful piece of evidence to defend the memory of the Confederacy, and a tool to maintain a system of white supremacy in the South.

Those who issued the pensions to the formerly enslaved would be shocked at recent attempts to present nonwhite pensioners on an equal footing with Confederate soldiers. Officials in charge of granting pensions did not see ex-slaves and servants as full soldiers worthy of the same rewards as white soldiers. For starters, while soldiers' widows were eligible for pensions, Class B pensions could not be transferred upon a pensioner's death. When the widow of John Gilmer, a former body servant from Forsyth County, requested a pension, the state auditor rejected her application, noting that "the legislature really intended the pension for the deserving colored men who went with their masters to the war, but the pension stops with them."[17] Indeed, a similar 1932 rejection to another Forsyth County widow noted that no widow of an African American could ever be eligible for a pension, "as there were no negro soldiers in the Confederate Army."[18]

African American pensioners' unequal treatment provides clear evidence of how these pensions were understood at the time. Unlike the expansions of pensions for white veterans in 1901 and 1903, there were few surviving men eligible to apply when Class B pensions were finally authorized in 1927, sixty-two years after the war ended. In 1928, only seventy-four of those "who in 1861–65 followed their masters" were reportedly receiving checks from North Carolina.[19] Fewer than two hundred black North Carolinians ever applied for Class B pensions.[20] Moreover, pensions for African Americans were also smaller than those given to white veterans, reinforcing Jim Crow–era social norms. In the 1930s, a North Carolina veteran would receive around $365 a year, a disabled widow $300, and an able-bodied widow (called a Class B widow) $100 a year. Servants' pensions were valued at $200 a year, which was actually a generous amount compared to some other states.[21]

North Carolina was not unique in providing smaller pensions for former slaves and free people of color that reinforced racial inequality. By 1927, four other states had passed similar laws providing pensions to former slaves who remained faithful to their Confederate owners when taken off to war.[22] In South Carolina, the maximum pensions for a servant was legally capped at twenty-five dollars annually, but in reality, even less was paid. In 1928, for example, an ex-slave could expect to receive $11 annually, while a white veteran might expect as much as $175, depending on his disability. South Carolina's white widows received an annual minimum of $110 and as much as $123, while widows of ex-slaves, being ineligible for a pension, received nothing.[23]

These pensions held up a worldview that African Americans deserved and required less than whites (and were happy about it) while simultaneously promulgating nostalgia for a time when blacks happily did whatever they were told for little or no pay.[24] While today these pensions are often cited to imply that the Confederacy was a place of racial harmony due to its commitment to equality, at the time they were issued, these pensions sent the opposite message: that racial harmony was premised on African Americans' acceptance of inequality. The lower payment, later authorization, lack of widows' pensions, and even the name made clear that the recipients of Class B pensions were considered a lower class of pensioners than Confederate veterans.

North Carolina pension authorities treated these pensions as secondary even in the manner in which they dealt with the paperwork. Unlike with widows' and soldiers' pensions, the state failed to produce standardized forms that fit the experiences of the formerly enslaved, leaving them to use the form designed for former soldiers.[25] In part, this was because there were so few applications, but it meant that county clerks were forced to modify existing forms for the small number of applicants. Despite using a form for soldiers, white officials filling out paperwork often made clear that they did not view these applicants as soldiers.[26] One clerk handwrote two words at the top of a form to turn "Soldier's Application For Pension" into "Soldier's Body Servant's Application for Pension."[27] The legislatures authorizing pensions similarly did not see these men as soldiers; Tennessee's law creating similar pensions was entitled "A Bill to Pension Negro Cooks and Servants," making clear the pensions were for noncombat services.[28]

A 1904 proposal to strike 318 African Americans from the pension roll in Mississippi, the one state that provided ex-slave pensions in the late nineteenth century, provides insight into how former slaves forced to work for the Confederacy were viewed. A Raleigh newspaper noted that black pensioners were cut because the state's limited funding for pensions was spread too thinly due to aging veterans; as former slaves "did not serve as soldiers" and it was wrong to cut the pensions of "those who saw actual service," African American pensioners must lose their pensions first, the paper explained. Even those who objected to the removal of black pensioners from the rolls noted that the money was for slaves of Confederate veterans and not black soldiers.[29]

To use pension documents to argue that slaves were Confederate soldiers ignores the context and content of the documents. Indeed, of the eighty-three Class B pensioners on the 1929 pension rolls, not one was listed as a soldier. Seventy received pensions as servants, ten as laborers, two as cooks, and one as a teamster. Even the specific application files commonly cited as evidence of black Confederates often show that white officials in the 1920s did not consider black pensioners to be former soldiers worthy of the same treatment given to veterans. When the state legislature granted a pension to the blind Elisha Howard through a private act in 1925, the Randolph County clerk of the court tasked with completing the necessary paperwork found himself confused. He left so many blanks on a standardized form designed for veterans that the application was returned for correction. The clerk had been unable to add a company, regiment, and enlistment date because the man had never enlisted. The clerk returned the corrected form to the state auditor, explaining that he "had the Blanks filled as best I could" but that "I do not understand how [the legislature] got the negro on [the] pension roll."[30]

Despite being for African Americans, Class B pensions still served to defend white supremacy. As Elna Green has pointed out, Confederate pensions "buttressed white supremacy" and "provided governmental financial support to the Lost Cause movement."[31] Pensions for slaves also supported the Lost Cause, providing the superficial appearance of a loyal (albeit silent and inferior) black population that accepted and supported a racial hierarchy putting whites, specifically those who fought for the Confederacy, on top. Quite the opposite of equality, these pensions recognized only former slaves who had stayed "in their place" below whites on the social ladder.

These pensions cost little to the state governments, and as Green points out, they "allowed southern whites to celebrate the loyalty of the South's slaves, further illustrating the precepts of the Lost Cause."[32]

Of course, a belief that slavery was benevolent was not based on reality. Slavery was an exploitive system premised on violence. But that was not how white southerners wished to remember it, so they fabricated an old South full of happy slaves. In 1941, the great critic of southern culture, journalist W. J. Cash, already recognized that white southerners' need to write a positive past was driven by the present. In his magnum opus, *The Mind of the South*, Cash wrote that "the South's perpetual need for justifying its career, and the will to shut away more effectually the vision of its mounting hate and brutality toward the black man" led to a nostalgia for a past that never existed. Cash felt that this nostalgia was driven by current concerns about criticisms of Jim Crow both from within the South and from outside the region. He argued that southern whites felt that "the Old South must be made not only the happy country but the happy country especially for the Negro." An erasure of the lash, of violence, and of unhappy African Americans was accomplished, according to Cash, by "one part fact and three parts fiction and the black man's miming, which subsisted in their minds under the denomination of the Good Negro."[33] Cash's depiction of the southern white mind may be the best way to understand one purpose these pensions served: they provided a real-life "Good Negro" as proof of the Lost Cause's validity.

It is no surprise that with one exception, the states that passed laws allowing pensions for African Americans did so in the 1920s, after Jim Crow was firmly established. These pensions were meant to reward African Americans who maintained a subservient role, as pensioners were used as real-life male equivalents of their fictional female contemporary, "Mammy."[34] The stereotype of the sweet black housekeeper was immortalized on the silver screen by Hattie McDaniel in *Gone with the Wind*, but the caricature had older roots, going back to the era of slavery. Not surprisingly, at the same time as these pensions were debated and authorized, the United Daughters of the Confederacy (UDC) attempted to build a national monument to the black mammy. The NAACP and other African American activists objected to this plan to place upon the landscape a stone statement that black women were meant to work as domestic help.[35]

Class B pensions served a contemporary political purpose in defending institutionalized racism in the South. As early as 1907, a resolution adopted by some Confederate veterans in Raleigh declared that pensioning the few remaining faithful slaves would "refute the theories held in some parts of the country that Southern white people hate their black fellow-citizens because of their color." These "theories" were based on the ongoing racial violence, disenfranchisement, and oppression occurring in North Carolina.[36] Once pensions were authorized, southern boosters followed through and used them to defend Jim Crow. In 1937, Alamance County's *Burlington Daily Times-News* celebrated the existence of black pensioners, stating outright that their existence "should blunt the edge of at least a part of the sectional rebuke which to this day stigmatizes Dixie as a region in which the Negro, under no circumstances, can receive justice."[37] The truth was that while justice was extremely hard to come by, a subservient, elderly, nonthreatening, obedient black man could in theory get a small semiannual payment by being perceived as a role model for other nonwhite people.

Pensions for former servants who remained loyal were a cheap investment by white southerners wanting to defend their region from accusations of being "indifferent to the fate of the negro." Despite the *Daily Times-News'* erroneous claim that "many Negroes refused to accept emancipation," as their "loyalty that was both brave and pathetic . . . refused to permit them to desert" their owners, the program found relatively few eligible pensioners. The small number of pensioners—exactly one in all of Alamance County—led the paper to assert that the scale of the program "does not in the least mar the spirit of such a gesture." The numbers make it clear, however, that Class B pensions were not much of a gesture.[38] Because there were so few black pensioners, the cost of providing welfare for former slaves was negligible. Just 1.6 percent of the state welfare provided to Alamance residents went to African Americans, while 98.4 percent went to white residents. In all, the state approved only around 121 pensions for African Americans. Statewide in 1928, these pensions accounted for 1 percent of pension expenditures, despite African Americans making up approximately 29 percent of the state's population. And this was a high percentage compared to some other southern states.[39]

South Carolina was even stingier. In that same year, black pensioners did not even receive one-half of 1 percent of the pensions paid out by state.[40] Indeed, South Carolina amended its law authorizing slave pensions after just one year so that only "body servants or male camp cooks" from South Carolina who had served six months or more were eligible because too many people applied. This meant that laborers, teamsters, and trench diggers lost their eligibility. In 1924, the year after the reduction in eligibility, South Carolina appropriated $750,000 for white pensioners while setting aside $3,000 for black pensioners.[41] Clearly, South Carolina's leaders did not consider African American pensioners as equal to Confederate veterans.

Not everyone welcomed the addition of black men to the pension rolls, and some ex-Confederates and white politicians opposed providing even the pittance being offered. Some veterans were infuriated about the inclusion of former slaves on the pension roles.[42] In 1921, a North Carolina legislator objected to a special pension bill that put a single black man on the rolls while the "widow of a white Confederate soldier" was left off.[43] Most Confederate veterans opposed any pensions for African Americans that might be viewed as equal to those of veterans. In 1901, controversy erupted in South Carolina when a former free person of color who served as a cook managed to get on the pension rolls, possibly because no one realized his race. One United Confederate Veterans camp unanimously adopted a resolution condemning this development, complaining that "free negroes are to be placed upon an equality with" white veterans.[44] Another South Carolinian saw any pensions for African Americans as a threat to white supremacy, arguing, "It can easily be seen that if the gap is once let down and negroes allowed to share with the white soldiers in receiving a pension there is no telling where it will end. And to place our mess cooks on an equal footing with our white brothers . . . is a little more than I can stand."[45] The issue was not that a black man might get money, but that he might be perceived as equal to whites. Equal pensions for former slaves challenged the racial hierarchy of the Jim Crow South. One former Confederate made clear that he objected because the former cook "was not the equal of the white men for whom he cooked," allowing that "a special law" might still be passed for exemplary former servants distinct from that rewarding Confederate veterans. The pension was revoked.[46] Only after clearly establishing that these pensions were not equal to those for whites and ensuring that all deserving white applicants were already cared for would many former Confederates come to support them.

These inferior pensions also reinforced white supremacy by perpetuating a myth of widespread loyal slaves. North Carolina newspapers abounded with articles recounting loyal slaves getting well-deserved pensions. Frequently, these stories spoke of the pensioners' service during and after the war. Some stories included a former slave trying to remain in slavery after emancipation or taking care of a former mistress even though freed. One story recounted how a former slave only grudgingly accepted freedom because his master told him that he "had so much sense that he could make something out of himself."[47] Stories of loyal slaves were designed to make clear that African Americans were not suited to democracy and were happiest when disenfranchised and untroubled by such concerns.

The remembrance of loyal slaves worked alongside other historical fabrications to uphold white supremacy. In a variety of ways, Class B pensions and accompanying anecdotes about slavery's supposed benevolence supported claims that contemporary racial strife arose from outsider meddling during Reconstruction. As noted in earlier chapters, Confederate monument builder Julian Carr frequently juxtaposed happy slaves against an imagined Reconstruction full of corruption. In his speeches, Carr used this contrasting imagery to justify disenfranchisement, which he claimed would help return race relations to their happy antebellum norm. For example, he claimed that during Reconstruction, "the enfranchisement of the ignorant negroes now bore its fruit. They became, under the influence of the Freedman's Bureau, in many sections, a menace to social order."[48] In the worldview that Carr propagated, disenfranchisement corrected a mistake. Implicitly, and at times explicitly, Lost Cause proponents made the point that southern whites should be left to govern their own affairs, as they knew what was best for all southerners, white and black.

Though neo-Confederates have used Class B pensions and tales of loyal slaves to try to refute slavery as the cause of the war, this was not the case in the 1920s. Indeed, stories of loyal slaves were one of the few places where Lost Cause boosters could easily admit the truth. For example, in recounting the tale of George Mills, who brought his owner's body home after the Battle of Antietam, the *Highpoint Enterprise* made no effort to deny the war's cause. A 1922 article noted that Mills's master "lost his life in the war over slavery that was fought between the states."[49] As with Carr's speeches, loyal slaves supporting their owners in a war about slavery made both their loyalty and the Confederates they served seem all the more remarkable.

The key aspect within many of these narratives was loyalty to one's master—often beyond the end of slavery—not devotion to the Confederacy. The article detailed how Mills attended the exhumation and reinternment of his former master sixty years after he brought the body home, portraying the elderly man as eternally loyal. Mills benefited from displays of devotion, as a year before the exhumation, the legislature had added him to the pension rolls by a special act.[50] By remaining loyal to the family that once owned him and even attending Confederate reunions as a former slave, Mills gained access to pension money before Class B pensions were even authorized.

Turn-of-the-century arguments for black pensions made clear that the loyalty being rewarded was to white slave owners rather than the Confederate state. A 1913 *Confederate Veteran* editorial arguing for ex-slave pensions claimed that "the negro slave delighted in serving his white folks," even though "the darky knew that the first consequence of the war in case of victory for the enemy would be his immediate 'freedom.'" These proposed pensions were intended to reward "black, ignorant, yet faithful" ex-slaves.[51] Shortly before Class B pensions were authorized, the state auditor noted that although he was not authorized to issue veterans' pensions to formerly enslaved men because "North Carolina had recognized no negro troops in the Confederacy," he felt that they deserved some sort of pensions "on account of their loyalty to the officers and men of the Confederacy."[52]

Pensions not only created evidence of slavery's benevolence by showing former slaves' devotion to their former masters but also served as a tool of social control that reinforced the color line. Class B pensions only rewarded those applicants claiming to be former slaves who remained obedient and subservient to whites *after* the conflict as well as during it. A legal requirement that "two reputable white persons" testify to an applicant's character ensured that only those who were accepting of the Jim Crow racial order were rewarded.[53] White witnesses, understanding this implicit intent, often stressed that the applicant was reliable and not a troublemaker. Witnesses routinely mentioned how pensioners were "peaceful, law-abiding, and industrious" and had an "honorable record." It was not uncommon to note how an applicant's children had been raised "honest and respectable."[54] These were all code for him and his family not upsetting societal expectations and the existing racial hierarchy. Similarly, a Greensboro newspaper recounted in 1928 how three local Class B pensioners were "polite as baskets of chips, uncomplaining and well known."[55] Requiring black pensioners to have white patrons kept them indebted and subservient to the white community. Newspapers portrayed one Class B pension applicant as deserving because the decrepit eighty-seven-year-old was "dreaming of the days when he would not be forced to work so hard—when the white folks would reward a faithful, polite old darkey, characteristic of the old south."[56] How much of this deference was internalized and how much merely a public façade is rarely clear, but white leaders clearly hoped that tales of loyal slaves and pensioners would provide examples of how to behave for the African American community. Additionally, the legal requirement for Class B pensioners to have white witnesses further supported a racial hierarchy by embedding inequality into state law even as it provided funds to a select few African Americans.

Ex-slave pensions were purposefully designed as tools of racial control. South Carolina's law explicitly considered a black applicant's postwar behavior, providing for later behavior to lead to a rejection, something with which white pensioners did not have to contend. While determining how to administer South Carolina's slave pensions, the state's assistant attorney general provided the following legal advice: "The purpose of the act is to reward the negroes who were faithful when the war was raging, and who have remained faithful through the years down to the present."[57]

The pension system can be seen as a continuation of older patronage systems that evolved out of slavery. In some ways, the pension system mirrored slavery, when elderly enslaved people were at the mercy of white enslavers for their most basic needs. After emancipation, those who stayed friendly with a former master might expect to receive protection and resources when needed. Eighty-year-old ex-slave Sarah Augustus recalled that she was the only one of her family still alive, adding, "I would not be living but I have spent most of my life in white folk's houses and they have looked after me."[58] Betty Cofer, another elderly North Carolinian, recalled how "if I ever wanted fore anthin' I just asked her [former mistress] and she give it to me or got it for me somehow."[59] During Reconstruction, white landowners could keep the Klan away from their workers, so acting loyally served as a survival strategy. By playing the happy slave, elderly African Americans frequently received charity from their former enslavers into the twentieth century.[60] However, as seen with Julian Carr in the first chapter, white charity remained premised upon kowtowing. The cost of these pensions was acquiescence to Jim Crow and being held up as an example.

In reality, both Cash's "Good Negro" and pensioners who at least tacitly claimed loyalty to their master were not necessarily displaying their actual feelings. Instead, many were "miming" to survive in an oppressive system that had left elderly and enfeebled men impoverished and unable to care for themselves. In exchange for survival, or perhaps even some privileges not accorded to other African Americans, black pensioners played a role and became an example that southern boosters could use to show that the South was not the cruel land of lynching that it actually was. When Cash died in July 1941, at least three ex-slaves were still receiving pensions in North Carolina.[61] While historians have rightly noted that "like black codes and racist violence, these myths [of loyal slaves] aided white southerners' attempts to shape and limit black freedom," it is important to consider how African Americans used these myths and deployed them to gain individually from an oppressive system. The belief in a past full of faithful slaves helped shape white views of domestic servants in the American South well into the twentieth century, yet it also provided pensioners with a way to support themselves.[62] African Americans used the fabrication of a mythic old South, and in the process of playing loyal slaves, sometimes they exaggerated their past, lied, or committed outright fraud.

Ex-slaves applying for pensions understood what role they were playing. Most applicants for Class B pensions in North Carolina avoided making any claim of loyalty toward the Confederacy, instead focusing on their past labor. The twenty-one North Carolina pension applications cited in one of the most popular books arguing for the existence of black Confederate troops provide clear evidence that pensioners did not see themselves as soldiers. Of the group, fourteen (or two-thirds) did not claim to have belonged to a Confederate unit.[63] Five applications included a unit on the official form but made clear in the application that they had worked as a servant, not as a soldier. As noted earlier, the county clerk only added the unit to

Elisha Howard's application when the state board returned the paperwork demanding that a unit be included.[64]

Leaving the spaces for units blank not only made sense to administrators but also likely made sense to the applicants. In 1931, when Thomas Farabee applied for a pension, he never claimed to have volunteered for the Confederate army. Quite the opposite: the clerk filling out the printed standardized application form replaced the wording "who" enlisted with a handwritten "whose master" enlisted. The application noted that Farabee "was carried by his master to the front, and used in constructing breast-works and in burying the dead."[65] This sort of passive voice worked for both the formerly enslaved and their former enslavers. Farabee avoided saying he had worked voluntarily, while the son of Farabee's former owner, who served as a witness, likely appreciated that the wording made an important distinction between the service of "a very worthy darky" and that of his father, who died "in the war as a Confederate Veteran."[66]

Ironically, those applications that included a claim that an ex-slave or free person of color had been a soldier were actually more likely to be rejected. Out of the twenty-one applications sampled, the only two that claimed to be for military service were filed by widows. As only widows of soldiers were eligible for pensions, the portrayal of their husbands as combatants makes sense. Even here, one of the applicants, Edith Bizzell, made clear that her late husband had not volunteered, stating that he had been a "negro slave who served as stated upon the orders of his master." The other, Sarah Venable, included a signed affidavit—presumably perjured—by her brother claiming that her late husband, who had been a free person of color, served in the 21st North Carolina and "that he was honorably discharged from service and made a good soldier and his widow is entitled to a pension."[67] Both applications were rejected.

At first glance, it may seem strange that so few applicants mentioned their loyalty, given that the pension bureau required two "reputable white persons" to testify to their service.[68] But a statement of loyalty to the Confederacy was unnecessary, or even suspect, in the minds of the all-white pension boards in 1930. Obedience and loyalty to their former master, not the Confederacy, was what qualified applicants for a Class B pension. Indeed, ex-slaves likely avoided saying they chose to serve, because slaves were not supposed to make choices. After all, African Americans had not been seen as citizens of the Confederacy but rather as property.[69]

Even in cases where Class B pensioners professed loyalty to the Confederacy, how should we interpret their statements? Given that white pensioners stretched the truth regarding their service, historians must ask themselves whether African American applicants might also have recognized and said what the authorities wanted to hear just to get a pension. Any survivor of slavery living in the Jim Crow South would have had ample practice hiding his emotions. It should not surprise us that some men played the "very honorable old colored man" or "very worthy darkie" as a means of manipulating white patrons through flattery, dissimulation, and outright lies.[70] For example, ex-slave Adam Moore made clear to pension officials that he understood his subservient station, beseeching in his 1931 application, "I know that I am not entitled [to a pension] unless the good white people will provide it for me."[71] Indeed, only those willing to engage in "miming," to use Cash's term, were likely to get a pension.[72] Sometimes, this miming went beyond emphasizing specific aspects of one's past and entered the realm of fraud.

Alfred "Uncle Teen" Blackburn was North Carolina's last Class B pensioner. In fact, by the time he died in 1951, he had outlived every Confederate veteran on the state's pension rolls.[73] Today, some neo-Confederates present him as the last Confederate veteran of North Carolina.[74] Blackburn's story perfectly encapsulated the legend of the loyal slave in 1950. After the war, he returned home to work for his old master. In interviews, the ex-slave recounted how well his master treated him. Blackburn even claimed he took up a sword at Bull Run to protect his master from a Yankee.[75] The only thing missing from the model loyal slave story was bringing home his slain owner's body.

There is a reason why Blackburn's tale encapsulated what whites were looking for in an old loyal slave: he played the system to garner a pension. When he died, Blackburn was not 109, as he claimed, but rather only 91. He was born in April 1860 in Iredell County, and Union cavalry rode through town signaling the end of the war just before his fifth birthday.[76] Although born into slavery, Blackburn never went to war. He appears in the 1860 Slave Schedule taken in late June 1860 as an unnamed, three-month-old infant.[77] By examining the censuses from 1870, 1900, 1910, and 1920, his real birth date is easily confirmed. In the first two, he is reported as being born in 1860. He aged slightly more quickly after the turn of the century, as his birth year dropped into the late 1850s, but not until 1929, when he applied for a pension, did Blackburn claim to have been born in the 1840s. Initially, Blackburn claimed to have been sixteen when he went to war, but by the time of his death, he maintained that his birthdate was in 1842, eighteen years earlier then was true.[78] Just as elderly white southerners fabricated a past for rewards, so too did elderly black men in need of assistance. Pensions helped elderly former slaves survive, and even flourish, in a Jim Crow South that presented few opportunities for support.

Though the evidence was there, no one recognized how Blackburn utilized Lost Cause myths to work the system before now, or at least no one spoke up. In 2015, a blog recounting how Blackburn was the last Confederate veteran affirmed that "though the Yankees delivered him from slavery, he was always a rebel at heart." The author, Tom Layton, acknowledged that "when talking about Uncle Teen, legend sometimes clouds the truth."[79] Like so many others who lauded Blackburn's memory, Layton missed the reason that new details appeared and aspects of his story shifted over time. For example, in 1938, Blackburn claimed to have protected his owner with a knife from another Confederate soldier. By his death in 1951, this story demonstrating his loyalty had morphed into fighting off Yankees, and the knife had grown into a sword.[80]

Though a Confederate widow testified on Blackburn's behalf, this is not indicative of him going to war. In fact, the white widow had herself committed fraud to receive a pension. When her own eligibility had been questioned, she had lied about when she married her late husband and altered her age, making a "correction" to her original form. At the time, only those who had wed a veteran before 1868 were eligible, and she had married her husband in 1872 at age nineteen, having been a child during the war.[81]

Blackburn and his witness were not the only ones stretching the truth to get pensions. Blackburn's brother, Wiley, also received a pension for his "service." In their respective applications, both Alfred (filed in 1929) and Wiley (filed in 1933) swore they were born in 1844. As Wiley claimed to have been born in March 1844 and Alfred in April of the same year, either they were a medical miracle or the birthdates they claimed were not accurate. Alfred actually testified to help Wiley's application, changing his birthdate once again so as not to contradict his brother.[82] Both brothers claimed to have accompanied the same master to war, a man who moved away from North Carolina shortly after the war and whose last visit to the state was around 1904, two years before his death.[83] With no one left to challenge them, their pensions were approved.

Wiley had long played a part for the white community of Statesville, North Carolina. Working as a newspaper salesman, he was well known around town. He would speak in a pidgin dialect as he hawked his newspapers, comically predicting the weather. Saying things like "De prognostifiers all ingecate dat if nothing happens dere is lible to be a chang in de wedder," he became popular with his white patrons by providing comic relief. His funny weather forecasts became so well known that the local newspaper routinely carried them. Asked to explain an extended drought, he replied, "I dun told you what's the matter. I cain't do nuthin by my self and Mr. Bob Tharpe [another local weather predictor] is too busy carring the mail to fool with it." Fortunately, Wiley accurately predicted the drought would end, as it would "rain one of these days."[84]

Wiley played a role as both the trickster and the tricked. In 1917, a newspaper recounted a comical story about Wiley fooling a fellow African American by making up a fake word. Asked to define the word himself, "Wiley laughed long and loud that no one knew the meaning of the word," refusing to define it. The article concluded comically that "Wiley was still the only one that really had his vocabulary up-to-date."[85] Dependent on whites for newspaper sales, Wiley also let them play pranks on him. In one story recounted years later, a customer looking at the headlines jokingly exclaimed to the reportedly illiterate Wiley, "Good gracious, hell has broke out in Georgia and the Tar River is burning." Without missing a beat, Wiley grabbed a paper and started shouting, "Hell has broke loose in Georgie and the Tar River is burning, Read all about it. Get a copy."[86]

Playing a caricature of an Uncle Remus–like character, at times full of folk wisdom but illiterate and inferior to whites, Wiley Blackburn's acting reified white supremacy, but he also profited and gained social status, using his minor celebrity status to sell newspapers. He was such a "noted paper vender" that he even appeared in a local newspaper advertisement for a hardware store.[87] For Wiley, being seen as a slave who had served his master loyally in the war likely helped him sell newspapers. It seems he never tired of stretching the truth, as toward the end of his life, he apparently claimed that his former master helped arrange his pension. In reality, Augustus Blackburn had died in 1906, almost thirty years earlier and twenty-one years before Class B pensions were even authorized.[88] In retrospect the Blackburns appear far smarter and less simpleminded than their acts let on.

Like the last white Confederate veterans, many of the last "black Confederates" lied in their applications. Both the first and the last pensions North Carolina paid to African Americans for wartime service were based on fraudulent claims or questionable loyalty, and many in between are also suspect.[89] For example, in 1933, Mose Fraser told the pension bureau that he was born September 15, 1842, and had served as the body servant for "Lt. Elias Fraser, an officer in the regiment of Col. John D. Wiley's 12th Regiment of South Carolina Troops . . . and was with his master at the 'Crater' or 'Blow up'" outside of Petersburg when the young officer was wounded. Fraser claimed to have carried the lieutenant home. To corroborate his claim, Fraser asked the former sheriff of neighboring Lancaster County, South Carolina, to testify on his behalf. His witness declared that although he "did not know of any living soldier who served with Elias Fraser," he "believe[d] that he is telling the truth" because he "always found

[Mose Fraser] to be a truthful, straight forward upright honest darky, and never any trouble at all."[90] In essence, the sheriff felt that because Fraser had behaved well after the war, he probably would not lie.

While not definitive, a number of holes in the story raise serious questions. Fraser confused units, battles, ranks, and even his master's fate. Elias never made it to the rank of lieutenant or to the Battle of Petersburg to be injured at the Crater. In fact, *Private* E. L. Frasier of the 12th Regiment was killed at Sharpsburg, two years earlier.[91] Additionally, circumstantial evidence indicates that Mose may never have gone to war at all. Upon his death in 1934, his grandchild reported that Mose had been born in 1854. Census records similarly indicate that his birth was most likely in September 1854 and almost certainly in the 1850s, not the early 1840s, as he claimed in his pension application.[92] While five different censuses could have incorrectly recorded his age, each time recording him as over a decade younger than he was, it seems the more likely explanation is that he was born around 1854. This would mean he went to war by age seven and carried his master's wounded or dead body home at age eight, or he lied. At the very least, he almost certainly added details to a partially true story to fit an expectation of how a loyal slave acted.

Because of how records were kept, it is harder to establish fraud among pensions for ex-slaves than those for former soldiers. Unlike with Confederate soldiers, there is rarely wartime evidence historians can use to confirm an enslaved person's wartime experiences. Lewis McGill successfully applied for a pension for serving the same master as Mose Fraser, although he recalled bringing his master's body home for burial. Perhaps McGill was telling the truth, but it is difficult to know, as once again there was "no living man who has actual knowledge of his service."[93] Though neither case provides a smoking gun proving fraud, both pensioners clearly played upon a set of expectations. Knowing that these pensions were meant to reward loyal slaves, both men highlighted bringing their master home. McGill and Fraser both employed a common trope of loyal slave tales to demonstrate their worthiness for a pension. Though fraud among ex-slaves is harder to establish, it seems reasonable to expect at least as high a rate of fraud among Class B pensioners as can be established among white veterans.

Even where fraud cannot be established, small falsehoods and inaccuracies can be found throughout the Class B pension records. Applicants often reported themselves as older than census records from decades earlier indicate. These fabrications were not necessarily always purposefully deceitful. Applicants could be too senile to know their right age, and so neighbors helped them fill out the forms. Many formerly enslaved people likely could not pinpoint the exact year they were born, although when someone was listed as nine or ten (or younger) in the 1870 Census, it seems unlikely that they accompanied their master to war. Some applicants may have served as body servants at a young age and adjusted details to make a legitimate claim more believable. For instance, when questions were raised about how young he had been at the end of the war, James Deal "corrected" his age on his application by subtracting five years from the birth year he had always had before.[94] Even women got into the act, changing the age of their late husbands in failed attempts to get widows' pensions.[95]

Exactly how many Class B pensioners lied will never be known, but the impact of their falsifications is easier to detect. An official North Carolina Civil War Trails marker at Windsor's Crossroads recounts Alfred Blackburn's whoppers as if they were true, promoting a whitewashed memory of slavery and the war.[96] Just as authorities' willingness to overlook fraud among white deserters silently buttressed white supremacy, so did their lack of concern for fraud among Class B pensioners. Fabricated tales and fraudulent pensioners helped legitimate a myth of widespread slave loyalty.

Though neo-Confederates like to see pensions as evidence of Confederate service and loyalty, records created decades later are inherently suspect for those studying wartime events. Pension applications do not provide reliable evidence of military service, loyalty to masters, or a sincere devotion to the Confederacy. Rather, they actually show that a few hundred indigent and elderly ex-slaves, in need of money, used a system designed to oppress them for their own uplift.

Even if pensions were an indicator of devotion, Class B pensions would still fail to indicate widespread support for the Confederacy among enslaved people. If every Class B pension represented a "black Confederate" soldier, then the level of African American support for the Confederacy would still remain statistically insignificant. It seems as if for every Eli Williamson impressed into service, reluctantly giving aid to the Confederacy to maintain what freedom he could, there are thousands more who actively fought against the Confederacy—men like Robert Smalls, an enslaved pilot who stole the CSS *Planter* and sailed it out of Charleston harbor to the Union blockade fleet and freedom. Compared to the roughly 180,000 African Americans who served in the Union army and the more than 400,000 who fled to Union lines, the 121 black pensioners in North Carolina or 2,807 black pensioners across the entire South would still show a paltry level of support for the Confederacy among enslaved southerners.[97] North Carolina alone provided the Union at least five thousand black soldiers.[98] The small number of pensions southern states granted for ex-slaves are swamped by the thousands of federal pensions for Union service that formerly enslaved southerners received.

Similarly, the few African Americans who attended Confederate reunions fail to compare to the tens of thousands who attended Emancipation Day and Memorial Day ceremonies held each year across the South.[99]

These Class B pensions and the accompanying tales of loyal slaves helped white southerners ignore slave resistance in popular memories of the war. As noted in chapter 1, southern whites have long defended themselves from outside criticism by denying the horrors of slavery. Because of this need to show that slaves were happy, the existence of runaways, black soldiers, and intelligent African Americans had little place in the Jim Crow–era Lost Cause narrative. Just as pensions given to deserters helped to erase white dissent from memory, Class B pensions for former slaves helped obliterate the memory of widespread African American resistance to the Confederacy.

The myth of the loyal slave played an important role in Jim Crow–era political battles. Historian Barbara Gannon argues that controlling "Civil War memory was crucial to [white] Southerners' battle to ensure Northern acquiescence to their answer to the race question—oppression of blacks. Propagandists of the 'Lost Cause' wanted Northerners to remember a Civil War that had nothing to do with emancipation and the social and political rights of African Americans." White supremacists saw it as critical that the war be recalled as one "waged by gallant white soldiers, all Americans who fought for their beliefs as African Americans stood idly by as 'faithful slaves' uninterested in fighting for freedom and unable to appreciate political and civil equality."[100] Indeed, as recounted in chapter 2, Governor Aycock justified disenfranchising African Americans by claiming that whites had earned the ballot through Confederate service and valor, while black southerners had not.[101] As part of the narrative of a war in which white valor was displayed by both sides, African American military service of any sort had to be erased.

While there was no room for black soldiers on either side of the conflict in the Lost Cause narrative of the early twentieth century, there were occasional tales of slaves fighting. Lost Cause advocates used stories of slaves taking up arms to protect their masters to reinforce the loyal slave myth, often belittling African American abilities and intelligence in the process. Even Julian Carr, speaking in 1903, repeated the questionable claim that "a colored body servant" had "killed the first Union officer to fall in the war."[102] In Carr's retelling, the "body servant" was not a soldier; instead, the concern of "the simple minded slave of 61" for his master—not love of the Confederacy—motivated the act. Carr and others who used these tales did not want stories of loyal black soldiers proving their manhood but instead of unintelligent and happy slaves, undesiring of freedom and incapable of participating in democracy. The entire story of white men fighting each other and African Americans standing by, happily serving or even protecting their beloved masters, was crucial to the larger narrative Carr presented to justify Jim Crow. Despite modern assertions of black Confederates by neo-Confederates, African Americans fighting bravely for the Confederacy would have undermined Carr's defense of Jim Crow almost as much as self-emancipating runaways fighting for the United States did.[103]

Attempts to erase black military service from history did not go unanswered. Some African Americans used this same definition of citizenship or "proof of manhood" through military service to appeal for black enfranchisement. In his 1935 account of the war and its aftermath, *Black Reconstruction*, W. E. B. Du Bois wrote, "Nothing else made Negro citizenship conceivable, but the record of the Negro soldier as a fighter," then provided a ten-page summary of black military service.[104] He argued that "the black worker won the war" by transferring their labor to the Union army by running away and enlisting. In essence, there had been a slave insurrection, he argued, but it was not accompanied by the "vengeance on unprotected women" that southern whites had feared.[105] But while African American civil rights activists pointed to their contributions in calling for protecting their rights, Lost Cause advocates ignored the existence of runaways and black soldiers by focusing on slave loyalty. In the late nineteenth and early twentieth centuries, loyal slave stories countered the appeals of black Union veterans that they deserved the fruits of victory, including life, liberty, and the ballot.[106]

Advocates for African American rights, including Du Bois, often combined elements of the myth of faithful slaves with the reality of Union military service, both reinforcing and challenging aspects of the Lost Cause. The federal ex-slave pension movement of the late nineteenth and early twentieth centuries, which advocated pensions for all former enslaved people, sought money owed for enslaved people's past labors. Advocates for these pensions pointed to how they "worked without wages and cultivated land and harvested crop, which did much to build up the country."[107] Mass meetings occurred across the United States as numerous ex-slave associations formed in the 1890s.[108] Walter Vaughan, who founded the Ex-Slave National Pension Club Association, played up the success of black military recruits, noting "the patriotism of the negro and his devotion to the Union cause" and how their "record . . . entitles the race to grand recognition." Not wanting to alienate the support of white southerners, he also implied that some slaves had wanted to fight for the Confederacy, which led Lincoln to recruit freedmen in the first place, though it supposedly took "months of war" to convince them to fight for the Union. Vaughan, the son of slaveholders, believed that enslaved people had been generally well treated, despite their lack of compensation, and explicitly said that slaveholders were not at fault for slavery. He even argued for pensions on the basis of freedpeople's living situation, which, he argued, "was made wretched by the act of emancipation" and not because they deserved back pay.[109]

By accepting some aspects of the Lost Cause while still asserting African American martial ability, Vaughan and other advocates for reparations played to the sensibilities of whites in both the North and the South to garner support. Advocates for federal ex-slave pensions appropriated numerous aspects of the Lost Cause in their appeals for reparations. In one such appeal, the author pointed out that the ex-slave "preserved the lives of the wives and children of his master" who went off to war. Comparing such service to that of Union soldiers, the writer declared that "both served in honorable battle" and both deserved pensions.[110] Not surprisingly, those opposed to ex-slave pensions also used the Lost Cause, arguing that slavery had benefited them, which should be payment enough.[111] In the end, this appeal for reparations came to naught and led to less principled individuals defrauding formerly enslaved people, promising them a pension if they paid an enrollment fee before disappearing with the money.[112]

For some former enslaved people, North Carolina's Class B pensions seemed like a form of back pay—or even reparations—for their years of unpaid labor, sixty-five years late. Isaac High, who had built defensive works near Raleigh and along the Cape Fear River, thought that was exactly what his pension represented. In 1931, at the age of ninety-six, High recalled that he "spent to the best of my memory eighteen months working for the Confederate army. I never received any compensation for the work rendered." High never said he enlisted in the army, only that he worked on fortifications because he "was sent by my master (I was a slave)."[113]

In many ways, pensions fabricated a past just as monuments did. Indeed, there were even a few loyal slave monuments.[114] In 1896, one such monument was erected in Fort Mill, South Carolina, because supposedly in that region, "the slaves remained at home and cared for the women and children, there was no insurrection, no runaways, and no trouble whatever." This claim of perfect loyalty by the local enslaved population was contradicted by documents from the war, but Class B pensioners provided living evidence of what monuments proclaimed.[115] Along with a narrative of noble battlefield heroics and widespread support from white southerners, the myth of loyal slaves helped create a memory in which a Solid South heroically fought for a Lost Cause, while African Americans stood by as bystanders who "did not ask for freedom nor the ballot with which to protect it," thus proving the justness of white supremacy.[116] Whether pensioners recognized it or not, accepting a Class B pension provided a form of reparations that required them to accede to elements of the Lost Cause, thus supporting white supremacy.

The fabrication of the past continues. A 1998 letter published in a Mississippi newspaper claimed that "some estimates conclude that as many 90 to 100 thousand soldiers of African descent filled the ranks of the Confederate army," which would mean somewhere in the order of 8 to 13 percent of the Confederate army was black. This particular proponent of black Confederates claimed that many Confederate soldiers could have been black because "unlike a racially-based United States Army, there was no place on the papers of enlistment to establish one who would be considered 'colored.'"[117] The claims have little grounding in documentation, there being no place for race on the forms because all enlistees to the Confederate army were assumed to be white. The numerous studies that have used census records to examine Confederate soldiers would have revealed such a large percentage of soldiers who were not white.[118] But reality is irrelevant to such arguments because the claim that Confederates "essentially did not care as long as they were willing to fight for independence" is politically useful when celebrating a memory of the Confederate States that is under attack as being racist.[119]

The idea that one-tenth of the Confederate army was black is ludicrous, as the entire premise of black troops was anathema to much of the Confederacy's founding principles, as well as to the Lost Cause narrative of the Jim Crow era. Many wartime politicians opposed arming black troops on the ground that they had seceded to save slavery, and this would defeat the purpose of the war.[120] Indeed, William Holden, a leader in North Carolina's peace movement and editor of the *Semi-Weekly Standard* pointed out that such a move "surrenders the great point upon which the two sections went to war."[121] Scholars have demonstrated repeatedly that not until the final weeks of the war were black soldiers even authorized by the Confederacy, and then only under protest of many white southerners. Throughout the war, groups of impressed laborers were a common sight in the South, as enslaved people were forced to dig trenches, move supplies, and perform various other forms of labor to support the Confederate war effort. While the impressment of enslaved people freed up whites to serve as troops, these laborers were not viewed as soldiers. The myth of black Confederates arose from and supported three key fabrications: first, a belief that slavery "was a mild, benign institution" that created loyal slaves; second, a false memory that southern masters trusted their slaves so much that they could arm thousands of them; and third, "that despite slavery's many virtues as an institution, it was never central to the Confederate cause." These three narrative tropes developed over time and were interconnected. As seen in previous chapters, by the early twentieth century, advocates of a Lost Cause narrative were already denying that slavery was both horrible and a cause of the Civil War.[122]

Tales of slaves being armed as soldiers, however, represent a more recent addition to the Lost Cause. Even in 1931, a member of the UDC— firmly entrenched in the Lost Cause—writing about the failed last-ditch attempt of Confederates to arm African Americans in 1865 noted that "the action came too late to be effective, and, with the exception of a limited number of troops, no negroes were armed, and these were never put into action."[123] Though authorized in March 1865, the Confederacy's failed black units were understood to be a footnote and not central to the war's history. This remained an understood consensus for decades, and while some early twentieth-century white southerners might have believed enslaved men would have fought for the Confederacy if allowed, the belief in large numbers of black Confederate soldiers is a creation of the last sixty years.[124]

Even at the midpoint of the twentieth century, Class B pensioners were not viewed as soldiers, though the first inklings of a shift from being seen as slaves to being seen as soldiers are visible. A 1950 *Greensboro Daily News* biographical piece on the last Class B pensioner, Alfred Blackburn, recounted how "in spite of fighting against it, [he] accepted freedom." Though presented as a happy slave who "fought in [the] Civil War," Blackburn's fabricated service as a body servant was not yet being equated to being a Confederate soldier.[125] A year earlier, another newspaper had recounted how only two Confederate veterans remained alive in North Carolina before mentioning Blackburn as "another survivor of Confederate days" also receiving a pension.[126] Though the memory of body servants had begun to shift from that of loyal slaves to pro-Confederate slaves, white southerners were still drawing a clear distinction between ex-slaves and Confederate soldiers when Blackburn died in 1951. His *Greensboro Daily News* obituary lamented "the last ex-slave of the state to die and one of the few Civil War 'veterans' left in America." The decision to put "veteran" in quotation marks highlighted the fact that Blackburn's service was distinct from that of white veterans. Only later would Confederate apologists present his service as equivalent to that of Confederate soldiers.[127]

The creation of a memory of loyal slaves, in part through pensions and pension fraud, laid the foundations for modern claims of black Confederates. As whites increasingly denied any attachment to or support for white supremacy after the civil rights movement, a myth of black Confederate soldiers becomes an increasingly useful tale. Black Confederates now often join states' rights as a means of denying that slavery (and now racism) had anything to do with the Confederacy. A leading authority on black Confederate myths, Kevin Levin, aptly describes how "if free and enslaved black men fought in Confederate ranks, alongside whites, neo-Confederates reasoned, the war could not have been fought to abolish slavery."[128] The argument that because one black person fought for the Confederacy, the war cannot have been about slavery is like claiming that a racist statement is not racist because "I have a black friend." That occasionally people seemingly act against their apparent self-interest or a group's interests should hardly surprise anyone who follows politics. Not only do these arguments faultily assume that people always act rationally—and that we can always understand their rationales—but such lines of logic also ignore the great mass of evidence that the overwhelming majority of enslaved people hoped and prayed for Union success. Even if historians established there were African Americans who volunteered for Confederate service, it would not change what started the war.

The addition of black Confederates makes celebrating the Confederacy less racially problematic in the eyes of many Lost Cause advocates. Black Confederate soldiers are often cited by neo-Confederates as "telling evidence that slavery was expendable" to Confederates.[129] Ironically, Jim Crow–era claims that African Americans happily accepted the antebellum racial hierarchy have morphed into evidence of enslaved people volunteering to defend an egalitarian Confederacy. Pension records, once used to demonstrate white supremacy, are now a favorite source for neo-Confederates seeking to "prove" that the Confederacy and its memory are not tainted by racist ideologies. The sources and tales that twenty-first-century neo-Confederates point to as evidence of black military valor for the Confederacy were originally used to deny that African Americans had participated in the war as combatants.[130]

Still, the myth of black Confederates remains part of a narrative that supports oppression. Just as stories of faithful slaves were originally used to rebut antebellum abolitionists, and then advocates for equality during Jim Crow, these tales serve a similar purpose today. As Micki McElya has pointed out, "The myth of the faithful slave lingers because so many white Americans have wished to live in a world in which African Americans are not angry over past and present injustices, a world in which white people were and are not complicit, in which the injustices themselves—of slavery, Jim Crow, and ongoing structural racism—seem not to exist at all."[131] The continued denial of slavery as a cause of the war, and of the horrors of the peculiar institution, through black Confederates and loyal slaves allows an ahistorical narrative to help shape present political debates around race.

Stories of black Confederates perpetuate institutionalized discrimination and inequality. If slavery were not so bad and the Confederacy not premised on racial hierarchy, the logic goes, then racism and discrimination are not at fault for any racial disparities in opportunity and achievement today. This slavery-denying narrative allows believers to see racial inequity as the fault of the African American community and not a product of institutional discrimination. Racial and economic disparities appear not as a product of history but as the fault of those that are poor. In this worldview, welfare and food assistance cause poverty instead of relieve impoverishment that has been inflicted on those trapped by economic circumstances. In essence, the denial of slavery as the war's cause and the propagation of myths about black Confederates serve as a form of victim blaming that transcends generations.

Neo-Confederate narratives provide an explanation for how we got where we are today that pretends racial discrimination does not continue to harm African Americans in the job and housing market or in how they are treated by police. Racism becomes solely a product of the heart, of the individual, and is easily erased by a colorblind society, which some neo-Confederates even claim existed in the past. Instead of declaring outright that African Americans are unequal, as the Lost Cause did in 1913, modern iterations pretend that African Americans receive equal opportunity when they do not—and thus efforts to address inequality seem unnecessary or even unjust. If African Americans were happy and well treated, then arguments for reparations make no sense. Affirmative action cannot be understood as leveling the playing field if the field was already level. The Confederacy's Lost Cause now supports the lie of the American Dream—that everyone has equal opportunity.

Tales of black Confederates are part of a larger whitewash of slavery and the history of race relations in the United States appearing within modern politics. During a 2017 special election for a Senate seat, former Alabama supreme court chief justice Roy Moore declared that he believed America "was great at the time when families were united—even though we had slavery—they cared for one another. . . . Our families were strong, our country had a direction."[132] That Moore could believe that families were united during slavery is a testament to how poor historical knowledge continues to shape public policy.[133] In fact, the opposite was true during the antebellum era for many families, specifically African American families. Unable to legally marry, enslaved people could be sold away from their loved ones at any moment. Families were routinely ripped apart by these sales. Children—some as young as four years old—were sold out of state, never to see their parents again. Twelve-year-old girls were openly advertised for sale as sex slaves in southern newspapers. Enslavers unashamedly branded enslaved people and advertised in newspapers higher rewards for the heads of runaways than they did for the return of the fugitive alive.[134] The reality of slavery was brutal and horrible, yet Moore's beliefs were not far outside the mainstream. A majority of white voters supported Moore, despite allegations of child molestation and his failure to understand American history. It was high turnout among African American voters that ultimately kept Moore from being elected.[135]

Fabricating false pasts to aid in selective forgetting has always been central to the creation of the Lost Cause. Alfred Blackburn, the last Class B pensioner, and his brother Wiley never mentioned their father's identity publicly. Only in death was he revealed. According to Wiley's death certificate, his father was their former master, Augustus Blackburn, the same man both brothers claimed they accompanied to war.[136] The Blackburns carefully crafted a story that appealed to white patrons, and a white father did not work when performing as a loyal slave. The Lost Cause narrative, obsessed as it was with racial purity, had no room for recounting the widespread rape of enslaved women. Claiming to have a white father would not fit the trope that the Blackburns were playing.

At times, formerly enslaved people played a part in the erasure of the horrors of slavery, but they likely felt they had little choice. In an era when black men could be lynched for the slightest suspicion of interracial sex and miscegenation was outlawed, honesty was dangerous. Survival sometimes required ex-slaves to forget that their former enslavers were their actual blood family and reminisce instead about how they merely treated them *like* family. Like so much of the Lost Cause, the Blackburns' stories were a product of the twentieth-century Jim Crow South.

5

The Soldiers Who Weren't

How Loyal Slaves Became "Black Confederates," 1910–2018

At the courthouse in Monroe, North Carolina, two monuments reflect two distinct narratives of the past. The first, a forty-foot-tall obelisk dedicated July 4, 1910, memorializing "the boys in gray from Union County who gave their all to the protection of home," is a typical Confederate monument from the Jim Crow era. In December 2012, over 102 years after the obelisk's unveiling, another marker was dedicated a few feet away. At the second dedication, some things remained the same from a century earlier: Confederate flags were flown, and the narrative presented during the dedication speeches presented a fabricated past for modern needs. But a century had changed the type of fabrication that was being done.

Monuments tell us more about the time they are erected than the events that they nominally commemorate, and these markers provide two snapshots of the evolving Lost Cause taken at moments over a century apart. The newer marker is a small granite rectangle set in the ground. Four feet long, with no statuary or imagery and surrounded by bricks, it contains only text. Viewed alongside the larger and older obelisk, its message appears less important. Indeed, the crowd in 2012 of around 250 people was much smaller than the over 3,000 who attended a century earlier. In 1910, the festivities included a parade, a bike race, a foot race, imported Japanese fireworks, and Confederate veterans.[1] As real Confederate veterans were unavailable in 2012, some attendees dressed up in reproduction uniforms.

In addition to the differences in aesthetics and enthusiasm, the narratives each monument attempted to immortalize differed. The new marker honored ten African American "Confederate Pensioners of Color" from Union County. As the first monument to African Americans who received Class B pensions for their service as laborers, slaves, and servants during the Civil War, it is unique. Unlike most earlier Confederate monument dedications, the keynote speaker was not a leading white political figure.

Instead, the keynote was given by an African American proponent of black Confederates, Earl Ijames, who "praised the men's courage" and stated, "The fact that there were Confederates of color cannot be denied."[2] Despite the fact that Ijames worked for the North Carolina Department of Cultural Resources, thus increasing his apparent credibility, his assertion actually could be denied. Indeed, the men who dedicated the original Confederate monument at the courthouse would have disagreed vehemently.

We know how the original monument builders felt about race and Confederate soldiers when they dedicated the Union County monument because they discussed it. The keynote speaker in 1910, future North Carolina governor Thomas Bickett, noted that Confederate soldiers provided examples of three virtues: "First, how to fight; second, how to fall; third, how to rise again." As Julian Carr would do three years later when dedicating the University of North Carolina's monument, Bickett celebrated not only the valor of veterans but also former Confederates' role overturning Reconstruction. He complimented the Confederate soldiers in front of him, saying, "You gave up your guns at Appomattox, that was all," and "You surrendered but, you did not quit." Those in attendance would have understood that Bickett meant that Confederate veterans had continued fighting for white supremacy even before he lauded them: "Immutable as the rocks and glorious as the stars they stood for a white civilization and a white race, and today North Carolina holds in trust for the safety of the nation the purest Anglo-Saxon blood to be found on the American shores." This was clearly the speech of a white supremacist who saw the monument and remembering the Confederacy as a tribute to Anglo-Saxon accomplishments, not the words of someone who believed in racial equality or that the Confederate army had included black soldiers.

Like so many other Confederate memorializers, Bickett used the remembrance of heroic Confederates to justify segregation and discrimination, condemning African American agency and political power. Before he concluded, he announced that "the Fifteenth Amendment was the most colossal blunder and crime in the history of the civilized world," and Reconstruction had showed the world that "the South, and only the South, is competent to deal with the race problem."[3]

In contrast, the 2012 biracial audience was told, "We are all brothers and sisters under one flag," and "these men, simply put, were 150 years ahead of their time" on race relations, a view of the past that did not mesh with Bickett's.[4] This was a form of fabrication, whether mendacious or just wishful, as most Confederate veterans would have been horrified at the claim that thousands of African Americans fought alongside them, let alone that the veterans believed in equality.

Today, neo-Confederate groups continue to fabricate new variations of the Lost Cause to serve present needs. Sometimes, the fabrications appear purposefully dishonest, while others appear innocent in intent if not impact. As seen in the previous chapter, pensions for former slaves were not indicators of Confederate service but rather a means for elderly, indigent men to gain an income. Examining the lives of these men raises questions. Multiple pensioners honored by the new marker had suspicious aspects to their applications and may have been frauds as well, but as old fabrications gave birth to new, loyal slaves became soldiers in the minds of Confederate memorializers.

The awkwardly worded 2012 tribute to "pensioners of color" represented a new iteration of the Lost Cause and historical fabrication, but it served many of the same purposes. Just as was true in the 1910s, fabrication remains crucial to defending the Confederacy's reputation and to maintaining and justifying a specific type of conservative worldview. As a genre that consists almost entirely of fabrications, tales of black Confederate soldiers provide one of the easiest lenses to see how falsehoods and fraud continue to shape neo-Confederate narratives of the past.[5]

This chapter aims to shed light on modern evolution of the Lost Cause and how the fabrication continues. By understanding the context of the evidence misused by neo-Confederate writers, we can better understand how the myth of the black Confederate formed, how historical narratives were used to justify segregation during the civil rights era, and how fabrication and fraud continue to influence the memory of Americans today. By examining the arguments of neo-Confederates, not only do we debunk falsehoods, but we are also able to understand a key purpose they still serve: upholding systems that support white supremacy.

In 1921, George Mills received a pension from North Carolina because "while not regularly mustered in or mustered out as a soldier, [he] did much valuable service during the four years that he was with the men who were fighting and dying in behalf of the Southern Confederacy."[6] Among Mills's notable actions was bringing his master's body home from Antietam. His situation was unusual enough that it required a special act of the state legislature for his individual pension, and the bill drew a clear distinction between white soldiers and the service that Mills provided. Even then, at least one legislator objected to him receiving any pension.[7]

As other formerly enslaved people did, Mills crafted an image of himself as a loyal slave to get the pension and additional support from Confederate veterans. His willingness to remain subservient led veterans to support his application for a pension.[8] Always appearing as a dutiful slave, he even accompanied his former master's body in 1922 when his grave was moved.[9] Mills even attended Confederate reunions, taking his daughter to at least three out of state, their expenses paid by local veterans.[10]

The case of George Mills presents one example of the evolution of a loyal slave into a Confederate soldier. By 1960, when the United Daughters of the Confederacy (UDC) first added a marker to Mills's grave on Confederate Memorial Day, he had morphed from "a laborer and servant" who was "determined to serve his master in death as faithfully as he had in life" into "a former slave who was a Confederate soldier."[11] While the 1921 bill granting him a pension mentioned that he had served soldiers in the Home Guard, by 1960, the UDC claimed he had actually enlisted in the Home Guard, a falsehood reflected on his gravestone.[12] The myth progressed to the point that by 1999 Mills was being honored as a "black Confederate soldier" who supposedly "joined the Confederate Army," not just the Home Guard.[13] In 2003, the local Sons of Confederate Veterans (SCV) camp changed its name from the Walter M. Bryson Camp (named after Mills's master) to the Walter M. Bryson–George Mills Camp.[14] Over ninety years, Mills morphed from a loyal slave to a veteran of a special class, to a full-fledged heroic Confederate soldier. Instead of being a slave devoted to his master despite his own self-interest in the Confederacy's defeat, as Mills was presented in 1921, he is now cited as a soldier devoted to the Confederacy and invested in its victory.

While it is hard to know the exact relationship between Mills and his master, the enslaved man has been used to present a specific spin on the Confederacy. Mills clearly displayed affection for his master and remained connected to many Confederate veterans, but whether this was because of a patronage relationship, genuine affection, or some combination remains unknown. Despite the lack of clarity, token examples of seemingly loyal slaves are consistently presented as soldiers by modern neo-Confederates to deny that the Confederacy had any racist intent. In 1999, one attendee to commemorative ceremonies arranged by the SCV told a reporter that Mills's relationship with his master in 1860 "was a typical relationship of that time," something with which few historians would agree. Additionally, the reporter repeated the false statistic "that between 38,000 to 90,000 blacks served in the Confederate army."[15]

As discussed in the previous chapter, false statistics and claims that African Americans fought for the Confederacy have been used in the late twentieth and early twenty-first centuries by neo-Confederates to claim that the war cannot have been about slavery.[16] Only after the last Confederate veterans were dead, however, did Confederate apologists begin claiming that thousands of black Confederates fought for the Confederacy. Historian

Kevin Levin pinpoints the increasing public acceptance of slavery as the war's cause alongside the release of *Roots* (1977) and *Glory* (1989) as the driving forces in a sudden search for loyal black Confederate soldiers.[17] Both *Roots* and *Glory* defied elements of the Lost Cause by challenging the premise that enslaved people were happy as well as presenting blacks as central actors in Civil War combat.

While the Jim Crow–era Lost Cause narrative presumed white supremacy—and indeed, was frequently cited to confirm its righteousness—today, some Confederate apologists seek to fabricate a postracial Confederacy, with black Confederates as a central piece of evidence. George Mills's transformation from loyal slave to comrade in arms is part of a larger whitewashing of the past, a process dependent upon poor historical interpretation, decontextualized documents, and outright lies.

"Evidence" of black Confederates continues to be created in a variety of ways, including misinterpreting legitimate historical documents. Pensions and twentieth-century newspaper stories about loyal slaves are far from the only sources used to argue that black Confederates exist. Sources from the war cited as examples of black Confederates are frequently decontextualized and easily shown, with a critical eye and research, to be misunderstood. Vague, unsubstantiated, reports in Civil War-era newspaper articles, as well as wartime rumors, are frequently presented as conclusive evidence of black Confederates.[18]

While a small number of free people of color tried enlisting for various reasons, sources pointed to as evidence of widescale acceptance of black enlistments by white Confederate troops often demonstrates the opposite. For example, Jackson Evans is often listed by neo-Confederates as a soldier in the 3rd North Carolina.[19] Looking at the records more carefully, it becomes clear that Evans was extremely light skinned and trying to pass for white. In the 3rd North Carolina's muster rolls, he appears only once, in the November–December 1862 roll. The document says that Evans "was substituted for one J. W. Cox . . . & proves to be a free negro." On the next muster roll, for January–February 1863, Evans is missing entirely, but John W. Cox appears, with a note that after being conscripted in July 1862, Cox "furnished Jackson Evans as substitute and Evans has since proven to be a free negro and [Cox] has reported for duty."[20] Evans had passed for white for a short time, but then when his race was revealed, his service was deemed unacceptable, and he was dismissed.[21] Overlooked testimony to the Southern Claims Commission in 1872 confirms what happened. Testifying under oath, Cox recalled how he had been forcibly conscripted in July 1862 but managed to acquire a substitute. He returned home and was left alone until February 1863, when a captain arrived to take him to rejoin his unit because "his substitute was not a white man" and was thus not eligible to serve. Fortunately for Cox, he joined the Quakers in March 1863; wartime muster rolls confirm his discharge after paying $500 dollars to gain a religious exemption.[22] The evidence actually shows that Evans, far from being a black Confederate accepted as a brother-in-arms, was rejected by the Confederate army specifically because of his race.

For Evans, service in the Confederate army represented a chance at social advancement. If he had successfully passed as white and fought, then he could have claimed the benefits of citizenship in the South. Ironically, fighting for the Confederacy was actually Evans's attempt to gain the rights that the Confederacy denied African Americans. Evans was not the only person later cited as a black Confederate who saw an opportunity to gain individual freedom through cooperation with the Confederacy. William Higginbotham, a free person of color from Georgia, agreed to work as a body servant for a Confederate soldier who feared his slaves would escape once near Union lines. In exchange, the soldier promised to sell Higginbotham's enslaved wife and children to him.[23]

War creates a massive amount of paperwork, so the idea that thousands of black Confederate soldiers could have somehow not made it into the records is hard to believe. The National Archives produced a carded name index of Confederate archival documents detailing where each soldier appeared in his unit's records, including muster roles. Finished in 1927, the Compiled Service Records, as this index is called, is frequently misread, misinterpreted, and misrepresented, and details are often ignored by seekers of black Confederates. Indeed, it is only a name index for countless archival sources, each of which must be interpreted in context—a fact that seekers of black Confederates ignore.

When a person of color does appear in the Compiled Service Records, as did Jackson Evans, it is frequently perceived to be a typical case instead of an exception that proves the rule. For example, the clerk of Company E, 5th North Carolina Cavalry, listed four "free Negros" employed as cooks on his unit's muster sheets. These men have since been pointed to as examples of volunteer Confederate soldiers, but those who want to hold them up as soldiers usually neglect to mention that two of the four deserted.[24] The unit's approach to record keeping was also unique. Perhaps the company commander was not paying attention to instructions on how to fill out the paperwork, or maybe the fact that they were free people of color and not enslaved led the men to stand out. Whatever the reason Company E's record keeper added these men to the muster rolls, their inclusion was clearly an aberration, not standard operating procedure in the Confederate army. One scholar examined twenty regiments, and Company E was the only company he found to include black cooks on their muster roll. In my own seeking, I discovered only two additional North Carolina companies that listed African American cooks on their muster roles, and in one of those cases, the name had been struck out by someone correcting the muster role to not include servants.[25] Indeed, none of the Class B pensioners discussed in the previous chapter appear in the Compiled Service Records. Most black cooks never made it on the muster rolls, including those in the rest of the 5th North Carolina. Indeed, Jesse Lynch, a "captain's cook," appears in the Compiled Service Records for the regiment's Company K, not because he appeared on any Confederate muster role but because the prisoner of war (POW) records created by the US Army show him slated "for release" in May 1863. Lynch promptly enlisted in the United States Colored Troops, joining the fight against the Confederacy.[26]

The reason that even hired cooks rarely appear in the Compiled Service Records is that they were not considered employees of the Confederacy but instead the responsibility of the soldiers who hired them. It is telling that although the Compiled Service Records were completed in the same year that North Carolina began giving pensions to black servants, the state pension bureau never wrote to the War Department asking for an ex-slave's service record. Former Confederates and the officials running the agency knew that muster rolls were unlikely to show enslaved servants and cooks. In a rare case where the state auditor did actually request information from the federal government for a Class B pension application, it was solely to establish the correct unit of Sam Griffin's former owner, not to confirm the formerly enslaved man's service.[27]

The fabrication of black Confederates from evidence within the Compiled Service Records is not always purposeful, though it still serves to distort history. For example, in 1931, Brinkley Bynum, born into slavery in Chatham County, received a pension for serving as a body servant for soldiers in the 15th North Carolina beginning in 1862.[28] Those wanting to find a black Confederate have confused him with another Brinkley Bynum, this one a white man from Chowan County who volunteered in 1861 with the 1st North Carolina.[29] The white soldier is easily found in the 1860 Census.[30] Ironically, even if the two men were the same, he would not be the hero sought. The white Bynum's Compiled Service Record shows that he "voluntarily" deserted to the Union in 1863 and hence would have been ineligible for a pension.[31]

Many of these cases are likely honest mistakes by overeager searchers. SCV websites about black Confederates, however, indicate that aspects of the Civil War might still be being fabricated out of thin air. Some SCV websites claim Company D, 34th Texas, included a black third sergeant named James Washington and was led by a Hispanic captain named Jose Rodriguez. The Texas branch of the SCV even named an award after Washington that is given to minority high school students. No documentation is cited, or apparently exists, to confirm a Washington ever served in the unit let alone was a sergeant. However, the rank facilitates the SCV's claim that African Americans achieved higher ranks in the Confederate army than in the United States Army. Similarly, the company had no Jose Rodriguez on its muster roles, let alone a captain. The only unit history of the 34th makes no mention of either of these individuals despite including a roster of the entire unit. At present Washington appears to have been entirely invented sometime in the last forty years. Some evidence that a Sergeant James Washington existed may conceivably appear in the future, but for now, he appears to be yet another fabrication.[32]

While some tales of black Confederates do not appear to have any primary sources attached to them at all, subtler means of manufacture are more common. The sloppy use of superficial or selective facts without looking at underlying causes is a form of historical fabrication common among neo-Confederates. Seekers of black Confederates rarely bother to look at the motives of the men they cite as veterans and often ignore counterevidence. They usually attempt to establish enslaved people's work for the Confederacy and equate it to support for the failed state. A belief that enslaved people were happy and maintained friendly ties with their owners without evidence or critical analysis runs throughout the search for black Confederates. For example, American studies professor Jay Hoar argues that those chosen to act as servants near the front were slaves who "had shown a wiliness and adeptness for literacy and gentle manners, who had often won the hearts of their owner-employers and enjoyed positions of trust and privilege. Often they were treated as family."[33] To Hoar, loyal slaves not only demonstrated their commitment to the Confederacy but also showed how kind their owners were.

Putting aside the absurdity of the term "owner-employer" and focusing on Hoar's evidence makes clear that examining the opinions of ex-slaves was not on the author's agenda. For example, Hoar cites William Henry Singleton as a "Black Confederate."[34] Fortunately, Singleton's life is well documented, and he even wrote a memoir. Singleton's memories of his wartime experience were quite different than the narrative Hoar presents. In reality, he did not have great feelings for his master, nor was he allowed to read. In fact, Singleton later wrote, he "was whipped simply because it was thought I had opened a book." Nor was Singleton treated like family, though he may have been just that—Singleton claimed to be the son of his master's brother. His parentage meant that because he "continually remind[ed] them of something they wanted to forget[, his] master sold [Singleton] to get [him] out of the way" when Singleton was about four years old.[35] He accompanied a Confederate unit at the start of the war after he begged to be allowed to go with an officer, as he "wanted to learn how to drill." He did not, however, want to drill *Confederate* soldiers. As soon as the unit arrived near the front, Singleton ran away and formed a company of formerly enslaved men, drilling them himself; his unit eventually was accepted into the 35th United States Colored Infantry. He fought for the United States for the rest of the war, rising to the rank of sergeant.[36] In no way was his accompanying his master to war "a matter of pride" for Singleton, but rather a means of escape.[37]

After the war, Singleton was unable to return home to North Carolina because "the Klu Klux Klan said they would shoot" him. Still, Singleton celebrated that he "saw the boys of my race take their place in the armies of the Republic and help save freedom for the world." He was proud of his part in ending slavery, writing later, "As a slave I was only property, something belonging to somebody else. I had nothing I could call my own. Now I am treated as a man. I am a part of society."[38] Singleton's memories of the war contradicted the Lost Cause narrative that Hoar embraced. Singleton would have objected to Hoar's characterization of him as a "centenarian Gray," especially given that he died of a heart attack shortly after participating in a Grand Army of the Republic parade, at the age of 103 in ninety-degree heat, presumably still wearing his blue uniform. There was a reason he received a United States pension and not a Confederate one.[39]

Singleton was not the only enslaved person who saw accompanying troops to the front as a way to escape. Judging from escaped slave advertisements, it seems that posing as a free person of color to be hired as a cook or body servant may have been a common way for enslaved people to reach Union lines.[40] Indeed, requesting to accompany the Confederate army, especially after the Emancipation Proclamation, likely raised the suspicions of slave-owners. At the very least, enslavers feared this method of escape, constantly suggesting it as a probable means of disguise for runaways. The historical record provides far more examples of cooks and body servants using their proximity to escape than examples of them claiming to support the Confederacy.[41]

Singleton is not the only United States soldier who has retroactively been transformed into a Confederate war hero. A cropped and photoshopped image of a group of United States Colored Troops taken in Philadelphia has been widely circulated online as a photographic proof of black

Confederates.[42] Turning US Army troops into black Confederates helps erase African American participation in the Union war effort, just as Julian Carr attempted to erase black troops by portraying the conflict as being only between whites.

This erasure of black soldiers in the US Army can be seen in the 2012 Union County monument to "pensioners of color." Though officially "In Honor Of Courage & Service By All African-Americans During The War Between The States (1861–65)," no mention is made of the African Americans from Union County who joined the United States Army, of which there were at least fifteen.[43] Instead, only those who supposedly "served with honor" in the Confederate army were commemorated.[44] By focusing on black Confederates, neo-Confederates still deflect attention from black southerners who opposed the Confederacy, allowing the conflict to appear as solely a sectional one.

Tales of African Americans supporting Confederate soldiers helped depict former Confederates heroically. Indeed, the common trope of slaves bringing the bodies of their masters home not only disguised the horrors of slavery but also demonstrated white sacrifice being appreciated by loyal slaves. As Micki McElya argues, "Enslaved people appeared faithful and caring not because they had to be or were violently compelled to be, but because their fidelity was heartfelt and indicative of their love for and dependence on their owners. At their core, stories of faithful slavery were expressions of the value, honor, and identity of whites."[45] Black Confederates are now similarly used to portray Confederate soldiers as worthy of admiration by all Americans.

The fabrication of black Confederates served to aid in the forgetting of awkward facts, but not just about the cause of the war. Lost Cause proponents have long avoided anything that might tarnish the legacy of Confederate soldiers, relying instead on widespread acceptance of "the alleged nobility of losers in a desperate struggle."[46] To that end, historians of memory have noted how memories that were "not conventionally heroic" were largely forgotten.[47] Scholars have also begun examining how race and racism shaped the Confederate war effort, revealing that both were central to the cause *and* conduct of Confederate soldiers.[48] As Mark Grimsley so aptly puts it, "Just as racism had helped to create the conflict, it also played a part in shaping it."[49]

On April 20, 1864, the Union-held town of Plymouth, North Carolina, fell. Overrun by Confederate infantry, United States soldiers surrendered en masse. Not all prisoners were treated equally. While the exact number remains unknown—estimates range from fifty to five hundred—numerous black prisoners of war were killed trying to surrender or were executed in the battle's immediate aftermath.[50] It was an act of terror, meant to ensure that African Americans stayed in their place. Eight days earlier, at Fort Pillow, Nathan Bedford Forrest's men killed hundreds of black US Army recruits, many of them as they tried to surrender. While not as well known as the Fort Pillow massacre, Plymouth was one of many racial massacres Confederate soldiers committed. At the Crater, Poison Springs, Olustee, Fort Pillow, and countless other smaller incidents, whenever Confederate troops came into battle with black troops, the likelihood of POWs being murdered increased.[51]

Rampant racism within the slaveholding South motivated the killing of black POWs. Antebellum southern culture provided guidance on how to respond to African Americans who opposed white control. In the eyes of Confederate soldiers, violence against the black body was the appropriate way to control African Americans. It is hardly surprising that people raised in a society that taught children it was acceptable to whip, brand, and rape slaves at will would react to armed black men with the type of violence usually reserved for a slave insurrection. Indeed, to white southerners, formerly enslaved men making war on the Confederacy appeared like a slave rebellion. It was even official Confederate policy that neither black prisoners nor their white officers were to be treated as POWs, and that the officers were to be punished as if "engaged in exciting servile insurrection."[52] In the eyes of Confederates, white officers leading black troops were on the same level as John Brown. Consider Nathan Bedford Forrest, who made his fortune selling slaves, then was in command at the most notorious racial massacre of the war, and finally became the head of the Ku Klux Klan. Within this single man's life, the continued impact can be seen of generations being taught that "the power of the master must be absolute, to render the submission of the slave perfect."[53]

Though some white southerners, fearing retaliation, denied that the massacre at Plymouth had occurred, other participants had no qualms boasting about it. One Confederate bragged in a letter to his father that his "brigade never takes any negro prisoners. Our soldiers would not even bury the Negroes." His father, feeling no embarrassment in his son's behavior, sent the account to the local paper for publication.[54] Still, despite participants bragging, some scholars still have denied racial killings occurred at Plymouth and other localities.[55] Denials of racial violence ring false to any real critical examination of the war. Even Edward Pollard, one of the foremost early Lost Cause proponents in Virginia, acknowledged that Confederate soldiers "maddened by the sight of negro troops" may have disobeyed orders at Fort Pillow and killed surrendering soldiers. Victim-blaming or hinting that the black soldiers' failure to surrender before the battle was responsible for any overreach by Confederates—a claim that would never be made about white troops refusing to surrender—appears frequently in assertions of innocence.[56]

The killing of surrendered soldiers does not fit within the memory of the Lost Cause, which still glorifies the gallantry with which Confederates fought. As Gregory Urwin points out, the forgetfulness of racial atrocity "was deliberately nurtured by the men who lost the war as they schemed to cheat their black neighbors of the fruits of emancipation," and that forgetting continues.[57] Massacres and racial animosity have been covered over with a fabricated memory of heroic gentlemanly valor. Indeed, after White House chief of staff John Kelly caused controversy in 2017 for calling Robert E. Lee "an honorable man," Allen Guelzo declared that Kelly had been right, as "no one was ever able to accuse [Lee] of ordering wartime atrocities." Though an authority on Gettysburg, Guelzo ignored Lee's historical connections to racial atrocities, including allowing his men to kidnap free African Americans to be sold into slavery during his invasion of Pennsylvania. While it is perhaps true that no written orders survived with Lee's name on them, scholars have shown that Lee almost certainly knew and made no effort to stop the actions of his men. Indeed, his second in command, James Longstreet, even issued orders regarding kidnapped civilians.[58] The erasure of atrocities worked in tandem with the expunging of black troops from the dominant narrative of the war to create a heroic conflict between white belligerents. Today, the inclusion of black Confederates makes racial massacres like Fort Pillow and Plymouth seem like the tragic "incidents" of any war, which inevitably include "some depredations," and not racially motivated war crimes that were a product of culture and policy.[59]

The effects of racism on the war's conduct were widespread. For example, the Confederacy's refusal to treat black prisoners equally led to the collapse of the Dix-Hill Cartel, which had lessened the suffering of prisoners by establishing a prisoner exchange. After the cartel was suspended, the need to house the ever-increasing number of unexchanged prisoners led to the creation of death traps like Andersonville Prison, where 12,920 (just under 29 percent) of prisoners died. It was no accident that Confederate veterans were defensive of Andersonville's legacy.[60] Explanations for the end of the prisoner exchange provide yet another example of fabrication. Accusations that Grant callously ended the cartel to gain a strategic advantage ignore chronology, as he was not yet in charge of US policy when the exchange ceased. There was a reason why a common refrain at Confederate monument dedications, Memorial Day ceremonies, and reunions was "No nation rose so white and fair, or fell so pure of crimes."[61] Avoiding blame for any unnecessary suffering became a pillar of Lost Cause narratives that

celebrated the moral superiority of whites. A denial of war crimes, especially racially motivated ones, remains central to remembering Confederate
soldiers as noble in their conduct.

How courageously and honorably Confederates fought matters. Neo-
Confederates are reliant upon a narrative of heroic deeds in their defense of
both the Confederate flag and the monuments that Carr and his associates
erected. When defenders of the Confederate flag declare that they are not
celebrating the cause but rather the courage and valor of their ancestors,
it is dependent on an agreement that such courage existed and that their
conduct was untarnished. As one 1947 defender of Forrest claimed, any
southerner who attacked Confederate behavior at Fort Pillow "denounced
his ancestors."[62] The death of prisoners due to racial animus contradicts
modern variations of the Lost Cause narrative that deny white supremacy's
role in the war as well as older versions that openly espoused white supremacy. Just as the cause of the war, dissent, desertion, the horrors of slavery,
murders, guerrilla conflict, torture, and the suffering of prisoners were
erased from the "true history" of the war, so too were battlefield massacres.
One major stumbling block for Lost Cause advocates wishing to engage in
honest considerations of white southern racial views during the war is that
such views led to racial massacres, thus undermining arguments that their
ancestors fought nobly, even if for a bad cause.

This denial of the horrors of war and of racism's role in propagating atrocity has helped create a nostalgia for what was actually a terribly
destructive conflict. In 1915, the *Asheville Weekly Citizen* published an article claiming that "incendiarism, rapine, plundering, the killing of prisoners and the slaughter of civilians were not ordinary accompaniments
of raid and invasion during the war" and that "the performance on the
Confederate side, at least, was strictly in accordance with the laws of war."
Although the author admitted, "It was the presence of colored troops at
Fort Pillow and elsewhere that put the humanity of the Confederates to the
sternest test," the article claimed that the Confederacy's threat to kill white
officers of black regiments "was never carried out." Assertions that Confederates always treated injured soldiers well and respectfully buried black
troops and their officers are contradicted by firsthand accounts given by
Confederates themselves. Only by erasing racial massacres, however, could
the newspaper claim that "no war ever furnished more stories of friendly
relations between combatants." Through forgetting and a fabricated past,
America's bloodiest war became America's friendliest.[63]

Black Confederates are part of this erasure of the worst parts of the war.
A belief in black Confederates allows neo-Confederates to deny both that
their ancestors held racist views and that those views shaped Confederate

conduct. Some neo-Confederates even absurdly argue that Forrest, slave trader and Klan leader that he was, should actually be seen as a "the first true civil rights leader." This claim is accompanied by factually incorrect assertions that the Confederate Army included "Black Southern Patriots, defending a free nation they firmly believed would one day offer them freedom and bring them into the bosom of the greatest Christian society every built."[64]

Black troops and racial massacres are still often overlooked and underemphasized in military histories. In a recent synthetic operational history of the war, the United States Colored Troops, which made up almost 10 percent of the US Army by war's end, only appear a couple of times in over five hundred pages. The Fort Pillow massacre is only mentioned in passing—in a quote, with no contextualization—when discussing why white soldiers from Wisconsin killed Confederate prisoners.[65] This is not a neo-Confederate work, addressing slavery as the cause of the war, rejecting a "Sambo" interpretation of slavery where the antebellum South was a place of "racial harmony," and tearing apart Lost Cause depictions of Grant the butcher and Sherman the home burner. Still, race is all but missing from the book's otherwise excellent discussion of the actual military conflict.[66] This reflects larger issues in the historiography, as white supremacists' old presentations of the war as a conflict between whites are still often mirrored in military histories, even those that are otherwise excellent at dismantling elements of the Lost Cause. By focusing exclusively on white troops or white veterans, historians of Union forces can unintentionally further this mythology's growth.

Though many historians shrug off accounts of black Confederates as hogwash, unworthy of study, they continue to be propagated, and not just on neo-Confederate websites. In 2010, controversy erupted when Virginia parents realized that a fourth-grade textbook claimed that there were thousands of black Confederates, including "two black battalions under the command of Stonewall Jackson."[67] The propagation of such myths should hardly have been surprising. Bookstores, including Barnes & Noble, still regularly carry James and Walter Kennedy's neo-Confederate scree *The South Was Right!* on their shelves. The book, written by men openly connected to the white nationalist League of the South, rejects slavery as the cause of the war, denies that slavery was premised on terror, and lists "Black Confederate Patriots."[68] Instead of scholarly history, readers learn about how we should "recognize African servitude as positive contribution to the development of America." In fairness, most neo-Confederate arguments are not so overtly proslavery as the Kennedys', but that does not mean they are not still racially problematic. While the overtly racist *The South Was Right!* snidely states that black Confederates "may prove a little embarrassing to those who claim that the North was fighting for blacks," tales of black Confederates also allow some Americans to celebrate Confederate soldiers without perceiving themselves as racist.[69] Indeed, it has become clear that the proliferation of proponents of black Confederates comes out of an "apparent desire to openly admire the Confederacy without appearing to favor a white supremacist society."[70]

Modern attempts to separate the Confederacy from racism extend into how neo-Confederates recall postwar commemorations of the war. Ahistorical claims that Confederate commemorations never had anything to do with racism ignore the Lost Cause's historical ties to white supremacy. As noted in earlier chapters, during the first half of the twentieth century, white supremacy was closely connected to celebrating the Confederacy; this remained true into the second half of the century as well. In 1955, at a Confederate Memorial Day ceremony in a Dunn, North Carolina, cemetery, Congressman F. Ertel Carlyle declared to a crowd of over one thousand that "while the Civil War was fought many years ago, we may perhaps today be facing some of the same trying principles that faced our grandfathers" before complaining about the Supreme Court "using authority it does not have: that it is unsurping [sic] in authority and is treading on the rights of the individual states." His allusion to court-ordered desegregation after *Brown v. Board of Education* was not missed by the audience. "He obviously was referring to the segregation issue," reported Lumberton, North Carolina's, *Robesonian*. Carlyle was not using just any public forum to mention his political agenda; he rhetorically connected the Confederacy and segregation, saying, "God forbid that we should limit our honor of our beloved dead to monuments and speeches. We must honor them by lives of patriotism and unselfish service to our state and to our country, and for the principles which we know to be good and enduring." For Carlyle, Confederate memory served as a rallying point to resist integration through appeals to states' rights.[71]

The rewriting of the cause of the war to be about states' rights remained useful to white supremacists throughout the civil rights movement. A century after Appomattox, segregationists used the Confederate flag as a symbol of their resistance. The banner celebrated white heroes who fought to hold up a way of life that kept whites on top, and Confederates were recalled as champions of states' rights—the same legal argument that segregationists championed in resisting integration. In 1957, in the midst of debates over federal civil rights legislation, one North Carolinian compared Senator Sam Ervin's opposition to the bill with the service of Confederate soldiers, seeing both as part of a long, ongoing fight to protect states' rights. Indeed, states' rights became nearly synonymous with segregation.[72]

Fears of federal intervention in southern race relations ran so deeply among some white southern politicians that states' rights became an all-encompassing creed. Ironically, a devotion to such rhetoric led South Carolina senator and ardent segregationist Strom Thurmond to oppose federal pensions for the last three men claiming to be Confederates—all of whom were frauds—on the grounds that such a move might invite "the encroachment of the federal government of state concern."[73] In yet another twist of memory, neo-Confederates now occasionally claim that a 1958 act authorizing pensions for Confederate widows and veterans proves that Confederate soldiers were actually US veterans. Not only is using Congress's opinion of the past a dubious approach to history, but the fact remains that no *actual* Confederate soldier ever legally received a federal pension for his Confederate service. Memory keeps evolving, based on the needs of the present. For example, in a move that would have horrified the founders of the UDC, who had been devoted to racial purity, Strom Thurmond's interracial daughter, her existence a closely held secret until his death, applied to join the organization in the early 2000s. The Daughters reportedly welcomed her application. Change comes slowly, though—Georgia's division of the UDC only gained their first African American member in 2014.[74]

Even as celebrating the Confederacy was being used to justify inequality, alternative memories of the war were used to demand desegregation. Ironically, a white southerner, President Lyndon Baines Johnson, provides one of the clearest examples of a countermemory, using Confederate defeat to highlight the need for the Voting Rights Act. Speaking to Congress in support of the bill in March 1965, Johnson noted, "At times, history and fate meet at a single time in a single place to shape a turning point in man's unending search for freedom. So it was at Lexington and Concord. So it was a century ago at Appomattox." It was no accident that he tied Lee's surrender to "man's unending search for freedom." He went on to note how the promise of Lincoln's Emancipation Proclamation remained unfulfilled. Later that year, Johnson signed the Voting Rights Act by symbolically recalling the destruction of slavery, holding the signing ceremony 104 years to the day after Lincoln signed the First Confiscation Act, which provided freedom to enslaved people impressed to work for the Confederacy. A precursor to the Emancipation Proclamation, the act provided a legal justification to begin freeing slaves. Johnson made the symbolism clear, signing the act during a ceremony similar to Lincoln's over a century earlier, even holding it in the same room. He addressed the press in front of a bust of Lincoln, and in case this was too subtle, Johnson's press secretary, Bill Moyers, draw attention to the parallels between the two events.[75]

Historical memories that upheld specific racial identities and ideologies influenced and were influenced by party realignment. After signing the Civil Rights Act of 1964, Johnson prophetically told Moyers, "I think we just delivered the South to the Republican party for a long time to come"[76] A long process of party realignment that began during the Roosevelt administration continued over the second half of the twentieth century, as Republicans increasingly took on the mantle of conservativism while the Democrats became known as a liberal party. Johnson's embrace of civil rights in 1964 accelerated this process, as seen by former Dixiecrat presidential candidate Strom Thurmond defecting to the Republican Party. In 1972, Nixon got four-fifths of white southerners' votes, winning the old Confederacy through racist appeals under his "southern strategy." A change in rhetoric accompanied the political shifts. After the failure of the short-lived States Rights Democratic Party, or Dixiecrat party, in 1948, appeals to "states' rights" increasingly became a tool of Republicans as party realignment progressed and the federal government increasingly sought to protect the civil rights of African Americans.[77]

As overt racism became increasingly frowned upon, appeals to states' rights became crucial dog whistles—code words—for white supremacy. For example, Ronald Reagan began his 1980 presidential campaign just outside Philadelphia, Mississippi, infamous for the lynching of three civil rights workers in 1964, declaring that he "believed in states' rights." During the campaign, Jimmy Carter complained that Reagan's use of the term was just a thinly veiled appeal to racism.[78] Despite claims by the Reagan administration that its appeals to states' rights were "part of a broad effort by the White House to resurrect and upgrade the doctrine of states' rights [and] change states' rights from a discredited code word for racial discrimination into the guiding principle of intergovernmental relations," leading Republicans knew better.[79] Lee Atwater, one of Reagan's senior advisers, acknowledged that Republicans used "coded racism" to win elections. In an off-the-record interview in 1981, Atwater admitted that appeals to racism had become more "abstract" as white supremacy became a dirty word. He explained, "By 1968 you can't say 'nigger'—that hurts you, backfires. So you say stuff like, uh, forced busing, states' rights, and all that stuff, and you're getting so abstract. Now, you're talking about cutting taxes, and all these things you're talking about are totally economic things and a byproduct of them is, blacks get hurt worse than whites." Atwater wanted to erase the taint of being called a racist while maintaining a constituency by using appeals to "economic issues." Similar campaigns decrying welfare fraud—which occurs at significantly lower levels than Confederate pension fraud did—continue Atwater's approach today.[80] Today, myths of black Confederates help separate dog whistles from their actual meaning, absolving appeals to racial identity and Confederate heritage from the taint of racism.

Lost Cause advocacy efforts have helped obscure the widespread belief in white supremacy held by southern whites during the antebellum, Jim Crow, and civil rights eras and the impact of those beliefs on Americans of all races. Instead of acknowledging a long history of whites violently supporting white supremacy, some modern Lost Cause supporters use tales of black Confederates to portray the racism that has historically been common among white southerners as abnormal aberrations, backward views that had little impact on society. In reality, the racism that justified and defended slavery with terror and atrocity survived beyond the last fake Confederate veteran. As many Black Lives Matter activists have tried to highlight in the twenty-first century, a society that has a history of controlling people of color with violence does not change its ways overnight. The same white supremacist ideology, or an evolution of it, that supported the use of violence against slaves also justified racial massacres during the war. Similar racist beliefs as to what constituted acceptable behavior and the appropriate response to African Americans who stepped out of their place survived beyond the war. White supremacist worldviews justified Klan killings during Reconstruction, lynching during the Jim Crow era, and the use of billy clubs, firehoses, and dogs on civil rights activists in the 1950s and '6os. Fear of black men causing whites to resort quickly to violence has a historical precedent that predated the war but survives today. That same strand of cultural continuity continues with the disproportionate police shootings of black men. In other words, the modern Lost Cause narrative largely overlooks not only the racism within the war but also the conflict's and slavery's continuing and disturbing impacts on American race relations.

The annual reunions of the United Confederate Veterans (UCV) were major events in the late nineteenth and early twentieth centuries. Cities lobbied to hold them, and at their peak they attracted hundreds of thousands of visitors.[81] In 1929, Charlotte, North Carolina, hosted the annual event, drawing former Confederates from around the country. Among the thousands of white Confederate veterans attending could be a found a handful of former slaves. The attendance of former slaves is perhaps the most confusing "evidence" of supposed progressive race relations in the Jim Crow South that seekers of black Confederates cite. Though these men are portrayed by neo-Confederates as veterans treated as equals by their white comrades, the reality was quite different. An examination of reunions shows that the racial hierarchy that Julian Carr and other former Confederates desired was not undermined but rather reinforced by the attendance and limited participation of a few former slaves.

Numerous aspects of the Charlotte reunion made clear that white attendees did not embrace equality. The governor of North Carolina declared to attendees that the aftermath of the war "was a long and bitter struggle and by the end of the century hope had returned and victory was in sight. And this story of the rebuilding of the south, carried on in the face of almost heartbreaking difficulties forms one of the most glorious chapters in the history of the Anglo-Saxon race." Another address, by the commander in chief of the UCV, similarly lauded the overturn of Reconstruction to "save civilization." A monument was even dedicated that celebrated Reconstruction's end and the preservation of "Anglo-Saxon Civilization."[82]

A close look at the small number of ex-slaves and the treatment they received also provides compelling evidence that Confederate veterans meant to reify white supremacy at the reunion. Often called "Uncle," these elderly black men were frequently described as an "old-time southern darkey" or a "colorful old darkey." Like Class B pensioners, newspapers held them up nostalgically as relics from a better time or remnants of a dying breed of African American who still knew his place.[83] Newspaper articles from the reunion even recounted a "negro who stayed a slave" continuing to serve his master by choice after emancipation.[84]

Uncle Steve Eberhart was described as the "most colorful of all" the attendees at the Charlotte reunion. He dressed in military regalia with every sort of embellishment, "enough medals and badges to outfit two or three Central American generals," wore a top hat covered in feathers, and even had tiny Confederate flags flying off his shoulders. Newspapers compared his absurd outfit to a "Christmas Tree." He carried roosters under his arms, "in his character of chicken thief," demonstrating how he caught them for his master during the war. Overly emotive, he claimed to have "remained loyal to his master" after the war, which helped account for why veterans from his home town of Rome, Georgia, paid for his annual trip. Over the years, his getup got progressively more absurd as he added additional ribbons, ropes, and medals. Supposedly, Eberhart even taught his rooster to crow "at every halt in the parade," calling it "the rebel yell."[85]

As black pensioners had done in shaping their narratives, Eberhart was clearly twisting reality, playing a role for an audience. Eberhart's real name was Steve Perry. Andy Hall has speculated that using a different name may be indicative of how much of a performance Perry was putting on by becoming Eberhart for white veterans.[86] Perry clearly played a loyal slave stereotype when going as Eberhart, doing what W. J. Cash called "miming."[87] The

Steve Eberhart, circa
1910. (Courtesy of
the Georgia Archives,
Vanishing Georgia
Collection)

former slaves attending the reunion in 1929 acted as simpletons, unable to
read and write, but always ready to compliment the veterans. They spoke
in pigeon English, constantly proclaiming the superiority of whites.[88] At
the mention of Henry Grady, for whom Eberhart sometimes claimed to
have been a valet, he "jumped to his feet, shouted and clapped his hands,
hugged himself until he grunted and then exclaimed as tears rolled down
his cheeks: 'Lordy white folks, I had the extinguished honor to dust off Mr.

Grady's coat and black his shoes.'" As part of acting like an ideal ex-slave, he made sure to show white observers that he remained obedient long after slavery ended, even loudly proclaiming himself to be a "lily white Democrat."[89] His thank-you card for those white citizens who paid for his trip to a reunion in Texas included the statement "I shall ever remain in my place, and be obedient to all the white people."[90]

Perry and other black attendees mimicked the words of white Lost Cause advocates. At one reunion, UCV leader Julian Carr declared to Confederate veterans, "The emancipation proclamation was a curse to the country, for it destroyed a system of dripline in industry, civilization, morals for heathens of an inferior race without parallel." Carr concluded, "America was a victim of social fanaticism; a million of choice citizens were disabled in a civil war in order to demolish the best school for black heathens ever organized and conducted."[91] At the Charlotte reunion, former slaves attending reportedly "proudly claim[ed] the title 'white man's nigger.'"[92] Perry's words, sincere or not, appealed to those enamored by the version of the past that Carr propagated.

How sincere Perry was when giving Eberhart's white supremacist views on race is unclear, but he obviously invented details to fit expectations. Aspects of his past changed between interviews, including the name of his owner and the number of reunions he had attended. In 1921, he claimed to have stayed with his master, Patrick Eberhart, ever since the war, but three years earlier, in 1918, he had reportedly been owned by the late James T. Moore. That year, the Moore family paid for his trip to the reunion. Other times, he claimed to have worked for additional individuals.[93] We know little about his life before 1865, though at various times he claimed to have served in Florida, Georgia, and Virginia.[94] Much like the last Confederate veterans, his age also changed over time. While he was likely born sometime in the late 1840s or early 1850s, once he began playing the role of Uncle Eberhart, his age began increasing faster than most people's. By 1918, he was publicly claiming to have been born in 1838. In Charlotte, his claims of being a centenarian helped him stand out from other "servants" attending the reunion. Two years later, he reportedly told one newspaper that he was 92 and another that he was 101.[95] Whether newspapers mangled his story or he told them different things remains unknown.

Like Wiley Blackburn, Perry used his performances of being less intelligent and loyal to profit, a fact that veterans recognized. Called a "slavery time darkey character" and known as "the mascot of the Confederate Veterans of Rome," it was an open secret that "in his attempts to attend every reunion of the Boys in Gray [Perry] collects a lot of money under various false pretenses, and gets away with it." White observers knew his kowtow-ing was just a performance, with one noting that "he carries himself with an erectile strut that immediately becomes a dissembling shamble when he wants to pass around the hat."[96] That his minstrel show might just be a performance did not matter to the audience, who found him comical and entertaining in ways that reinforced their racial expectations. The clearly exaggerated act also demonstrated his reliance on whites, thus demonstrat-ing their power.

Perry's deference and performance as the bumbling loyal slave, morally less developed than white people, was lucrative. According to one account of him, "These old veterans all know Steve, as do their sons and daughters, and it's not often that he returns home without some evidence of their kindly remembrance and regard." Gifted with clothing, money, and free trips, he also gained social capital.[97] But the fact that at times he was treated better by the veterans than other African Americans does not mean that he was treated equally. Neither Perry nor former Confederates pretended that the veterans saw him as an equal.

Scholars have recognized that African Americans and whites "did not gather at reunions and other public events as equals" but instead that the UCV "used these occasions to reinforce the racial hierarchy."[98] Even during the parade, former slaves were segregated; instead of parading with their state's delegation, the former slaves "trailed" the procession of veter-ans as a separate group at the end, clearly relegated to an inferior status. In melodramatic fashion, the former slaves were "the most emotional" participants of Charlotte's parade.[99] Only old, clownish African Americans vocally loyal to whites and accepting an inferior status were invited to par-ticipate and receive the spoils. During the 1931 Richmond reunion, one former servant actually gave an impromptu speech. Ridiculously dressed like Eberhart with feathers in both his hat and pockets—it may have been Eberhart, had he shifted his age yet again—the man told the crowd, "I am one hundred and seven years old. I have always been a white folks nigger, and the Yankees can't change me, suh."[100] Upheld as examples to other African Americans, these men provided a contrast with the noble Confederate veterans. Like tales of loyal slaves and Class B pensions, their presence and acceptance at reunions served to make Confederate soldiers even worthier of admiration.

Attempts by African Americans to act like equals were unwelcome. William Mack Lee attended multiple Confederate reunions before being outed as a fraud in 1927 by *Confederate Veteran* after he claimed to have been friends with his supposed master, Robert E. Lee. Mack Lee tried to gain notoriety by being linked to a famous Confederate but overstepped the bounds of a proper slave in the eyes of ex-Confederates. The idea that Robert E. Lee, of all people, would be friends with a slave was tantamount to slander.[101] Despite being exposed, Mack Lee continued to be invited to celebrations, including the unveiling of the largest monument to Robert E. Lee, the carving at Stone Mountain.[102] Though modern scholars have also questioned his credentials, neither modern scholars nor the *Confederate Veteran*'s denouncement deterred the SCV from placing a Confederate marker on his grave in 2016.[103] Like the fabricated stories that Julian Carr told, the story was too useful to modern political needs. In exchange for standing in as a loyal slave, Mack Lee continued to get to travel around the country and received a pension from the state of Virginia.[104]

Most African Americans were not invited to participate in reunions. In 1903, for example, the UCV rejected the offer of unionized bands in New Orleans to provide the music for their upcoming reunion, instead paying significantly more to import out-of-town bands, all to avoid having black performers. The UCV's refusal to "march behind negro bands" almost resulted in a general strike. In the end, no union bands performed in the parade, but the city's other unions failed to boycott. Some veterans actually supported having black bands, but historian Mark Johnson points out that those veterans did so because they felt black performers "entailed no threat to white supremacy but instead might reinforce it." Indeed, they compared the inclusion of black musicians entertaining veterans to happy slaves performing music for their masters.[105]

Reunions were political events full of white supremacist politics. At an 1894 reunion, for example, Alabama senator John Morgan, a Confederate veteran himself, declared, "I hope to see the day when none but Americans, white men, shall be allowed to cast a ballot."[106] Whether white or black, those who challenged white supremacy were unlikely to be welcomed. Looking at reunions of guerrilla units, Matthew Hulbert found that the act of denouncing the Democratic Party led one former Confederate to be blacklisted from future events, while gunplay over a stolen pet raccoon was reported as a reflection of how the old veterans were colorful characters. The fate of the raccoon remains unknown.[107]

While we often think of the Lost Cause as solely a product of whites, Eberhart, Class B pensioners, and ex-slaves at reunions shaped the Lost Cause and profited from it. Just as their attendance at reunions helped sculpt the memory of the war in the early twentieth century, so do the descendants of former slaves help rewrite the past today. Nelson Winbush, grandson of a former slave named Louis Napoleon Nelson, who also attended the Charlotte reunion, claimed in the early 2000s that "in the Confederate Army, blacks and whites as well as Indians fought together, prayed together and died together. They cared for each other. Everybody was family. The blacks who were left behind looked out for and guarded the misses and the children."[108] His claim might have surprised Confederate soldiers in 1864.[109] Much like his ancestor, Winbush was feted by the SCV, whose white members now saw him as proof that they were not racist.

The racism within the modern Lost Cause is not the same racism of Julian Carr that acknowledged its belief in white supremacy. Instead, the modern variation often upholds a twenty-first-century form of racism that denies it is even racist, failing to recognize the Lost Cause's racially problematic roots and function. Indeed, it is with complete sincerity that the Lt. F. C. Frazier Camp of the Sons of Confederate Veterans can state that it "rejects any group whose actions demean or distort the image of the Confederate soldier's good name, or their reasons for fighting. We do not support, condone, or embrace any group whose philosophy involves racism."[110] Many, perhaps most, SCV members who say they do not approve of white supremacy are not saying this in bad faith.

Those who believe the Lost Cause narrative often do not recognize how the historical memory they propagate focuses almost entirely on white men. As Tara McPherson points out, the "overt images of blackness or explicit expressions of racism" of earlier white supremacists are often publicly rejected by today's "neo-Confederates [who] focus almost exclusively on whiteness, albeit a whiteness that is naturalized and taken for granted." With race not discussed, or explained away with tales of black Confederates, a focus on preserving "white masculinity" without using racialized language can at times provide a form of "covert racism" that proclaims ownership of the past without explicitly mentioning who is excluded.[111]

While some may object to my use of the term "racist," racism is not limited to an individual hatred due to skin tone but rather includes a series of beliefs and actions that supports and upholds structures that are oppressive to people of color, intentionally or not. Hate is not necessary for racism. The idea that Jim Crow and segregation were solely driven by hatred is mistaken. Julian Carr believed African Americans were inferior to him and that whites should be above them, but he did not have to hate anyone to hold those beliefs. As noted earlier, Carr frequently stated that he was "a friend of the negro" so long as every black man was "in his place."[112] White supremacist ideology has often been more about how society should be ordered than about hatred. A belief that racism is only a problem of the heart and does not include structures of society that privilege and oppress avoids addressing the legacy of America's problematic history with race. Alexis Okeowo describes how there is a "peculiarity of racial relations in America, where a person who has racist beliefs believes himself to be absolved if he doesn't consider himself racist." Okeowo argues this modern-day "self-deception" is just a continuation of one that "has been around since Reconstruction, when Southern whites who considered themselves well meaning could perform charitable deeds for, or often hire, their black neighbors, as long as those black people knew their place and stayed there."[113] The Lost Cause narrative still often provides a basis for a worldview in which modern civil rights activists do not have legitimate reasons to protest.

A white supremacist narrative of the past still grounds Confederate apologists' remembrances in a subtler manner. Modern uses of the loyal slave and fabricated black Confederates continue to create an imagined old South without racial strife, which buttresses skewed views of Reconstruction. At the end of the nineteenth century, Julian Carr declared, "Take the ballot from the ignorant vicious negro and you will do more to restore the old-before-the-war feeling between the white man and the colored man than anything else that can be done." His remembrance of Reconstruction as the cause of racial strife was key to his argument for disenfranchisement, paternalistically claiming that "for the Negro[']s own good, I would therefore eliminate him from politics."[114] Without a positive version of slavery, a belief in racial superiority, and a negative construction of Reconstruction, Carr's argument for how disenfranchisement would solve the problems of the South fell apart. Writing in 2001, Wayne Austerman, a proponent of black Confederates, still blamed "Reconstruction and the crude attempt at social engineering that accompanied it" for driving "a wedge between the races, inspiring far deeper bitterness and mistrust than ever had existed during the war. The appearance of hooded nightriders and the passage of Jim Crow law were two of the results." While not necessarily celebrating the racial violence that ended Reconstruction, neo-Confederates often still excuse it as an inevitable result of the South losing and the North providing rights to blacks. The Lost Cause has remained tied to a conservative viewpoint, as both Carr's and Austerman's views were premised on a belief that African Americans were happy without the vote and their freedom should be considered less important than maintaining the status quo. Both put responsibility for racial strife upon northern interference in local southern matters. Both viewed antebellum race relations as something to aspire to, providing them with a regressive roadmap to achieving better race relations. Both prioritized peace for whites over justice and equality for African Americans.[115]

There are two major versions of neo-Confederate memory, one of which denies ties to white supremacy. Today, many defenders of the Confederacy insist that secession, the war, and Confederate flags have no connections to upholding a racial hierarchy. In 2015, the chief of heritage operations for the SCV, Ben Jones (who played Cooter on *Dukes of Hazzard*), declared, "To those 70 million of us whose ancestors fought for the South, [the flag] is a symbol of family members who fought for what they thought was right in their time, and whose valor became legendary in military history. This is not nostalgia. It is our legacy." This use of vague language sounds much like Carr's description of the war, even as Jones claimed that "racists have appropriated and desecrated" Confederate symbols, which he believed had previously been pure from any stain of racism.[116] The problem with such statements is that the Confederacy became "legendary" in part because of "what they thought was right in their time," white supremacy.

Though on the surface this seems a complete reversal, the new narrative serves many of the same purposes and still justifies policies that maintain inequality. Neo-Confederate historical narratives are used by conservative politicians to garner support for policies that are racially discriminatory in function if not design. Just as with Atwater in the 1980s, the racism is hidden in an "abstract" manner, allowing proponents to not even recognize racism's role in their understanding of history or the world around them. It should not be surprising that the Lost Cause tends to support a conservative worldview that resists change and aims to preserve the privileges whites have held for centuries. It was no coincidence that during the 2016 election, Donald Trump supporters flew Confederate flags at rallies and Hillary Clinton's did not. The Lost Cause has always been tied to efforts to maintain white privilege, and denying that whites have privilege helps maintain that privilege.

The fabrication of the past paints a skewed picture of the present. The racism within the Trump campaign was not just a visceral hatred and fear of others—although that existed, too. Many voters were motivated by a less visible form of racism based on a historical narrative that told white voters that they were being discriminated against, even though study after study showed otherwise. Conservative rhetoric that white men are heavily discriminated against obscures reality but remains widely accepted. Fifty-four percent of Trump supporters saw discrimination against whites as a bigger issue than discrimination against racial minorities.[117] For those who feel left behind economically, politically, or culturally, a version of the past that posits them and their racial group as the victims had a very real appeal.

This sense of being left behind is often tied to a racial identity. In their eyes, they deserve more but have been denied it because of their race. For those who believe equality has already been achieved, movement toward greater equality provides the appearance of reverse discrimination. In reality, greater equality means less unshared privilege for those who are most advantaged. The Lost Cause facilitates a failure to recognize privilege. In essence, a fabricated history creates a false appearance of discrimination.[118]

But not all neo-Confederates want to be separated from white supremacist and hate groups. A second strand of neo-Confederate memory embraces white supremacy and white nationalism. Neo-Confederate Facebook pages attract racist, anti-Semitic, and bigoted comments. Many of the most vehement pro-monument activists are also openly neo-Nazis, some bearing racist tattoos like the SS bolts. The overlap in membership and activism means that neo-Confederate heritage organizations—which have the appearance of just being about history—often serve as a gateway to extremist white supremacist organizations.[119] Because "group membership, personal identity, and memory are mutually dependent," narratives of the past provide a crucial means of radicalization.[120]

The past has been weaponized, and historians must adapt to fight lies and fabricated memories. Technology has allowed a democratization of history but has also furthered the fabrication of the past. While online resources allow anyone to do research more easily, they also circumvent traditional guardians of quality like peer review and editors. Anyone can make up a story or interpretation without any critical consideration and post it online. Exaggerations and fabrications spread more easily, and the internet allows neo-Confederates to respond in alarming ways to scholars who disagree with them. Efforts to debunk black Confederates raise deep anger in some Confederate apologists, and scholars who have pushed back on these myths are frequently insulted online for their willingness to engage in debate.[121] Attempts to silence critics harken back to the UDC's attempts to limit what versions of the past could be recounted in the early twentieth century.

Public outreach by historians is crucial. False narratives will not disappear just because historians speak out in academic monographs. Ultimately, blogging, popular histories, public lectures, working with museums and historic sites, and teaching in the classroom are all needed to counter these myths. Getting historians on local and state school boards or reaching out to public officials to make sure educational materials are accurate should be seen as a professional obligation. At the turn of the twentieth century, the Confederate veterans and their supporters demanded that white southerners "give our descendants a true history" of the war that uncritically celebrated the Confederacy.[122] Historians must answer with our own demand that history, critical thought, and research dictate how we teach and recall the past instead of fabrications. Trained to consider the past objectively, historians often worry about being viewed as political, but when addressing objectively unhistorical narratives being used politically, efforts to correct the narrative cannot help but be political. Indeed, writing history remains as connected to politics today as it was in 1900.

Epilogue

Why the Lost Cause Still Needs to Lose

On August 12, 2017, white supremacists converged on Charlottesville, Virginia, to protest the removal of a monument to Robert E. Lee. Counterprotesters decrying racism and the presence of Nazis took to the street. Violence ensued. Street fights that seemed to belong in 1930s Germany and not the twenty-first-century United States broke out in the normally quiet college town. Amid the chaos and violence, an act of terrorism was committed: a neo-Nazi drove a car into a crowd of counterprotesters, killing Heather Heyer and injuring nineteen others who were demonstrating against racism. Americans watched in horror as a white supremacist rally became a white supremacist terror attack.

Many Americans, not just politicians, denounced the violence. In the aftermath of this racist act of terror, thousands of Americans tweeted the hashtag #ThisIsNotUS.[1] The intent of the tweet was clear: we deny that your ideology belongs here. With the notable exception of the president, most major political figures rushed to condemn both the rally and the terror attack as un-American. Even Attorney General Jefferson Beauregard Sessions III, a man who is no stranger to accusations of racism himself, said, "When such actions arise from racial bigotry and hatred, they betray our core values."[2] But what are America's core values?

The problem with a hashtag like #ThisIsNotUS was not that it represented feel-good slacktivism but rather that it actively denied that racism remains a powerful force in the United States. While the intent was admirable and reminded the nation that many Americans reject racist ideologies, it denied an important historical reality by making white supremacist violence appear to be a fringe event in isolation from the rest of American society and history. Jelani Cobb accurately pointed out that a more appropriate hashtag would be "This is not who we want to be."[3] Though commentators claimed that racial violence was un-American, historically such violence has been profoundly American.

Aspirations rarely meet reality. One of Sessions's own namesakes, Jefferson Davis, led the Confederacy, a nation founded on the belief that races were not equal. In 1858, Davis argued that nonwhites were unable to make Democracy work because "that standard of civilization is above their race."[4] Sessions's other namesake, Pierre Gustave Toutant Beauregard, ordered the first shots of a war to protect slavery. Indeed, throughout the nineteenth and twentieth centuries, white supremacy was a core value of many white southerners—and Americans, for that matter; these ideologies remained very much alive in 2017.[5] Indeed, some Americans saw history as justifying the violence in Charlottesville. One self-described Nazi explained, "We are assembled to defend our history, our heritage and to protect our race to the last man," a statement that would have fit in Julian Carr's mouth a hundred years earlier.[6]

Just as the views espoused by white supremacists were not new, so was the use of terror to maintain white supremacy not a historical aberration. Violence against people opposed to white supremacy goes back to the days of slavery, when the terror of the lash was used to control labor. Confederates fought a war in their effort to maintain white supremacy, during which they murdered African American prisoners of war. After the war, terrorism and vigilante violence were used to overthrow Reconstruction and reassert white supremacy. Lynching and race riots in the Jim Crow South were a form of terrorism meant to maintain control of African American populations. During the civil rights movement, government-sponsored violence against protestors of color, bombings of churches, and the assassinations of civil rights leaders and activists were all acts of terror meant to keep change from occurring. In 1995, the terrorists who killed 168 people, 19 children among them, and wounded over 600 in Oklahoma City had links to white supremacists as well. They were not alone. The 1996 Olympic bombing in Atlanta was committed by a white nationalist who also attacked abortion clinics and gay bars. The memory of the Confederacy and ideologies of white supremacy have long motivated terrorism. Two years before Charlottesville, a white supremacist inspired by southern history murdered nine African Americans praying at Charleston's Emanuel AME Church.[7]

White supremacists who rallied in Charlottesville felt like they belonged in America. For all their setbacks over the past 150 years, marchers believed they were still victorious enough to appear without hiding their faces. This feeling of empowerment did not just magically appear from the victory of Donald Trump nine months earlier, though his election surely reinforced it. Shouts of "Heil Trump" were just the most obvious connection between his presidency and a racialized ideology. Indeed, Trump rose to political prominence in large part due to his role in the birther movement, which could not fathom that a black man could be president, let alone an American. In an effort to delegitimize Barack Obama's presidency, members of the Republican Party trafficked in repeatedly debunked conspiracy theories, capitalizing on racist expectations of what an "American" looked like. The white supremacists' belief that they would not suffer consequences for their views came from four hundred years of history in which white supremacists had the privilege of not suffering consequences for their racist beliefs. As one white nationalist at Charlottesville said, "We just want to preserve what we have."[8] The catch, of course, was that what they had was premised on others not having it.

Intentionally or not, Trump's rhetoric, actions, and policies encouraged white supremacists. At the Charlottesville rally, David Duke, former grand wizard of the Ku Klux Klan, declared that whites had voted for Trump because "he said he's going to take our country back." Trump's statements after the rally further encouraged Duke. Trump asserted there was "violence on many sides," resulting in criticism by politicians across the spectrum. After two days of equivocating and pressure from his staff and party, Trump finally declared that "this display of hatred, bigotry, and violence . . . has no place in America." Two days later however, Trump walked back his second statement by saying there were "some very fine people" among the white nationalists in Charlottesville. Not surprisingly, Trump's equivocating further encouraged white supremacists to see him as an ally.[9]

Trump's presidency did not create the white supremacist movement, nor is it coincidental that Confederate monuments still attract white supremacists. Celebrating white heroics was a major purpose in building Confederate monuments. Given that one of their original purposes was tied to a "heritage of hate," we should hardly be surprised that monuments continue to be used to similar ends.[10] These contests over monuments are symbolic of larger political fights, as some Americans seek to maintain both control of the landscape and a privileged status in society.

Today, when cries of "Confederate heritage" are heard, Lost Cause memory is frequently being used to unite whites against perceived outsiders, just as it was in the early twentieth century. Instead of overt appeals to race, as occurred in 1898 and 1900, racism today often appears in Lee Atwater's more "abstract" manner.[11] For instance, during the 2017 Virginia gubernatorial race, Republican candidate Corey Stewart made the Confederate flag one of his main campaign issues, declaring, "It's time that we embrace our history, we embrace our heritage and we take back Virginia."[12] Exactly whom they were taking the state back from and to whom that heritage belonged was left unsaid, but to a ballroom full of people in period garb, Stewart's message was clear. His language could have come from the mouths of white supremacists during Reconstruction, the Jim Crow era, or the 1950s and '60s. When Stewart stood in front of that Confederate flag, he was not appealing to middle-class black voters with conservative views on fiscal policy. The heritage invoked by Stewart, a Minnesotan by birth, was inherently racial and meant to attract votes from whites. Dog whistles, appeals to implicit biases, and the rhetoric of victimhood have become the calling card of the Republican Party since the party realignment that occurred in the second half of the twentieth century. In recent years, those appeals have often become less "abstract."

Politicians continue to weaponize the past to mobilize support through appeals to a shared identity and memory, just as they did in the 1890s. At an August 2017 rally, Donald Trump told a crowd of cheering fans that those wanting to remove Confederate monuments were "trying to take away our culture. They're trying to take away our history," and that the media was "trying to take away our history and our heritage."[13] Whose heritage was it? Trump's family did not fight in the war—they still lived in Europe at the time. It seems unlikely that Trump was actually concerned about history, having never shown any affection for accurate history. In yet another example of fabrication, Trump invented an entire Civil War battlefield on one of his golf courses, even installing a plaque that bogusly claimed, "The casualties were so great that the water would turn red and thus became known as 'The River of Blood.'"[14] In his appeals to monuments just days after the Charlottesville attack, Trump mobilized heritage and white resentment for political gain. He used identity politics—in this case, a white racial identity—to rally his base.

Not all supporters of Confederate monuments and flags are aware of the ties between these symbols, narratives of history, and white supremacy. Often, the connections between pro-Confederate rhetoric and race are not even clear to those who find Trump's words appealing. The disassociation of the war from slavery, the whitewashing of how enslavement is recalled, the erasure of black troops, the celebration of states' rights, and the heroization of Confederate soldiers all aid in disconnecting the Lost Cause from issues of race. The fact that Confederates were white becomes almost incidental, and with the invention of black Confederates, even that aspect of the past can be forgotten.

Sometimes, however, white supporters employ the Lost Cause as a shared past, appealing to clannish racism in an overt fashion. Similar rhetoric about taking back the country can be seen in the Charleston shooter's appeals to start a race war. As he reloaded during the June 17, 2015, massacre at Mother Emanuel Church in Charleston, South Carolina, the white terrorist told a survivor that he had "to do it" because African Americans "rape our women" and are "taking over our country."[15] The "our" clearly referred to white Americans. The rhetoric about using violence against African Americans to protect white women has not changed.[16] That the shooter had a Confederate flag license plate and took photos of himself with the flag was not a coincidence. It is hardly surprising that someone who valorized fighting to protect white women attached himself to the Lost Cause, which also portrayed white men fighting nobly to protect home and hearth from invasion. Julian Carr's explanation that black rapists caused lynching would fit right into the shooter's mouth. Those who erected Confederate monuments wanted to leave their descendants a "legacy" and "heritage" of a white-controlled South where white supremacy reigned supreme. Efforts to maintain a South that privileged whites was justified by a specific historic memory that blended facts with misinterpretation, exaggeration, outright lies, and wishful thinking. As seen in both Charlottesville and Charleston, the Lost Cause's lies still have deadly consequences.

Whether Charlottesville and Charleston will be turning points in the fight over the symbolic landscape or one step in a longer process remains unclear. What to do with monuments remains a problem without a clear solution. Even among those who recognize that these monuments are connected to white supremacy, there remains no consensus. Some want to maintain them as a tool to educate the public about America's history of white supremacy, while others wish to tear them down. While the destruction of monuments might obscure the long history of using the Confederacy to justify Jim Crow and segregation, leaving them up maintains a narrative that celebrates selective parts of the past and can at times support white supremacy. It seems unlikely that any one solution will be used everywhere. Some locations are pursuing contextualization through interpretive signage providing the history of a monument, while others may try to turn monuments into memorials through the addition of new plaques or inscriptions. Each community and monument is distinct. A monument sends a different message in front of a courthouse than it does in a cemetery. Perhaps some communities will do as Lithuania did in creating a "Stalin World," where Soviet-era monuments were collected and placed together in a park for visitors to learn about the period.[17] Who is included in the process of determining each monument's future is a continuation of earlier struggles over access to the ballot and inclusion in the political process.

Augmenting Confederate monuments by placing a parallel memory for African Americans next to them seems unlikely to solve these controversies. Allowing two histories to exist side by side is not an easy process because it creates a contradictory commemorative landscape. For example, in 2005, the University of North Carolina put up a memorial to its "unsung founders—the people of color bound and free—who helped build the Carolina that we cherish today." A black granite table surrounded by five seats is held up by tiny bronze figurines representing the slaves and free people of color who helped build the school. The monument was an abject failure. Its location just a few hundred feet from the much larger Confederate memorial (pulled down in 2018) presented a stark contrast in visual and symbolic importance. Even without the juxtaposition, the monument would have remained problematic. Many students failed to even recognize that it was a memorial, sitting on the chairs and unknowingly kicking the tiny figures holding the table up. Instead of a place to sit and contemplate the role of slavery at the state's premier university, it was used as a place to eat lunch or change a baby's diaper.[18] The memorial has, not surprisingly, been viewed as unequal and tokenistic.

Still, any monument celebrating nineteenth-century African American resistance to white supremacy will inherently challenge the Lost Cause. As seen throughout this book, controlling the past is not just about remembering one's heroic ancestors but about determining what others can commemorate as well. In 1988, with no trace of irony, the commander in chief of the Sons of Confederate Veterans (SCV) told a historian that advocating for new monuments honoring United States Colored Troops would "further racial divisions," while the organization simultaneously pushed narratives about "Black Confederates."[19] This situation is testament to the stakes and the inability of two fundamentally contradictory narratives to coexist. Long before Barack Obama's 2017 designation of the Reconstruction Era National Monument, the SCV had opposed efforts to create a national monument devoted to Reconstruction. For example, in 2010, a member of the SCV told a journalist reporting on an earlier proposal that "if the park service is talking about opening a site to celebrate Reconstruction, we're going to have a hard time with that. What was done to the South was horrible."[20] A park celebrating black accomplishments and freedom, many of which were overturned during "Redemption," would have undermined the Lost Cause version of the past that presented Reconstruction's excesses as the cause of racial strife today. The same SCV member's declaration the he felt "no shame or regret over the action those men took" to overturn Reconstruction might have been challenged by a national historic site that discussed how those actions included voter fraud, vigilante violence, torture, murder, and terrorism.[21] The SCV's commander in chief emeritus wanted any such site to recount "how the United States Congress illegally passed the 14th Amendment that was designed to punish the South."[22] To him, the South included only southern whites, and requiring equal protection under the law was a punishment to southerners. Indeed, maintaining a commemorative landscape that only celebrates white heroes continues to allow neo-Confederates to see themselves as having a unique claim on the South inherited from their ancestors.

The Lost Cause relies upon a form of cultural exclusion that continues to divide Americans. Its narrative celebrates white accomplishments by portraying white men as superhuman in their valor, endurance, and accomplishments. The complete erasure of any flaw in the Confederacy and simultaneous snubbing of African American agency leaves southern history the heroic realm of white people. The exclusionary nature of our commemorative landscape reflects the historical power dynamics in the South.

Historians can accidently contribute to this exclusion at times. Scholars still routinely use "southerner" as shorthand for white southerner or even white Confederate-supporting southerner. This often negatively impacts their interpretation of the past.[23] In 2017, a professor of history told a reporter that "if there's something the generation that put up (the monuments) could all agree on, it was that [Confederate monuments] were testaments to the men who fought and did their duty." In reality, these monuments have divided communities since their erection. Statements that a generation "could all agree on" the need for Confederate monuments erases African Americans and others who opposed them. Indeed, some African Americans felt that the United Daughters of the Confederacy should not even be allowed to exist, given that they were essentially honoring treason. Continuing his erasure of nonwhite Americans, the historian celebrated Confederate monuments as "part of the reunification of our country," providing another example of an exclusionary "our."[24]

The modern Lost Cause narrative supports ideologies that justify opposing active efforts to address racism within society. An understanding of the past that fails to include African Americans as historically disadvantaged and discriminated against provides the historical underpinnings for inaccurate beliefs that white men are victims of reverse discrimination. Presenting racism as solely a product of individual bigotry and not a product of history helps maintain inequality, disguising the impact and roots of institutionalized racism. Unrelenting, uncritical defense of all things Confederate often helps provide a historical justification for ignoring institutionalized racism, disparities in opportunity, and continued discrimination. Even neo-Confederates who sincerely deny having a racist bone in their body are often unknowingly propagating a selective, ahistorical, and fabricated narrative of the past that buttresses inequality within America.

These larger questions of historical memory are unlikely to disappear from American politics anytime soon. In 2005, Fitzhugh Brundage predicted that "current trends in southern politics suggest we can anticipate further corrosive debates over the past."[25] He appears to have been correct, as these fights accelerated at the same time partisan politics became increasingly polarized. These debates about the past are as much about identity as they are about history. To revise their understanding of the past would not just upset a neo-Confederate's sense of history but would challenge his or her place in the world. In an era when white privilege is increasingly recognized and under attack, fears of cultural and demographic change overlap with the changing landscape of modern-day race relations. Fears of losing political supremacy are attached to a corresponding loss of cultural hegemony in the public sphere.

No solution for the monument question will make racism disappear overnight, nor can dealing with monuments solve all of America's problems. Memories of the Confederacy and the neo-Confederate movement have supported ideologies of white supremacy, but so have many other aspects of American society. Confederate monuments are part of a larger ongoing struggle. Until Americans—both those in favor of and opposed to removing monuments—are able to acknowledge and address the larger historical connections between white supremacy and American society, the underlying issues that make Confederate monuments controversial will continue to cause controversy, division, and struggle.

Historians have an important role in providing needed context for debates about monuments and memory. We have the ability to call attention to how the past has been used and manipulated. As each community decides what it wishes to celebrate and remember, historians can help provide the context needed to make decisions. Historians of the Civil War are increasingly engaging neo-Confederate fabrications in the public sphere through letters to the editor, blog posts, media interviews, Twitter, works aimed at the public, and their teaching.

In North Carolina, historians have already played a role. As seen with the example of the University of North Carolina's Silent Sam, scholars are increasingly taking part in public debates about monuments. The pulling down of Silent Sam did not happen in a vacuum. The press consulted numerous historians, myself included, about the monument's history, and the media often cite Carr's racist dedication speech. That speech helped shift the question from whether the monument represented fighting for slavery to whether the statue has Jim Crow–era connections to white supremacy.[26] For those raised on the Lost Cause, the first assertion that the monument has ties to slavery seems easily—if inaccurately—challenged. But Carr's description of the monument and of whipping a woman to reassert white supremacy makes it nearly impossible to argue that the monument has no racist ties. The best that can be leveled is the erroneous assertion that Carr's opinion is not representative of other Confederate memory makers.

More broadly, the speech has become a key talking point in North Carolina's debates around Confederate monuments and has even been cited in proposals to change the town of Carrboro's name.[27] In 2017, Durham Public Schools renamed their Carr building.[28] The following year, Duke University's History Department, housed in the Carr building, requested that the university change the building's name, citing this very book (which was still forthcoming at the time). The board of trustees agreed and approved a renaming—proving that historical research can change the world, or at least a building's name.[29]

Teaching and writing history are inherently political. In my first few weeks after arriving in Charleston, South Carolina, as a new professor, a local resident asked me if I "teach a southern view of the war or a northern view of the war." Her hoped-for answer was clear. Caught off guard, I could only reply, "I teach a historical view of the war." Whom we include in our writing and our teaching matters. Focusing a Civil War class entirely on white southerners' wartime actions erases other groups' claims to the legacy of the Civil War and American history more broadly. Indeed, teaching both a Confederate and a white northern view of the past still neglects large parts of the country's wartime experience, including those of African Americans, Native Americans, and southern Unionists, to name just a few. An exclusionary history full of white valor that erased African American military participation helped justify North Carolina's disenfranchisement of black voters in 1900. Similarly, the Lost Cause narrative still protects white ownership of the past to maintain a privileged place in the future. Historians bear a professional obligation to engage those who would abuse the past and to not contribute to that abuse's continuation. Civil War historians who ignore dissent, desertion, and other aspects of the past that contradict the Lost Cause, or who focus solely on decontextualized battlefield heroics, can at times unintentionally help propagate a false past capable of uniting white southerners along racial lines through a shared memory of honor.

If nothing else, in an era when "fake news," "alternative facts," and increasing polarization of the news imperils democratic institutions, history can remind people that facts should matter, even if they have not always mattered in the past. The story of how the Lost Cause movement created the mythic marble soldier seen on monuments across the southern landscape, as well as in textbooks and historical monographs, shows that rewriting and fabricating narratives of the past out of thin air is not new and that the threat from allowing lies to stand unchallenged should not be underestimated. Lies have been used to justify disenfranchisement, oppression, killings, terrorism, and racist policies in the past, and they will be so used again. The acceptance of fabricated narratives that Americans should know to be false from their own lived experience is not a recent phenomenon. In fact, fabricating a past with lies and fraud might just be an essential component of American history.

Acknowledgments

I did not originally intend to write this book.

First, this book would not have been created if not for the student activists who pushed me—though they may not have known it—to write it. When I first stumbled upon the Julian Carr's 1913 dedication speech in the archives, I failed to comprehend the psychological impact that the University of North Carolina's (UNC's) Silent Sam had upon students and faculty of color, nor the power that Carr's words would have. I thought the speech was just a neat little primary source that might provide a means of teaching about Jim Crow and Civil War memory, not realizing that it might play a part in changing the name of at least two buildings, become a national news story, and help motivate activists to pull down a monument, ultimately leading to a university chancellor resigning. Activists made me realize the power and importance of this story. Their work in North Carolina eventually led me to put aside my dissertation revisions and write this book first.

Second, this book would never have been written without a flood. On arriving at the North Carolina State Archives to do some research, I was told that the documents I wanted to look at were not accessible due to standing water on the bottom floor of the building. Turning to my notes, I remembered a small lead that I had wanted to follow up on regarding a pension for a deserter. That day, I found substantial evidence of widespread pension fraud—the seeds for chapters 3 and 4.

Finally, this book is the result of the recent change in American politics. My work in this volume was initially no more than a couple of articles, but the 2016 election convinced me that a book on lies and white supremacy might be timely.

Now that it is written, I have so many people to thank, and I apologize in advance to anyone I forget. Hilary Green, Phyllis Jestice, George Roupe, and Lauren Simpson read the entire manuscript. While I'd like to claim any mistakes are their fault, the truth is, any errors are likely the result of me not listening to them. Fitz Brundage, Joseph Glatthaar, Barbara Gannon, Jennifer Kosmin, Ethan Kytle, and Karen Cox all provided valuable feedback on parts of the book. I am confident that they made this book better.

This project would not have happened without archivists. First up, Matt Turi and Laura Hart at UNC have helped a generation of scholars find the sources they need. The staff of Commemorative Landscapes of North Carolina, especially Natasha Smith, Erin Corrales-Diaz, Kami LaBerge, and Peter Zasowski, made this project possible. Doug Brown, Chris Meekins, and Michael Hill in Raleigh not only helped me find the documents I needed but also talked out their implications with me.

My colleagues at the College of Charleston supported my decision to put aside my dissertation and write a different book, believing in me and encouraging me throughout the process. I wish to thank especially Bernard Powers, Briana McGinnis, Brittany Lehman, Chris Boucher, Gibbs Knotts, Irina Erman, Jerry Hale, Karyn Amira, Mary Jo Fairchild, Rebecca Shumway, Shari Rabin, Shyam Sriram, Simon Lewis, and Sandi Slater. My students deserve a shout out, as they helped me work out ideas in classes; special thanks to Maaike Kooijman, Marina Conner, and Lilah Grace Mullis, who helped find crucial primary sources for the book. To the College of Charleston Interlibrary Loan Office, thank you, and I am sorry for the overdue books I still need to return. I'll bring them in tomorrow, I swear.

Many scholars, friends, and strangers, assisted me in a variety of ways, including Pearl Young, Bruce Baker, Blain Roberts, David Silkenat, Vernon Burton, Will Sturkey, Robert Colby, Eric Burke, Brian Fennessy, Brian Jordan, Chris Barr, Evan Kutzler, Willie Griffin, Jim O'Hara, Elizabeth Lundeen, Angela Riotto, Angela Diaz, Angie Zombek, Michael Gray, Frances Pierce, Bill Barney, Wayne Lee, David Blight, Dan Sherman, Malinda Lowery, Alex Ruble, Julie Ault, Thavolia Glymph, John Chasteen, Dominic Bryan, Peter Gray, Manisha Sinha, Simon Lewis, Kelly Mezurek, Sarah Beetham, Scott Nesbit, Amanda Brickell Bellows, Barton Myers, Andrew Frank, James Wilkey, Garrett Wright, Lindsay Ayling, Samuel Finesurrey, Alyssa Bowen, Maya Little, Marcellene Lindsey, Andrew Mackie, Jasmin Howard, Andy Slap, Marjorie Spruill, Don Doyle, Victoria Bynum, Lorien Foote, Warren Milteer, Laura Sandy, Kevin Levin, Patrick Lewis, and David Hamilton. Beatrice Burton ensured I had an excellent index. For years, Alex Remington, Margy Kohn, and Mya Chasanow have provided me a place to sleep when researching and listened to me ramble about my findings.

The wonderful folks at the University of Virginia Press who believed in this project from the start deserve the utmost praise. Dick Holway understood the vision for the book and supported me throughout the process.

Helen Chandler and Niccole Leilanionapae'aina Coggins made sure things stayed on schedule and kept me from making mistakes. Though hard on me, the two peer review readers made this book significantly better. I truly can say I thanked them even as I cursed them.

I am fortunate to have a supportive family and wonderful friends. Without my sisters and parents, this book would not exist, and I would likely not have graduated college. To my nephews, Eli and Matthew, thank you for motivating me to write. Though you can't read this yet, I wrote this book in the hope that it might help ensure you grow up in a more equal and just world. The support of Maddie Domby, Maisie Domby, Bruno Pritchard-Su, Ethel Rodes, Gussie Sherrill, Cassie Flores, Lola Foley, and Lexington Domby-Kosmin made this book possible, though they are unlikely to ever read it.

Finally, I must thank Jennifer. You were with me throughout this entire project, you listened to me talk about it, you helped me work out the hard paragraphs, and you have lived with this book as long as anyone. You read drafts and encouraged me when I became frustrated with the book. Thank you most of all for the love and support. I could not have written this without you.

Notes

Abbreviations and Short Titles

Carr Papers	Julian Shakespeare Carr Papers
CSR	Compiled Service Records
Federal Census Collection	Population Schedules of Censuses via Ancestry.com
NARA	National Archives and Record Administration, Washington DC
NCDAH	North Carolina Department of Archives and History, Raleigh NC
SCC Approved	Southern Claims Commission Approved Claims, 1871–1880, RG 217, NARA
SCC Disallowed	Southern Claims Commission Barred and Disallowed Claims, NARA Microfilm M1407
SHC	Southern Historical Collection, Wilson Library, University of North Carolina, Chapel Hill, NC
UA	University Archives
UNC	Wilson Library, University of North Carolina at Chapel Hill
USCT	United States Colored Troops

Introduction

1. Antonia Noori Farzan, "'Silent Sam': A Racist Jim Crow–Era Speech Inspired UNC Students to Topple a Confederate Monument on Campus," *Washington Post*, August 21, 2018; interview by author with Alyssa Bowen, Lindsay Ayling, Samuel Finesurrey, January 6, 2019; "Editorial: UNC's Stature Threatened by System Board's Mediocrity," WRAL.com, January 16, 2019, https://www.wral.com/editorial-unc-s-stature-threatened-by-system-board-s-mediocrity/18127160/.

2. For a good history of the monument see Jane Stancill and Andrew Carter, "The Unfinished Story of Silent Sam, from 'Soldier Boy' to Fallen Symbol of a Painful Past," *News and Observer* (Raleigh, NC), August 25, 2018; "'Silent Sam' Sparks Conversation at UNC," WRAL.com, April 23, 2003, https://www.wral.com/news/local/story/104969/.

3. I had actually found the speech in December 2009 but did not publish about it until 2011.

4. David Blight, "The Battle for Memorial Day in New Orleans," *Atlantic*, May 29, 2017.

5. Blight, *Beyond the Battlefield*, 1.

6. For the best works on Civil War memory and the Lost Cause, see Blight, *Race and Reunion;* Janney, *Remembering the Civil War;* Cox, *Dixie's Daughters;* Brundage, *Southern Past;* Kytle and Roberts, *Denmark Vesey's Garden;* Gannon, *Americans Remember Their Civil War;* Goldfield, *Still Fighting the Civil War;* Cobb, *Away Down South;* McPherson, *Reconstructing Dixie;* Cook, *Civil War Memories;* Janney, *Burying the Dead but Not the Past;* Harris, *Across the Bloody Chasm;* Blight, *American Oracle;* Foster, *Ghosts of the Confederacy;* Savage, *Standing Soldiers, Kneeling Slaves;* Blair, *Cities of the Dead;* Hulbert, *Ghosts of Guerrilla Memory;* Baker, *What Reconstruction Meant;* Blight, *Beyond the Battlefield;* Cook, *Troubled Commemoration;* Gardner, *Blood and Irony;* Marshall, *Creating a Confederate Kentucky;* Poole, *Never Surrender;* Reardon, *Pickett's Charge in History and Memory;* Wilson, *Baptized in Blood;* Goleman, *Your Heritage Will Still Remain;* McElya, *Clinging to Mammy*. There are numerous excellent edited volumes on southern memory, including Mills and Simpson, *Monuments to the Lost Cause;* Emberton and Baker, *Remembering Reconstruction;* Brundage, *Where These Memories Grow;* Gallagher and Nolan, *Myth of the Lost Cause and Civil War History*. For works focused on alternative memories of the war, see Gannon, *The Won Cause;* Clark, *Defining Moments;* Bynum, *Long Shadow of the Civil War;* Bynum, *Free State of Jones;* Lee, *Claiming the Union;* Noe, "Toward the Myth of Unionist Appalachia"; Inscoe, "Guerrilla War and Remembrance"; Sarris, *Separate Civil War;* Starnes, "'Stirring Strains of Dixie.'"

7. Scholars often focus on Virginia, Georgia, and South Carolina. There have been efforts to expand focus and examine local variation of the Lost Cause. For examples, see Marshall, *Creating a Confederate Kentucky;* Hulbert, *Ghosts of Guerrilla Memory;* Goleman, *Your Heritage Will Still Remain*.

8. Cecil-Fronsman, *Common Whites*, 204.

9. Moore, *Conscription and Conflict in the Confederacy*, 107; Williard, "Executions, Justice, and Reconciliation in North Carolina's Western Piedmont, 1865–1866," 37; Paludan, *Victims*, 49; Myers, *Rebels against the Confederacy*, 119; Browning, "Visions of Freedom and Civilization Opening before Them," 85; Williard, "North Carolina in the Civil War."

10. Barrett, *Civil War in North Carolina;* Myers, *Rebels against the Confederacy;* Barrett, *Sherman's March through the Carolinas;* Hartley, *Stoneman's Raid*.

11. Beckel, *Radical Reform*, 3–16.

12. Brundage, *Southern Past*, 4.

13. Cobb, *Away Down South*, 140; see also Cox, *Dixie's Daughters*, 106.

14. Cobb, *Away Down South*, 316–17.

15. Blight, *Race and Reunion*, 292.

16. Woodward, *Origins of the New South*, 154–55; on objectivity, see Burke, *Varieties of Cultural History*, 44.

17. Goldfield, *Still Fighting the Civil War*, 21. History also evolves and is influenced by the present but is bound by sources.

18. Savage, *Standing Soldiers, Kneeling Slaves*, 131. See also Goldfield, *Still Fighting the Civil War*, 20.

19. Goldfield, *Still Fighting the Civil War*, 2.

20. For the best work on the memory of slavery and loyal slaves, see McElya, *Clinging to Mammy;* Kytle and Roberts, *Denmark Vesey's Garden.* On the memory of Reconstruction, see Baker, *What Reconstruction Meant;* Emberton and Baker, *Remembering Reconstruction,* esp. Prince, "Jim Crow Memory."

21. Young, *Bunk*, esp. 184.

22. Nora, "Between Memory and History," 8.

23. Brundage, *Southern Past*, 5.

24. Kytle and Roberts, *Denmark Vesey's Garden*, 83.

25. Gessen, "Autocrat's Language."

26. Lowenthal, *Past Is a Foreign Country—Revisited,* 296, 500.

27. Brundage, *Southern Past*, 32; see also Cox, *Dixie's Daughters;* Foster, *Ghosts of the Confederacy,* 140–44, 194–95; Goldfield, *Still Fighting the Civil War,* 21, 195–97; Wilson, *Baptized in Blood,* esp. xii–xiv, 100–104, 109, 117–18.

28. Cobb, *Away Down South*, 316–17.

29. Clifton, "Trump and Putin's Strong Connection." For more on the distinction between truth and lies and why their uses matter, see Sithole and Mkhize, "Truth or Lies?," 70. On how the South can be seen as authoritarian enclaves, see Mickey, *Paths Out of Dixie.*

30. For an exception to that rule see John Stauffer, "Yes, There Were Black Confederates. Here's Why," *The Root*, January 20, 2015, https://www.theroot.com/yes-there-were-black-confederates-here-s-why-1790858546; Ta-Nehisi Coates, "Black Confederates at Harvard," *Atlantic*, September 2, 2011; Kevin M. Levin, "What I Learned About Black Confederates at Harvard," *Civil War Memory*, August 31, 2011, http://cwmemory.com/2011/08/31/what-i-learned-about-black-confederates-at-harvard; Corydon Ireland, "Black Confederates," *Harvard Gazette*, September 1, 2011.

31. The Dunning school viewed Reconstruction as well as the emancipation and enfranchisement of African Americans as a mistake. Dunning and his followers assumed African Americans were not fit to lead and were manipulated by white northerners. Modern interpretations rarely have the overt claims that African Americans were incapable of participating in democracy but instead merely ignore nonwhite southerners as political actors, instead only considering white conservative viewpoints. For examples of neo-Dunning arguments or sentiments slipping into histories, see Herron, *Framing the Solid South;* McIlwain, *1865 Alabama.* McIlwain largely ignores the agency or perspective of African Americans, assuming only white populations mattered in political decisions. Additionally, his tone is Dunning-esque, for example arguing Alabama was "haunted" by the "emancipation of slaves" in 1865. For analysis of neo-Dunning writings, see Burton, "Reconstructing South Carolina's Reconstruction," 24.

32. Clara Turnage, "Most Republicans Think Colleges Are Bad for the Country. Why?," *Chronicle of Higher Education*, July 10, 2017; Charles Bethea, "Teaching Southern and Black History under Trump," *New Yorker*, February 2, 2017. For more on the myth of Confederate constitutionalism see Neely, *Southern Rights.*

33. Pew Research Center, "Civil War at 150"; Marist College Institute for Public Opinion, "A Nation Still Divided." For two examples playing out in the public sphere, see Kevin Levin, "The Myth of the Black Confederate Soldier," *Daily Beast*, August 8, 2015, http://www.thedailybeast.com/the-myth-of-the-black-confederate-soldier;

Adam Serwer, "The Secret History of the Photo at the Center of the Black Confederate Myth," *Buzz Feed*, April 17, 2016, https://www.buzzfeed.com/adamserwer/the -secret-history-of-the-photo-at-the-center-of-the-black-c.

34. Chris Joyner, "Georgia Lawmaker Punished for Civil War Mailer," *Atlanta Journal-Constitution*, June 16, 2017.

35. My views are heavily influenced by Masha Gessen; see, for example, Clifton, "Trump and Putin's Strong Connection"; Gessen, "Autocrat's Language."

36. Joel Brown, "Chapel Hill Removes Monuments Honoring Confederacy, Black History," ABC11, February 23, 2019, https://abc11.com/chapel-hill-removes -monuments-honoring-confederacy-black-history/5152565.

1. Rewriting the Past in Stone

1. "University Finals at Chapel Hill," *Wilmington Morning Star*, June 3, 1913, 1. The exact number remains unknown, but Gerrard Hall, where the speeches were given, currently holds 380 people. A photo shows over 280 people at the unveiling. Board of Trustee's Minutes, Oversize Volume 11: May 1904–September 1916, 482, series 1. Minutes, 1789–1932, in the Board of Trustees of the University of North Carolina Records #40001, UA, UNC; S. R. Winters, "Notable Events Mark Class Day at the University," *News and Observer* (Raleigh, NC), June 3, 1913, 1. For most of the key sources about this monument, see "Archival Resources"; "Confederate Monument, UNC (Chapel Hill)," Commemorative Landscapes of North Carolina, https://docsouth.unc.edu/commland/monument/41.

2. "Programme at the Unveiling of the Confederate Monument at the University of North Carolina"; CSR for Henry London, 32nd North Carolina, NARA M270; Smith, "London, Henry Armand"; "Clasping Hands at Appomattox," *North Carolinian* (Raleigh, NC), April 12, 1905, 1, 2; "An Appomattox Veteran Tells of Closing Scenes," *North Carolinian* (Raleigh, NC), April 12, 1905, 1, 3; "Veterans Going," *Farmer and Mechanic* (Raleigh, NC), March 26, 1907. In 1903, London nominated Carr at a Democratic convention. "No Senator Was Named By Caucus Last Night," *Farmer and Mechanic* (Raleigh, NC), January 13, 1903, 6.

3. London, "Thirty-Second Regiment"; Smith, "London, Henry Armand"; London, "Bryan Grimes."

4. Cox, *Dixie's Daughters*, 1; Caroline Janney built upon Cox's work to show that the UDC was continuing what the Ladies' Memorial Associations began in the decades after the war. See Janney, *Burying the Dead but Not the Past*, 3. For monuments and women, see Mills and Simpson, *Monuments to the Lost Cause*; Bishir, "Landmarks of Power"; Brundage, *Southern Past*, esp. 12–54; Vincent, "'Evidence of Womans Loyalty, Perseverance, and Fidelity'"; Foster, *Ghosts of the Confederacy*, esp. 40–41, 44, 127, 129–30, 158. For the Lost Cause more generally, see Blight, *Race and Reunion*; Blight, *Beyond the Battlefield*; Reardon, *Pickett's Charge in History and Memory*; Janney, *Remembering the Civil War*; Cook, *Civil War Memories*; Gannon, *Americans Remember Their Civil War*. This chapter focuses on monuments built after 1890, as monuments moved from graveyards to public spaces. On North Carolina monuments, see Brown, "Civil War Monuments"; Bishir, "North Carolina's Union Square." Commemorative Landscapes of North Carolina, a digital humanities project of UNC, provides a database of monuments, primary sources, and scholarly essays.

5. Mrs. Henry London, "Working for the Monument Fund," *Evening Chronicle* (Charlotte, NC), April 1, 1911, 3; "Programme at the Unveiling of the Confederate Monument at the University of North Carolina."

6. Cox, *Dixie's Daughters*, 2; Rosenburg, *Living Monuments*, xiii.

7. London, "Dedication of Monument," typed presentation speech, 1913, North Carolina Collection, UNC; "Programme at the Unveiling of the Confederate Monument at the University of North Carolina." A few scholars previously noted the speech, notably Weare, *Black Business in the New South*, 41; and Webb, *Jule Carr*, 26. Neither connected the monument's meaning to the violence, instead citing it as evidence of Carr's participation in an assault. Brown, *Upbuilding Black Durham*, 4, cites Weare to discuss the assault.

8. Gannon, *Americans Remember Their Civil War*, 8, 104. For women writers' role, see Gardner, *Blood and Irony*.

9. Foster, *Ghosts of the Confederacy*, 8.

10. Tammy Grubb, "Confederate Flags Could Fly over Multiple Orange County Sites. One's in Hillsborough," *Herald Sun* (Durham, NC), February 9, 2018.

11. Webb, *Jule Carr*, is the only full-length biography. Turner, "Oral History Interview with Viola Turner"; for evidence of donations, see *Semi-Weekly Messenger* (Wilmington, NC), March 30, 1899, 4; "North Carolina Letter. Julian S. Carr for Governor in 1884," *New York Globe*, January 1, 1883, 1; "Praises Southern Negro," *Washington Bee*, February 4, 1911, 1; "Durham's Great Work," *Washington Bee*, August 7, 1909, 1.

12. "With Petition over 100 Yards in Length Memphis Secures Reunion; Haldeman New Head of Veterans," *Asheville Citizen-Times*, April 13, 1923, 1.

13. Webb, *Jule Carr*, 97–98; Craig, *Josephus Daniels*, 73–80, 95, 101, 134–36; Steward, *David Schenck and the Contours of Confederate Identity*, 92–96.

14. "General Carr's Speech," *Standard* (Concord, NC), October 18, 1900, 4.

15. Webb, *Jule Carr*, 191–96; "General Metts Promoted," *Wilmington Morning Star*, October 22, 1915, 4; "Miss Gorman Maid of Honor," *Richmond Times Dispatch*, October 5, 1919, part 4, 6; M. M. Buford, "The Surrender of Johnston's Army," *Herald and News* (Newbury, SC), June 15, 1920, 3; "North Carolina Veteran's Association," *Lenoir Topic*, October 9, 1889, 2; "The Most Valuable Bull in the World," *News and Observer* (Raleigh, NC), April 5, 1896, 13. Carr lost his reelection campaign in 1916 but returned in 1917 as head of the Department of the Army of Northern Virginia—responsible for all veterans residing in Virginia, West Virginia, Kentucky, Tennessee, and the Carolinas—until he was elected to head the national organization in 1921. In 1889 he presided over the Confederate Pensioners' Convention and served as the first president of the North Carolina Confederate Veterans Association, founded to build the state's old soldiers' home. He also headed up the National Association of the Blue and the Gray and the Battle Abbey Association. See "Carr," *Raleigh Christian Advocate*, July 16, 1889, 3; "Julian S. Carr Re-Elected," *Sun* (Baltimore, MD), July 18, 1907, 12; John A. Livingstone, "General Carr Believes in Pep and Will Practice It as Command of Veterans," *News and Observer* (Raleigh, NC), November 6, 1921, second section, 1.

16. "Durham County North Carolina Cemeteries: Maplewood [Durham City Owned]—Surname Starts with C," Cemetery Census, May 29, 2017, http://cemeterycensus.com/nc/durh/cem058c.htm.

17. Julian Carr, "Unveiling of Confederate Memorial at University, July 2, 1913," in Folder 26, Addresses, 1912–1914, Carr Papers, SHC.

18. Brian K. Fennessy, "Silent Sam and Other Civil War Monuments Rose on Race," *News and Observer* (Raleigh, NC), November 23, 2017.

19. Julian Carr, "Unveiling of Confederate Monument at University, June 2, 1913," in Folder 26, Addresses, 1912–1914, Carr Papers, SHC.

20. In many ways, the violence of Reconstruction displays "aspects of the guerrilla war that Confederates rejected in 1865." Rubin, *Shattered Nation*, 145. See also Cobb, *Away Down South*, 61; Janney, *Remembering the Civil War*, 9.

21. "1929 Confederate Reunion Marker, Charlotte," Commemorative Landscapes of North Carolina, http://docsouth.unc.edu/commland/monument/600/.

22. S. R. Winter, "Marshall Is Heard by Some 2,000 Tar Heels," *News and Observer* (Raleigh, NC), June 5, 1913, 5. Carr was not the first UCV leader with Klan ties. Indeed, the UCV had been tied to the original Klan since their founding as the organization's first commander, John Gordon, had led Georgia's Klan during Reconstruction. The fifth commander was a founding member of the Klan. Other UCV and SCV leaders clearly had similar affiliations or at least leanings. Richard Sneed, for example, who became the commanding general of the UCV in 1930, had led his county's Klan organization. Wilson, *Baptized in Blood*, 111–12; James B. Clark, "Ku-Klux-Klan," *Montgomery (AL) Advertiser*, October 18, 1908, 11 (there are two page 11s in this edition, the article is on the second one); "A Ku Klux Leader," *Greensboro Patriot*, September 7, 1911, 11; "Commander in Chief of Confederates Dead," *Austin American-Statesman*, August 10, 1911, 1; "The Confederacy Well Represented," *Palestine (TX) Daily Herald*, November 29, 1907, 2; "Jackson Ku Klux Challenged Scalawags," *Jackson (TN) Sun*, November 28, 1948, Section 6, 12; Hattaway, "Stephen Dill Lee," 258. Nathan Bedford Forrest II, who led the SCV, was also a Klan leader. "Forrest Tells Aims of Ku Klux College," *New York Times*, September 12, 1921, 15.

23. Brundage, *Southern Past*, 29–32; Baker, *Gospel According to the Klan*; Wilson, *Baptized in Blood*, 100–101, 117–18.

24. Meehan, "Craig, Locke."

25. "Monument to Sir Walter Raleigh," *Economist* (Elizabeth City, NC), November 1, 1901, 1; "With Patriotic Fervor Raleigh Honors Itself," *News and Observer* (Raleigh, NC), November 23, 1901, 1; "20,000 Persons Witness Unveiling of the Bagley Monument in Raleigh," *Greensboro Daily News*, May 21, 1907, 1; Johnson, *History of Negro Soldiers in the Spanish-American War*, 30. See also Bishir, "Landmarks of Power," esp. 20–21; Cox, *Dixie's Daughters*, 14; Baker, *What Reconstruction Meant*, 38–43.

26. Beckel, *Radical Reform*, 6.

27. Mabry, "Negro Suffrage and Fusion Rule in North Carolina," 81; "The General Assembly," *News and Observer* (Raleigh, NC), November 17, 1886, 4; "Result of the Official Count For Congress," *Greensboro North State*, December 9, 1886, 3. Despite garnering around 55 percent of the vote in the state's US House races, Democrats won 78 percent of districts that year.

28. Anderson, *Race and Politics in North Carolina*; Beckel, *Radical Reform*, esp. 3–7; Mabry, "Negro Suffrage and Fusion Rule in North Carolina."

29. Edmonds, *Negro and Fusion Politics in North Carolina*; Beckel, *Radical Reform*; for short summaries of Fusionism, see Graham, "1898 Election in North Carolina"; Faulkner, "Fusion Politics."

30. Natalie Ring argues scholars should pay attention to "how broader social and political changes in the late nineteenth and early twentieth centuries, such as the Progressive movement and American imperialism, influence the memory of the war and Reconstruction." Ring, "New Reconstruction for the South," 176.

31. Mills, introduction, xvii. On why public monuments came later, see Bishir, "Landmarks of Power," 14–19; Foster, *Ghosts of the Confederacy*, 129–31, sets the date in the 1880s. In North Carolina, the increase of monuments really began in 1887–88 with cemetery monuments. The switch to public squares began in 1892 but only took off after 1900. See Vincent, "'Evidence of Womans Loyalty, Perseverance, and Fidelity,'" 64.

32. Commemorative Landscapes of North Carolina, http://docsouth.unc.edu /commland, has a database of over 920 monuments in the state (234 Civil War monuments as of January 2019). "North Carolina Civil War Monuments Survey," North Carolina Civil War Monuments, http://ncmonuments.ncdcr.gov, also provides data on dedications and monuments.

33. Janney, *Burying the Dead but Not the Past*; Cox, *Dixie's Daughters*; Foster, *Ghosts of the Confederacy*. Once proposed, it often took years to get a monument funded, purchased, and dedicated.

34. Trelease, "Fusion Legislatures of 1895 and 1897," 297–98, 309. See also Bishir, "Landmarks of Power," 14–18.

35. "William Gaston Vickers," *Durham Sun*, July 12, 1900, 1; "The People Know Him," *Durham Daily Sun*, July 27, 1900, 3; "Black Thursday," *Semi-Weekly Messenger* (Wilmington, NC), February 28, 1895, 1; "Our Humiliation," *Wilmington Messenger*, February 24, 1895, 5; *Roxboro Courier*, March 13, 1895, 2; "Crowning Shame," *Oxford Public Ledger*, March 1, 1895, 2. See also Bishir, "Strong Force of Ladies," 477–81, 489–90; Bishir, "North Carolina's Union Square"; Edmonds, *Negro and Fusion Politics in North Carolina*, esp. 41–43, 120–23; Gilmore, *Gender and Jim Crow*, 82–92. Carr paid travel costs for Durham's Confederate veterans who attended the dedication.

36. J. S. Carr, "The Veterans in Gray," *Dispatch* (Lexington, NC), October 22, 1902, 6.

37. "The Boss Is 'Biling,'" *Goldsboro Daily Argus*, March 2, 1895, 1; "Russell's Got a Job," *Goldsboro Daily Argus*, March 8, 1895, 1; "Wake's Disgrace" and "Don't Take It," *News and Observer* (Raleigh, NC), March 10, 1895, 4.

38. "Black Thursday," *Semi-Weekly Messenger* (Wilmington, NC), February 28, 1895, 1; "Special to the Messenger," *Semi-Weekly Messenger* (Wilmington, NC), March 14, 1895, 3; "The General Assembly," *Western Sentinel* (Winston-Salem, NC), March 7, 1895, 1; Trelease, "Fusion Legislatures of 1895 and 1897," 297–98, 309; *Journal of the Senate of the General Assembly of the State of North Carolina at Its Session of 1895*, 384, 409; "Under the Dome," *News and Observer* (Raleigh, NC), March 2, 1895, 5; *Journal of the House of Representatives of the General Assembly of the State of North Carolina at Its Session of 1895*, 895; "Senate," *Semi-Weekly Messenger* (Wilmington, NC), March 7, 1895, 3; "A Touching Scene," *News and Observer* (Raleigh, NC), March 2, 1895, 2.

39. "For White Supremacy: State Democratic Ticket," *Weekly Star* (Wilmington, NC), July 13, 1900, 2; "The Banners Presented," *Semi-Weekly Messenger* (Wilmington, NC), August 17, 1900, 3; "A Campaign Factor: White Supremacy Clubs in Every Township," *Morning Post* (Raleigh, NC), May 16, 1900, 5; "Democratic Convention," *Durham Recorder*, April 16, 1900, 1; see also Webb, *Jule Carr*, 171.

40. J. W. Faison, "Dr. Faison for General Carr," *Charlotte Observer,* October 11, 1900, 2; see also J. M. Wolfe, "The Senatorial Contest," *Charlotte Observer,* October 2, 1900, 2.

41. "North Carolina Letter. Julian S. Carr for Governor in 1884," *New York Globe,* January 1, 1883, 1; "Praises Southern Negro," *Washington Bee,* February 4, 1911, 1; W. E. B. Du Bois, "The Upbuilding of Black Durham. The Success of the Negroes and Their Value to a Tolerant and Helpful Southern City," *World's Work* 23 (January 1912): 336, accessed at http://docsouth.unc.edu/nc/dubois/dubois.html.

42. Webb, *Jule Carr,* 183–84; On Carr's relationship with African Americans, see Weare, *Black Business in the New South,* 40–42, 51, 82.

43. Quote from Peter A. Coclanis, "Yes, Carr Was Racist. And Much More," *Herald Sun* (Durham, NC), November 3, 2017.

44. Carr, *Issues of the Campaign Stated,* 12.

45. Anderson, *Education of Blacks in the South,* 98–99, 122–23, 198, 280.

46. "Bryan Stevenson Club in Session," *Asheville Daily Citizen,* September 22, 1900, 5. On Waddell and the race riot, see Gilmore, *Gender and Jim Crow,* 108–13; Hossfeld, *Narrative, Political Unconscious and Racial Violence in Wilmington, North Carolina,* 32, 37–44, 55–56; Bishir, "Landmarks of Power," 9–13, 15–22; Cecelski and Tyson, *Democracy Betrayed,* esp. 16–33.

47. Quoted in Webb, *Jule Carr,* 169.

48. Prince, "Jim Crow Memory," 19; Baker, *What Reconstruction Meant,* esp. 21–27.

49. Key, *Southern Politics in State and Nation,* 205; Bailey, "Textbooks of the 'Lost Cause,'" 533.

50. "Insult to Vets," *Salisbury Weekly Sun,* August 1, 1900, 3.

51. Blight, *Race and Reunion,* 293–94.

52. "White Supremacy," *Newton Enterprise,* March 23, 1900, 2.

53. Prince, "Jim Crow Memory," 20–21; Redding, *Making Race, Making Power,* 19–21, 37, 75; Smith, "London, Henry Armand."

54. County-level canvas returns and registration numbers found in *Journal of the Constitutional Convention of the State of North-Carolina, at Its Session 1868,* 114–18; my conservative estimate is based on the assumption that 100 percent of eligible African Americans voted for the convention. A similar number of North Carolinians (93,086) voted for ratification of the document as well, while 74,016 voted against it. White Republican votes were critical to the ratification. See Faulkner, "Convention of 1868."

55. Camp, *American Year-Book and National Register for 1869,* 234–35; "Letter of the General of the Army of the United States." For more Lost Cause memory makers inaccurately recalling voter turnout and the extent of disenfranchised ex-Confederates, see Herbert et al., *Why the Solid South?,* 76–77. See also Prince, "Jim Crow Memory."

56. Beckel, *Radical Reform,* 3.

57. Edmonds, *Negro and Fusion Politics in North Carolina,* 112, 121–23, 219–20.

58. Hamilton, *Reconstruction in North Carolina,* 228; *Journal of the Constitutional Convention of the State of North-Carolina, at Its Session 1868,* 114–18. Over 45 percent of Forsyth County's registered whites supported the convention in 1867. Domby, "'Loyal to the Core from the First to the Last,'" 82–83.

59. Hamilton, *Reconstruction in North Carolina,* 204, 213. See also Baker, *What Reconstruction Meant,* 69, 71.

60. Baker, *What Reconstruction Meant*, 33–36; Gardner, *Blood and Irony*, 163.

61. Anderson, *Imagined Communities*.

62. "White Supremacy," *Newton Enterprise*, March 23, 1900, 2; "The Man for State Treasurer," *Morning Post* (Raleigh, NC), February 1, 1900, 2.

63. Alex J. Field, "The Political Record of Gen. Carr and Mr. Simmons Contrasted," *Raleigh Post*, November 1, 1900, 8.

64. Julian Carr, "Gentlemen, Fellow Democrats, Lovers of North Carolina Better Than Lovers of Party, and Members of the Convention" in Folder 35a, Addresses, undated, Carr Papers, SHC. The speech was likely given between 1894 and 1900. Even in 1955, scholars recognized how a memory of "Redemption" justified overturning populism. Woodward, *Strange Career of Jim Crow*, 6.

65. Webb, *Jule Carr*, 169; Edmonds, *Negro and Fusion Politics in North Carolina*, 148–49, 171, 205.

66. Julian Carr, "General Julian S. Carr's Address at Lexington, Va.," June 3, 1916, in Folder 27, Addresses, 1915–1918, Carr Papers, SHC; "Mr. Overman to Attend Trinity Commencement," *Greensboro Daily News*, June 6, 1916, 10. For the horrors of slavery, see Williams, *Help Me to Find My People;* Baptist, *Half Has Never Been Told;* Johnson, *Soul by Soul;* Camp, *Closer to Freedom;* Owens, *Medical Bondage*, esp. 42–72. The connections between politics and a false memory of slavery were noted in 1955 in Woodward, *Strange Career of Jim Crow*, 13–14. See also Duck, "Woodward's Southerner," 38.

67. Julian Carr, untitled speech given at Southern Pines, in Folder 34a, Addresses, undated, Carr Papers, SHC. The speech was likely given within a few years of 1910.

68. On these imaginations of race relations, see Kytle and Roberts, *Denmark Vesey's Garden*, esp. 124–30; Brundage, *Southern Past*, 33; McElya, *Clinging to Mammy*, 11, 54–55, 171–72. For an example of nostalgia making it into history books, see Webb, *Jule Carr*, 168, 195.

69. Foner, *Fiery Trial*, 167; Glatthaar, *Forged in Battle*, x, 227, 250.

70. Julian Carr, untitled speech in Folder 21, Addresses, 1896–1899, Carr Papers, SHC. Based on its content, the speech seems to be from around 1900. Emancipation was often portrayed as a "crime" worse than slavery. See also Cox, *Dixie's Daughters*, 105–7; Janney, *Remembering the Civil War*, 208; Cook, *Civil War Memories*, 68; Goleman, *Your Heritage Will Still Remain*, 114–20.

71. Julian Carr, untitled speech, in Folder 21, Addresses, 1896–1899, Carr Papers, SHC.

72. Cobb, *Away Down South*, 62.

73. Dew, *Apostles of Disunion*, 10.

74. Lincoln, "Second Inaugural Address."

75. "A Declaration of the Immediate Causes Which Induce and Justify the Secession of the State of Mississippi from the Federal Union."

76. Janney, *Remembering the Civil War*, 8, 206–11; Blight, *Race and Reunion*, 282–84; Kytle and Roberts, *Denmark Vesey's Garden*, 119–21.

77. Julian Carr, "Unveiling of Confederate Monument at University, June 2, 1913," in Folder 26, Addresses, 1912–1914, Carr Papers, SHC.

78. Julian Carr, "Ladies of the Memorial Association, Comrades of the Confederacy and Fellow Citizens: Windsor," in Folder 41b, Addresses, undated, Carr Papers, SHC; Carr was quoting Benjamin Andrews of Brown University.

79. "Stately Shaft Unveiled," *Charlotte Daily Observer*, May 11, 1906, 1, 10.

80. Julian Carr, "Fellow-Countrymen, Veterans of North Carolina, Ladies and Gentleman," in Folder 34b, Addresses, undated, Carr Papers, SHC; for similar claims, see Janney, *Remembering the Civil War*, 208–9; Cook, *Civil War Memories*, 66–67; on memory of slavery, see Kytle and Roberts, *Denmark Vesey's Garden*.

81. Carr, *Peace with Honor*, 9; the original can be found in Julian Carr, untitled speech, in Folder 41d, Addresses, undated, Carr Papers, SHC. See also Silkenat, *Raising the White Flag*, 283–85.

82. Janney, *Remembering the Civil War*, 8. See also Kytle and Roberts, *Denmark Vesey's Garden*, 125–27.

83. Christian and McGuire, *Confederate Cause and Conduct in the War between the States*, 180.

84. Janney, *Remembering the Civil War*, 153.

85. W. E. B. Du Bois, "Robert E. Lee," *Crisis*, March 1928, republished at Kevin M. Levin, "W. E. B. Du Bois on Robert E. Lee," *Civil War Memory*, May 30, 2017, http://cwmemory.com/2017/05/30/w-e-b-dubois-on-robert-e-lee.

86. Janney, *Remembering the Civil War*, 143, 145, 170–71, 189, 194; Domby, "Captives of Memory," 289.

87. Michael Trouche, "Letter: Leave Statues Alone," *Post and Courier* (Charleston, SC), September 6, 2017; Powers, "Monumental Challenges in Charleston." My views here were heavily influenced by Bernard Powers's writings and subsequent conversations with him.

88. Blight, *Race and Reunion*, 282–84; Woodward, "Marching Masters," 20.

89. Julian Carr, untitled speech given at Southern Pines, in Folder 34a, Addresses, undated, Carr Papers, SHC.

90. Julian Carr, untitled speech given at Southern Pines, in Folder 34a, Addresses, undated, Carr Papers, SHC.

91. Rose, *Ku Klux Klan or Invisible Empire*, dedication, introduction, endorsement, 13, 16; S. E. F. Rose, "Ku Klux Klan Booklet," *Our Heritage* (West Point, MS), October 1, 1913, 8. See also Cox, *Dixie's Daughters*, 96–110.

92. Janney, *Remembering the Civil War*, 256.

93. Rutherford, *Measuring Rod to Test Text Books*, 3.

94. Rutherford, *Measuring Rod to Test Text Books*, 2, 9, 10. See also Janney, *Remembering the Civil War*, 276; John A. Livingstone, "General Carr Believes in Pep and Will Practice It as Command of Veterans," *News and Observer* (Raleigh, NC), November 6, 1921, second section, 1. On historical writing and policing narratives, see Gardner, *Blood and Irony*, esp. 6, 69, 150, 162–69; Cox, *Dixie's Daughters*, 94–98, 101–8, 114–17, 125, 157; Bailey, "Textbooks of the 'Lost Cause'"; Blight, *Race and Reunion*, 280–85; Kytle and Roberts, *Denmark Vesey's Garden*, 131–35.

95. Rutherford, *Truths of History*, 91.

96. Equal Justice Initiative, *Lynching in America*; Brundage, *Lynching in the New South*; Brundage, *Under Sentence of Death*; Feimster, *Southern Horrors*.

97. Julian Carr, untitled speech, in Folder 30b, Addresses, undated, Carr Papers, SHC.

98. Julian Carr, untitled speech, in Folder 35b, Addresses, undated, Carr Papers, SHC.

99. McPherson, *Reconstructing Dixie*, 45.

100. Julian Carr, "Befo' Da Wah," in Folder 33b, Addresses, undated, Carr Papers, SHC.

101. Julian Carr, "Befo' Da Wah," in Folder 33b, Addresses, undated, Carr Papers, SHC. Italics added.

102. Julian Carr, "Befo' Da Wah," in Folder 33b, Addresses, undated, Carr Papers, SHC. On threatening African Americans with reminders about Reconstruction, see Baker, *What Reconstruction Meant*, 27. For African American response to threats, see Clark, *Defining Moments*, 194–207.

103. "No Civil War," *Afro-American* (Baltimore, MD), June 22, 1929, 6. Willie Griffin brought this to my attention. For examples of African Americans pushing back, see "Neither Traitors Nor Rebels," *Washington Bee*, June 30, 1883, 2; "Why Not," *Washington Bee*, November 30, 1912, 4; "Federal Monuments in the South," *Savannah Tribune*, June 1, 1895, 2. There remains a need for research into African Americans' pushback against the Lost Cause.

104. Pike, *Address at the Celebration of Emancipation Day*, 2, 5.

105. Edmonds, *Negro and Fusion Politics in North Carolina*, 181; Leak, *Freedom's Jubilee*, 8, 11–13; "Negroes of Raleigh Adopt Some Notable Resolutions," *Morning Post* (Raleigh, NC), January 2, 1903, 5; "Home Folks," *Semi-Weekly Messenger* (Wilmington, NC), January 10, 1899, 2; "Raleigh Negroes 'Resolute,'" *Weekly Star* (Wilmington, NC), April 9, 1903, 1; "Emancipation Day," *Henderson Gold Leaf*, January 5, 1905, 2; Clark, *Defining Moments*, 201–2.

106. "Local Briefs," *Tarborough Southerner*, April 11, 1901, 3; "North Carolina News," *Alamance Gleaner* (Graham, NC), April 18, 1901, 3.

107. *News Reporter* (Littleton, NC), April 12, 1901, 1; "Good Advice," *News and Observer* (Raleigh, NC), April 14, 1901, 8.

108. Clark, *Defining Moments*, 195, 202–7; Silkenat, *Raising the White Flag*, 278.

109. Christian and McGuire, *Confederate Cause and Conduct in the War between the States*, 173–90. The claim about northern ownership evolved into the false claim that no southerner ever owned a slave ship, seen at "U.C.V. Commander-in-Chief Seeking Truth in History," *Charlotte Observer*, June 6, 1929, 10.

110. John S. Mosby to Samuel Chapman, June 4, 1907, Gilder Lehrman Institute of American History. On Mosby and memory, see Blight, *Race and Reunion*, 296–99.

111. John S. Mosby to Samuel Chapman, June 4, 1907, Gilder Lehrman Institute of American History.

112. Trevor Baratko, "Virginia Sen. Dick Black Says No Confederate Soldiers Died Fighting for Slavery," *Loudoun Times-Mirror* (Leesburg, VA), September 14, 2017; Tammy Grubb, "Confederate Rally to Defend UNC's Silent Sam Coming to Chapel Hill," *News and Observer* (Raleigh, NC), October 24, 2015.

113. Julian Carr, untitled speech given at Southern Pines, in Folder 34a, Addresses, undated, Carr Papers, SHC.

114. Carr, *Problem of the Hour*, 8.

115. Julian Carr, untitled speech, in Folder 38a, Addresses, undated, Carr Papers, SHC; "Among Former Enemies," *Henderson Gold Leaf*, May 16, 1901, 1.

116. "Ellender Warns against Carpetbagger's Return," *Rocky Mount Telegram* (NC), March 18, 1956, 1; "George Wallace on Segregation, 1964," Gilder Lehrman Institute of American History. On memory of Reconstruction during Civil Rights movement, see Cook, *Civil War Memories*, 148–49, 154; Baker, *What Reconstruction Meant*, esp. 145–62.

117. Jane Stancill, "Cooper Tells UNC Leaders They Can Remove Silent Sam If There's 'Imminent Threat,'" *News and Observer* (Raleigh, NC), August 21, 2017, updated August 22, 2017.

118. Chris Joyner, "Georgia Lawmaker Famous for 'Klan' Remark Named to Civics Committee," *Atlanta Journal-Constitution*, June 5, 2017, archived version accessible at https://web.archive.org/web/20170608132016/http://investigations.blog.ajc.com/2017/06/05/benton-named-to-civics-committee.

119. Chris Joyner, "Georgia Lawmaker Punished for Civil War Mailer," *Atlanta Journal-Constitution*, June 16, 2017. Benton sponsored bills renaming Atlanta's Martin Luther King Boulevard after Confederate general and Klan leader John B. Gordon (whom the street had previously been named after); he requested his name not be included alongside the other members of the legislature on a monument to King. Jim Galloway, "Lawmaker Chastised for Confederate Views Doesn't Want His Name on MLK Statue," *Atlanta Journal-Constitution*, June 20, 2017.

120. Tom Crawford, "Lawmaker Is Fighting an Old War He Can't Win," *Gainesville (GA) Times*, June 21, 2017.

121. Kytle and Roberts, *Denmark Vesey's Garden*, 11.

122. Pew Research Center, "Civil War at 150"; Marist College Institute for Public Opinion, "A Nation Still Divided."

123. Marist College Institute for Public Opinion, "A Nation Still Divided"; see also Elon Poll, "Opinion of North Carolina Voters on State Issues," 2, 13.

124. Since 1992, Democrats have increasingly viewed the flag negatively, while Republicans have seen a slight uptick in support for it. Jones, "Democrats' Views on Confederate Flag Increasingly Negative."

125. Coski, *Confederate Battle Flag*, 49–50.

126. "Confederate Handouts Are Sticking Point for Many at State Fair," WRAL.com, October 21, 2017, http://www.wral.com/confederate-handouts-are-sticking-point-for-many-at-state-fair/17035741.

2. Inventing Confederates

1. "Monument to Student Soldiers," *Wilmington Morning Star*, June 15, 1913, 11.

2. Julian Carr, "Unveiling of Confederate Monument at University, June 2, 1913," in Folder 26, Addresses, 1912–1914, Carr Papers, SHC. Building on another common Lost Cause claim, Carr declared Stonewall Jackson "the world's greatest strategist."

3. Julian Carr, fragment of speech, in Folder 30a, Addresses, undated, Carr Papers, SHC. This was likely part of the UNC monument speech, as it is from the same typewriter and has "Chapel Hill" written at the top of a page.

4. Goldfield, *Still Fighting the Civil War*, 27.

5. "Unveiling of the Student's War Monument at the University," *Fayetteville Weekly Observer*, June 11, 1913, 4.

6. Wilson, "Pettigrew, James Johnston."

7. Sowder, "'In Defense of My Country,'" 19–21; John Halliburton to Juliet Halliburton, April 22, 1861, John Wesley Halliburton Papers (#4414-z), SHC; Graham, "UNC's Union Veterans"; "Conferring of War Class Degrees," *University Record* 93 (June 1911): 56.

8. Graham, "UNC's Union Veterans"; *Official Army Register for 1863*, 118; Battle, *Sketches of the History of the University of North Carolina*, 95, 227.

9. For more about London's college life, see his diaries in the Henry Armand London Papers (#868-z), SHC.

10. Henry A. London to Lilla London, February 16, 1864, Henry Armand London Papers (#868-z), SHC.

11. Henry London, diary, entries for October 30 and 31, 1864, Henry Armand London Papers (#868-z), SHC. London also notes disagreements about "going back into the Union" on November 23.

12. S. R. Winters, "Notable Events Mark Class Day at the University," *News and Observer* (Raleigh, NC), June 3, 1913, 1.

13. Webb, *Jule Carr*, 20, 201; John A. Livingstone, "General Carr Believes in Pep and Will Practice It as Command of Veterans," *News and Observer* (Raleigh, NC), November 6, 1921, third section, 1; file for Julian S. Carr, "Unfiled Papers and Slips Belonging in Confederate Compiled Service Records," NARA Microfilm M347.

14. Murray and Hsieh, *Savage War*, 53.

15. On white southerners fighting for the Union, see Current, *Lincoln's Loyalists*, esp. 218. On dissent and Unionism, see Merritt, *Masterless Men;* Auman, *Civil War in the North Carolina Quaker Belt;* Bynum, *Free State of Jones*; Bynum, *Long Shadow of the Civil War;* Myers, *Executing Daniel Bright;* Paludan, *Victims;* Souders and Chamberlin, *Between Reb and Yank;* Sarris, *Separate Civil War;* Myers, *Rebels against the Confederacy;* Browning, *Shifting Loyalties;* Williams, Williams, and Carlson, *Plain Folk in a Rich Man's War;* Lee, *Claiming the Union;* Domby, "War within the States"; Hebert, "Civil War and Reconstruction Era Cass/Bartow County, Georgia"; Bohannon, "Northeast Georgia Mountains during the Secession Crisis and Civil War."

16. *Chatham Record* (Pittsboro, NC), June 4, 1913, 2.

17. Julian Carr, "Unveiling of Confederate Monument at University, June 2, 1913," in Folder 26, Addresses, 1912–1914, Carr Papers, SHC; S. R. Winters, "Notable Events Mark Class Day at the University," *News and Observer* (Raleigh, NC), June 3, 1913.

18. These letters can all be found in Folder 987, 16–24 May 1913, and Folder 988, 26–31 May 1913, University of North Carolina Papers #40005, UA, UNC.

19. Julian Carr to Dr. F. P. Venable, May 16, 1913, in Folder 987, 16–24 May 1913, University of North Carolina Papers #40005, UA, UNC; Dr. F. P. Venable to General Julian S. Carr, May 17, 1913, in Folder 987: 16–24 May 1913, University of North Carolina Papers #40005, UA, UNC; Thomas M. Gorman, private sec. to J. S. Carr, to Dr. F. P. Venable, May 27, 1913, in Folder 988, 26–31 May 1913, University of North Carolina Papers #40005, UA, UNC; President [Venable] to General Julian S. Carr, May 28, 1913, University of North Carolina Papers #40005, UA, UNC; Battle, "University of North Carolina in the War, 1861–'65," 647–52; Battle, *History of the University of North Carolina*, 749–51.

20. Vickers, *Chapel Hill*, 64. Vickers provides no footnotes, so where his numbers come from remain unclear. Based on Battle's count of total students who attended UNC, had Carr's claims been correct, 64 percent of all graduates (living and dead) from 1830 to 1867 served in the Confederate army. Carr announced in his speech that "about 1800 entered the Confederate army, of whom 842 belonged to the generation of 1850–1862," taking the 842 from Battle's essay. This meant

Carr only inflated the numbers of other classes and were Carr correct, the classes of 1830–49 and 1863–67 would have served at a rate of 69 percent, while the men in prime age for service served at a rate of only 57 percent. The claim that nearly 70 percent of fifty-year-olds served is hard to believe.

21. On wartime loyalty, see Auman, "Neighbor against Neighbor"; Bynum, *Long Shadow of the Civil War;* Myers, *Rebels against the Confederacy;* Kruman, "Dissent in the Confederacy"; Scarboro, "North Carolina and the Confederacy"; Moore, *Conscription and Conflict in the Confederacy,* esp. 107; Domby, "War within the States"; Tatum, *Disloyalty in the Confederacy;* Escott and Crow, "Social Order and Violent Disorder."

22. Julian Carr, untitled speech, in Folder 31b, Addresses, undated, Carr Papers, SHC; Julian Carr, untitled speech, in Folder 35a, Addresses, undated, Carr Papers, SHC; Julian Carr, untitled speech given at Southern Pines, in Folder 34a, Addresses, undated, Carr Papers, SHC.

23. Julian Carr, "Unveiling of Confederate Monument at University, June 2, 1913," in Folder 26, Addresses, 1912–1914, Carr Papers, SHC. He used this exact line repeatedly, including during his Senate campaign. Julian Carr, untitled speech dated May 21, 1900, in Folder 22, Addresses, 1900–1902, Carr Papers, SHC.

24. "Virginia's Glory Guarded by the History Committee," *Times Dispatch* (Richmond, VA), November 1, 1903, C10.

25. Christian and McGuire, *Confederate Cause and Conduct in the War between the States,* 141, 146.

26. "Virginia's Glory Guarded by the History Committee," *Times Dispatch* (Richmond, VA), November 1, 1903, C10; Christian and McGuire, *Confederate Cause and Conduct in the War between the States,* 151–67.

27. North Carolina Literary and Historical Association, *Five Points in the Record of North Carolina in the Great War of 1861–65.*

28. Ashe, "Number and Losses of North Carolina Troops." This number was refuted by Christian and McGuire, *Confederate Cause and Conduct in the War between the States,* 145–48; McKim, *Numerical Strength of the Confederate Army,* 56–57. Ashe actually claimed 102,607 troops from North Carolina in Confederate service, which increased to 125,000 if Home Guard, state reserves, and militia were included. In time, this became conflated to 125,000 Confederate soldiers. Historians relying on secondary sources for their statistics often disseminate this questionable statistic unknowingly. For examples of excellent historians citing potentially faulty numbers due to secondary literature, see Escott, *Many Excellent People,* 53; Downs, *Declarations of Dependence,* 16; Myers, *Rebels against the Confederacy,* 102. For state-by-state estimates of troop numbers from 1864, see *The War of the Rebellion: A Compilation of the Official Records of the Union and Confederate Armies,* series IV, vol. 3, section 1, 95–103.

29. Silkenat, *Raising the White Flag,* 108, 127–31.

30. Quoted in Trudeau, *Gettysburg,* 521; Linenthal, *Sacred Ground,* 92.

31. Hess, *Pickett's Charge,* 354, 360.

32. "How Pickett's Division Was 'Cut All to Pieces': Its Support Ran," *Abingdon Virginian,* August 7, 1863, 1.

33. "General Pettigrew's Brigade," *Daily Progress* (Raleigh, NC), August 1, 1863, 2.

34. "Governor Locke Craig Speaks at the Unveiling of Monument Erected to Memory of the Chapel Hill Students," *Asheville Citizen-Times,* June 3, 1913, 1, 7.

35. Hess, *Pickett's Charge*, xiii.

36. Desjardin, *These Honored Dead*, 174.

37. Christian and McGuire, *Confederate Cause and Conduct in the War between the States*, 155, 159; see also Reardon, *Pickett's Charge in History and Memory*, 171–72.

38. Reardon, *Pickett's Charge in History and Memory*, esp. 131–75; Hess, *Pickett's Charge*, 182, 248; Guelzo, *Gettysburg*, 423. Military historian Earl Hess does not even bother to debate who went farthest in Hess, *Pickett's Charge*, 248, 183, 188. For a discussion on the root of the phrase "farthest at Gettysburg," see Linenthal, *Sacred Ground*, 107–10.

39. Reardon, *Pickett's Charge in History and Memory*, 11–15.

40. Quoted in Reardon, *Pickett's Charge in History and Memory*, 207.

41. Quoted in Desjardin, *These Honored Dead*, 153. On Buehler, see Vanderslice, *Gettysburg*, 217, 218, 228–29.

42. Reardon, *Pickett's Charge in History and Memory*, 186–87.

43. Hess, *Pickett's Charge*, 183, 188–90, 360; Guelzo, *Gettysburg*, 422.

44. Christian and McGuire, *Confederate Cause and Conduct in the War between the States*, 165; Hess, *Pickett's Charge*, 408. Brockenbrough's troops took the lightest casualties of all units engaged in the charge. Hess, *Pickett's Charge*, 334.

45. Reardon, *Pickett's Charge in History and Memory*, 133.

46. Bond, *Pickett or Pettigrew*, 56. To give an idea of how long this debate lasted, the original version was published in 1888, and the third edition came out in 1901. On Pettigrew's retreat, see Guelzo, *Gettysburg*, 425.

47. Silkenat, *Raising the White Flag*, 128.

48. Hess, *Pickett's Charge*, 333–35.

49. Neal, "Surrendered," 1; Silkenat, *Raising the White Flag*, 2. As 247,769 Confederates were paroled on the field, this means that as many as 214,865 spent time as prisoners. Some may have surrendered multiple times, so the exact number of individuals who spent time in prison is likely lower.

50. Silkenat, *Raising the White Flag*, 124, 130–31.

51. CSR for Henry London, 32nd North Carolina, NARA M270.

52. "Clasping Hands at Appomattox," *North Carolinian* (Raleigh, NC), April 13, 1905, 1–2; Henry A. London, "An Appomattox Veteran Tells of Closing," *North Carolinian* (Raleigh, NC), April 13, 1905, 1, 3.

53. "Objection by Virginians," *Washington Post*, March 24, 1905, 5; Christian and McGuire, *Confederate Cause and Conduct in the War between the States*, 144–45.

54. London, "Bryan Grimes," 508–9.

55. On remembering surrender, see Silkenat, *Raising the White Flag*, 270–94.

56. "Aycock in Iredell," *Henderson Gold Leaf*, July 12, 1900, 1.

57. "Aycock in Iredell," *Henderson Gold Leaf*, July 12, 1900, 1. Carr made similar arguments to justify the grandfather clause providing illiterate whites the right to vote.

58. Julian Carr, "Befo' Da Wah," in Folder 36a, Addresses, undated, Carr Papers, SHC.

59. On the Confederate monument at Arlington, they even put a black servant in the background. See Cox, "Confederate Monument at Arlington," 158.

60. "Mr. Warren Speaks," *Standard* (Concord, NC), July 5, 1900, 2.

61. Mary Belle Gary, "The Spirit of Liberty That Characterizes North Carolinians," *Henderson Gold Leaf*, June 13, 1901, 4. On how the Lost Cause taught "reverence"

for white supremacy, see Cox, *Dixie's Daughters,* 91; Goldfield, *Still Fighting the Civil War,* 22.

62. D. H. McLean, "Memorial Address of Hon. D. H. McLean," *Fayetteville Weekly Observer,* May 17, 1900, 1.

63. Current, "That Other Declaration." For examples of claims about North Carolina being first, see "First Things," *Newton Enterprise,* May 27, 1898, 1; Walter W. Moore, "Vanguard of the Revolution," *Newton Enterprise,* May 27, 1898, 1; John E. Taylor, "The Battle of Alamance," *News and Observer* (Raleigh, NC), January 10, 1896, 3.

64. Brundage and Domby, "Evolution of Landscape"; "Colonial Column (Battle of Alamance), Burlington," Commemorative Landscapes of North Carolina, https://docsouth.unc.edu/commland/monument/25/; Henderson, *Kings Mountain and Its Campaigns,* 23.

65. Smith, "Civil War Desertion." On deserters, see Glatthaar, *General Lee's Army,* 408–420; Giuffre, "First in Flight"; Bardolph, "Inconstant Rebels"; Reid, "A Test Case of the 'Crying Evil'"; Auman, *Civil War in the North Carolina Quaker Belt;* Lonn, *Desertion during the Civil War;* Tatum, *Disloyalty in the Confederacy;* Weitz, *Higher Duty;* Weitz, *More Damning Than Slaughter;* Escott, *After Secession,* 125–34; Bynum, *Long Shadow of the Civil War.*

66. Glatthaar, *General Lee's Army,* 413; Smith, "Civil War Desertion."

67. Glatthaar, *General Lee's Army,* 409.

68. On dissent, see Myers, *Rebels against the Confederacy;* Tatum, *Disloyalty in the Confederacy;* Crofts, *Reluctant Confederates;* Kruman, "Dissent in the Confederacy."

69. *Official Records of the Union and Confederate Navies in the War of the Rebellion,* series I, vol. 6, 725.

70. Alfred M. Waddell, speech given to "Ladies of the James B Gordon Chapter United Daughters of the Confederacy," [October 3, 1905], in Folder 13, Alfred M. Waddell Papers (#743), SHC.

71. Domby, "War within the States."

72. Julian Carr, "Winston-Salem, Oct. 28 1903," in Folder 23, Addresses, 1903–1905, Carr Papers, SHC. This myth's widespread acceptance can be seen in Webb, *Jule Carr,* 194.

73. Bond, *Pickett or Pettigrew?,* 58–59.

74. Bond, *Pickett or Pettigrew?,* 58–59.

75. Glatthaar, *General Lee's Army,* 412–13.

76. For an example, see Gallagher, *Confederate War,* 31–32. Desertion was more complex than most scholars depict it, and some have pushed back at overly simplistic understandings. For an example of a good study that supports the understanding that desertion was caused by devotion to family using statistical data, see Glatthaar, "Everyman's War," 232, 236, 241–42. Glatthaar goes into more depth and nuance about the many causes of desertion in *General Lee's Army,* esp. 408–20. Bearman, "Desertion as Localism," 340, challenges the interpretation that family led to desertion.

77. Julian Carr, speech fragment, in Folder 32a, Addresses, undated, Carr Papers, SHC; Julian Carr, "Raleigh Monument to Confederate Women," in Folder 32b, Addresses, undated, Carr Papers, SHC; another variation can be found in Folder 30a of Carr's papers. This last fragment may actually be part of the UNC monument speech, as on the first page, it has "Chapel Hill" written on it, and the color of the ink is similar and appears to be from the same typewriter.

78. Julian Carr, speech fragment, in Folder 32a, Addresses, undated, Carr Papers, SHC.

79. Julian Carr, speech fragment, in Folder 32a, Addresses, undated, Carr Papers, SHC.

80. Men who deserted as many as three times still sometimes received lighter sentences than death. See Glatthaar, *General Lee's Army*, 419. On punishments, see Bunch, *Military Justice in the Confederate States Armies*, 88–131.

81. Perry, *Civil War Courts-Martial of North Carolina Troops*, 8–9.

82. Many deserters did not have a trial but were administratively punished by their commanding officers. For a comprehensive list of trials, see Bunch, *Roster of the Courts-Martial in the Confederate States Armies*.

83. Perry, *Civil War Courts-Martial of North Carolina Troops*, 318, 320.

84. On Lee's elevation to near sainthood, see Fellman, *Making of Robert E. Lee*, esp. 129–30, 173–74. See also Hall, "Fantasizing Lee as a Civil Rights Pioneer," for more lies about Lee.

85. "A Beautiful Story," *Virginian-Pilot* (Norfolk, VA), October 9, 1874, 1.

86. "A Confederate Story," *San Francisco Bulletin*, October 13, 1874, 3.

87. For examples, see "'Twixt Love and Duty," *Las Cruces (NM) Sun-News*, July 1, 1898, 3; "Confederate States vs. Edward Cooper, Deserter," *Greensboro Patriot*, November 18, 1903, 8; "Confederate States vs. Edward Cooper, Deserter," *News And Observer* (Raleigh, NC), November 8, 1903, 15; "The Booming Cannon," *Waterloo (IN) Press*, September 20, 1906, 3; "Affecting Incident of the Civil War," *Independent Record* (Helena, MT), August 9, 1878, 1; "Two Specimen Cases of Desertion," *Southern Historical Society Papers* 8, no. 1 (January 1880): 29–31. On the Southern Historical Society shaping Confederate memory, see Blight, *Race and Reunion*, esp. 78–80, 151, 158–260.

88. "Mercy for a Deserter," *Great Falls (MT) Tribune*, May 14, 1904, 7. Gordon and other former generals repeating these tales knew that courts-martial had no requirement to convict.

89. "Edward Cooper and His Wife Mary," *Confederate Veteran* 18, no. 7 (July 1919): 330.

90. "The Lee Monument," *Staunton (VA) Spectator*, August 31, 1887, 2; "The Great Rebel General," *San Francisco Chronicle*, October 28, 1887, 1. For histories of Monument Avenue and the Lee monument, see Edwards, Howard, and Prawl, *Monument Avenue*, esp. 12–19; Driggs, Wilson, and Winthrop, *Richmond's Monument Avenue*.

91. "Evening Sermon," *Register and Leader* (Des Moines, IA), December 14, 1914, 7; "After Death, Judgment, Evangelist's Warning," *Philadelphia Inquirer*, February 15, 1915, 11; "All Must Die, Warns Sunday and after Death, Judgment," *Colorado Springs Gazette*, July 6, 1914, 5–6. In 1961, during the centennial, it reappeared in a Petersburg newspaper, again leaving off his death. "Confederate Military Judges Weep as Deserter's Letter Read," *Progress-Index* (Petersburg, VA), April 23, 1961, 6.

92. "Horne Monument Presented to State," *Charlotte Observer*, June 11, 1914, 1, 3.

93. Julian Carr, "Raleigh Monument to Confederate Women," in Folder 32b, Addresses, undated, Carr Papers, SHC.

94. "Death of Edward Cooper," *News and Observer* (Raleigh, NC), July 23, 1890, 1.

95. "The Story of Edward Cooper," *News and Observer* (Raleigh, NC), July 27, 1890, 2.

96. For examples of excellent scholars being misled by faulty secondary literature, see Paludan, *Victims*, 81; Jones, *Dispossessed*, 61–62; Burton, *Age of Lincoln*,
208. For examples of historians who cite questionable sources, see Weitz, *Higher
Duty*, 97–98; Barret, *Civil War in North Carolina*, 191. Weitz claims Cooper was
from Alabama. His mistake likely derives from the fact that Battle first told the story
in Alabama. For additional examples, see Tate, *Jefferson Davis*, 203; Förster, *On the
Road to Total War*, 447; Barefoot, *Let Us Die like Brave Men*, 180–83. Burton and
others often provide additional evidence alongside Cooper's story to support their
assertions that home-front concerns influenced desertion.

97. For example community studies, see Auman, *Civil War in the North Carolina
Quaker Belt*; Durrill, *War of Another Kind*; Bynum, *Free State of Jones*; Bynum, *Long
Shadow of the Civil War*; Kenzer, *Kinship and Neighborhood in a Southern Community*;
Myers, *Executing Daniel Bright*; Paludan, *Victims*; Souders and Chamberlin, *Between
Reb and Yank*; Sarris, *Separate Civil War*; Myers, *Rebels against the Confederacy*;
Browning, *Shifting Loyalties*; Williams, Williams, and Carlson, *Plain Folk in a Rich
Man's War*; Lee, *Claiming the Union*; Domby, "War within the States"; Hebert, "Civil
War and Reconstruction Era Cass/Bartow County, Georgia"; Bohannon, "Northeast
Georgia Mountains during the Secession Crisis and Civil War."

98. "Lee Jackson Day Beautiful Exercises," *Charlotte News*, January 19, 1910, 2.

99. "Carr's Services in the Trenches," *Daily Free Press* (Kinston, NC), October 16,
1900, 1; Alex J. Field, "The Political Record of Gen. Carr and Mr. Simmons Contrasted," *Eastern Courier* (Edenton, NC), November, 1, 1900, 5; Wiley G. Riddick,
"From Gen. Carr's Lieutenant," *News and Observer* (Raleigh, NC), October 21, 1900,
5; Paul B. Means, "General Carr's War Record," *Oxford Public Ledger*, October 25,
1900, 4. A similar exaggeration was made in 1888 in a Durham paper claiming that
reports that he never served were incorrect and that he served in the early years of
the war. Quoted in *News and Observer* (Raleigh, NC), November 23, 1888, 2.

100. John A. Livingstone, "General Carr Believes in Pep and Will Practice It as
Command of Veterans," *News and Observer* (Raleigh, NC), November 6, 1921, third
section, 1.

101. "Protest against Using Confederate Veterans Association in Politics," *Eastern Courier* (Edenton, NC), November 1, 1900, 5.

102. Hill, "Forty-First Regiment," 772. The unit was also known as the 41st
North Carolina State Troops.

103. CSR for Alfred M. Waddell, 3rd North Carolina Cavalry, NARA M270.

104. Chas. F. Warren, "The Winchester Fund," *Washington (NC) Gazette*, March
19, 1896, 3; "Celebration at Manteo," *Charlotte (NC) News*, July 22, 1902, 3.

105. Bragaw, "Presentation of the Portrait of Charles Frederick Warren to the
Supreme Court of North Carolina," 860.

106. Pryor, *Reading the Man*, 437, 462–64.

107. Bragaw, "Presentation of the Portrait of Charles Frederick Warren to the
Supreme Court of North Carolina," 861–62.

108. Cited in Driggs, Wilson, and Winthrop, *Richmond's Monument Avenue*, 49;
and Savage, *Standing Soldiers, Kneeling Slaves*, 151.

109. "Contradicts Speaker at Memorial Exercises," *Richmond Times-Dispatch*,
June 4, 1916, 10.

110. Marvel, "Great Imposters" ; Smith, "Cases of Francis Marion Lundy and
William Allen Lundy, Father and Son," 3–23.

111. Hoar, *South's Last Boys in Gray*, 26, 383–89, 470–516.

112. "Oldest Person Ever," *Guinness World Records*, http://www.guinnessworld records.com/world-records/oldest-person.

113. "Colonel Mosby in Town," *Baltimore Sun*, October 12, 1910, 14. Mosby only attended one reunion. His role in Republican politics may have made him feel unwelcome. He also expressed concerns that reunions kept the nation from healing. See "Noted Guerrilla Survives the Knife," *Liberty (TX) Vindicator*, January 26, 1912, 7; "War Ought to Be Forgotten," *Montgomery (AL) Advertiser*, July 11, 1910, 5.

114. "'Mosby's Men,'" *Tazewell (VA) Republican*, November 17, 1910, 3. See also Jennifer van der Kleut, "Herndon's 1910 Mosby's Ranger Reunion," *Herndon Patch*, September 8, 2013.

115. "Governor Locke Craig Speaks at the Unveiling of Monument Erected to Memory of the Chapel Hill Students," *Asheville Citizen-Times*, June 3, 1913, 1,7.

116. This point is made by Goldfield, *Still Fighting the Civil War*, 2.

117. Newell, *Regular Army before the Civil War*, 50, 52. About 20 percent of the officers joined the Confederacy.

118. Collins, "Confederate Identity and the Southern Myth," 41.

119. See both Glatthaar, *General Lee's Army;* and Glatthaar, *Soldiering in the Army of Northern Virginia*.

120. Hess, *Civil War Infantry Tactics*, 236.

121. Nolan, "Anatomy of the Myth," 24–25. See also Goleman, *Your Heritage Will Still Remain*, 112.

122. Murray and Hsieh, *Savage War*, 13, 15, 33, 46, 49.

123. Murray and Hsieh, *Savage War*, 55, 56. For similar claims about Confederate perseverance, see Gallagher, *Confederate War*, 27–31.

124. Quoted in Gordon, *Broken Regiment*, 3.

125. Gallagher, *Confederate War*, 66.

126. Gordon, *Broken Regiment*, 2, 13–14.

127. London, "Thirty-Second Regiment," 523, 529.

128. Col. E. C. Brabble to Capt. John W. Reily, December 19, 1862, in CSR for Edward C. Brabble, 32nd North Carolina, NARA, M270.

129. Sword, "Franklin," 130.

130. Julian Carr, speech headed "C & M," in Folder 31a, Addresses, undated, Carr Papers, SHC; Julian Carr, untitled speech, in Folder 32a, Addresses, undated, Carr Papers, SHC.

131. Sword, "Franklin," 107; Hood and John Bell Hood Historical Society, "What Kind of Courage?"; Kevin M. Levin, "A Holy War against Wiley Sword?," *Civil War Memory*, July 6, 2009, http://cwmemory.com/2009/07/06/a-holy-war-against -wiley-sword.

132. Donald, "Confederate as a Fighting Man," 193.

133. Gallagher and Meier, "Coming to Terms with Civil War Military History." The need for memory studies inclusion can be seen in the article's unfortunate disdain for guerrilla and community studies.

134. Sheehan-Dean, "Blue and the Gray in Black and White,"16–17.

135. Hess, "Where Do We Stand?," 393.

136. Gallagher, *Confederate War*, 13. Gallagher's dismissal of community studies as being selective and not representative ignores his own selectivity. Ironically, Gallagher warns against community studies lumping "together upcountry, piedmont,

and lowland yeomen" (23) even as he lumps diverse southern whites into a nearly solid mass.

3. The Loyal Deserters

1. Pension File for D. P. Yokley (Davidson County), NCDAH; Brock Barkley, "Confederate Pension List in the State Is Reduced 750 by Deaths in Past Year; Widows Now Outnumber the Veterans," *Asheville Citizen-Times*, December 14, 1923, 1.

2. "The Pension List about Complete," *North Carolinian* (Raleigh, NC), October 3, 1901, 8.

3. Claim of Samuel Yokeley (#10959), Davidson County, SCC Approved; Files for Joseph Yokley and D. P. Yokley, *Union Provost Marshals' File of Papers Relating to Individual Civilians*, NARA M345.

4. Pension File for D. P. Yokley (Davidson County), NCDAH; Pension File for Joseph Yokeley (Forsyth Country), NCDAH; "Widows Entitled to Forsyth County Pensions"; General Assembly of North Carolina, "Chapter 189: An Act to Amend and Consolidate the Pension Laws," in *Public Laws and Resolutions of the State of North Carolina Passed by the General Assembly at its Session in 1921*, 481–87.

5. Inscoe, "Guerrilla War and Remembrance," 76. On the erasure of Unionists, see Sarris, *Separate Civil War*; Starnes, "'Stirring Strains of Dixie.'"

6. "Headq's 48th Regt., Centerville Road, September 3, 1862," *Raleigh Register*, September 24, 1862, 1; "D. P. Yokeley Succumbs at Home Near Walburg," *Charlotte Observer*, August 8, 1926, 3.

7. CSR for D. P. Yokley, Joseph Yokeley, and Jefferson Yokeley of the 48th North Carolina Infantry, NARA M270; Claim of Samuel Yokeley (#10959), Davidson County, SCC Approved.

8. "Davidson County," *Tri-Weekly Era* (Raleigh, NC), April 18, 1872, 2–3.

9. Pension File for D. P. Yokley (Davidson County), NCDAH. Additionally, David married in 1890, which made his widow ineligible, as marriages had to have occurred before 1880 at the time. Baxter Durham to E. C. Byerly, January 23, 1931, in Folder Davidson, 1931–1932, Correspondence, Pension Bureau, State Auditor, NCDAH. Later, when her pension application was revisited, the county pension board inquired about her age and wealth. On David's application see letters in Folder Forsyth 1931–1932, Correspondence, Pension Bureau, State Auditor, NCDAH. Yearly pension lists for each county at NCDAH confirm a pension was paid.

10. Forsyth County Pension Lists, 1924–1926, NCDAH; Baxter Durgham to C. M. McKaughan, July 5, 1927, in Folder Forsyth, 1927–1928, Correspondence, Pension Bureau, State Auditor, NCDAH; Pension File for Joseph Yokeley (Forsyth County), NCDAH; Davidson County Marriage Bond Abstracts, Davidson County Marriage Bonds—Series II, 161, in North Carolina County Registers of Deeds, Microfilm, Record Group 048, NCDAH, accessed in *North Carolina, Marriage Records, 1741–2011*, via https://www.ancestry.com/interactive/60548/42091_331547 -00271.

11. Sturken, "Wall, the Screen, and the Image," 137. See also Sturken, *Tangled Memories*.

12. Marshall, *Creating a Confederate Kentucky*, 5.

13. J. S. Carr, "The Veterans in Gray," *Dispatch* (Lexington, NC), October 22, 1902, 6.

14. Jones and Kenzer, "Confederate Pensions."

15. Thomas Rhodes, "The Status of Veterans," *Greensboro Patriot*, July 10, 1901, 11; CSR for Thomas Rhodes of the 27th North Carolina Infantry, NARA M270. Though Thomas Rhodes claimed to have deserted, his military record does not reveal his desertion, demonstrating that at times, relying on the CSRs used in this chapter to determine the war record of pensioners may undercount absence without leave and desertion. The only indicator of disciplinary trouble was a hospital record that says, "This man was turned over to his captain."

16. "State Press," *Semi-Weekly Messenger* (Wilmington, NC), November 21, 1902, 7. In 1876, Republican gubernatorial candidate Thomas Settle had recognized two types of deserters: those who "deserted from bad motives" and those "who would rather have been shot than to have fought against the flag of our fathers." "The Great Contest," *Union Republican* (Winston, NC), August 24, 1876, 2. This alternative Unionist memory of deserters as either pro-Union or with bad motives failed to fit the lived experience of many deserters.

17. The depiction of deserting to care for their families likely does describe many deserters, perhaps even the majority, but this depiction took on a mythic life of its own and remains in the historiography today.

18. "Wires to Go under Ground," *Charlotte Daily Observer*, August 5, 1901, 8.

19. "Regarding Pensions," *Union Republican* (Winston-Salem, NC), June 25, 1903, 4.

20. "The New Pension Law," *Union Republican* (Winston-Salem, NC), April 16, 1903, 2.

21. Pension File for George E. Dull (Forsyth County), NCDAH; CSR for George Dull of the 52nd North Carolina Infantry, NARA M270.

22. Pension File for Jefferson Younts (Davidson County), NCDAH; Davidson County Pension List, 1936, NCDAH.

23. Pension File for Michael Swain (Davidson County), NCDAH.

24. "State News," *Progressive Farmer* (Winston-Salem, NC), April 30, 1901, 3.

25. "The Prodigal's Return," *Dispatch* (Lexington, NC), March 27, 1901, 4.

26. "Wake Pension List," *North Carolinian* (Raleigh, NC), July 11, 1901, 8. The article includes the subheading "Are Any Names on It That Ought Not Be There?"

27. "Instructions to Pension Boards," *Asheville Daily Citizen*, April 16, 1901, 2; "Looking Up Deserters," *Daily Journal* (New Bern, NC), April 16, 1901, 1.

28. "The Pensions Are Here," *Dispatch* (Lexington, NC), December 17, 1902, 1.

29. For estimates of deserters, see "Looking Up Deserters," *Daily Journal* (New Bern, NC), April 16, 1901, 1.

30. To determine the list of ineligible pensions, I cross-referenced CSRs, Watford, *Civil War Roster of Davidson County, North Carolina*, as well as the Davidson County Pension Applications files and Davidson County pension lists kept at NCDAH organized by year and county. Lists of pensioners were also gleaned from "The Davidson Pensioners," *Dispatch* (Lexington, NC), December 1, 1909, 2. By 1919, at least 11 percent of Davidson County pensioners would have been ineligible due to their service record under the strict 1901 standard. At least 6 percent of that year's pensioners should not have been approved under the 1919 laws. For an additional list of pensioners in 1919, see "Pensioners Are Here," *Dispatch* (Lexington, NC), December 19, 1919, 1. My research likely underestimates the number of deserters. Some soldiers may have returned to duty—although most of the examples used in this

chapter clearly did not—but no records survived the war to indicate it. While it is true that record keeping fell apart at the end of the war, so did the Army of Northern Virginia. Records are worst for the last year of the war, when desertion was highest. So for every soldier who returned to his unit in the last months of the war but did not get recorded, at least one, if not two, likely deserted without leaving a trace in the historical record. Record keeping could be better or worse throughout the conflict, depending on the unit. The CSRs likely underreport desertion and AWOL soldiers. For example, in Bladen County, John Tedder was marked as a deserter in 1902 but does not show any sign of desertion in his very brief CSR. Bladen County Pension List 1902, NCDAH; CSR for John Tedder, 2nd North Carolina Artillery, NARA M270. While Watford notes if an individual deserted, due to name duplication, confusion, and incomplete service records, some individuals who deserted may have been missed by me as well.

31. Pension lists and pension applications of Davidson County, NCDAH; Watford, *Civil War Roster of Davidson County, North Carolina;* CSRs. Some of the forty-six approved were initially rejected. The two rejected for their service records were Valentine Hill and Jacob Yokley, discussed later in the chapter. Each pension file contains every application based on an individual's service. A veteran's and his widow's applications would be in the same file, and sometimes people applied multiple times. I counted by file, not by individual application.

32. See, for example, Mantovani, Williams, and Pflieger, *Extent of Trafficking in the Supplemental Nutrition Assistance Program,* iii.

33. Davidson County Pension Lists, 1901, 1902, NCDAH. Bladen County, for example, discovered three deserters on the list in 1902.

34. Davidson County Pension Lists 1901, 1902, 1904, NCDAH; Pension File for Thomas Smith (Davidson County), NCDAH.

35. Yancey County Pension Lists, 1901–1906, NCDAH.

36. Pension File for R. G. Gordon (Davidson County), NCDAH; CSR for R. G. Gordon, 18th North Carolina Infantry, NARA M270.

37. "Favor Anti-Cigarette Law," *Charlotte Observer,* February 27, 1903, 3.

38. "Wires to Go under Ground," *Charlotte Daily Observer,* August 5, 1901, 8.

39. Pension File for Thomas E. Johnson (Wilkes County), NCDAH; CSR for Thomas E. Johnson, 18th North Carolina Infantry, NARA M270; Pension File for L. C. Byrd (Wilkes County), NCDAH; CSR for Lyndolph C. Byrd, 54th North Carolina Infantry, NARA M270; Wilkes County Pension Lists, 1910, 1912, 1913, 1915, NCDAH. Byrd deserted twice, and the second time, he does not appear to have returned.

40. Members of the pension board can be established by examining signatures on pension applications. Pension files and CSRs were used to determine the service record of each board member.

41. Burgess Gallimore (Company G), for example, had his pension application signed by a member of the 14th North Carolina.

42. Moore, "Moore, John Wheeler."

43. For an example of Moore's *Roster of North Carolina Troops in the War between the States* being checked by officials, see State Auditor to Z. T. Bynum, July 14, 1926, in Folder Forsyth, 1925–1926, Correspondence, Pension Bureau, State Auditor, NCDAH.

44. Moore, *Roster of North Carolina Troops in the War between the States,* 3:1.

45. Pension File for Robert B. Black (Davidson County), NCDAH. No contemporary record of Robert B. Black in the 14th North Carolina or any other North Carolina unit has yet been found.

46. "Paring Down State Pensioners," *Charlotte News*, September 7, 1901, 3; "Local News," *Dispatch* (Lexington, NC), September 11, 1901, 3. For an example of a deserter rejected due to insufficient disability, see Pension File for Seth W. Ward (Davidson County), NCDAH; CSR for Seth W. Ward, 44th North Carolina Infantry, NARA M270.

47. "Confederate Pensions," *Chatham Record* (Pittsboro, NC), June 11, 1903, 3; *Chatham Record* (Pittsboro, NC), June 18, 1903, 2. County pension lists from 1903 and 1904 show numerous crossed-off Home Guard members. In Davidson County, at least eleven applicants were rejected for being in the Home Guard. Another eight in Davidson were rejected for not serving in the actual army but having been on work details. Rejected applications also included those who hired substitutes.

48. Pension File for John Chappell (Surry County), NCDAH.

49. Daniel Eaker, "Chapter of Another Soldier's Experience," *Lincoln County News* (Lincolnton, NC), April 2, 1915, 4.

50. Daniel Eaker, "Chapter of Another Soldier's Experience," *Lincoln County News* (Lincolnton, NC), April 2, 1915, 4.

51. CSR for Daniel Eaker, 34th North Carolina Infantry, NARA M270; CSR for Daniel Eaker in "Confederate Prisoners of War Who Enlisted in the US Army," in *Alphabetical Card Index to the Compiled Service Records of Volunteer Union Soldiers Belonging to Union Organizations Not Raised by States or Territories*, NARA M1290; Pension File for Daniel Eaker, 1st US Volunteers, NARA; Pension File for Daniel Eaker (Gaston County and Lincoln County), NCDAH. Claiming the same disability was a product of Union and Confederate services, he used Lincoln County for his Union application and applied for his Confederate pensions through Gaston County.

52. 1901 and 1902 Gaston County Pension Lists, NCDAH. Daniel's brother Jesse similarly received a pension for his Confederate service even though he also tried to join the Union army.

53. Gaston County Pension Lists, NCDAH; Pension File for Daniel Eaker, 1st US Volunteers, NARA; Andrew L. Eaker, "Application for Headstone for Daniel Edward Eaker," June 7, 1930, *Applications for Headstones for U.S. Military Veterans, 1925–1941*, NARA Microfilm M1916, accessed at https://www.ancestry.com/interactive/2375/40050_2421401696_0342-03303.

54. Pension File for Elkanah Wall (Forsyth County and Randolph County), NCDAH; CSR for Elkana Wall, 33rd North Carolina Infantry, NARA M270; 1910 Census, Federal Census Collection. Wall was wounded in 1862.

55. Green, "Protecting Confederate Soldiers and Mothers," 1079.

56. "Forsyth County Exhibit, 1892," *Western Sentinel* (Winston-Salem, NC), December 8, 1892, 5; "Forsyth County Exhibit, 1894," *Western Sentinel* (Winston-Salem, NC), January 17, 1895, 5.

57. On how pensions functioned as welfare, see Gorman, "Confederate Pensions as Social Welfare," 24–39; Skopol, *Protecting Soldiers and Mothers*. For more on pensions see Marten, *Sing Not War*, esp. 215–22.

58. Pension File for Jesse Wall (Forsyth County), NCDAH; CSR for Jesse Wall, 33rd North Carolina Infantry, NARA M270; "County Pension Board Approve More Applicants," *Union Republican* (Winston-Salem, NC), August 8, 1901, 6.

59. "The New Pension Law," *Union Republican* (Winston-Salem, NC), April 16, 1903, 2. The limit was later increased to $2,000.

60. E. C. Byerly to Baxter Durham, April 9, 1924, in Folder Davidson, 1923–1924, Correspondence, Pension Bureau, State Auditor, NCDAH; E. C. Byerly to Baxter Durham, July 7, 1925, in Folder Davidson, 1925–1927, Correspondence, Pension Bureau, State Auditor, NCDAH; E. C. Byerly to Baxter Durham, December 31, 1923, in Folder Davidson, 1923–1924, Correspondence, Pension Bureau, State Auditor, NCDAH; Baxter Durham to W. E. Church, August 6, 1931, in Folder Forsyth 1931–1932, Correspondence, Pension Bureau, State Auditor, NCDAH; Reece and Hall to Baxter Durham, June 20, 1931, in Folder Yadkin 1931–1933, Correspondence, Pension Bureau, State Auditor, NCDAH.

61. Pension File for John Chappell (Surry County), NCDAH.

62. Pension Files for Z. N. Stafford (Forsyth County), NCDAH (there are two); CSRs for Zadock Stafford, 21st North Carolina Infantry and 9th Battalion, North Carolina Sharp Shooters, NARA M270.

63. "Pension Warrants for Old Soldiers," *Winston-Salem Journal*, December 16, 1911, 1. For examples of pensioners who previously received funds as paupers, see "Forsyth County Exhibit, 1893," *Western Sentinel* (Winston-Salem, NC), January 4, 1894, 5; Pension File for Emanuel Binkley (Forsyth County), NCDAH; Pension File for Moses Fulp (Forsyth County), NCDAH.

64. CSR for Henry B. Newby, 10th Battalion, North Carolina Heavy Artillery, NARA M270; "Davidson Confederate Veteran Passes Away," *Winston-Salem Journal*, April 9, 1928, 10; "Thomasville U.D.C. Feasts Old Soldiers," *Greensboro Daily News*, December 8, 1927, 2; "Thomasville Department," *Dispatch* (Lexington, NC), June 22, 1922, 7; Bunch, *Roster of the Courts-Martial in the Confederate States Armies*, 256.

65. "Thomasville Department," *Dispatch* (Lexington, NC), June 22, 1922, 7; "Thomasville Department," *Dispatch* (Lexington, NC), June 13, 1917, 8.

66. CSR for John Meredith, 7th North Carolina Infantry, NARA M270; "Register of Prisoners Ordered to Be Released, Compiled by the Office of the Commissary General of Prisoners, 1865," *Selected Records of the War Department Relating to Confederate Prisoners of War, 1861–1865*, NARA Microfilm M598, roll 8, 90–91; Pension File for John Meridith (Davidson County), NCDAH.

67. Pension File for Henry Grubb (Davidson County), NCDAH; Watford, *Civil War Roster of Davidson County, North Carolina*, 91; CSR for Henry Grubb, 15th North Carolina Infantry, NARA M270. Doug Brown at the NCDAH pointed out this phenomenon.

68. Pension File for Franklin Everhart, NCDAH; CSR for Franklin Everhart, 6th North Carolina Infantry, NARA M270; CSRs of the 48th North Carolina, NARA M270.

69. Pension File for Jacob Barley (Davidson County), NCDAH.

70. "Civil War Vet Dies at 100; 2 Left in State," *Asheville Citizen-Times*, April 2, 1949, 14. Pension File for Aaron Scales Cockerham (Surry County), NCDAH; Federal Census Collection; Death Certificate for Aaron Scales Cockerham (Surry County), April 1, 1949, *North Carolina, Death Certificates, 1909–1976*, accessed at https://www.ancestry.com/interactive/1121/S123_346-0406/1960040; Aaron S. Cockerham to Susan C. Thompson, March 24, 1883, Surry County Marriage Register (1853–1940), in North Carolina County Registers of Deeds, Microfilm, Record

Group 048, NCDAH, found in *North Carolina, Marriage Records, 1741–2011*, accessed at https://www.ancestry.com/interactive/60548/42091_343299-00016/2903148. His death certificate lists him as serving in the Civil War, but the birth year has been scratched off twice with the final entry being 1859; this may have been corrected years later.

71. On the politicization of pensions (especially federal), see Skopol, *Protecting Soldiers and Mothers*, 115–18, 120–30, 139, 148, 151.

72. McClurken, *Take Care of the Living*, 144.

73. Jeffrey Vogel argues that the very "meaning of the Civil War" was central to debates around Union pensions, and the same can be said about Confederate pensions. Vogel, "Redefining Reconciliation," 74. Pensions, issued by the state, also legitimated Confederates claims to have fought patriotically for their country, thus keeping them from being recalled as traitors.

74. Eli and Salisbury, "Patronage Politics and the Development of the Welfare State." Using a different approach, Eli and Salisbury also find ties between political patronage, pensions, and Democratic politics.

75. "The Political Record of General Carr and Mr. Simmons Contrasted," *Standard* (Concord, NC), November 1, 1900, 7; "Our Raleigh Letter," *Henderson Gold Leaf*, December 20, 1900, 2.

76. State Auditor to Z. T. Bynum, July 14, 1926, in Folder Forsyth, 1925–1926, Correspondence, Pension Bureau, State Auditor, NCDAH.

77. J. C. Pinnix to B. F. Dixon, January 31, 1903, in Folder Yadkin, 1886–1903, Correspondence, Pension Bureau, State Auditor, NCDAH; B. F. Dixon to J. C. Pinnix, February 4, 1903, in Folder Yadkin, 1886–1903, Correspondence, Pension Bureau, State Auditor, NCDAH. Smith's CSR does not indicate he was a deserter.

78. Frank T. Baldwin to B. F. Dixon, December 28, 1901, in Folder Forsyth, 1885–1914, Correspondence, Pension Bureau, State Auditor, NCDAH; John M. Greenfield to B. F. Dixon, January 1, 1902, in Folder Forsyth, 1885–1914, Correspondence, Pension Bureau, State Auditor, NCDAH.

79. A. N. Bulla to W. P. Wood, October 24, 1912, and Auditor to A. N. Bulla, October 24, 1912, both in Pension File for James M. Fields (Randolph County), NCDAH; Randolph County Pension Lists, 1909, 1912, NCDAH.

80. Clerk to B. F. Dixon, November 3, 1909, attached to the 1909 Randolph County Pension List, NCDAH.

81. "Soldier and Pensions," *Courier* (Asheboro, NC), September 29, 1910, 1; "About Particular Pensions," *Courier* (Asheboro, NC), October 27, 1910, 1; *Randolph Bulletin* (Asheboro, NC), October 6, 1910, 4; "J. M. Fields, Confederate Veteran," *Randolph Bulletin* (Asheboro, NC), November 3, 1910, 1; "The Confederate Soldier and Pensions," *Randolph Bulletin* (Asheboro, NC), October 6, 1910, 1.

82. Pension File for James M. Fields (Randolph County), NCDAH; CSR for J. Fields, 1st North Carolina Junior Reserves, NARA M270.

83. An Old Soldier, "An Old Soldier Has a Grievance," *Union Republican* (Winston-Salem, NC), January 9, 1902, 7. On the board member, see CSR for Augustin E. Shore, 33rd North Carolina infantry, NARA M270; "N.C. House of Representatives," *Daily Concord Standard*, November 17, 1892, 1. For another example of party membership being appealed to, see Pension File for C. R. Bradford (Yancey County), NCDAH.

84. An Old Soldier, "An Old Soldier Has a Grievance," *Union Republican* (Winston-Salem, NC), January 9, 1902, 7. In fairness, his admission to deserting actually did make him ineligible until 1903.

85. Pension File for Jacob H. Yokley (Davidson County), NCDAH. For a full accounting of the investigation, see letters in Folder Davidson, 1925–1927, Correspondence, Pension Bureau, State Auditor, NCDAH.

86. J. K. P. Thomas and J. A. Eller, affidavit, December 16, 1925, in Folder Davidson 1925–1927, Correspondence, Pension Bureau, State Auditor, NCDAH.

87. W. E. Conrad, V. S. Briles, and H. H. Hodge, "In Re Pension Allowance for Jacob H. Yokley," affidavit, December 15, 1925, in Folder Davidson 1925–1927, Correspondence, Pension Bureau, State Auditor, NCDAH.

88. For another individual whose marriage records indicate he was born in the mid-1850s and not the 1840s, see Pension File for C. R. Bradford (Yancey County), NCDAH.

89. E. C. Byerly et al. to Baxter Durham, "In Re Jacob H. Yokley Pension," December 30, 1925, in Folder Davidson 1925–1927, Correspondence, Pension Bureau, State Auditor, NCDAH.

90. For an example of a recusant conscript dressing as a woman, see Claim of Ransom Phipps (10716), Guilford County, NC, SCC Disallowed.

91. Pension File for Valentine Hill (Davidson County), NCDAH; CSR for Valentine Hill, 4th US Volunteers, NARA M1017; CSR for Valentine Hill, 21st North Carolina Infantry, NARA M270; CSR for Samuel Hill, 21st North Carolina Infantry, NARA M270; Pension File for Valentine Hill, 4th US Volunteers, NARA.

92. CSR for James J. Young, 14th North Carolina Infantry, NARA M270; CSR for James J. Young, 1st US Volunteers, NARA M1017; Pension File for James J. Young, 1st US Volunteers, NARA ; Pension File for James J. Young (Davidson County), NCDAH.

93. "Davidson County Pensioners," *Dispatch* (Lexington, NC), November 6, 1901, 1; Davidson County Pension Lists, NCDAH. Attempts at double-dipping may not have been as rare as one might suppose. Larkin H. Edwards had his North Carolina pension turned down because he was already receiving a federal pension. Pension File for Larkin H. Edwards (Johnston County), NCDAH. Under US pension laws, Edwards was eligible because he had lost his hearing from a fall off a horse *during his service* in the US Army. In 1895, he lost part of his pension due to his Confederate service. Pension File for Larkin H. Edwards, 4th US Volunteers, NARA. The law was further amended in 1902 and interpreted in 1903 to allow pensions for some galvanized Yankees. Bureau of Pensions, *Laws of the United States Governing the Granting of Army and Navy Pensions Together with the Regulations Relating Thereto*, 95–96.

94. "A Correct Position," *Farmer and Mechanic* (Raleigh, NC), August 26, 1902, 4; "Looking Backward," *Rutherfordton Tribune*, November 6, 1902, 2; "The Deserters' Pensions," *Wilmington Morning Star*, October 17, 1902, 2. For more on galvanized Yankees see Brown, *Galvanized Yankees*.

95. "Pension Rolls Show Fraud," *Augusta Chronicle*, November 2, 1906, 1; "$42,5000 Deficit in Pension Fund," *Atlanta Constitution*, June 30, 1907, 1; "Lindsay Makes Strong Appeal," *Atlanta Constitution*, March 21, 1909, 6; "Alleged Frauds on Pension Rolls," *Atlanta Constitution*, January 31, 1909, 2.

96. "Pension Fraudes," *Times and Democrat* (Orangeburg, SC), February 18, 1911, 1; A. W. Jones, "The Pension Matter Again," *Keowee Courier* (Pickens, SC),

March 1, 1911, 3; A. S. Salley Jr., "More about Pension Matter," *State* (Columbia, SC), March 23, 1911, 9.

97. "'Mosby's Men,'" *Tazewell (VA) Republican*, November 17, 1910, 3.

98. Claim of Samuel Yokeley (#10959), Davidson County, SCC Approved; see also Hartley, *Stoneman's Raid*, 207–8.

99. Because of the complexity of wartime loyalties, I often use the term *dissenter* where others might use *Unionist*. *Dissenter* encompasses anyone who resisted Confederate authority at any point during in the war. *Dissenter* as a term does not presume to define motivations.

100. Auman, "Neighbor against Neighbor," esp. 83, 243–44, 258–60, 380–81, 390, 395, 449, 460. See also *People's Press* (Salem, NC) and *Western Sentinel* (Winston, NC) during the war for newspaper accounts of the community. For an account of one Forsyth dissenter being shot, see "Your Affectionate Mother" to "My Dear Son," October 29, 1863, Jarrett-Puryear Family Papers, David M. Rubenstein Rare Book and Manuscript Library, Duke University. On the murder of five dissenters, see Williard, "Executions, Justice, and Reconciliation in North Carolina's Western Piedmont, 1865–1866."

101. On the SCC, see Lee, *Claiming the Union;* Myers, *Rebels against the Confederacy*.

102. "Unionist" became a negotiated postwar identity during Reconstruction. The debate over what made one a Unionist is easily seen in testimony and decisions of the SCC. My conception of identity is largely shaped by Malinda Lowery, with identity as "conversation between insiders and outsiders; these categories themselves are not fixed, and the labels represent heterogeneous populations." Lowery, *Lumbee Indians in the Jim Crow South*, xii.

103. On the formation of Unionist coalition, political organizing, and complexities of loyalty, see Domby, "'Loyal to the Core from the First to the Last'"; Domby, "War within the States," 229–53; Nash, *Reconstruction's Ragged Edge;* Fennessy, "Reconstruction of Memory and Loyalty in North Carolina."

104. Claim of Samuel Yokeley (#10959), Davidson County, SCC Approved; Confederate Citizens File for Samuel Yokeley, *Confederate Papers Relating to Citizen or Business Firms*, NARA Microfilm M346; *Slave Schedule, Eighth Census of the United States, 1860*, NARA Microfilm M653; Agricultural Schedule for Davidson County North Carolina, in *Agricultural and Manufacturing Census Records of Fifteen Southern States for the Years 1850, 1860, 1870 and 1880*.

105. "Whig Convention," *Weekly Raleigh Register*, April 20, 1859 [3]; Claim of Samuel Yokeley (#10959), Davidson County, SCC Approved.

106. Claim of Samuel Yokeley (#10959), Davidson County, SCC Approved; CSR for John Gilmer of 21st North Carolina, NARA M270.

107. Claim of Samuel Yokeley (#10959), Davidson County, SCC Approved.

108. Claim of Samuel Yokeley (#10959), Davidson County, SCC Approved.

109. For an example of those attacking Confederates, see the Dial family in Forsyth County. Auman, "Neighbor against Neighbor," 242–44, 407, 433; Domby, "War within the States," 34–38, 44–48, 218–19.

110. The Yokleys were not unique in their willingness to take up arms to protect family. In February 1865, another "band of brother deserters" released two prisoners from the stagecoach along the same road. The next month, a local paper reported that "it has become a common occurrence for the stagecoach, on the High

Point Road, to be attacked, and any deserter that might be on transportation turned loose." "Rescued," *People's Press* (Salem, NC), February 9, 1865, 1; "Deserters Shot," *Western Sentinel* (Winston, NC), March 2, 1865, 2.

111. Claim of Andrew Yokeley (#10729), Davidson County, SCC Disallowed; Claim of Samuel Yokeley (#10959), Davidson County, SCC Approved.

112. Claim of Samuel Yokeley (#10959), Davidson County, SCC Approved; Claim of Andrew Yokeley (#10729), Davidson County, SCC Disallowed; Claim of Jacob Charles (#10957), Forsyth County, SCC Disallowed; CSRs of D. P. Yokley, Joseph Yokeley, and Jefferson Yokeley of the 48th North Carolina, NARA M270; CSR for Andrew J. Yokley, 7th Missouri Cavalry (US), NARA M405; Claim of Jackson M. Jones (#2797), Davidson County, and Claim of Charles Long (#2707), Davidson County, both in SCC Approved. Some sources indicate that another relative, John Yokley, was also in hiding. Watford, *Civil War in North Carolina*, 116.

113. On definitions of *loyalty*, see Domby, "War within the States," 224–27.

114. For other examples of expanding the Lost Cause to include previously unwelcome whites, see Gardner, *Blood and Irony*, 139.

115. Vogel, "Redefining Reconciliation," 70. For more about federal pensions see Jordan, *Marching Home*.

116. On the memory of Unionism in North Carolina, see Myers, "Rebels against a Rebellion," 221–56; Paludan, *Victims;* Inscoe, *Race, War, and Remembrance in the Appalachian South;* Domby, "'Loyal to the Core from the First to the Last'"; Fennessy, "Re-construction of Memory and Loyalty in North Carolina"; Bynum, *Long Shadow of the Civil War;* Crow, "Thomas Settle Jr., Reconstruction, and the Memory of the Civil War"; McKinney, "Zebulon Vance and His Reconstruction of the Civil War in North Carolina"; Nash, "Immortal Vance."

117. Burgess L. Gallimore to "Ginerl in Command of the Military Department of N.C.," September 4, 1866, in File for Burgess L. Gallimore, *Union Provost Marshals' File of Papers Relating to Individual Civilians*, NARA M345.

118. "Died," *Dispatch* (Lexington, NC), May 23, 1921, 1; Pension File for Burgis L. Gallimore (Davidson County), NCDAH. For another example, see "Died," *Dispatch* (Lexington, NC), February 18, 1914, 1; Pension File for Ransom Essick (Davidson County), NCDAH; CSR for Ransom Essick, 49th North Carolina, NARA M270.

119. CSRs for Augustin Crouch and John C. Crouch, 48th North Carolina Infantry, NARA M270; Pension File for John C. Crouch (Davidson Country), NCDAH. Both were drafted in 1862 in a county draft held just before general conscription began. On the Crouch family, see Domby, "War within the States," 36, 211; Perry, *Civil War Courts-Martial of North Carolina Troops*, 96.

120. Domby, "War within the States," 36; "The Draft-Volunteering," *People's Press* (Salem, NC), March 14, 1862, 2; Kathy Merris Mills and Dan Stevenson, "Augustin Crouch," Find a Grave, April 27, 2007, http://findagrave.com/cgi-bin/fg.cgi/http%22//fg.cgi?page=gr&GRid=19113724. Exactly when the gravestone was placed is unknown.

121. Pension File for Andrew J. Yokley, 7th Missouri Cavalry (USA) NARA; CSR for Andrew J. Yokley, 7th Missouri Cavalry (USA), NARA M405.

122. Kestler, "Amos Yokley," 639. Genealogists seem to have missed Andrew's real story. As of August 2016, Ancestry.com had no family trees that accurately listed Andrew's death date. The one online hint that the Civil War may have played

a role in his death is a genealogical entry that asks, "Did [his son] Andrew die during the Civil War?" Kathy Merris Mills and Dan Stevenson, "Samuel David Yokeley," Find a Grave, 2007, http://www.findagrave.com/cgi-bin/fg.cgi?page=gr&GRid= 18063568. On James, see Stiles, *Jesse James*. In 1997, a family member recalled hearing about "Austin Yokeley" (even his name had been forgotten by that point), who "supposedly . . . was killed in a wheat field in Missouri by Jesse James." She noted that all her information came from "hear-say" and the family knew little about "Austin." Lauten, "Austin Yokeley." On how guerrillas became recalled as bandits, see Hulbert, *Ghosts of Guerrilla Memory*.

4. Playing the Faithful Slave

1. Parker, *Recollections of a Naval Officer*, 230–36; Olson, "The *Curlew*"; Olson, "Investigations of the CSS *Curlew*," 28–33; Simonds, "A Determination Worthy of a Better Cause."

2. Parker, *Recollections of a Naval Officer*, 230. Parker recalled Hunter excitedly trying to hail him as the *Curlew* turned toward shore but could not hear his words.

3. Mallison, *Civil War on the Outer Banks*, 75; Olson, "Investigations of the CSS *Curlew*," esp. 31–33.

4. *Official Records of the Union and Confederate Navies in the War of the Rebellion*, series I, vol. 6, 594.

5. On Williamson, see Milteer, *Hertford County North Carolina's Free People of Color and Their Descendants*, 53, 62, 70.

6. State Auditor to C. M. McKaughan, June 19, 1922, in Folder Forsyth, 1919–1922, Correspondence, Pension Bureau, State Auditor, NCDAH. One of these was to a woman who served as a nurse in Raleigh.

7. "Respected Old Negro Dies in Washington," *Albemarle Observer* (Edenton, NC), April 2, 1915, 4; Geo. H. Withy, "An Appeal in Behalf of a Worthy Colored Man Formerly Known throughout This Section, Pilot Eli Williamson," *Albemarle Observer* (Edenton, NC), October 16, 1914, 4.

8. Harper, "Black Loyalty under the Confederacy," 20.

9. Claim of Ely Williamson (#9429), Hertford County, SCC Approved.

10. Geo. H. Withy, "An Appeal in Behalf of a Worthy Colored Man Formerly Known throughout This Section, Pilot Eli Williamson," *Albemarle Observer* (Edenton, NC), October 16, 1914, 4.

11. "Eli Williamson Dies at the Age of Ninety," *Evening Star* (Washington, DC), March 14, 1915, 5; "Afro-American Cullings," *Bystander* (Des Moines, IA), April 3, 1915, 2; "Afro-American Cullings," *Uniontown (AL) News*, April 2, 1915, 6.

12. "Respected Old Negro Dies in Washington," *Albemarle Observer* (Edenton, NC), April 2, 1915, 4.

13. "Afro-American Cullings," *Kansas City Sun*, April 3, 1915, 2; Geo. H. Withy, "An Appeal in Behalf of a Worthy Colored Man Formerly Known throughout This Section, Pilot Eli Williamson," *Albemarle Observer* (Edenton, NC), October 16, 1914, 4; 1870 Census, Federal Census Collection. On the ship's history, see Olson, "The *Curlew*." Though a skilled pilot, Williamson was paid less than the white pilot, being paid the wage of a seaman instead. Evidence of Williamson's lower pay can be found at: Tho. T. Hunter, "Cash Account of the CSS *Curlew*," November 20, 1861, in NA Complements Rolls, Lists of Persons Serving in or with Vessels or

Stations," in "N-Personal," *Subject File of the Confederate States Navy, 1861–1865*, NARA Microfilm M1091.

14. "Obituary Notice of Eli Williamson," A. O. & Dorothy Steele Collection, John C. Smith University, accessed at https://cdm16324.contentdm.oclc.org/digital /collection/p15170coll8/id/441.

15. Janney, *Remembering the Civil War*, 210. See also Cook, *Civil War Memories*, 101. For excellent summaries on the truth behind these claims of black Confederates, see Martinez, *Confederate Slave Impressment in the Upper South*, 159–63; Levin, "Black Confederates Out of the Attic and into the Mainstream." On Confederate views of African Americans see Levine, *Confederate Emancipation;* Woodward, *Marching Masters*. For examples of claims that black Confederates were real, see Segars and Barrow, *Black Southerners in Confederate Armies;* Barrow, Segars, and Rosenburg, *Forgotten Confederates*, later republished as *Black Confederates*. For good updates about these debates, see Kevin M. Levin, "Searching for Black Confederates," *Civil War Memory*, August 31, 2010, http://cwmemory.com/book/black-confederate-resources.

16. Levin, "Black Confederates Out of the Attic and into the Mainstream," 628.

17. State Auditor to C. M. McKaughan, July 28, 1926, in Folder Forsyth, 1925–1926, Correspondence, Pension Bureau, State Auditor, NCDAH.

18. Baxter Durham to Sallie Wilson, February 29, 1932, in Folder Forsyth, 1931–1932, Correspondence, Pension Bureau, State Auditor, NCDAH. Tennessee had a similar policy, as seen in Pension File for Louis Nelson Pension, scanned copy accessed courtesy of Andy Hall, *Dead Confederates, A Civil War Era Blog*, https://deadconfederates.files.wordpress.com/2012/12/louisnelsonpensionfile.pdf. On Nelson, see Andy Hall, "Pension Records for Louis Napoleon Nelson," *Dead Confederates, A Civil War Era Blog*, December 14, 2012, https://deadconfederates.com/2012/12/16/pension-records-for-louis-napoleon-nelson.

19. "Pension Checks Sent Out by State Auditor," *Greensboro Daily News*, December 15, 1928, 18.

20. Martinez, *Confederate Slave Impressment in the Upper South*, 161.

21. "Three Who Wore the Gray in the Sixties Now Survive in County," *Daily Times-News* (Burlington, NC), December 15, 1937, 10.

22. Ratchford and Heise, "Confederate Pensions," 212.

23. "Pension Money for Veterans," *Evening Post* (Charleston, SC), April 13, 1928, 20. In earlier years, African Americans had received as little as seven dollars per year.

24. On mammies and domestic servants, see McElya, *Clinging to Mammy*, 208–30.

25. Pension File for Elisha Howard (Randolph County), NCDAH.

26. One neo-Confederate proponent has even claimed that this modification of forms was part of a "cover up." Who he believed committed the cover-up remains unknown. Williams, "Black Confederates."

27. Pension File for Thomas Farabee (Davidson County), NCDAH.

28. "Tennessee Will Pension Negro Confederates," *Broad Ax* (Chicago), June 18, 1921, 1.

29. "Negro Pensioners," *Morning Post* (Raleigh, NC), February, 4, 1904, 6. A year earlier a newspaper noted that "the negroes to whom pensions are given were, of course, servants of the Confederate soldiers and sailors." "More Pensioners," *Clarke*

County Times (Enterprise, MS), October 31, 1903, 2. See also "State Pensions to War Servants," *Daily Herald* (Biloxi, MS), February 9, 1904, 2.

30. Pension File for Elisha Howard (Randolph County), NCDAH; *Journal of the House of Representatives of the General Assembly of the State of North Carolina, Session 1925*, 525.

31. Green, "Protecting Confederate Soldiers and Mothers," 1079.

32. Green, *This Business of Relief*, 125.

33. Cash, *Mind of the South*, 127–28.

34. Hollandsworth, "Black Confederate Pensioners after the Civil War"; McElya, *Clinging to Mammy*.

35. McElya, "Commemorating the Color Line," 203–18.

36. "Negro Pensions Proposed," *Weekly Clarion-Ledger* (Jackson, MS), January 17, 1907, 4. The article acknowledged that the number of faithful slaves "was not large, and it is growing less day by day."

37. "Justice from the Past for the Negro 'Veteran,'" *Daily Times-News* (Burlington, NC), December 21, 1937, 4.

38. "Justice from the Past for the Negro 'Veteran,'" *Daily Times-News* (Burlington, NC), December 21, 1937, 4.

39. "Pensions Checks Sent Out by State Auditor," *Greensboro Daily News*, December 15, 1928, 18. Demographics from 1930 Census taken from Steven Manson, Jonathan Schroeder, David Van Riper, and Steven Ruggles, IPUMS National Historical Geographic Information System: Version 12.0 (database) (Minneapolis: University of Minnesota, 2017.)

40. "Pension Money for Veterans," *Evening Post* (Charleston, SC), April 13, 1928, 20.

41. Helsley, "Notes and News from the Archives," 184; Helsley, *South Carolina's African American Confederate Pensioners*, 7, 11.

42. "Negroes on Confederate Role," *Anglo-Saxon* (Rockingham, NC), April 11, 1901, 1.

43. *Journal of the House of Representatives of the General Assembly of the State of North Carolina, Session 1921*, 660. See also O. J. Peterson, "Mr. Petersan Pleads for Widow of Veteran," *News and Observer* (Raleigh, NC), February 28, 1921, 7. Exactly why the Confederate widow's pension was rejected is unclear, though there is evidence that her husband may have deserted. CSR for Marshall Pope, Captain Moseley's Company (Sampson Artillery), North Carolina, NARA M270.

44. "Camp Pulliam," *Greenville Daily News*, April 5, 1901, 8; "Protest Presented," *State* (Columbia, SC), March 23, 1901, 8.

45. Chas. M. Calhoun, "A Communication," *Greenwood Index*, April 18, 1901, 1.

46. *Greenwood Index*, April 18, 1901, 1.

47. Brock Barkley, "Governor McLean Determined to Get Pension for Negro Man," *Winston-Salem Journal*, May 31, 1926, 15.

48. Julian Carr, untitled speech given at Southern Pines, in Folder 34a, Addresses, undated, Carr Papers, SHC.

49. "Negro Slave Sees Owner Disinterred," *High Point Enterprise*, May 5, 1922, 8; CSR for Walter M. Bryson, 35th North Carolina Infantry, NARA M270.

50. *Journal of the House of Representatives of the General Assembly of the State of North Carolina, Session 1921*, 636, 660.

51. "Pension Slaves Who Served in the War," *Confederate Veteran* 21, no. 10 (October 1913): 481; Andy Hall, "How—and Why—Real Confederates Endorsed Slave Pensions," *Dead Confederates, A Civil War Era Blog*, June 13, 2012, https://deadconfederates .com/2012/06/13/how-real-confederates-endorsed-slave-pensions.

52. Baxter Durham to C. M. McKaughan, March 30, 1926, in Folder Forsyth, 1925–1926, Correspondence, Pension Bureau, State Auditor, NCDAH.

53. Baxter Durham to W. E. Church, August 29, 1934, in Folder Forsyth, 1933–1934, Correspondence, Pension Bureau, State Auditor, NCDAH.

54. Pension File for Ned Byrd (Union County), NCDAH.

55. "Three Negroes, Age Total of 249, Ask Confederate Pensions," *Greensboro Daily News*, July 12, 1928, 5.

56. "Pension Saves Old Slave from Pauper's Suffering," *Winston-Salem Journal*, January 16, 1926, 15. The subtitle, "Clyde Hoey Aids Shelby Negro to Get Reward for Faithfulness to White Masters during Days of the Civil War," made clear why the former slave was getting a pension.

57. "Negro Pension La wconstred [*sic*]," *Cherokee Times* (Gaffney, SC), April 9, 1923, 3.

58. Augustus, "Sarah Louise Augustus," 51.

59. Cofer, "Negro Folk Lore of the Piedmont," 172.

60. Moring, "Ex-Slave Story," 141.

61. Bob Thompson, "North Carolina Has Only 35 Confederate Veterans," *High Point Enterprise*, February 12, 1942, 15.

62. McElya, *Clinging to Mammy*, 11.

63. "Confederate Military Records," 53–54; "Confederate Pension Applications, U.C.V. Camp Records, & Reunions," 121; examining additional pensions reveals the same thing.

64. Pension File for Elisha Howard (Randolph County), NCDAH.

65. Pension File for Thomas Farabee (Davidson County), NCDAH; E. C. Byerly to Baxter Durham, September 4, 1931, in Folder Davidson, 1931–1932, Correspondence, Pension Bureau, State Auditor, NCDAH.

66. Pension File for Thomas Farabee (Davidson County), NCDAH.

67. Pension File for John W. Venable (Forsyth County), NCDAH; Pension File for Agrippe Bizzell (Sampson County), NCDAH. Though often conflated, census records and probate records from 1862 confirm that a John T. Venable in the CSRs is not the John W. Venable appearing in the pension records. The company and enlistment dates are wrong, and John T. died in 1861, while John W. survived until 1920. Federal Census Collection; Probate File for John T. Venable, Estate Records, Stokes County, *North Carolina, Wills and Probate Records, 1665–1998*, NCDAH, accessed at https://www.ancestry.com/interactive/9061/007641324_01608; Record of Wills, book 8, 217, Forsyth County, *North Carolina, Wills and Probate Records, 1665–1998*, NCDAH accessed at https://www.ancestry.com/interactive/9061/004779965 _00426. CSR for John T. Venable, 21st North Carolina Infantry, NARA M270. Census records also confirm the identity of John Sawyer, who signed the affidavit. For more on this conflation see Kevin M. Levin, "Was John Venable a Black Confederate Soldier?," *Civil War Memory*, May 18, 2009, updated May 20, 2009, http://cwmemory.com/2009/05/18/was-john-venable-a-black-confederate/.

68. Baxter Durham to W. E. Church, August 29, 1934, in Folder Forsyth, 1933–1934, Correspondence, Pension Bureau, State Auditor, NCDAH.

69. For another example, see Pension File for Wyatt Cunningham (Union County), NCDAH.

70. These quotes were used by white advocates for Class B pensioners. C. M. McKaughan to Baxter Durham, March 19, 1826, in Folder Forsyth 1925–1926, Correspondence, Pension Bureau, State Auditor, NCDAH; Pension File for Thomas Farabee (Davidson County), NCDAH.

71. Pension File for Adam Moore (Lincoln County), NCDAH.

72. Cash, *Mind of the South*, 127–28.

73. Burke Davis, "Mrs. Norris Guardian of Confederate Pension Rolls," *Greensboro Daily News*, November 18, 1951, feature section, 1; Pension File for Alfred Blackburn (Yadkin County), NCDAH.

74. Hoar, *South's Last Boys in Gray*, 461–62; Tom Layton, "Guess Where NC's Last Rebel Came From!," *Stoneman Gazette*, April 1, 2015, http://stonemangazette.blogspot.com/2015/04/guess-where-ncs-last-rebel-was-born.html; Tom Layton, "First in War, Last in Peace, and Still Sipping Taxes," *Stoneman Gazette*, April 14, 2016, http://stonemangazette.blogspot.com/2016/04/first-in-war-last-in-peace-and-still.html.

75. Frances H. Casstevens, "One of Yadin County's Most Unusual Citizens: Alfred (Uncle Teen) Blackburn," *Yadkin County Historical and Genealogical Society Journal* 9, no. 1 (March 1990): 23; "Teen Blackburn," *Winston-Salem Journal*, November 1, 1998, B2; "109-Year-Old Ex-Slave Dies," *Asheville Citizen-Times*, December 17, 1951, 5.

76. Pension File for Alfred Blackburn (Yadkin County), NCDAH; Federal Census Collection. The 1870 Census places Alfred, age ten, as living with his old master's family and with his brother Wiley, who was four years older. Unless a thirty-something-year-old was mistaken for a fourteen-year-old and a twenty-eight-year-old was mistaken for a ten-year-old, Wiley and Alfred both lied to get pensions. It seems unlikely that the census taker in 1870 was reporting grown men as young boys. It is worth noting that in his pension record and in many stories, Alfred presented himself as a "husky, stalwart youth" capable of doing a day's labor while still in his teens, so we would expect to find him reported as older than he actually was in 1870, not younger.

77. His mother and brothers also appear in the 1860 Census. See *Slave Schedule, Eighth Census of the United States, 1860*, NARA Microfilm M653.

78. "Teen Blackburn Dead at 109," *Statesville Daily Record*, December 17, 1951, [24]. He was reportedly nearly twenty by 1861, according to J. C. Brown, "Magnolia Trees at Hamptonville and Uncle Teen Grew Up Together," *Greensboro Daily News*, December 3, 1950, Women's Section, 16.

79. Tom Layton, "Guess Where NC's Last Rebel Came From!," *Stoneman Gazette*, April 1, 2015, http://stonemangazette.blogspot.com/2015/04/guess-where-ncs-last-rebel-was-born.html.

80. "Teen Blackburn," *Winston-Salem Journal*, November 1, 1998, B2; "109-Year-Old Ex-Slave Dies," *Asheville Citizen-Times*, December 17, 1951, 5.

81. Pension File for Alfred Blackburn (Yadkin County), NCDAH; Pension File for John A. Hampton (Yadkin County), NCDAH; Death Certificate for C. Carolina Hampton (Yadkin County), August 3, 1929, *North Carolina, Death Certificates, 1909–1976*, accessed at https://www.ancestry.com/interactive/1121/S123_238-0631; Marriage License for John A. Hampton and Cynthia Carolina Brown, November 21, 1872

(Yadkin County), *North Carolina, Marriage Records, 1741–2011,* accessed at https://www.ancestry.com/interactive/60548/42091_343663-00424. Census records and her headstone further confirm she lied. Federal Census Collection; "Cynthia Caroline Brown Hampton," Find a Grave, https://www.findagrave.com/memorial/76186076. Whether she knew Blackburn was lying remains unknown. Indeed, it is unclear if they even knew each other before the war ended, as census records indicate they lived in different counties in 1860. The information she provided may have been given to her secondhand and she repeated it as firsthand knowledge. She clearly knew her marriage date, as it is reported accurately in Blackburn's pension file but not her own. On how laws regarding widow eligibility evolved see Jones and Kenzer, "Confederate Pensions."

82. Pension File for Wiley Blackburn (Iredell County), NCDAH.

83. "Death of Miss Sallie Bostick Blackburn," *Statesville Record and Landmark,* January 26, 1900, 3; *Statesville Record and Landmark,* July 31, 1906, 3.

84. "Wiley Explains What's the Matter with the Weather," *Statesville Record and Landmark,* September 9, 1932, 1. Numerous other weather articles can be found in the *Statesville Record and Landmark* and other local papers from 1922 to 1933.

85. "What Does Zit Mean," *Statesville Sentinel,* July 7, 1917, 7.

86. Ralph Sloan, "Statesville—Then and Now," *Statesville Record and Landmark,* November 24, 1967, 7-B. For another funny story where the joke was on Wiley, see "Wiley Blackburn Is to Beard the Wild Santer," *Statesville Record and Landmark,* August 17, 1931, 5.

87. "We Have the Hardware," *Statesville Record and Landmark,* October 18, 1926, 3.

88. *Statesville Record and Landmark,* June 20, 1935, 6.

89. For another attempt at changing age, see Pension File for Sidney Hayes (Durham County), NCDAH.

90. Pension File for Mose Fraser (Union County), NCDAH.

91. CSR for E. L. Frasier, 12th South Carolina Infantry, NARA M267; CSR for E. L. Frasier, 9th South Carolina Infantry, NARA M267. Captain John D. Wiley was never in the 12th South Carolina, but rather in the 9th (later part of the 5th) South Carolina. Wartime records show that in 1861, the sixteen-year-old Elias Frasier initially enlisted in John Wylie's Lancaster Greys, but his name was then removed from the muster role. Instead, he ended up serving in the 12th South Carolina. None of these units fought at the Battle of the Crater.

92. Death Certificate for Moses Fraizer (Union County), December 19, 1934, *North Carolina, Death Certificates, 1909–1976,* accessed at https://www.ancestry.com/interactive/1121/S123_1123-2514; Federal Census Collection.

93. Pension File for Lewis McGill (Union County), NCDAH.

94. Pension File for James Deal (Macon County), NCDAH. Based on extremely consistent census records it appears that in reality, he was born around 1854, not 1850. Federal Census Collection. Deal may have been lying about his service as well, as no record of his supposed master, Colonel Clinton Ugee, has been found.

95. Though marriage records note he was born in 1854, Steve Bryson's widow claimed her late husband accompanied "his master in South Carolina" off to war. Pension File for Steve Bryson (Swain County), NCDAH; Stephen Bryson and Jane Dehart, October 27, 1880, Marriage Register (1871–1958), Swain County, North Carolina County Registers of Deeds, Microfilm, Record Group 048, NCDAH, accessed

in *North Carolina, Marriage Records, 1741–2011,* accessed at https://www.ancestry .com/interactive/60548/42091_343304-00032.

96. Wilcox, "Windsor's Crossroads."

97. Glatthaar, *Forged in Battle,* x; Manning, *Troubled Refuge,* 34; Hollandsworth, "Black Confederate Pensioners after the Civil War." Some estimates put the number of fleeing slaves at closer to a million. Silkenat, *Driven from Home,* 8.

98. Browning, "Visions of Freedom and Civilization Opening before Them," 85; Williard, "North Carolina in the Civil War."

99. On emancipation celebrations, see Clark, *Defining Moments.*

100. Gannon, "Sites of Memory, Sites of Glory," 166–68; see also Domby, "Captives of Memory," 269–70; Janney, *Remembering the Civil War,* 206–11. For more on uniting whites nationally along racial lines see Blum, *Reforging the White Republic.*

101. "Aycock in Iredell," *Henderson Gold Leaf,* July 12, 1900, 1.

102. Julian Carr, "Chapel Hill, May 11, 1902," in Folder 23, Addresses, 1903–1905, Carr Papers, SHC. Carr shared this speech with other Confederate speakers. "Portion of Macon Speech Used by Asheley Horne," in Folder 35b, Addresses, undated, Carr Papers, SHC.

103. "Portion of Macon Speech Used by Asheley Horne," in Folder 35b, Addresses, undated, Carr Papers, SHC. For more on manhood and obscuring a memory of black heroics see Levin, *Remembering the Battle of the Crater,* esp. 2–3, 70–75, 84–85, 101–5.

104. Du Bois, *Black Reconstruction,* 104–14.

105. Du Bois, *Black Reconstruction,* 55, 66.

106. Gannon, "Sites of Memory, Sites of Glory," 166–68; Gannon, *Won Cause,* 193.

107. "An Ex-Slave Would Organize the Ex-Slaves to Demand Pensions," *St. Louis Post-Dispatch,* December 11, 1898, [39].

108. "Hutchinson Notes," *National Reflector* (Wichita, KS), July 18, 1896, 3.

109. Vaughan, *Vaughan's "Freedmen's Pension Bill,"* vii, 14–15, 21, 43, and copyright page; Araujo, *Reparations for Slavery and the Slave Trade,* 95–99; Kendi, *Stamped from the Beginning,* 270.

110. Josephine Ghant-Carlisle, "Pensions for Ex-Slaves!," *Freeman* (Indianapolis, IN), June 6, 1896, 7.

111. "Ex Slave Pension Bill," *Recorder* (Indianapolis, IN), March 25, 1899, 2–3.

112. "North State News," *Daily Free Press* (Kinston, NC), May 20, 1903, 1; "An Infamous Outrage," *Cleveland Gazette,* February 26, 1898, 2; "Plan for Swindling Negros," *New Bern Weekly Journal,* November 3, 1905, 1. There is some question as to whether the government overprosecuted in their efforts to stop fraud. Araujo, *Reparations for Slavery and the Slave Trade,* 102–5.

113. Pension File for Isaac High (Wake County), NCDAH. High, who did not consider himself a member of any Confederate unit, left the space for his unit blank.

114. Johnston and Wise, "Commemorating Faithful Slaves, Mammies, and Black Confederates"; see also Janney, *Remembering the Civil War,* 8; McElya, "Commemorating the Color Line," 203–18.

115. "Two Unique Monuments," *Hutchinson (KS) News,* August 3, 1896, 4; J. H. Faulkner, "50 Dollars Reward," *Evening Bulletin* (Charlotte, NC), October 10, 1863, 3. See also Janney, *Remembering the Civil War,* 208–10.

116. "A Southern Patriot," *Burlington (VT) Weekly Free Press,* November 26, 1891, 14. See also Domby, "Captives of Memory," 269–70. For this argument being used

during debates over women's suffrage, see Rollo S. Minn, "Wants Women to Work for Ballot," *Trenton (NJ) Evening Times*, November 4, 1909, 10.

117. John R. Blackmon, "Confederates Honor Black History," *Columbian-Progress* (Columbia, MS), February 26, 1998, 3A.

118. The best such study is Glatthaar, *General Lee's Army*, which failed to discover a single black Confederate in a large statistical sample. See also Levine, "In Search of a Useable Past," 201–2.

119. John R. Blackmon, "Confederates Honor Black History," *Columbian-Progress* (Columbia, MS), February 26, 1998, 3A.

120. Levine, *Confederate Emancipation*, 40–59. See also Woodward, *Marching Masters*, 155–79.

121. "Exciting and Eventful Times!," *Semi-Weekly Standard* (Raleigh, NC), February 3, 1865, 2. See also Levine, *Confederate Emancipation*, 55.

122. Levine, *Confederate Emancipation*, 6; Harper, "Black Loyalty under the Confederacy," 26. For additional works beyond Levine on the debates around authorizing the enlistment of troops, see Martinez, *Confederate Slave Impressment in the Upper South*, 132–56; McCurry, *Confederate Reckoning*, 324–57.

123. Mrs. H. J. Burkhardt, "Judah P. Benjamin: A Statement of the Confederate States," *Confederate Veteran* 37, no. 7 (July 1931): 254.

124. Janney, *Remembering the Civil War*, 210.

125. J. C. Brown, "Magnolia Trees at Hamptonville and Uncle Teen Grew Up Together," *Greensboro Daily News*, December 3, 1950, Women's Section, 16.

126. "Only Two Vets in N.C., Memorial Day," *Robesonian* (Lumberton, NC), May 10, 1949, 1.

127. "Rites are Planned for Ex-Slave, 109," *Greensboro Daily News*, December 18, 1951, section 2, 4; Burke Davis, "Mrs. Norris Guardian of Confederate Pension Rolls," *Greensboro Daily News*, November 18, 1951, feature section, 1; Hoar, *South's Last Boys in Gray*, 461–62.

128. Kevin M. Levin, "Searching for Black Confederate Soldiers: The Civil War's Most Persistent Myth," *Civil War Memory*, http://cwmemory.com/searching-for-black-confederate-soldiers-the-civil-wars-most-persistent-myth; Levin, "Black Confederates Out of the Attic and into the Mainstream," 627–36. For an example of this see Roger K. Broxton, "Abraham Lincoln Said War Was over Taxes, Not Slavery," AL.Com, June 26, 2015, http://www.al.com/opinion/index.ssf/2015/06/war-over-slavery_rhetoric_is_i.html.

129. Kelly, Segars, and Rosenburg, *Black Confederates*, 26.

130. Janney, *Remembering the Civil War*, 210. See also Cook, *Civil War Memories*, 101.

131. McElya *Clinging to Mammy*, 3.

132. Lisa Mascaro, "In Alabama, the Heart of Trump Country, Many Think He's Backing the Wrong Candidate in Senate Race," *Los Angeles Times*, September 21, 2017.

133. An alternative reading is that Moore's reference to "our families" included only white families.

134. On the slave trade, family separation, and the horrors of slavery, see Williams, *Help Me to Find My People*; Johnson, *Soul by Soul*; Genovese, *Roll, Jordan, Roll*; Rothman, *Slave Country*. For examples of primary sources, see "Valuable Family Servant at Auction," *Times-Picayune* (New Orleans), March 15, 1856, 5; Micajah

Ricks, "$20 Reward," *Weekly Standard* (Raleigh, NC), July 18, 1838, 3; Jas. P. Moore, "State of North Carolina," *Wilmington Journal*, August 16, 1860, 1.

135. Scott Clement and Emily Guskin, "Exit Poll Results: How Different Groups Voted in Alabama," *Washington Post*, December 13, 2017.

136. Death Certificate for Wiley Blackburn (Iredell County), April 25, 1936, *North Carolina, Death Certificates, 1909–1976*, accessed at http://search.ancestry.com/cgi -bin/sse.dll?indiv=1&db=NCdeathCerts&h=1799396.

5. The Soldiers Who Weren't

1. "The Monument Unveiled," *Monroe Journal*, July 5, 1910, 1.

2. Adam Bell, "Monroe Ceremony Honors Slaves Who Served in Confederate Army," *Charlotte Observer*, December 8, 2012; UCPMF, "You are Invited to Join Us."

3. [Thomas Bickett], "The Fine Speech of Attorney General Bickett," *Monroe Journal*, July 19, 1910, 3, 7; "The Monument Unveiled," *Monroe Journal*, July 5, 1910, 1. Bickett's speech would easily have fit in the first two chapters of this book.

4. Adam Bell, "Monroe Ceremony Honors Slaves Who Served in Confederate Army," *Charlotte Observer*, December 8, 2012. One of the individuals honored was a free person of color, while the others were enslaved. For more on this monument, see "Memorial for Confederate Pensioners of Color, Monroe," Commemorative Landscapes of North Carolina, http://docsouth.unc.edu/commland/monument /353; Martinez, "Jaime Amanda Martinez"; Kevin M. Levin, "Black North Carolinians Plan to Erect Faithful Slave Marker," *Civil War Memory*, May 15, 2010, http:// cwmemory.com/2010/05/15/black-north-carolinians-plan-to-erect-faithful-slave -monument.

5. On academic historians rarely studying the topic, see Madsen-Brooks, "'I Nevertheless Am a Historian,'" esp. 56. There are some key exceptions, and some historians have studied it. See, for example, Levine, *Confederate Emancipation;* Levine, "In Search of a Useable Past"; Levin, "Black Confederates Out of the Attic and into the Mainstream," 627–36; Martinez, *Confederate Slave Impressment in the Upper South*, esp. 159–64, which represent some of the few peer-reviewed works discussing the creation of Black Confederates among neo-Confederates. Kevin M. Levin's blog *Civil War Memory* and Andy Hall's *Dead Confederates, A Civil War Era Blog* both routinely post on this topic. Brooks Simpson's blog *Crossroads*, https://cwcrossroads .wordpress.com, has occasionally posted about Black Confederates and argues that the best response is to properly teach African American history.

6. State of North Carolina, *Public Laws and Resolutions Passed by the General Assembly at Its Session of 1921*, 430–31.

7. *Journal of the House of Representatives of the General Assembly of the State of North Carolina, Session 1921*, 660. His wife applied for a pension in 1929 but never received payment. Pension File for George Mills (Henderson County), NCDAH.

8. State of North Carolina, *Public Laws and Resolutions Passed by the General Assembly at Its Session of 1921*, 430–31.

9. "George Mills Reverently Reviews Casket Buried in Methodist Cemetery," *News of Henderson County* (Hendersonville, NC), May 9, 1922, 3; "Civil War Hero's Grave Is Moved," *Western North Carolina Times* (Hendersonville, NC), April 28, 1922, 1.

10. "Veterans of Confederacy Enjoy Feast," *News of Henderson County* (Hendersonville, NC), June 7, 1922, 1; "Veterans Annual Dinner," *Hendersonville Visitor*, June

5, 1917, 1; "Hendersonville Is Ready for the Day," *Asheville Citizen-Times*, June 5, 1917, 2; Davis, *Black Heritage of Western North Carolina*, 15; FitzSimons, *From the Banks of the Oklawaha*, 115–19.

11. State of North Carolina, *Public Laws and Resolutions Passed by the General Assembly at Its Session of 1921*, 430–31; "Negro Slave Sees Owner Disinterred," *High Point Enterprise*, May 5, 1922, 8; Jeannette C. St. Amand, "UDC Chapters in North Carolina Observe Confederate Memorial Day," *High Point Enterprise*, May 22, 1960, 5b.

12. Sadie Smathers Patton, "Tribute to Be Paid George Mills, Faithful to Master and the South," *Asheville Citizen-Times*, May 8, 1960, D5.

13. John Boyle, "Ceremony to Honor Black Confederate," *Asheville Citizen-Times*, May 30, 1999, C1, C9.

14. "Camp Changes Name to Honor Soldier," BlueRidgeNow.com, May 17, 2006, http://www.blueridgenow.com/news/20060517/camp-changes-name-to-honor-soldier.

15. John Boyle, "Ceremony to Honor Black Confederate," *Asheville Citizen-Times*, May 30, 1999, C1, C9.

16. Wrobel, "Civil War Was NOT over Slavery"; see also King, "10 Causes of the War between the States."

17. Kevin M. Levin, "Searching for Black Confederate Soldiers: The Civil War's Most Persistent Myth," *Civil War Memory*, http://cwmemory.com/searching-for-black-confederate-soldiers-the-civil-wars-most-persistent-myth; Levin, "Ngram Tracks Black Confederates and Black Confederates," *Civil War Memory*, December 20, 2010, http://cwmemory.com/2010/12/20/ngram-tracks-black-confederates-and-black-confederate; Levin, "Black Confederates Didn't Exist in 1914," *Civil War Memory*, October 25, 2010, http://cwmemory.com/2010/10/25/black-confederates-didnt-exist-in-1914.

18. Kevin M. Levin, "John Stauffer Goes Looking for Black Confederates and Comes Up Empty . . . Again," *Civil War Memory*, January 20, 2015, http://cwmemory.com/2015/01/20/john-stauffer-goes-looking-for-black-confederates-and-comes-up-empty-again.

19. "Confederate Military Records," 53.

20. CSRs for Jackson Evans and John W. Cox, 3rd North Carolina Infantry, NARA M270.

21. CSR for John W. Cox, 3rd North Carolina Infantry, NARA M270.

22. Neuse Monthly Meeting, "Men's Minutes, 1841–1875," p. 118, 7th Day of 3rd Month 1863, Wayne County, NC, North Carolina Yearly Meeting Archives, Friends Historical Collection, Guilford College, accessed via U.S., Quaker Meeting Records, 1681–1935, accessed at https://www.ancestry.com/interactive/2189/40642_290989-00075; CSR for John W. Cox, 3rd North Carolina Infantry, NARA M270.

23. Dixon, "To Laugh in One Hand and Cry in the Other," 14, 17; "Returned," *Rome (GA) Tri-Weekly Courier*, August 6, 1861, 3; Domby, "War within the States," 198; "Impressing Free Negroes," *Rome (GA) Tri-Weekly Courier*, February 11, 1864, 2; Russ McClanahan, "Museum Wants Civil War Stories of Black Romans," *Rome (GA) News-Tribune*, June 19, 2010; Battey, *History of Rome and Floyd County*, 142; "Old 'Black Men in the Confederate Army': What the Newspapers Said—1861–1865."

24. "Confederate Military Records," 53; CSRs of William Rudd, William Lynch, Willis Dove, and William H. Dove, 5th North Carolina Cavalry, NARA M270.

Willis is not listed as a free negro in the records but appears as a "Mulatto" in the census.

25. Andy Hall, "Were Cooks Enlisted in the Confederate Army?," *Dead Confederates, A Civil War Era Blog,* July 17, 2011, https://deadconfederates.com/2011/07/17/were-cooks-enlisted-in-the-confederate-army; Andy Hall, "Soldiers All," *Dead Confederates, A Civil War Era Blog,* July 6, 2011, https://deadconfederates.com/2011/07/06/everyones-a-soldier. See CSR for Robert Richardson, 56th North Carolina Infantry, NARA M270; CSRs for John Stewart, Alexander Cobb, Marl Morgan, Coswell Henton, 31st North Carolina Infantry, NARA M270.

26. CSR for Jesse Lynch, 35th USCT, NARA M1992; CSR for Jesse Lynch, 5th North Carolina Cavalry, NARA M270. One company in the 32nd North Carolina had five servants accompanying eighty-two soldiers in it, according to a scrap of paper in CSR for Edward C. Brabble, 32nd North Carolina Infantry, NARA, M270. I was unable to find any servants in the CSRs for that unit.

27. Pension File for Sam Griffin (Wake County), NCDAH

28. Pension File for Brinkley Bynum (Orange County), NCDAH.

29. "Confederate Military Records," 53; "Brinkley Bynum," Find a Grave, August 26, 2009, https://www.findagrave.com/cgi-bin/fg.cgi?page=gr&GRid=41192956. Family trees on Ancestry.com similarly have this issue. "Brinkley Bynum," Smith Family Tree, https://www.ancestry.com/family-tree/person/tree/23622072/person/1493235528/facts.

30. Federal Census Collection.

31. CSR for Brinkley Bynum, 1st North Carolina Infantry, NARA M270.

32. "Sergeant James Washington Memorial Award"; Williams, "Black Confederates." The same author claims elsewhere that Washington served in the 35th Cavalry. Williams, "On Black Confederates." For the unit history see Spencer, *Terrell's Texas Cavalry.* The fabrication even made it into Sutherland, *African Americans at War,* 389, which only cites Spencer despite Spencer's never mentioning Washington. No record is found for either man in the CSRs, including CSRs for 37th Cavalry (Terrell's Regiment, 34th Cavalry), NARA M323.

33. Hoar, "Aged Body Servants among the Last Survivors of the Confederate Army," 71.

34. Hoar, "Aged Body Servants among the Last Survivors of the Confederate Army," 71, 73.

35. Singleton, *Recollections of My Slavery Days,* 2. Some scholars believe he may have been mistaken about his parentage. Charon and Cecelski, introduction, 12–19. It was common for enslaved people to be related to their enslavers.

36. Singleton, *Recollections of My Slavery Days,* 7–9.

37. Hoar, "Aged Body Servants among the Last Survivors of the Confederate Army," 71.

38. Singleton, *Recollections of My Slavery Days,* 9, 1, 10.

39. Hoar, "Aged Body Servants among the Last Survivors of the Confederate Army," 73; "Only Negro Commissioned Civil War Vet Dies at 103," *Plaindealer* (Kansas City, KS), September 16, 1938, 1; Pension File for Henry Singleton, 35th USCT (1st North Carolina Colored), NARA M1992.

40. Assorted runaway advertisements, *Richmond Dispatch,* January 21, 1862, 4. Scott Nesbit's talk, "Mapping Journeys Out of Wartime Slavery," at the Society For Civil War History Conference, Chattanooga, TN, June 3, 2016, inspired me to look

at escaped slave advertisements to find them running to Union lines. For references to cooks escaping, see University of Richmond, Digital Scholarship Lab, "Visualizing Emancipation."

41. McCurry, *Confederate Reckoning*, 242, 244–50, 267–68, 279–81, 289, 356; Camp, *Closer to Freedom*, 9–11, 117–38; see also Silkenat, *Driven from Home;* Manning, *Troubled Refuge;* Martinez, *Confederate Slave Impressment in the Upper South.*

42. Handler and Tuite, "Retouching History."

43. Martinez, "Jaime Amanda Martinez"; USCT soldiers found via search of U.S., Colored Troops Military Service Records, 1863–1865, NARA, on Ancestry.com. Eight men list Union County as their birthplace, and seven list Monroe or Monroe County, NC. Because of record-keeping norms and slave illiteracy, it is likely that there were more from Union County.

44. Pam Evans, "Memorial Dedication for Confederate Pensioners of Color," *Times Examiner* (Greenville, SC), December 19, 2012.

45. McElya, *Clinging to Mammy,* 6.

46. Blight, *Race and Reunion,* 89.

47. Gordon, *Broken Regiment,* 228.

48. Woodward, *Marching Masters.*

49. Urwin, "Introduction," 13.

50. Jordan and Thomas, "Massacre at Plymouth," 153–202; Gordon, *Broken Regiment,* 141–42, 144, 147. Some white southerners in the US Army, known as "Buffaloes," were also executed at Plymouth. Browning, "'Little Souled Mercenaries'?"

51. Frisby, "Remember Fort Pillow"; see also Urwin, *Black Flag over Dixie;* Levin, *Remembering the Battle of the Crater.*

52. Jordan and Thomas, "Massacre at Plymouth," 166; Domby, "Captives of Memory," 258.

53. *State v. Mann,* quoted in Gikandi, *Slavery and the Culture of Taste,* 225.

54. "Gen. Ransom's Expedition," *Evening Bulletin* (Charlotte, NC), March 18, 1864, 1; Jordan and Thomas, "Massacre at Plymouth," 167.

55. Jordan and Thomas, "Massacre at Plymouth," 153–54.

56. Cimprich, *Fort Pillow,* 109–12.

57. Urwin, "Introduction," 2. See also Levin, *Remembering the Battle of the Crater,* for more on the memory of atrocity.

58. Allen Guelzo, "Honor and Compromise, and Getting History Right," *American Interest,* November 6, 2017, https://www.the-american-interest.com/2017/11/06/honor-compromise-history-kelly; Brasher, "Do We Really Have to Keep Doing This?"; Paradis, *African Americans and the Gettysburg Campaign,* 39; Green, "Persistence of Memory"; Giesberg, *Keystone State in Crisis,* 48–50.

59. [Ladnier], "General Nathan Bedford Forrest—the First True Civil Rights Leader"; Ladnier, "Lt. Gen. Nathan Bedford Forrest: An Essay." On racial massacres, see Urwin, *Black Flag over Dixie;* Woodward, *Marching Masters,* 130–54; Fellman, *In the Name of God and Country,* 66–73; Fellman, *Views from the Dark Side of American History,* 69–70, 144.

60. Domby, "Captives of Memory," 258; Frisby, "Remember Fort Pillow," 121; Barr, "Loathsome Diseases and Principles," 105–9. On POWs and memory, see Gray, *Crossing the Deadlines;* Cloyd, *Haunted by Atrocity;* Riotto, "Beyond 'the Scrawl'd, Worn Slips of Paper'"; Horwitz, *Confederates in the Attic,* 318–31; Jordan, *Marching Home,* esp. 131–51.

61. For an example, see "A Pleasant Reunion," *Semi-Weekly Messenger* (Wilmington, NC), October 26, 1897, 7. The quote is inscribed on a monument in Montezuma, Georgia, ten miles from Andersonville.

62. Quoted in Cimprich, *Fort Pillow*, 119.

63. "Frightfulness Never a Policy during War between the States," *Asheville Weekly Citizen*, October 6, 1915, 5.

64. [Ladnier], "General Nathan Bedford Forrest—the First True Civil Rights Leader." For a similar claim about Lee, see Hall, "Fantasizing Lee as a Civil Rights Pioneer."

65. Murray and Hsieh, *Savage War*, 241, 247, 463.

66. Murray and Hsieh, *Savage War*, 10–11, 101, 523–24, 535–38. Emancipation is also largely missing.

67. Kevin Sieff, "Virginia 4th-Grade Textbook Criticized over Claims on Black Confederate Soldiers," *Washington Post*, October 20, 2010.

68. Ben Terris, "Scholars Nostalgic for the Old South Study the Virtues of Secession, Quietly," *Chronicle of Higher Education*, December 6, 2009; Kennedy and Kennedy, *South Was Right!*, 92.

69. Kennedy and Kennedy, *South Was Right!*, 84, 94.

70. Madsen-Brooks, "I Nevertheless Am a Historian," 51.

71. Hoover Adams, "Carlyle Raps High Court," *Robesonian* (Lumberton, NC), May 10, 1955, 5.

72. R. S. Meroney, "Principle of States Rights Will Reassert Itself in Years to Come," *Asheville Citizen-Times*, July 21, 1957, D3. For Civil War memory and the civil rights movement, see Cook, *Troubled Commemorations*, esp. 51–57, 76, 194–97, 202–3, 209–10; Blight, *American Oracle*; Gannon, *Americans Remember Their Civil War*, 61–84.

73. "Thurmond Scores Bill to Let U.S. Aid Vets of Gray," *Asheville Citizen*, February 4, 1954, 7.

74. Rowland Nethaway, "Don't Adopt All Strom's Lessons," *Rocky Mount (NC) Telegram*, August 12, 2004, 4; Chuck Mobley, "African American Savannah Woman Takes Her Place among United Daughters of the Confederacy," *Savannah Morning News*, February 22, 2014.

75. Lyndon Baines Johnson, "Johnson's Speech," *Philadelphia Inquirer*, March 16, 1965, 1, 22. Also accessible at "Lyndon B. Johnson: Voting Rights Act Address," *Great American Documents*, https://www.greatamericandocuments.com/speeches/lbj-voting-rights; "Johnson Signs Voting Rights Bill into Law," *High Point Enterprise*, August 6, 1965, 1; "Justice Department Ready to Enforce Negro Voting Rights," *Alexandria (IN) Times Tribune*, August 6, 1955, 1; "Johnson to Sign Voting Bill Today," *Asheville Citizen*, August 6, 1965, 21; Berman, *Give Us the Ballot*, 36–38.

76. Moyers, *Moyers on America*, 136.

77. Knotts, "Grassroots Republicanism"; Gilliland, "Calculus of Realignment," 432; Schickler, *Racial Realignment*, esp. 1–10; Maxwell, *Indicted South*, 26, 237–45.

78. López, *Dog Whistle Politics*, 58; "Racism Issue Dominates President's Press Session," *Marion (OH) Star*, September 19, 1980, 13; Berman, *Give Us the Ballot*, 123–25.

79. Howell Raines, "Reagan and States' Rights," *New York Times*, March 4, 1981, 1.

80. Interview accessible at Rick Perlstein, "Exclusive: Lee Atwater's Infamous 1981 Interview on the Southern Strategy," *Nation*, November 13, 2012, https://www.thenation.com/article/exclusive-lee-atwaters-infamous-1981-interview-southern-strategy; see also López, *Dog Whistle Politics*, 55–61; Jay Willis, "The Trump Administration's 'States' Rights' Rhetoric Is an Insidious Dog Whistle for Something Far Worse," *GQ*, February 22, 2017.

81. "New Orleans Plans to Receive 250,000 Visitors at the Confederate Reunion," *St. Louis Republic*, May 17, 1903, [20]; "The Great Re-union," *Daily Clarion-Ledger* (Jackson, MS), May 16, 1903, 1; Hattaway, "United Confederate Veterans in Louisiana," 14; Foster, *Ghosts of the Confederacy*, 168–69.

82. "Gardner Praises Men and Women of Confederacy," *Charlotte Observer*, June 5, 1929, 17; "Veterans Hear Gen. Goodwyn," *Columbia (SC) Record*, June 5, 1929, 2; "1929 Confederate Reunion Marker, Charlotte," Commemorative Landscapes of North Carolina, https://docsouth.unc.edu/commland/monument/600.

83. "Forrest's Valet Admits Lee and Jackson Were Good Too," *Charlotte Observer*, June 5, 1929, 10; Jack Bates, "Aged Negro Is a Typical Character of Old South," *Augusta Chronicle*, June 18, 1929, 5.

84. "Negro Who Stayed a Slave," *Evansville (IN) Press*, June 9, 1929, section C, 2; "Master and Slave," *Hemet (CA) News*, July 5, 1929, 16. See also Foster, *Ghosts of the Confederacy*, 140.

85. "Confederate Bodies Hold Joint Session," *Tennessean* (Nashville), June 5, 1929, 5; "Reunion All Set Now; Uncle Steve Eberhart Is in Town," *Charlotte Observer*, June 5, 1929, 10; "With the Veterans," *Washington Times*, June 5, 1917, 3; "Reunion Sidelights," *Charlotte Observer*, June 8, 1929, section 2, 13; "'Champ' Chicken Stealer," *Edwardsville (IL) Intelligencer*, June 4, 1931, 1; Hilliard H. Wimpee, "Uncle Eberhart Happy on His 100th Birthday," *Atlanta Constitution*, March 31, 1929, 5F; "United Confederate Veterans at Camp Stephens," *Clarion-Ledger* (Jackson, MS), June 12, 1931, 14; "North Carolina Governor Greets Gray Veterans," *Tennessean* (Nashville), June 5, 1929, 1, 5. Much of the following section is based on the work of Andy Hall and Kevin M. Levin. In addition to his blog Levin has a forthcoming book, *Searching for Black Confederates: The Civil War's Most Persistent Myth*, that promises to definitively debunk the myth.

86. Andy Hall, "Steve Perry and 'Uncle Steve Eberhart,'" *Dead Confederates, A Civil War Era Blog*, November 11, 2011, https://deadconfederates.com/2011/11/11/everyone-laughs-both-at-and-with-steve.

87. Cash, *Mind of the South*, 128.

88. Andy Hall, "Steve Perry: Thanks for the Slavery!," *Dead Confederates, A Civil War Era Blog*, May 8, 2018, https://deadconfederates.com/2018/05/08/steve-perry-thanks-for-the-slavery. In one video clip (of unconfirmed provenance, but likely the Library of Congress), Perry appears to be saying at the 1930 reunion that whites saved African Americans from the jungles of Africa and that southern white men had "made a human out of me." Johnny Reb, "Black Confederate Veterans at the 1930 UCV Reunion In Biloxi, Mississippi," YouTube, https://www.youtube.com/watch?v=zzxhQjogxqw; see also Fergus M. Bordewich, "Civil War Veterans Come Alive in Audio and Video Recordings," Smithsonian.com, October 4, 2011, http://www.smithsonianmag.com/history/civil-war-veterans-come-alive-in-audio-and-video-recordings-97841665.

89. Battey, *History of Rome and Floyd County*, 252, 302. William Mack Lee also declared he always voted Democratic. "Old Age Formula," *Index-Journal* (Greenwood, SC), June 10, 1927, 4.

90. Battey, *History of Rome and Floyd County*, 302.

91. Julian Carr, "Fellow-Countrymen, Veterans of North Carolina, Ladies and Gentleman," in Folder 34b, Addresses, undated, Carr Papers, SHC; see also Janney, *Remembering the Civil War*, 208–9.

92. "Vets Air Political Views along with Battle Yarns," *News and Observer* (Raleigh, NC), June 7, 1929, 8.

93. "Uncle Steve Civil War 'Gunga Din' Drops In," *St. Louis Post-Dispatch*, September 24, 1918, 7; "Ex-Slave Still Loyal to Old Master," *Charlotte News*, December 15, 1921, 10. He also claimed to have worked for Florida colonel Abraham Eberhart during the war and for Henry Grady after the war. Battey, *History of Rome and Floyd County*, 252, 370; Kevin M. Levin, "'Ex-Slaves' Attend Confederate Veterans Reunion," *Civil War Memory*, September 27, 2015, http://cwmemory.com/2015/09/27/ex-slaves-attend-confederate-veterans-reunion; Kevin M. Levin, "What Did They Call Steve Perry (Eberhart)?," *Civil War Memory*, December 9, 2016, http://cwmemory.com/2016/12/09/what-did-they-call-steve-perry-eberhart; Andy Hall, "Steve Perry and 'Uncle Steve Eberhart,'" *Dead Confederates, A Civil War Era Blog*, November 11, 2011, https://deadconfederates.com/2011/11/11/everyone-laughs-both-at-and-with-steve.

94. "With the Veterans," *Washington Times*, June 5, 1917, 3; Andy Hall, "Steve Perry and 'Uncle Steve Eberhart,'" *Dead Confederates, A Civil War Era Blog*, November 11, 2011, https://deadconfederates.com/2011/11/11/everyone-laughs-both-at-and-with-steve. A P. S. Eberhart served in Echols Light Artillery.

95. "Reunion Sidelights," *Index-Journal* (Greenwood, SC), June 5, 1929, 3; "Chickens Were in Danger as Steve Roamed," *Orlando Evening Star*, June 4, 1911, 1; "United Confederate Veterans at Camp Stephens," *Town Talk* (Alexandria, LA), June 8, 1931, 7. Inexplicably, upon his death in 1936, Perry's daughter reported his age as "approximately" sixty-four. His death certificate can be found at Pat Millican and Bev, "Steve Eberhardt 'Uncle Steve' Perry," Find a Grave, December 12, 2004, https://www.findagrave.com/cgi-bin/fg.cgi?page=gr&GRid=10072318.

96. Battey, *History of Rome and Floyd County*, 370, 372.

97. Andy Hall, "Steve Perry and 'Uncle Steve Eberhart,'" *Dead Confederates, A Civil War Era Blog*, November 11, 2011, https://deadconfederates.com/2011/11/11/everyone-laughs-both-at-and-with-steve; Kevin M. Levin, "What Did They Call Steve Perry (Eberhart)?," *Civil War Memory*, December 9, 2016, http://cwmemory.com/2016/12/09/what-did-they-call-steve-perry-eberhart.

98. Kevin M. Levin, "William Mack Lee Outed in Confederate Veteran," *Civil War Memory*, May 27, 2016, http://cwmemory.com/2016/05/27/william-mack-lee-outed-in-confederate-veteran. See also Foster, *Ghosts of the Confederacy*, 140.

99. "Confederate Host Moves Homeward after Reunion," *Asheville Citizen*, June 8, 1929, 1; "Reunion Sidelights," *Charlotte Observer*, June 8, 1929, section 2, 13.

100. James Dinkins, "Snapshot from the Reunion," *Confederate Veteran* 11, no. 8 (August 1932): 289.

101. Kevin M. Levin, "William Mack Lee Outed in Confederate Veteran," *Civil War Memory*, May 27, 2016, http://cwmemory.com/2016/05/27/william-mack-lee

-outed-in-confederate-veteran; Levin, "The Making of a Black Confederate Soldier," *Civil War Memory*, May 23, 2016, http://cwmemory.com/2016/05/24/the-making -of-a-black-confederate-soldier; Levin, "William Mack Lee Conned the UCV & SCV," *Civil War Memory*, June 2, 2016, http://cwmemory.com/2016/06/02/william-mack -lee-conned-the-ucv-scv.

102. "Lee Memorial to Be Unveiled Today," *Cincinnati Enquirer*, April 9, 1928, 3; "Gen. Lee's Figure on Stone Mountain to Be Unveiled Today," *Tennessean* (Nashville), April 9, 1928, 1, 5; "A Shining Light Goes Out," *Every Evening* (Wilmington, DE), November 12, 1932, 8; "General Lee's Servant Dies," *Kingsport (TN) Times*, November 10, 1932, 7.

103. Kevin M. Levin, "The Making of a Black Confederate Soldier," *Civil War Memory*, May 23, 2016, http://cwmemory.com/2016/05/24/the-making-of-a-black -confederate-soldier. Pryor, *Reading the Man*, 562 takes apart Mack Lee's story.

104. "General Lee's Cook Given Added Pension," *Daily Press* (Newport News, VA), February 15, 1928, 1.

105. Johnson, "'Red Flag before an Army of Old Vets,'" 328–35.

106. "Birmingham News," *Huntsville (AL) Gazette*, May 5, 1894, 2.

107. Hulbert, *Ghosts of Guerrilla Memory*, 96–97.

108. Jim Robison, "Black Family Holds onto Confederate Heritage," *Orlando Sentinel*, March 21, 2004, Osceola section, K8. Winbush distorted the meaning of the term "bodyguard" to claim that he protected his master instead of being a servant. Jim Robison, "2 Take Opposite Views of War," *Orlando Sentinel*, April 18, 2004, Seminole section, K1, K3.

109. Levine, *Confederate Emancipation*, 44; McCurry, *Confederate Reckoning*, 324–57.

110. Lt. F. C. Frazier Camp, "About Us."

111. McPherson, *Reconstructing Dixie*, 110–12.

112. Carr, *Issues of the Campaign Stated*, 12; see also "Jule Carr a Friend," *Everything* (Greensboro, NC), September 26, 1914, 3.

113. Alexis Okeowo, "Witnessing a Rally for a Brand-New Confederate Monument," *New Yorker*, August 29, 2017.

114. Julian Carr, untitled speech, in Folder 21, Addresses, 1896–1899, Carr Papers, SHC.

115. Austerman, "Black Confederates," 49; see also Levine, "In Search of a Usable Past," 193.

116. Ben Jones, "The Confederate Flag Is a Matter of Pride and Heritage, Not Hatred," *New York Times*, December 22, 2015.

117. Scott Clement, "Discrimination against Whites Was a Core Concern of Trump's Base," *Washington Post*, August 2, 2017.

118. McPherson, *Reconstructing Dixie*, 114.

119. "Neo Confederate," Southern Poverty Law Center, https://www.splcenter .org/fighting-hate/extremist-files/ideology/neo-confederate.

120. Baker, *What Reconstruction Meant*, 76.

121. Madsen-Brooks, "I Nevertheless Am a Historian," 51, 54–55; Kevin M. Levin, "Black Confederates Didn't Exist in 1914," *Civil War Memory*, October 25, 2010, http:// cwmemory.com/2010/10/25/black-confederates-didnt-exist-in-1914; "Andy Hall— Hypocrite and Liberal Bullshitter," Jerryd14, December 12, 2014, accessed at https://

web.archive.org/web/20160408193656/https://jerryd14.wordpress.com/2014/12/12
/andy-hall-hypocrite-and-liberal-bullshitter.

122. "The Six Hundred to Meet in Louisville," *Confederate Veteran* 8, no. 3 (March 1900): 116.

Epilogue

1. "'New Yorker' Writer: #ThisIsNotUs Downplays History of Racism in U.S.," *All Things Considered*, August 14, 2017, http://www.npr.org/2017/08/14/543477439 /new-yorker-writer-thisisnotus-downplays-history-of-racism-in-u-s.

2. Charlie Savage, "A Hate Crime? How the Charlottesville Car Attack May Become a Federal Case," *New York Times*, August 13, 2017.

3. "'New Yorker' Writer: #ThisIsNotUs Downplays History Of Racism In U.S.," *All Things Considered*, August 14, 2017, http://www.npr.org/2017/08/14/543477439 /new-yorker-writer-thisisnotus-downplays-history-of-racism-in-u-s.

4. Davis, *Speeches of the Hon. Jefferson Davis*, 12.

5. On racial views of white southerners during the war, see Woodward, *Marching Masters*.

6. Joe Heim, Ellie Silverman, T. Rees Shapiro, and Emma Brown, "One Dead as Car Strikes Crowds amid Protests of White Nationalist Gathering in Charlottesville; Two Police Die in Helicopter Crash," *Washington Post*, August 13, 2017.

7. Neely Tucker and Peter Holley, "Dylann Roof's Eerie Tour of American Slavery at Its Beginning, Middle and End," *Washington Post*, July 1, 2015.

8. Petula Dvorak, "Trump Lit the Torches of White Supremacy in Charlottesville. We Must Extinguish Them," *Washington Post*, August 13, 2017; David Edwards, "'I'm Not the Angry Racist They See': Alt-Righter Became Viral Face of Hate in Virginia—and Now Regrets It," Raw Story, August 13, 2017, http://www.rawstory.com /2017/08/im-not-the-angry-racist-they-see-alt-righter-became-viral-face-of-hate-in -virginia-and-now-regrets-it.

9. Woodward, *Fear*, 238–52; William Cummings, "Former KKK Leader David Duke Praises Trump for His 'Courage,'" *USA Today*, August 15, 2017; "Trump: Racism 'Has No Place in America,'" *Washington Post*, August 14, 2017; A. J. Willingham, "Trump Made Two Statements on Charlottesville. Here's How White Nationalists Heard Them," CNN, August 15, 2017; Rosie Gray, "Trump Defends White-Nationalist Protesters: 'Some Very Fine People on Both Sides,'" *Atlantic*, August 15, 2017. Trump's delay in condemning racism was not the only dog whistle some observers noted. Even in his statement's language, Trump showed a different standard than he used for attacks inspired by the Islamic State; instead of calling it a "white supremacist terror attack," he referred to a "car attack."

10. Kevin M. Levin, "Virginia Flaggers Bring Heritage of Hate to Lexington," *Civil War Memory*, January 14, 2017, http://cwmemory.com/2017/01/14/virginia -flaggers-bring-heritage-of-hate-to-lexington.

11. Rick Perlstein, "Exclusive: Lee Atwater's Infamous 1981 Interview on the Southern Strategy," *Nation*, November 13, 2012, https://www.thenation.com/article /exclusive-lee-atwaters-infamous-1981-interview-southern-strategy; see also López, *Dog Whistle Politics*, 55–61.

12. Jill Palermo, "Republican Supervisor Criticizes Corey Stewart's Defense of the Confederate Flag," *Prince William Times* (Warrenton, VA), April 20, 2017.

13. Gregory Kreig, "Rally Trump vs. Teleprompter Trump," CNN, August 23, 2017.

14. Nicholas Fandos, "In Renovation of Golf Club, Donald Trump Also Dressed Up History," *New York Times*, November 24, 2015. Mirroring Trump's later moral equivocating of "many sides," the plaque he put up claimed, "Many great American soldiers, both of the North and South, died at this spot," furthering a narrative that the Civil War was a story of equally brave sides in which the cause had little relevance.

15. Raf Sanchez and Peter Foster, "'You Rape Our Women and Are Taking Over Our Country,' Charleston Church Gunman Told Black Victims," *Telegraph* (UK), June 18, 2015.

16. For more on the use of sexuality and gender to justify lynching, see Feimster, *Southern Horrors*.

17. Budapest has a similar park. Levinson, *Written in Stone*, 70–73.

18. "Unsung Founders Memorial, UNC (Chapel Hill)," Commemorative Landscapes of North Carolina, http://docsouth.unc.edu/commland/monument/45.

19. Urwin, "Introduction," 3.

20. Bill Rauch, "Can the South Make Room for Reconstruction," *Atlantic*, September 17, 2016.

21. Katherine Q. Seelye, "Celebrating Secession without the Slaves," *New York Times*, November 29, 2010; Jennifer Schuessler, "President Obama Designates First National Monument Dedicated to Reconstruction," *New York Times*, January 12, 2017; Jennifer Schuessler, "Taking Another Look at the Reconstruction Era," *New York Times*, August 24, 2015.

22. Bill Rauch, "Can the South Make Room for Reconstruction?," *Atlantic*, September 17, 2016.

23. For an example, see Herron, *Framing the Solid South*; for explanation of terminology, see Brundage, *Southern Past*, 2.

24. Adam Parker, "Two Sides, One Past Pride and Prejudice," *Post and Courier* (Charleston, SC), May 27, 2016; Janney, *Remembering the Civil War*, 137–38, 219–22, 256–59, 260–62, 264–65. An entire generation of Americans did not agree that monuments were needed. In addition to African Americans, many northern veterans and some white southerners objected to Confederate monuments. On the use of exclusionary language, see McPherson, *Reconstructing Dixie*, 110, 114.

25. Brundage, *Southern Past*, 338.

26. Emma Pettit "For Historians, the Business of Studying Monuments Like UNC's Silent Sam Takes a Toll," *Chronicle of Higher Education*, August 21, 2018.

27. For a selection of articles about the debate that mention the speech, see Mark Schultz, "NAACP President Says NC Leaders Fostering Hate," *News and Observer* (Raleigh, NC), August 6, 2015; Tammy Grubb, "Confederate Rally to Defend UNC's Silent Sam Coming to Chapel Hill," *News and Observer* (Raleigh, NC), October 24, 2015; Zaina Alsous, "Silent Sam Still Matters," *Daily Tar Heel* (Chapel Hill, NC), October 28, 2012; Daniel Lockwood, "Institutional Racism at UNC," *Daily Tar Heel* (Chapel Hill, NC), February 20, 2015; Stephanie Lamm, "Police Investigate Silent Sam Vandalism," *Daily Tar Heel* (Chapel Hill, NC), July 5, 2015; Shannon Brien, "Letter: Contextualization Is Not Deconstruction," *Daily Tar Heel* (Chapel Hill, NC),

August 25, 2015; Shelby Eden Dawkins-Law, "Letter: A Poem Questioning University Day," *Daily Tar Heel* (Chapel Hill, NC), October 12, 2015; Sarah Crump, "Former Mayor Requests Carrboro Name Change," *Daily Tar Heel* (Chapel Hill, NC), April 20, 2016.

28. Greg Childress, "It's Unanimous. The Confederate Flag Is Now Banned in Durham Public Schools," *Herald Sun* (Durham, NC), August 24, 2017. Carr's UNC speech, not his 1900 election campaign or racist speeches given in Durham, was cited as the justification for the name change.

29. "Text of History Department Request on Building Name," *Duke Today*, August 31, 2018, https://today.duke.edu/2018/08/text-history-department-request -building-name.

Selected Bibliography

Archival Sources

David M. Rubenstein Rare Book and Manuscript Library,
Duke University, Durham, NC

Jarrett-Puryear Family Papers
Julian Shakespeare Carr Papers

Friends Historical Collection, Guilford College, Guilford, NC

North Carolina Yearly Meeting Archives, accessed via "U.S., Quaker Meeting Records, 1681–1935" on Ancestry.com

John C. Smith University, Charlotte, NC

A. O. & Dorothy Steele Collection (accessed via http://cdm16324.contentdm.oclc .org/cdm/landingpage/collection/p15170coll8)

National Archives and Records Administration, Washington, DC (NARA)

Record Group 15 Records of the Veterans Administration

Pension Files

Record Group 217 Records of the Accounting Officers of the Department of the Treasury

Southern Claims Commission Approved Claims, 1871–1880, accessed via fold3.com

NARA Microfilm

Orders and Circulars Issued by the Army of the Potomac and the Army and Department of Northern Virginia, C.S.A, 1861–1865, NARA Microfilm M921, accessed at NARA.

Compiled Service Records Accessed via fold3.com (cited as CSR with name and unit and microfilm number)

Alphabetical Card Index to the Compiled Service Records of Volunteer Union Soldiers Belonging to Union Organizations Not Raised by States or Territories, NARA Microfilm M1290.

Compiled Service Records of Confederate Soldiers Who Served in Organizations from the State of North Carolina, NARA Microfilm M270.

Compiled Service Records of Confederate Soldiers Who Served in Organizations from the State of South Carolina, NARA Microfilm M267.

Compiled Service Records of Confederate Soldiers Who Served in Organizations from the State of Texas, NARA Microfilm M323.

Compiled Service Records of Former Confederate Soldiers Who Served in the 1st through 6th U.S. Volunteer Infantry Regiments, 1864–1866, NARA Microfilm M1017.

Compiled Service Records of Volunteer Union Soldiers Who Served in Organizations from the State of Missouri, NARA Microfilm M405.

Compiled Military Service Records of Volunteer Union Soldiers Who Served with the United States Colored Troops: Infantry Organizations, 31st through 35th, NARA Microfilm M1992.

Additional NARA Microfilm Accessed via fold3.com

Confederate Papers Relating to Citizen or Business Firms, 1861–1865, NARA Microfilm M346.

Southern Claims Commission Barred and Disallowed Claims, NARA Microfilm M1407.

Subject File of the Confederate States Navy, 1861–1865, NARA Microfilm M1091.

Unfiled Papers and Slips Belonging in Confederate Compiled Service Records, NARA Microfilm M347.

Union Provost Marshals' File of Papers Relating to Individual Civilians, NARA Microfilm M345.

NARA Microfilm Accessed via Ancestry.com

Applications for Headstones for U.S. Military Veterans, 1925–1941, NARA Microfilm M1916.

Federal Census Collection, including

Population Schedules, Seventh Census of the United States, 1850, NARA Microfilm M432.

Population Schedules, Eighth Census of the United States, 1860, NARA Microfilm M653.

Population Schedules, Ninth Census of the United States, 1870, NARA Microfilm M593.

Population Schedules, Tenth Census of the United States, 1880, NARA Microfilm T9.

Population Schedules, Twelfth Census of the United States, 1900, NARA Microfilm 623.

Population Schedules, Thirteenth Census of the United States, 1910, NARA Microfilm T624.

Population Schedules, Fourteenth Census of the United States, 1920, NARA Microfilm T625.

Population Schedules, Fifteenth Census of the United States, 1930, NARA Microfilm T626.

Population Schedules, Sixteenth Census of the United States, 1940, NARA Microfilm T627.

Selected Records of the War Department Relating to Confederate Prisoners of War, 1861–1865, NARA Microfilm M598.

Slave Schedule, Eighth Census of the United States, 1860, NARA Microfilm M653.

U.S., Colored Troops Military Service Records, 1863–1865, including

 Compiled Military Service Records of Volunteer Union Soldiers Who Served with the United States Colored Troops: Artillery Organizations, NARA Microfilm M1818.

 Compiled Service Records of Volunteer Union Soldiers Who Served with the United States Colored Troops: Infantry Organizations, 8th through 13th, Including the 11th (New), NARA Microfilm M1821.

 Compiled Military Service Records of Volunteer Union Soldiers Who Served with the United States Colored Troops: Infantry Organizations, 26th through 30th, Including the 29th Connecticut (Colored), NARA Microfilm M1824.

 Compiled Military Service Records of Volunteer Union Soldiers Who Served with the United States Colored Troops: Infantry Organizations, 41st through 46th, NARA Microfilm M1994.

 Compiled Military Service Records of Volunteer Union Soldiers Who Served with the United States Colored Troops: Infantry Organizations, 47th through 55th, NARA Microfilm M2000.

North Carolina Department of Archives and History, Raleigh, NC (NCDAH)

Pension Application Files, Office of the State Auditor (accessed via http://digital.ncdcr.gov/cdm/landingpage/collection/p16062coll21/)

Correspondence, Pension Bureau, Office of the State Auditor

County Pension Lists, Office of the State Auditor

NCDAH Documents Accessed via Ancestry.com

North Carolina, Marriage Records, 1741–2011

North Carolina, Death Certificates, 1909–1976

North Carolina, Wills and Probate Records, 1665–1998

Wilson Library, University of North Carolina, Chapel Hill, NC

North Carolina Collection

London, Bettie Jackson. "Dedication of Monument." Typed presentation speech, 1913 (accessed via https://archive.org/details/aschairmanofmonuoolond)

Southern Historical Collection, Wilson Library, UNC Chapel Hill (SHC, UNC)

Alfred M. Waddell Papers, #743 (accessed via http://finding-aids.lib.unc.edu/00743/)
Henry Armand London Papers, #868-z (accessed via http://finding-aids.lib.unc
.edu/00868/)
John Wesley Halliburton Papers, #4414-z (accessed via http://finding-aids.lib.unc
.edu/04414/)
Julian Shakespeare Carr Papers, #141 (accessed via http://finding-aids.lib.unc.edu
/00141/)
Southern Oral History Program Collection #4007

University Archives, Wilson Library, University of North Carolina at Chapel Hill

Board of Trustees of the University of North Carolina Records, 1789–1932, #40001
(accessed via http://finding-aids.lib.unc.edu/40001/)
University of North Carolina Papers, #40005 (accessed via http://finding-aids.lib
.unc.edu/40005/)

Selected Online Databases

Ancestry, https://ancestry.com
Cemetery Census, http://cemeterycensus.com/
Commemorative Landscapes of North Carolina, https://docsouth.unc.edu
/commland/
Fold3, https://www.fold3.com
Find a Grave, https://www.findagrave.com
Genealogy Bank, https://www.genealogybank.com/
Guinness World Records, www.guinnessworldrecords.com/
Manson, Steven, Jonathan Schroeder, David Van Riper, and Steven Ruggles. IPUMS
National Historical Geographic Information System: Version 12.0 (database).
Minneapolis: University of Minnesota, 2017. https://www.nhgis.org/
Newspapers.com, https://www.newspapers.com
North Carolina Civil War Monuments, http://ncmonuments.ncdcr.gov/
University of Richmond, Digital Scholarship Lab. "Visualizing Emancipation,"
http://dsl.richmond.edu/emancipation/

Federal Government Reports and Publications

*Agricultural and Manufacturing Census Records of Fifteen Southern States for the Years
1850, 1860, 1870 and 1880.* Chapel Hill, NC: Microfilmed by University of North
Carolina Library.
Bureau of Pensions. *Laws of the United States Governing the Granting of Army and
Navy Pensions Together with the Regulations Relating Thereto, Corrected to January
1, 1921.* Washington, DC: Government Printing Office, 1921.
"Letter of the General of the Army of the United States." Ex. doc. no. 53, 40th Congress, 2nd Session.
Mantovani, Richard, Eric Sean Williams, and Jacqueline Pflieger. *The Extent of Trafficking in the Supplemental Nutrition Assistance Program: 2009–2011.* Prepared by

ICF International for the US Department of Agriculture, Food and Nutrition Service, August 2013. Accessed at https://www.fns.usda.gov/ops/research-and -analysis.

Official Army Register for 1863. Washington, DC: Adjutant General's Office, 1863.

Official Records of the Union and Confederate Navies in the War of the Rebellion. Series I, vol. 6. Washington, DC: Government Printing Office, 1897.

The War of the Rebellion: A Compilation of the Official Records of the Union and Confederate Armies, 1861–1865. Series IV, vol. 3. Washington, DC: Government Printing Office, 1900.

Other Primary Sources

Ashe, S. A. "Number and Losses of North Carolina Troops." In *Five Points in the Record of North Carolina in the Great War of 1861–65,* edited by North Carolina State Department of Archives and History, 73–79. Raleigh: E. M. Uzzell, 1904.

Augustus, Sarah Louise. "Sarah Louise Augustus." In *The American Slave: A Composite Autobiography,* vol. 14, *North Carolina Narratives, Part 1,* edited by George P. Rawick, 50–57. Westport, CT: Greenwood, 1972.

Austerman, Wayne. "The Black Confederates." In *Black Confederates,* edited by Charles Kelly Barrow, J. H. Segars, and R. B. Rosenburg, 37–50. Gretna, LA: Pelican, 2001.

Barrow, Charles Kelly, J. H. Segars, and R. B. Rosenburg, eds. *Black Confederates.* Gretna, LA: Pelican, 2001.

———, eds. *Forgotten Confederates: An Anthology about Black Southerners.* Atlanta: Southern Heritage, 1995.

Battey, George Magruder, Jr. *A History of Rome and Floyd County, 1500–1922.* Atlanta: Webb and Vary, 1922.

Battle, Kemp P. *Sketches of the History of the University of North Carolina: Together with a Catalogue of Officers and Students, 1789–1889.* University of North Carolina, 1889.

———. "The University of North Carolina in the War, 1861–'65." In *Histories of the Several Regiments and Battalions from North Carolina, in the Great War, 1861–'65,* edited by Walter Clark, 5:647–52. Raleigh: E. M. Uzzell, 1901.

Bond, W. R. *Pickett or Pettigrew: North Carolina at Gettysburg.* 3rd ed. Scotland Neck, NC: W. L. L. Hall, 1901.

Bragaw, Stephen C. "Presentation of the Portrait of Charles Frederick Warren to the Supreme Court of North Carolina, September 1, 1914." In *North Carolina Reports: Cases Argued and Determined in the Supreme Court of North Carolina,* 169:859–67. Raleigh, NC: Edward and Broughton, 1916.

Camp, David N., ed. *The American Year-Book and National Register for 1869.* Hartford, CT: O. D. Case, 1869.

Carr, Julian S. *The Issues of the Campaign Stated: An Open Letter to Van B. Sparrow, Patterson Township, Durham County.* 1898.

———. *Peace with Honor: Unveiling Bennet House Memorial, November 8, 1923.* Durham, NC: Seeman, [1923].

———. *The Problem of the Hour: Will the Colored Race Save Itself from Ruin.* Durham, NC: Seeman, 1899.

Christian, George L., and Hunter McGuire. *The Confederate Cause and Conduct in the War between the States.* Richmond: L. H. Jenkins, 1907.

Clark, Walter, ed. *Histories of the Several Regiments and Battalions from North Carolina in the Great War, 1861–'65.* Vol 2. Goldsboro, NC: Nash Brothers, [1901].

———, ed. *Histories of the Several Regiments and Battalions from North Carolina, in the Great War, 1861–'65.* Vol 5. Raleigh: E. M. Uzzell, 1901.

Cofer, Aunt Betty. "Negro Folk Lore of the Piedmont." In *The American Slave: A Composite Autobiography,* vol. 14, *North Carolina Narratives, Part 1,* edited by George P. Rawick, 165–75. Westport, CT: Greenwood, 1972.

"Confederate Military Records." In *Black Confederates,* edited by Charles Kelly Barrow, J. H. Segars, and R. B. Rosenburg, 51–60. Gretna, LA: Pelican, 2001.

"Confederate Pension Applications, U.C.V. Camp Records, & Reunions." In *Black Confederates,* edited by Charles Kelly Barrow, J. H. Segars, and R. B. Rosenburg, 113–26. Gretna, LA: Pelican, 2001.

Davis, Jefferson. *Speeches of the Hon. Jefferson Davis, of Mississippi: Delivered during the Summer of 1858.* Baltimore: John Murphy, 1859.

"A Declaration of the Immediate Causes Which Induce and Justify the Secession of the State of Mississippi from the Federal Union." Accessed at http://avalon.law .yale.edu/19th_century/csa_missec.asp.

"Despite Growing Opposition, Richmond Mayor Pushes to Add PC 'Context' to Confederate Monuments." *Virginia Flaggers,* June 22, 2017. http://vaflaggers.blogspot .com/2017/06/richmond-mayor-pushes-to-add-context-to.html.

FitzSimons, Frank L. *From the Banks of the Oklawaha.* Vol. 1. Hendersonville, NC: Golden Glow, 1976.

"George Wallace on Segregation, 1964." Gilder Lehrman Institute of American History. https://www.gilderlehrman.org/history-by-era/civil-rights-movement /resources/george-wallace-segregation-1964.

Hamilton, J. G. de Roulhac. *Reconstruction in North Carolina.* Raleigh, NC: Edwards and Broughton, 1906.

Harper, Charles W. "Black Loyalty under the Confederacy." In *Black Confederates,* edited by Charles Kelly Barrow, J. H. Segars, and R. B. Rosenburg, 7–30. Gretna, LA: Pelican, 2001.

Henderson, W. A. *Kings Mountain and Its Campaigns.* Greensboro, NC: Guilford Battleground, 1903.

Herbert, Hilary A., et al. *Why the Solid South? Or Reconstruction and Its Results.* Baltimore: R. H. Woodward, 1890.

Hill, Joshua B. "Forty-First Regiment." In *Histories of the Several Regiments and Battalions from North Carolina in the Great War, 1861–'65,* edited by Walter Clark, 2:767–88. Goldsboro, NC: Nash Brothers, [1901].

Hoar, Jay S. "Aged Body Servants among the Last Survivors of the Confederate Army." In *Black Confederates,* edited by Charles Kelly Barrow, J. H. Segars, and R. B. Rosenburg, 71–92. Gretna, LA: Pelican, 2001.

———. *The South's Last Boys in Gray: An Epic Prose Elegy, A Substudy of Sunset and Dusk of the Blue and the Gray.* Bowling Green, OH: Bowling Green State University Popular Press, 1986.

Hood, S. M., and John Bell Hood Historical Society. "What Kind of Courage?" www.swordexposed.com, 2009. Accessed at https://web.archive.org/web /20101117011248/http://swordexposed.com/.

Journal of the Constitutional Convention of the State of North-Carolina, at Its Session 1868. Raleigh: Joseph W. Holden, 1868. Accessed at http://docsouth.unc.edu/nc /convi868/convi868.html.

Journal of the House of Representatives of the General Assembly of the State of North Carolina, at Its Session of 1895. Winston, NC: M. I. and J. C. Steward, 1895.

Journal of the House of Representatives of the General Assembly of the State of North Carolina, Session 1921. Raleigh, NC: Mitchell, 1921.

Journal of the House of Representatives of the General Assembly of the State of North Carolina, Session 1925. Raleigh, NC: Capital, 1925.

Journal of the Senate of the General Assembly of the State of North Carolina at Its Session of 1895. Winston, NC: M. I. and J. C. Steward, 1895.

Kennedy, James Ronald, and Walter Donald Kennedy. *The South Was Right!* Gretna, LA: Pelican, 2004.

Kestler, Francis Y. "Amos Yokley." In *The Heritage of Davidson County, 1982,* 639. Lexington, NC: Genealogical Society of Davidson County, 1982.

King, James W. "The 10 Causes of the War between the States." Confederate American Pride. http://www.confederateamericanpride.com/10causes.html.

[Ladnier, Gene]."General Nathan Bedford Forrest—the First True Civil Rights Leader." SouthernHeritage411.com, http://www.southernheritage411.com/true history.php?th=039.

Ladnier, Gene. "Lt. Gen. Nathan Bedford Forrest: An Essay." The Forrest Preserve, 2000. Accessed at https://web.archive.org/web/20010415140103/http://www .nbforrest.com/nbf_essay_gl_01.htm.

Lauten, Donna. "Austin Yokeley." On "Those Who Also Rode," *Pony Express Home Station,* February 1997. https://web.archive.org/web/20160315022945/http:// www.xphomestation.com/others.html

Leak, R. H. W. *Freedom's Jubilee: Celebration of the 31st Anniversary of the Proclamation of Emancipation at Raleigh, N.C., January 1, 1894.* Raleigh, NC: Barnes Bros., 1894.

Lincoln, Abraham. "Second Inaugural Address." March 4, 1865. *Atlantic Monthly* 284, no. 3 (September 1999): 60. Accessed at https://www.theatlantic.com/past /docs/issues/99sep/9909lincaddress.htm.

London, Henry A. "Thirty-Second Regiment." In *Histories of the Several Regiments and Battalions from North Carolina in the Great War, 1861–'65,* edited by Walter Clark, 2:521–36. Goldsboro, NC: Nash Brothers, [1901].

———. "Bryan Grimes." In *Lives of Distinguished North Carolinians: With Illustrations and Speeches,* edited by W. J. Peele, 495–512. Raleigh: North Carolina Publishing Society, 1898.

Lt. F. C. Frazier Camp. "About Us." Lt. F. C. Frazier Camp #668 SCV. http:// fraziercamp.org/.

Moore, John W. *Roster of North Carolina Troops in the War between the States: During the Years 1861, 1862, 1863, 1864 and 1865.* Vol. 3. Raleigh, NC: Ashe and Gatling, 1882.

Moring, Richard C. "Ex-Slave Story." In *The American Slave: A Composite Autobiography,* vol. 15, *North Carolina Narratives, Part 2,* edited by George P. Rawick, 138–42. Westport, CT: Greenwood, 1972.

Mosby, John S., to Samuel Chapman, June 4, 1907. Gilder Lehrman Institute of American History. https://www.gilderlehrman.org/sites/default/files/inline -pdfs/t-03921-21.pdf.

North Carolina Literary and Historical Association. *Five Points in the Record of North Carolina in the Great War of 1861–65*. Goldsboro, NC: Nash Brothers, 1904.

"Old 'Black Men in the Confederate Army': What the Newspapers Said—1861–1865." Civil War Talk, October 26, 2016. https://civilwartalk.com/threads /old-black-men-in-the-confederate-army-what-the-newspapers-said-1861-1865 .127333/page-29.

Parker, William Harward. *Recollections of a Naval Officer, 1841–1865*. New York: Charles Scribners' Sons, 1883.

Pike, H. L. *Address at the Celebration of Emancipation Day, Delivered by Col. H. L. Pike, at Raleigh, January, 1870*. Raleigh, NC: Standard, 1870.

"Programme at the Unveiling of the Confederate Monument at the University of North Carolina, June 2, 1913, 3:30 p.m." Accessed at "Program for the Dedication of the Confederate Monument, 1913," UNC Libraries, https://exhibits.lib.unc .edu/items/show/3687.

Rawick, George P., ed. *The American Slave: A Composite Autobiography*. Vol. 14, *North Carolina Narratives, Part 1*. Westport, CT: Greenwood, 1972.

———. ed. *The American Slave: A Composite Autobiography*. Vol. 15, *North Carolina Narratives, Part 2*. Westport, CT: Greenwood, 1972.

Rose, S. E. F. *The Ku Klux Klan or Invisible Empire*. New Orleans: Graham, 1914.

Rutherford, Mildred Lewis. *A Measuring Rod to Test Text Books, and Reference Books in Schools, Colleges and Libraries*. Athens, GA: Mildred Lewis Rutherford, [1920].

———. *Truths of History: A Fair, Unbiased, Impartial, Unprejudiced and Conscientious Study of History*. Accessed at https://archive.org/details/truthsofhistoryfooruth.

Segars, J. H., and Charles Kelly Barrow, eds. *Black Southerners in Confederate Armies: A Collection of Historical Accounts*. Gretna, LA: Pelican, 2007.

"Sergeant James Washington Memorial Award." Sons of Confederate Veterans Texas Division. http://scvtexas.org/Washington_Memorial_Awar.html.

Singleton, William Henry. *Recollections of My Slavery Days*. Peekskill, NY: Highland Democrat, 1922. Accessed at http://docsouth.unc.edu/neh/singleton/singleton .html.

State of North Carolina. *Public Laws and Resolutions of the State of North Carolina Passed by the General Assembly at Its Session in 1921*. Raleigh, NC: Mitchell, 1921.

Turner, Viola. "Oral History Interview with Viola Turner, April 17, 1979." Interview by Walter Weare. Interview C-0016. Southern Oral History Program Collection (#4007), University of North Carolina, accessed at http://docsouth.unc.edu /sohp/C-0016/excerpts/excerpt_9340.html.

UCPMF. "You are Invited to Join Us: New Confederate Monument Memorial Service Dedication and Unveiling." http://www.fraziercamp.org/new_site/pdfs /monroe.pdf.

Vaughan, Walter Raleigh. *Vaughan's "Freedmen's Pension Bill." Being an Appeal in Behalf of Men Released from Slavery. A Plea for American Freedmen and a Rational Proposition to Grant Pensions to Persons of Color Emancipated from Slavery*. Chicago, 1891. Accessed at http://hdl.handle.net/2027/dul1.ark:/13960/t3905q07c.

Wilcox, Michael C. "Windsor's Crossroads: Stoneman's Raiders Pass By." Historical Marker Database, May 13, 2012, last revised June 16, 2016. https://www.hmdb .org/marker.asp?marker=55343.

Williams, Scott. "Black Confederates." Sons of Confederate Veterans. http://www .scv.org/new/contributed-works/black-confederates/.

———. "On Black Confederates." SouthernHeritage411.com. http://www
.southernheritage411.com/bc.php?nw=020.

Wrobel, Amy M. "The Civil War Was NOT over Slavery." Confederate American
Pride. http://www.confederateamericanpride.com/notslavery.html.

Secondary Sources

Anderson, Benedict. *Imagined Communities: Reflections on the Origin and Spread of
Nationalism.* Rev. ed. New York: Verso, 2006.

Anderson, Eric. *Race and Politics in North Carolina, 1872–1901: The Black Second.*
Baton Rouge: Louisiana State University Press, 1980.

Anderson, James D. *The Education of Blacks in the South, 1860–1935.* Chapel Hill:
University of North Carolina Press, 1988.

Araujo, Ana Lucia. *Reparations for Slavery and the Slave Trade: A Transnational and
Comparative History.* London: Bloomsbury, 2017.

"Archival Resources." *A Guide to Resources about UNC's Confederate Monument.*
https://exhibits.lib.unc.edu/exhibits/show/silent-sam/archives.

Auman, William T. *Civil War in the North Carolina Quaker Belt: The Confederate
Campaign against Peace Agitators, Deserters and Draft Dodgers.* Jefferson, NC:
McFarland, 2014.

———. "Neighbor against Neighbor: The Inner Civil War in the Central Counties of Confederate North Carolina." PhD diss., University of North Carolina at
Chapel Hill, 1988.

Bailey, Fred Arthur. "The Textbooks of the 'Lost Cause': Censorship and the Creation of Southern State Histories." *Georgia Historical Quarterly* 75, no. 3 (Fall
1991): 507–33.

Baker, Bruce. *What Reconstruction Meant: Historical Memory in the American South.*
Charlottesville: University of Virginia Press, 2007.

Baker, Kelly J. *Gospel According to the Klan: The KKK's Appeal to Protestant America,
1915–1930.* Lawrence: University Press of Kansas, 2011.

Baptist, Edward E. *The Half Has Never Been Told: Slavery and the Making of American
Capitalism.* New York: Basic Books, 2016.

Bardolph, Richard. "Inconstant Rebels: Desertion of North Carolina Troops in the
Civil War." *North Carolina Historical Review* 41, no. 2 (April 1964): 163–89.

Barefoot, Daniel W. *Let Us Die like Brave Men: Behind the Dying Words of Confederate
Warriors.* Winston-Salem, NC: John F. Blair, 2005.

Barr, Chris. "Loathsome Diseases and Principles: Conceptualizing Race and Slavery in Civil War Prisons." In *Crossing the Deadlines: Civil War Prisons Reconsidered,* edited by Michael P. Gray, 101–24. Kent, OH: Kent State University Press,
2018.

Barrett, John Gilchrist. *The Civil War in North Carolina.* Chapel Hill: University of
North Carolina Press, 1995.

———. *Sherman's March through the Carolinas.* Chapel Hill: University of North Carolina Press, 2014.

Bearman, Peter S. "Desertion as Localism: Army Unit Solidarity and Group Norms
in the U.S. Civil War." *Social Forces* 70, no. 2 (December 1991): 321–42.

Beckel, Deborah. *Radical Reform: Interracial Politics in Post-Emancipation North Carolina.* Charlottesville: University of Virginia Press, 2010.

Berman, Ari. *Give Us the Ballot: The Modern Struggle for Voting Rights in America.* New York: Farrar, Straus and Giroux, 2015.

Bishir, Catherine W. "Landmarks of Power: Building a Southern Past, 1885–1915." *Southern Cultures* 1, no. 1 (1993): 5–45.

————. "North Carolina's Union Square." Commemorative Landscapes of North Carolina, 2012. http://docsouth.unc.edu/commland/features/essays/bishir_two/.

————. "A Strong Force of Ladies: Women, Politics, and Confederate Memorial Associations in Nineteenth-Century Raleigh." *North Carolina Historical Review* 77, no. 4 (October 2000): 455–91.

Blair, William. *Cities of the Dead: Contesting the Memory of the Civil War in the South, 1865–1914.* Chapel Hill: University of North Carolina Press, 2004.

Blight, David W. *American Oracle: The Civil War in the Civil Rights Era.* Cambridge, MA: Belknap Press of Harvard University Press, 2011.

————. *Beyond the Battlefield: Race, Memory and the American Civil War.* Amherst: University of Massachusetts Press, 2002.

————. *Race and Reunion: The Civil War in American Memory.* Cambridge, MA: Belknap Press of Harvard University Press, 2001.

Blum, Edward J. *Reforging the White Republic: Race, Religion, and American Nationalism, 1865–1898.* Baton Rouge: Louisiana State University Press, 2007.

Bohannon, Keith S. "The Northeast Georgia Mountains during the Secession Crisis and Civil War." PhD diss., Pennsylvania State University, 2001.

Brasher, Glenn David. "Do We Really Have to Keep Doing This?" *History Headlines,* November 15, 2017. https://historyandthenews.wordpress.com/2017/11/15/do-we-really-have-to-keep-doing-this/.

Brown, Dee. *The Galvanized Yankees.* Lincoln: University of Nebraska Press, 1963.

Brown, Leslie. *Upbuilding Black Durham: Gender, Class, and Black Community Development in the Jim Crow South.* Chapel Hill: University of North Carolina Press, 2008.

Brown, Thomas. "Civil War Monuments." Commemorative Landscapes of North Carolina, 2012. http://docsouth.unc.edu/commland/features/essays/brown/.

Brown, Yvonne. "Tolerance and Bigotry in Southwest Louisiana: The Ku Klux Klan, 1921–23." *Louisiana History* 47, no. 2 (Spring 2006): 153–68.

Browning, Judkin. "'Little Souled Mercenaries'? The Buffaloes of Eastern North Carolina during the Civil War." *North Carolina Historical Review* 77, no. 3 (July 2000): 337–63.

————. *Shifting Loyalties: The Union Occupation of Eastern North Carolina.* Chapel Hill: University of North Carolina Press, 2011.

————. "Visions of Freedom and Civilization Opening before Them: African Americans Search for Autonomy during the Military Occupation in North Carolina." In *North Carolinians in the Era of the Civil War and Reconstruction,* edited by Paul D. Escott, 69–100. Chapel Hill: University of North Carolina Press, 2012.

Brundage, W. Fitzhugh. *Lynching in the New South: Georgia and Virginia, 1880–1930.* Urbana: University of Illinois Press, 1993.

————. *The Southern Past: A Clash of Race and Memory.* Cambridge, MA: Belknap Press of Harvard University Press, 2005.

————, ed. *Where These Memories Grow: History, Memory, and Southern Identity.* Chapel Hill: University of North Carolina Press, 2000.

————, ed. *Under Sentence of Death: Lynching in the South.* Chapel Hill: University of North Carolina Press, 1997.

Brundage, W. Fitzhugh, and Adam H. Domby. "Evolution of Landscape: Changing Conceptions of Commemoration at Guilford Courthouse Battleground." *Commemorative Landscapes of North Carolina*, 2012. https://docsouth.unc.edu /commland/features/essays/brundage_domby.

Bunch, Jack A. *Military Justice in the Confederate States Armies*. Shippensburg, PA: White Mane Books, 2000.

———. *Roster of the Courts-Martial in the Confederate States Armies*. Shippensburg, PA: White Mane Books, 2001.

Burke, Peter. *Varieties of Cultural History*. Ithaca, NY: Cornell University Press, 1997.

Burton, Orville Vernon. *The Age of Lincoln*. New York: Hill and Wang, 2007.

———. "'Reconstructing South Carolina's Reconstruction': Keynote, South Carolina Historical Association, 2017." *Proceedings of the South Carolina Historical Association* (2018): 7–40.

Bynum, Victoria E. *The Free State of Jones: Mississippi's Longest Civil War*. Chapel Hill: University of North Carolina Press, 2001.

———. *The Long Shadow of the Civil War: Southern Dissent and Its Legacies*. Chapel Hill: University of North Carolina Press, 2013.

Camp, Stephanie M. H. *Closer to Freedom: Enslaved Women and Everyday Resistance in the Plantation South*. Chapel Hill: University of North Carolina Press, 2004.

Cash, W. J. *The Mind of the South*. New York: Vintage Books, 1991.

Casstevens, Frances H. "One of Yadin County's Most Unusual Citizens: Alfred (Uncle Teen) Blackburn." *Yadkin County Historical and Genealogical Society Journal* 9, no. 1 (March 1990): 23.

Cecelski, David S., and Timothy B. Tyson, eds. *Democracy Betrayed: The Wilmington Race Riot of 1898 and Its Legacy*. Chapel Hill: University of North Carolina Press, 1998.

Cecil-Fronsman, Bill. *Common Whites: Class and Culture in Antebellum North Carolina*. Lexington: University Press of Kentucky, 1992.

Charon, Katherine Mellen, and David S. Cecelski. Introduction to *Recollections of My Slavery Days*, by William Henry Singleton, 12–19. Raleigh: Division of Archives and History, North Carolina Department of Cultural Resources, 1999.

Cimprich, John. *Fort Pillow, A Civil War Massacre, and Public Memory*. Baton Rouge: Louisiana State University Press, 2005.

Clark, Kathleen Ann. *Defining Moments: African American Commemoration and Political Culture in the South, 1863–1913*. Chapel Hill: University of North Carolina Press, 2005.

Clifton, Denise. "Trump and Putin's Strong Connection: Lies." *Mother Jones*, October 19, 2017. Accessed at https://www.motherjones.com/politics/2017/10 /trump-and-putin-strong-connection-lies/.

Cloyd, Benjamin G. *Haunted by Atrocity: Civil War Prisons in American Memory*. Baton Rouge: Louisiana State University Press, 2010.

Cobb, James C. *Away Down South: A History of Southern Identity*. New York: Oxford University Press, 2005.

Collins, Bruce. "Confederate Identity and the Southern Myth." In *Legacy of Disunion: The Enduring Significance of the American Civil War*, edited by Susan-Mary Grand and Peter J. Parish, 30–47. Baton Rouge: Louisiana State University Press, 2003.

Cook, Robert J. *Civil War Memories: Contesting the Past in the United States since 1865*. Baltimore: John Hopkins University Press, 2017.

———. *Troubled Commemoration: The American Civil War Centennial, 1961–1965.* Baton Rouge: Louisiana State University Press, 2007.

Coski, John M. *The Confederate Battle Flag: America's Most Embattled Emblem.* Cambridge, MA: Harvard University Press, 2009.

Cox, Karen L. "The Confederate Monument at Arlington: A Token of Reconciliation." In *Monuments to the Lost Cause: Women, Art, and the Landscapes of Southern Memory,* edited by Cynthia Mills and Pamela H. Simpson, 149–62. Knoxville: University of Tennessee Press, 2003.

———. *Dixie's Daughters: The United Daughters of the Confederacy and the Preservation of Confederate Culture.* Gainesville: University Press of Florida, 2003.

Craig, Lee A. *Josephus Daniels: His Life and Times.* Chapel Hill: University of North Carolina Press, 2013.

Crofts, Daniel W. *Reluctant Confederates: Upper South Unionists in the Secession Crisis.* Chapel Hill: University of North Carolina Press, 1989.

Crow, Jeffrey J. "Thomas Settle Jr., Reconstruction, and the Memory of the Civil War." *Journal of Southern History* 62, no. 4 (1996): 689–726.

Current, Richard N. *Lincoln's Loyalists: Union Soldiers from the Confederacy.* Boston: Northeastern University Press, 1992,

———. "That Other Declaration: May 20, 1775–May 20, 1975." *North Carolina Historical Review* 54, no. 2 (April 1977): 169–91.

Davis, Lenwood G. *The Black Heritage of Western North Carolina.* Asheville: Grateful Steps Foundation, 2012.

Desjardin, Thomas A. *These Honored Dead: How the Story of Gettysburg Shaped American Memory.* Cambridge, MA: De Capo, 2003.

Dew, Charles. *Apostles of Disunion: Southern Secession Commissioners and the Causes of the Civil War.* Charlottesville: University of Virginia Press, 2001.

Dixon, David T. "To Laugh in One Hand and Cry in the Other: W. B. Higginbotham and the Black Community in Civil War Rome." *Georgia Backroads,* Winter 2011, 14–19.

Domby, Adam H. "Captives of Memory: The Contested Legacy of Race at Andersonville National Historic Site." *Civil War History* 63, no. 3 (September 2017): 253–94.

———. "Loyal to the Core from the First to the Last: Remembering the Inner Civil War of Forsyth County, North Carolina, 1862–1876." MA thesis, University of North Carolina at Chapel Hill, 2015.

———. "War within the States: Loyalty, Dissent, and Conflict in Southern Piedmont Communities, 1860–1876." PhD diss., University of North Carolina at Chapel Hill, 2015.

Donald, David. "The Confederate as a Fighting Man." *Journal of Southern History* 25, no. 2 (May 1959): 178–93.

Downs, Gregory P. *Declarations of Dependence: The Long Reconstruction of Popular Politics in the South, 1861–1908.* Chapel Hill: University of North Carolina Press, 2011.

Driggs, Sarah Shields, Richard Guy Wilson, and Robert P. Winthrop. *Richmond's Monument Avenue.* Chapel Hill: University of North Carolina Press, 2001.

Du Bois, W. E. B. *Black Reconstruction in America, 1860–1880.* New York: Simon and Schuster, 1999.

Duck, Leigh Anne. "Woodward's Southerner: History, Literature and the Question of Identity." In *The Ongoing Burden of Southern History: Politics and Identity in the*

Twenty-First-Century South, edited by Todd Shields, Jeannie Whayne, and Angie Maxwell, 31–61. Baton Rouge: Louisiana State University Press, 2012.

Durrill, Wayne K. *War of Another Kind: A Southern Community in the Great Rebellion.* New York: Oxford University Press, 1990.

Edmonds, Helen G. *The Negro and Fusion Politics in North Carolina, 1894–1901.* New York: Russell and Russell, 1973.

Edwards, Kathy, Esme Howard, and Toni Prawl. *Monument Avenue: History and Architecture.* National Park Service, 1992.

Eli, Shari, and Laura Salisbury. "Patronage Politics and the Development of the Welfare State: Confederate Pensions in the American South." *Journal of Economic History* 76, no. 4 (December 2016): 1078–1112.

Elon Poll. "Opinion of North Carolina Voters on State Issues: Registered Voters in North Carolina, September 25–29th, 2017." https://www.elon.edu/e/CmsFile /GetFile?FileID=1137.

Emberton, Carole, and Bruce Baker, eds. *Remembering Reconstruction: Struggles over the Meaning of America's Most Turbulent Era.* Baton Rouge: Louisiana State University Press, 2017.

Equal Justice Initiative. *Lynching in America: Confronting the Legacy of Racial Terror.* Equal Justice Initiative, 2017. Accessed at https://lynchinginamerica.eji.org /report/.

Escott, Paul D. *After Secession: Jefferson Davis and the Failure of Confederate Nationalism.* Baton Rouge: Louisiana State University Press, 1992.

———. *Many Excellent People: Power and Privilege in North Carolina, 1850–1900.* Chapel Hill: University of North Carolina Press, 2012.

Escott, Paul D., and Jeffrey J. Crow. "The Social Order and Violent Disorder: An Analysis of North Carolina in the Revolution and the Civil War." *Journal of Southern History* 52, no. 3 (August 1986): 373–402.

Faulkner, Ronnie W. "Fusion Politics." North Carolina History Project. http:// northcarolinahistory.org/encyclopedia/fusion-politics/.

———. "Convention of 1868." *NCpedia,* 2006. https://www.ncpedia.org/govern ment/convention-1868. Originally from *Encyclopedia of North Carolina,* edited by William S. Powell.

Feimster, Crystal Nicole. *Southern Horrors: Women and the Politics of Rape and Lynching.* Cambridge, MA: Harvard University Press, 2009.

Fellman, Michael. *In the Name of God and Country: Reconsidering Terrorism in American History.* New Haven, CT: Yale University Press, 2010.

———. *The Making of Robert E. Lee.* Baltimore: John Hopkins University Press, 2000.

———. *Views from the Dark Side of American History.* Baton Rouge: Louisiana State University Press, 2011.

Fennessy, Brian. "The Re-construction of Memory and Loyalty in North Carolina, 1865–1880." MA thesis, University of North Carolina at Chapel Hill, 2014.

Foner, Eric. *The Fiery Trial: Abraham Lincoln and American Slavery.* New York: W. W. Norton, 2010.

Förster, Stig. *On the Road to Total War: The American Civil War and the German Wars of Unification, 1861–1871.* Cambridge: Cambridge University Press, 2002.

Foster, Gaines M. *Ghosts of the Confederacy: Defeat, the Lost Cause, and the Emergence of the New South, 1865 to 1913.* New York: Oxford University Press, 1987.

Frisby, Derek W. "Remember Fort Pillow: Politics, Atrocity Propaganda, and the Evolution of Hard War." In *Black Flag over Dixie: Racial Atrocities and Reprisals in the Civil War,* edited by Gregory J. W. Urwin, 104–32. Carbondale: Southern Illinois University Press, 2004.

Gallagher, Gary W. *The Confederate War.* Cambridge, MA: Harvard University Press, 1997.

Gallagher, Gary W., and Alan T. Nolan, eds. *The Myth of the Lost Cause and Civil War History.* Bloomington: Indiana University Press, 2000.

Gallagher, Gary W., and Kathryn Shively Meier. "Coming to Terms with Civil War Military History." *Journal of the Civil War Era* 4, no. 4 (December 2014): 487–508.

Gannon, Barbara A. *Americans Remember Their Civil War.* Santa Barbara, CA: Praeger, 2017.

———. "Sites of Memory, Sites of Glory: African American Grand Army of the Republic Posts in Pennsylvania." In *Making and Remaking Pennsylvania's Civil War,* edited by William A. Blair and William A. Pencak, 165–88. University Park: Pennsylvania State Press, 2001.

———. *The Won Cause: Black and White Comradeship in the Grand Army of the Republic.* Chapel Hill: University of North Carolina Press, 2011.

Gardner, Sarah E. *Blood and Irony: Southern White Women's Narratives of the Civil War, 1861–1937.* Chapel Hill: University of North Carolina Press, 2006.

Genovese, Eugene D. *Roll, Jordan, Roll: The World the Slaves Made.* New York: Vintage 1976.

Gessen, Masha. "The Autocrat's Language." *New York Review of Books,* May 13, 2017. https://www.nybooks.com/daily/2017/05/13/the-autocrats-language/.

Giesberg, Judith. *Keystone State in Crisis: The Civil War in Pennsylvania.* Mansfield: Pennsylvania Historical Association, 2013.

Gikandi, Simon. *Slavery and the Culture of Taste.* Princeton, NJ: Princeton University Press, 2011.

Gilliland, Jason W. "The Calculus of Realignment: The Rise of Republicanism in Georgia, 1964–1992." *Georgia Historical Quarterly* 96, no. 4 (Winter 2012): 413–52.

Gilmore, Glenda Elizabeth. *Gender and Jim Crow: Women and the Politics of White Supremacy in North Carolina, 1896–1920.* Chapel Hill: University of North Carolina Press, 1996.

Giuffre, Katherine A. "First in Flight: Desertion as Politics in the North Carolina Confederate Army." *Social Science History* 21, no. 2 (Summer 1997): 245–63.

Glatthaar, Joseph T. "Everyman's War: A Rich and Poor Man's Fight in Lee's Army." *Civil War History* 54, no. 3 (September 2008): 229–46.

———. *Forged in Battle: The Civil War Alliance of Black Soldiers and White Officers.* Baton Rouge: Louisiana State University Press, 2000.

———. *General Lee's Army: From Victory to Collapse.* New York: Free Press, 2008.

———. *Soldiering in the Army of Northern Virginia: A Statistical Portrait of the Troops Who Served under Robert E. Lee.* Chapel Hill: University of North Carolina Press, 2011.

Goldfield, David. *Still Fighting the Civil War: The American South and Southern History.* Baton Rouge: Louisiana State University Press, 2004.

Goleman, Michael J. *Your Heritage Will Still Remain: Racial Identity and Mississippi's Lost Cause.* Jackson: University Press of Mississippi, 2017.

Gordon, Lesley J. *A Broken Regiment: The 16th Connecticut's Civil War.* Baton Rouge: Louisiana State University Press, 2014.

Gorman, Kathleen. "Confederate Pensions as Social Welfare." In *Before the New Deal: Social Welfare in the South, 1830–1930,* edited by Elna C. Green, 24–39. Athens: University of Georgia Press, 1999.

Graham, Nicholas. "The 1898 Election in North Carolina: An Introduction." The 1898 Election in North Carolina, June 2005. https://exhibits.lib.unc.edu /exhibits/show/1898/history.

———. "UNC's Union Veterans." *For the Record: News and Perspective from University Archives and Records Management Service,* May 17, 2017. http://blogs.lib.unc .edu/uarms/index.php/2017/05/uncs-union-veterans/.

Gray, Michael P., ed. *Crossing the Deadlines: Civil War Prisons Reconsidered.* Kent, OH: Kent State University Press, 2018.

Green, Elna C., ed. *Before the New Deal: Social Welfare in the South, 1830–1930.* Athens: University of Georgia Press, 1999.

———. *This Business of Relief: Confronting Poverty in a Southern City, 1740–1940.* Athens: University of Georgia Press, 2003.

———. "Protecting Confederate Soldiers and Mothers: Pensions, Gender, and the Welfare State in the U.S. South, a Case Study from Florida." *Journal of Social History* 39, no. 4 (Summer 2006): 1079–1104.

Green, Hilary. "The Persistence of Memory: African Americans and Transitional Justice Efforts in Franklin County, Pennsylvania." In *Reconciliation after Civil Wars: Global Perspectives,* edited by Paul Quigley and James Hawdon, 131–49. New York: Routledge, 2019.

Guelzo, Allen. *Gettysburg: The Last Invasion.* New York: Alfred A. Knopf, 2013.

Hall, Andy. *Dead Confederates, A Civil War Era Blog.* https://deadconfederates.com/.

———. "Fantasizing Lee as a Civil Rights Pioneer." *Civil War Monitor,* July 23, 2012. https://www.civilwarmonitor.com/blog/fantasizing-lee-as-a-civil-rights -pioneer.

Handler, Jerome S., and Michael L. Tuite Jr. "Retouching History: The Modern Falsification of a Civil War Photograph." N.d. http://people.virginia.edu/~jh3v /retouchinghistory/essay.html.

Harris, M. Keith. *Across the Bloody Chasm: The Culture of Commemoration among Civil War Veterans.* Baton Rouge: Louisiana State University Press, 2014.

Hartley, Chris J. *Stoneman's Raid, 1865.* Winston-Salem, NC: John F. Blair, 2010.

Hattaway, Herman. "Stephen Dill Lee: A Biography." PhD diss., Louisiana State University, 1969.

———. "The United Confederate Veterans in Louisiana." *Louisiana History* 16, no. 1 (Winter 1975): 5–37.

Hebert, Keith Scott. "Civil War and Reconstruction Era Cass/Bartow County, Georgia." PhD diss., Auburn University, 2007.

Helsley, Alexia Jones. *South Carolina's African American Confederate Pensioners, 1923–1925.* South Carolina Department of Archives and History, 1998.

———. "Notes and News from the Archives: Black Confederates." *South Carolina Historical Magazine* 74, no. 3 (July 1973): 184–88.

Herron, Paul E. *Framing the Solid South: The State Constitutional Conventions of Secession, Reconstruction, and Redemption, 1860–1902.* Lawrence: University Press of Kansas, 2017.

Hess, Earl J. *Civil War Infantry Tactics: Training, Combat, and Small-Unit Effective-ness*. Baton Rouge: Louisiana State University Press, 2015.

———. *Pickett's Charge: The Last Attack at Gettysburg*. Chapel Hill: University of North Carolina Press, 2001.

———. "Where Do We Stand? A Critical Assessment of Civil War Studies in the Sesquicentennial Era." *Civil War History* 60, no. 4 (December 2014): 371–403.

Hollandsworth, James G., Jr. "Black Confederate Pensioners after the Civil War." *Mississippi History Now*, http://mshistorynow.mdah.state.ms.us/articles/289/.

Horton, James Oliver, and Lois E. Horton, eds. *Slavery and Public History: The Tough Stuff of American Memory*. New York: New Press, 2006.

Horwitz, Tony. *Confederates in the Attic: Dispatches from the Unfinished Civil War*. New York: Vintage Books, 1999.

Hossfeld, Leslie H. *Narrative, Political Unconscious and Racial Violence in Wilming-ton, North Carolina*. New York: Routledge, 2005.

Hulbert, Matthew C. *The Ghosts of Guerrilla Memory: How Civil War Bushwhackers Became Gunslingers in the American West*. Athens: University of Georgia Press, 2016.

Inscoe, John C. "Guerrilla War and Remembrance." *Appalachian Journal* 34, no. 1 (Fall 2006): 74–97.

———. *Race, War, and Remembrance in the Appalachian South*. Lexington: University Press of Kentucky, 2008.

Janney, Caroline E. *Burying the Dead but Not the Past: Ladies' Memorial Associations and the Lost Cause*. Chapel Hill: University of North Carolina Press, 2008.

———. *Remembering the Civil War: Reunion and the Limits of Reconciliation*. Chapel Hill: University of North Carolina Press, 2013.

Johnson, Edward A. *History of Negro Soldiers in the Spanish-American War, and Other Items of Interest*. Raleigh, NC: Capital, 1899.

Johnson, Mark A. "'Red Flag before an Army of Old Vets': Black Musicians and the United Confederate Veterans Reunion in New Orleans, 1903." *Louisiana History* 56, no. 3 (July 2015): 315–43.

Johnson, Walter. *Soul by Soul: Life inside the Antebellum Slave Market*. Cambridge, MA: Harvard University Press, 1999.

Johnston, Angelina Ray, and Robinson Wise. "Commemorating Faithful Slaves, Mammies, and Black Confederates." Commemorative Landscapes of North Carolina, 2013. http://docsouth.unc.edu/commland/features/essays/ray_wise/.

Jones, Garett, and Robert C. Kenzer. "Confederate Pensions." *NCpedia*, 2006. https://ncpedia.org/confederate-pensions. Originally from *Encyclopedia of North Carolina*, edited by William S. Powell.

Jones, Jacqueline. *The Dispossessed: America's Underclasses from the Civil War to the Present*. New York: Basic Books, 1992.

Jones, Jeffrey M. "Democrats' Views on Confederate Flag Increasingly Negative." *Gallup*, July 8, 2015. https://news.gallup.com/poll/184040/democrats-views -confederate-flag-increasingly-negative.aspx.

Jordan, Brian. *Marching Home: Union Veterans and Their Unending Civil War*. New York: Liveright, 2014.

Jordan, Weymouth T., Jr., and Gerald W. Thomas. "Massacre at Plymouth: April 20, 1864." In *Black Flag over Dixie : Racial Atrocities and Reprisals in the Civil War*, edited by Gregory J. W. Urwin, 153–202. Carbondale: Southern Illinois University Press, 2014.

Kendi, Ibram X. *Stamped from the Beginning: The Definitive History of Racist Ideas in America*. New York: Nation Books, 2016.

Kenzer, Robert C. *Kinship and Neighborhood in a Southern Community: Orange County, North Carolina, 1849–1881*. Knoxville: University of Tennessee Press, 1987.

Key, V. O., Jr. *Southern Politics in State and Nation*. New ed. Knoxville: University of Tennessee Press, 1984.

Knotts, H. Gibbs. "Grassroots Republicanism: Evaluating the Trickle Down Realignment Theory in North Carolina." *Politics & Policy* 33, no. 2 (June 2005): 330–45.

Kruman, Marc W. "Dissent in the Confederacy: The North Carolina Experience." *Civil War History* 27, no. 4 (December 1981): 293–313.

Kytle, Ethan J., and Blain Roberts. *Denmark Vesey's Garden: Slavery and Memory in the Cradle of the Confederacy*. New York: New Press, 2018.

Layton, Tom. *The Stoneman Gazette: Reliving the Tales of Stoneman's Raid, 1865*. http://stonemangazette.blogspot.com.

Lee, Susanna Michele. *Claiming the Union: Citizenship in the Post–Civil War South*. Cambridge: Cambridge University Press, 2014.

Levin, Kevin M. "Black Confederates Out of the Attic and into the Mainstream." *Journal of the Civil War Era* 4, no. 4 (2014): 627–35.

———. *Civil War Memory: The Online Home of Kevin M. Levin*. http://cwmemory.com.

———. *Remembering the Battle of the Crater: War as Murder*. Lexington: University Press of Kentucky, 2012.

Levine, Bruce. *Confederate Emancipation: Southern Plans to Free and Arm Slaves during the Civil War*. Oxford: Oxford University Press, 2006.

———. "In Search of a Useable Past: Neo-Confederates and Black Confederates." In *Slavery and Public History: The Tough Stuff of American Memory*, edited by James Oliver Horton and Lois E. Horton, 187–212. New York: New Press, 2006.

Levinson, Sanford. *Written in Stone: Public Monuments in Changing Societies*. Durham, NC: Duke University Press, 2018.

Linenthal, Edward Tabor. *Sacred Ground: Americans and Their Battlefields*. Urbana: University of Illinois Press, 1993.

Lonn, Ella. *Desertion during the Civil War*. New York: Century, 1928.

López, Ian Haney. *Dog Whistle Politics: How Coded Racial Appeals Have Reinvented Racism and Wrecked the Middle Class*. Oxford: Oxford University Press, 2015.

Lowenthal, David. *The Past Is a Foreign Country—Revisited*. Cambridge: Cambridge University Press, 2015.

Lowery, Malinda Maynor. *Lumbee Indians in the Jim Crow South: Race, Identity, and the Making of a Nation*. Chapel Hill: University of North Carolina Press, 2010.

Mabry, William Alexander. "Negro Suffrage and Fusion Rule in North Carolina." *North Carolina Historical Review* 12, no. 2 (April 1935): 79–102.

Madsen-Brooks, Leslie. "'I Nevertheless Am a Historian': Digital Historical Practice and Malpractice around Black Confederate Soldiers." In *Writing History in the Digital Age*, edited by Jack Dougherty and Kristen Nawrotzki, 49–63. Ann Arbor: University of Michigan Press, 2013.

Mallison, Fred M. *The Civil War on the Outer Banks: A History of the Late Rebellion along the Coast of North Carolina from Carteret to Currituck.* Jefferson, NC: McFarland, 1998.

Manning, Chandra. *Troubled Refuge: Struggling for Freedom in the Civil War.* New York: Alfred A. Knopf, 2016.

Marist College Institute for Public Opinion. "A Nation Still Divided: The Confederate Flag." August 6, 2015. http://maristpoll.marist.edu/wp-content/misc/usapolls/us150722/CivilWar/McClatchy-Marist%20Poll_National%20Release%20and%20Tables_The%20Confederate%20Flag_August%202015.pdf.

Marshall, Anne E. *Creating a Confederate Kentucky: The Lost Cause and Civil War Memory in a Border State.* Chapel Hill: University of North Carolina Press, 2010.

Marten, James. *Sing Not War: The Lives of Union and Confederate Veterans in Gilded Age America.* Chapel Hill: University of North Carolina Press, 2011.

Martinez, Jaime Amanda. *Confederate Slave Impressment in the Upper South.* Chapel Hill: University of North Carolina Press, 2013.

———. "Jaime Amanda Martinez: Why Exactly Are We Commemorating 'Confederate Pensioners of Color'?" *UNC Press Blog,* December 4, 2013. https://uncpressblog.com/2013/12/04/Jaime-amanda-martinez-why-exactly-are-we-commemorating-confederate-pensioners-of-color/.

Marvel, Andrew. "The Great Imposters." *Blue and Gray Magazine* 8, no. 3 (1991): 32–33.

Maxwell, Angie. *The Indicted South: Public Criticism, Southern Inferiority, and the Politics of Whiteness.* Chapel Hill: University of North Carolina Press, 2014.

McClurken, Jeffrey W. *Take Care of the Living: Reconstructing Confederate Veteran Families in Virginia.* Charlottesville: University of Virginia Press, 2009.

McCurry, Stephanie. *Confederate Reckoning: Power and Politics in the Civil War South.* Cambridge, MA: Harvard University Press, 2012.

McElya, Micki. *Clinging to Mammy: The Faithful Slave in Twentieth-Century America.* Cambridge, MA: Harvard University Press, 2007.

———. "Commemorating the Color Line: The National Mammy Monument Controversy of the 1920s." In *Monuments to the Lost Cause: Women, Art, and the Landscapes of Southern Memory,* edited by Cynthia Mills and Pamela H. Simpson, 203–18. Knoxville: University of Tennessee Press, 2003.

McIlwain, Christopher Lyle, Sr. *1865 Alabama: From Civil War to Uncivil Peace.* Tuscaloosa: University of Alabama Press, 2017.

McKim, Randolph Harrison. *The Numerical Strength of the Confederate Army: An Examination of the Argument of the Hon. Charles Francis Adams and Others.* New York: Neale, 1912.

McKinney, Gordon B. "Zebulon Vance and His Reconstruction of the Civil War in North Carolina." *North Carolina Historical Review* 75, no. 1 (1998): 69–85.

McPherson, Tara. *Reconstructing Dixie: Race, Gender, and Nostalgia in the Imagined South.* Durham, NC: Duke University Press, 2003.

Meehan, James. "Craig, Locke." *NCpedia,* 1979. https://www.ncpedia.org/biography/craig-locke. Originally from *Dictionary of North Carolina Biography,* edited by William S. Powell.

Merritt, Keri Leigh. *Masterless Men: Poor Whites and Slavery in the Antebellum South.* Cambridge: Cambridge University Press, 2017.

Mickey, Robert. *Paths Out of Dixie: The Democratization of Authoritarian Enclaves in America's Deep South, 1944–1972.* Princeton, NJ: Princeton University Press, 2015.

Mills, Cynthia. Introduction to *Monuments to the Lost Cause: Women, Art, and the Landscapes of Southern Memory,* edited by Cynthia Mills and Pamela H. Simpson, xv–xxx. Knoxville: University of Tennessee Press, 2003.

Mills, Cynthia, and Pamela H. Simpson, eds. *Monuments to the Lost Cause: Women, Art, And the Landscapes of Southern Memory.* Knoxville: University of Tennessee Press, 2003.

Milteer, Warren Eugene, Jr. *Hertford County North Carolina's Free People of Color and Their Descendants.* Burlington, NC: Milteer, 2016.

Moore, Albert Burton. *Conscription and Conflict in the Confederacy.* Columbia: University of South Carolina Press, 1996.

Moore, James Elliott. "Moore, John Wheeler." *NCpedia,* 1991. http://ncpedia.org/biography/moore-john-wheeler. Originally from *Dictionary of North Carolina Biography,* edited by William S. Powell.

Moyers, Bill D. *Moyers on America: A Journalist And His Times.* Edited by Julie Leininger Pycior. New York: Anchor Books, 2005.

Murray, William, and Wayne Wei-Siang Hsieh. *A Savage War: A Military History of the Civil War.* Princeton, NJ: Princeton University Press, 2016.

Myers, Barton A. *Executing Daniel Bright: Race, Loyalty, and Guerrilla Violence in a Coastal Carolina Community, 1861–1865.* Baton Rouge: Louisiana State University Press, 2009.

———. "'Rebels against a Rebellion': Southern Unionists in Secession, War and Remembrance." PhD diss., University of Georgia, 2009.

———. *Rebels against the Confederacy: North Carolina's Unionists.* New York: Cambridge University Press, 2014.

Nash, Steven E. "The Immortal Vance: The Political Commemoration of North Carolina's War Governor." In *North Carolinians in the Era of the Civil War and Reconstruction,* edited by Paul D. Escott, 269–94. Chapel Hill: University of North Carolina Press, 2008.

———. *Reconstruction's Ragged Edge: The Politics of Postwar Life in the Southern Mountains.* Chapel Hill, University of North Carolina Press, 2016.

Neal, James R. "Surrendered: The Prisoner-of-War Condition in the American Civil War." PhD diss., University of Nevada, Reno, 2015.

Neely, Mark E. *Southern Rights: Political Prisoners and the Myth of Confederate Constitutionalism.* Charlottesville: University Press of Virginia, 1999.

Newell, Clayton R. *The Regular Army before the Civil War, 1845–1860.* Washington, DC: Center for Military History, 2014.

Noe, Kenneth W. "Toward the Myth of Unionist Appalachia, 1865–1883." *Journal of the Appalachian Studies Association* 6 (1994): 73–80.

Nolan, Alan T. "The Anatomy of the Myth." In *The Myth of the Lost Cause and Civil War History,* edited by Gary W. Gallagher and Alan T. Nolan, 11–34. Bloomington: Indiana University Press, 2000.

Nora, Pierre. "Between Memory and History: Les Lieux de Mémoire." *Representations* no. 26 (Spring 1989): 7–24.

Olson, Christopher. "Investigations of the CSS *Curlew:* A Victim of the Battle of Roanoke Island, North Carolina." In *Underwater Archeology Proceedings from the*

Society for Historical Archaeology Conference, edited by Paul Forsythe Johnston, 28–33. Washington, DC: Society of Historical Archeology, 1995.

———. "The *Curlew:* The Life and Death of a North Carolina Steamboat, 1856–1862." *North Carolina Historical Review* 83, no. 2 (April 2006): 139–64.

Owens, Deirdre Cooper. *Medical Bondage: Race, Gender, and the Origins of American Gynecology.* Athens: University of Georgia Press, 2017.

Paludan, Phillip Shaw. *Victims: A True Story of the Civil War.* Knoxville: University of Tennessee Press, 2004.

Paradis, James M. *African Americans and the Gettysburg Campaign.* Sesquicentennial ed. Lanham, MD: Scarecrow, 2013.

Perry, Aldo S. *Civil War Courts-Martial of North Carolina Troops.* Jefferson, NC: McFarland, 2012.

Pew Research Center. "Civil War at 150: Still Relevant, Still Divisive." April 8, 2011. http://assets.pewresearch.org/wp-content/uploads/sites/5/legacy-pdf/04-08-11 %20Civil%20War%20Release%20.pdf.

Poole, W. Scott. *Never Surrender: Confederate Memory and Conservatism in the South Carolina Upcountry.* Athens: University of Georgia Press, 2004.

Powers, Bernard. "Monumental Challenges in Charleston." *Studying the South: C of C's Program in Southern Studies,* September 19, 2017. http://blogs.cofc.edu /southern-studies-minor/2017/09/19/charlestons-monumental-task/.

Prince, K. Stephen. "Jim Crow Memory: Southern White Supremacists and the Regional Politics of Remembrance." In *Remembering Reconstruction: Struggles over the Meaning of America's Most Turbulent Era,* edited by Carole Emberton and Bruce Baker, 17–34. Baton Rouge: Louisiana State University Press, 2017.

Pryor, Elizabeth Brown. *Reading the Man: A Portrait of Robert E. Lee through His Private Letters.* New York: Viking 2007.

Ratchford, B. U., and K. C. Heise. "Confederate Pensions." *Southern Economic Journal* 5, no. 2 (October 1938): 207–17.

Reardon, Carol. *Pickett's Charge in History and Memory.* Chapel Hill: University of North Carolina Press, 1997.

Redding, Kent. *Making Race, Making Power: North Carolina's Road to Disfranchisement.* Urbana: University of Illinois Press, 2010.

Reid, Richard. "A Test Case of the 'Crying Evil': Desertion among North Carolina Troops during the Civil War." *North Carolina Historical Review* 58, no. 3 (July, 1981): 234–62.

Ring, Natalie J. "A New Reconstruction for the South." In *Remembering Reconstruction: Struggles over the Meaning of America's Most Turbulent Era,* edited by Carole Emberton and Bruce Baker, 173–202. Baton Rouge: Louisiana State University Press, 2017.

Riotto, Angela. "Beyond 'the Scrawl'd, Worn Slips of Paper': Union and Confederate Prisoners of War and Their Postwar Memories." PhD diss., University of Akron, 2018.

Rosenburg, R. B. *Living Monuments: Confederate Soldiers' Homes in the New South.* Chapel Hill: University of North Carolina Press, 1993.

Rothman, Adam. *Slave Country: American Expansion and the Origins of the Deep South.* Cambridge, MA: Harvard University Press, 2005.

Rubin, Anne Sarah. *A Shattered Nation: The Rise and Fall of the Confederacy, 1861–1868.* Chapel Hill: University of North Carolina Press, 2005.

Sarris, Jonathon Dean. *A Separate Civil War: Communities in Conflict in the Mountain South.* Charlottesville: University of Virginia Press, 2006.

Savage, Kirk. *Standing Soldiers, Kneeling Slaves: Race, War, and Monument in Nineteenth-Century America.* Princeton, NJ: Princeton University Press, 1997.

Scarboro, David D. "North Carolina and the Confederacy: The Weakness of States' Rights during the Civil War." *North Carolina Historical Review* 56, no. 2 (April 1979): 133–49.

Schickler, Eric. *Racial Realignment: The Transformation of American Liberalism, 1932–1965.* Princeton, NJ: Princeton University Press, 2016.

Sheehan-Dean, Aaron. "The Blue and the Gray in Black and White: Assessing the Scholarship on Civil War Soldiers." In *The View from the Ground: Experiences of Civil War Soldiers,* edited by Aaron Sheehan Dean, 9–30. Lexington: University Press of Kentucky, 2007.

Silkenat, David. *Driven from Home: North Carolina's Civil War Refugee Crises.* Athens: University of Georgia Press, 2016.

———. *Raising the White Flag: How Surrender Defined the American Civil War.* Chapel Hill: University of North Carolina Press, 2019.

Skopol, Theda. *Protecting Soldiers and Mothers: The Political Origins of Social Policy in United States.* Cambridge, MA: Belknap Press of Harvard University Press, 1992.

Simonds, Lucas Samuel. "A Determination Worthy of a Better Cause: Naval Action at the Battle of Roanoke Island, 7 February 1862." MA thesis, East Carolina University, 2012.

Simpson, Brooks D. *Crossroads: Where History, Scholarship, the Academic Life, and Other Stuff Meet.* https://cwcrossroads.wordpress.com.

Sithole, Jabulani, and Sibongiseni Mkhize. "Truth or Lies? Selective Memories, Imagings, and Representations of Chief Albert John Luthuli in Recent Political Discourses." *History and Theory* 39, no. 4 (December 2000): 69–85.

Smith, Claiborne T., Jr. "London, Henry Armand." *NCpedia,* January 1, 1991, http://www.ncpedia.org/biography/london-henry-armand. Originally from *Dictionary of North Carolina Biography,* edited by William S. Powell.

Smith, Michael Thomas. "Civil War Desertion." *NCpedia,* 2006. http://www.ncpedia.org/desertion-civil-war. Originally from *Encyclopedia of North Carolina,* edited by William S. Powell.

Smith, Scott R. "The Cases of Francis Marion Lundy and William Allen Lundy, Father and Son: Self-Declared Confederate Veterans and Bogus Pensioners." *Pea River Trails,* Winter 2015, 3–23.

Souders, John M., and Taylor M. Chamberlin. *Between Reb and Yank: A Civil War History of Northern Loudoun County, Virginia.* Jefferson, NC: McFarland, 2011.

Sowder, Hugo. "'In Defense of My Country': Slavery, Secession, Civil War and the Students Who Served the Confederacy from the University of North Carolina." Senior thesis, University of North Carolina Asheville, 2016.

Spencer, John W. *Terrell's Texas Cavalry.* Burnet, TX: Eakin, 1982.

Starnes, Richard. "'The Stirring Strains of Dixie': The Civil War and Southern Identity in Haywood County, North Carolina." *North Carolina Historical Review* 74, no. 3 (July 1997): 237–59.

Steward, Rodney. *David Schenck and the Contours of Confederate Identity.* Knoxville: University Tennessee Press, 2012.

Sturken, Marita. *Tangled Memories: The Vietnam War, the AIDS Epidemic, and the Politics of Remembering.* Berkeley: University of California Press, 1997.

———. "The Wall, the Screen, and the Image: The Vietnam Veterans Memorial." *Representations* no. 35 (Summer 1991): 118–42.

Stiles, T. J. *Jesse James: Last Rebel of the Civil War.* New York: Alfred A. Knopf, 2002.

Sutherland, Jonathan. *African Americans at War: An Encyclopedia.* Santa Barbara, CA: ABC-CLIO, 2004.

Sword, Wiley. *The Confederacy's Last Hurrah: Spring Hill, Franklin, and Nashville.* Lawrence: University Press of Kansas, 1993.

———. *Courage under Fire: Profiles in Bravery from the Battlefields of the Civil War.* New York: St. Martin's, 2011.

———. "Franklin: The Thunder Drum of War." In *Border Wars: The Civil War in Tennessee and Kentucky,* edited by Kent T. Dollar, Larry H. Whiteaker, and W. Calvin Dickinson, 130–44. Kent, OH: Kent State University Press, 2015.

Tate, Allen. *Jefferson Davis: His Rise and Fall, A Biographical Narrative.* Nashville: J. S. Sanders, 1998.

Tatum, Georgia Lee. *Disloyalty in the Confederacy.* Chapel Hill: University of North Carolina Press, 1934.

Trelease, Allen W. "The Fusion Legislatures of 1895 and 1897: A Roll-Call Analysis of the North Carolina House of Representatives." *North Carolina Historical Review* 57, no. 3 (July 1980): 280–309.

Trudeau, Noah Andre. *Gettysburg: A Testing of Courage.* New York: HarperCollins, 2002.

Urwin, Gregory J. W., ed. *Black Flag over Dixie: Racial Atrocities and Reprisals in the Civil War.* Carbondale: Southern Illinois University Press, 2004.

———. "Introduction: Warfare, Race, and the Civil War in American Memory." In *Black Flag over Dixie: Racial Atrocities and Reprisals in the Civil War,* edited by Gregory J. W. Urwin, 1–18. Carbondale: Southern Illinois University Press, 2014.

Vanderslice, John M. *Gettysburg: A History of the Gettysburg Battle-field Memorial Association.* Philadelphia: Memorial Association, 1897.

Vickers, James. *Chapel Hill: An Illustrated History.* Chapel Hill: Barclay, 1985.

Vincent, Tom. "'Evidence of Womans Loyalty, Perseverance, and Fidelity': Confederate Soldiers' Monuments in North Carolina, 1865–1914." *North Carolina Historical Review* 83, no. 1 (January 2006): 61–90.

Vogel, Jeffrey E. "Redefining Reconciliation: Confederate Veterans and the Southern Responses to Federal Civil War Pensions." *Civil War History* 51, no. 1 (March 2005): 67–93.

Watford, Christopher M. *The Civil War in North Carolina: Soldiers' and Civilians' Letters and Diaries, 1861–1865.* Jefferson, NC: McFarland, 2003.

———. *The Civil War Roster of Davidson County, North Carolina: Biographies of 1,996 Men before, during, and after the Conflict.* Jefferson, NC: McFarland, 2001.

Weare, Walter B. *Black Business in the New South: A Social History of the North Carolina Mutual Life Insurance Company.* Durham, NC: Duke University Press, 1993.

Webb, Mena. *Jule Carr: General without an Army.* Chapel Hill: University of North Carolina Press, 1987.

Weitz, Mark A. *A Higher Duty: Desertion among Georgia Troops during the Civil War.* Lincoln: University of Nebraska Press, 2000.

———. *More Damning Than Slaughter: Desertion in the Confederate Army*. Lincoln: University of Nebraska Press, 2008.

"Widows Entitled to Forsyth County Pensions." Reprinted in *Forsyth County Genealogical Society Journal* 23, no. 2 (Winter, 2005): 134–35.

Williams, David, Teresa C. Williams, and R. David Carlson. *Plain Folk in a Rich Man's War: Class and Dissent in Confederate Georgia*. Gainesville: University Press of Florida, 2002.

Williams, Heather Andrea. *Help Me to Find My People: The African American Search for Family Lost in Slavery*. Chapel Hill: University of North Carolina Press, 2012.

Williard, David C. "Executions, Justice, and Reconciliation in North Carolina's Western Piedmont, 1865–1866." *Journal of the Civil War Era* 2, no. 1 (March 2012): 31–57.

———. "North Carolina in the Civil War." *NCpedia*, 2010, https://www.ncpedia.org/history/cw-1900/civil-war.

Wilson, Charles Reagan. *Baptized in Blood: The Religion of the Lost Cause, 1865–1920*. Athens: University of Georgia Press, 2009.

Wilson, Clyde. "Pettigrew, James Johnston." *NCpedia*, 1994, https://www.ncpedia.org/biography/pettigrew-james-johnston. Originally from *Dictionary of North Carolina Biography*, edited by William S. Powell.

Woodward, Bob. *Fear: Trump in the White House*. New York: Simon and Schuster, 2018.

Woodward, C. Vann. *Origins of the New South, 1877–1913*. Baton Rouge: Louisiana State University Press, 2006.

———. *The Strange Career of Jim Crow*. New York: Oxford University Press, 1955.

Woodward, Colin Edward. *Marching Masters: Slavery, Race, and the Confederate Army during the Civil War*. Charlottesville: University of Virginia Press, 2014.

———. "Marching Masters: Slavery, Race, and the Confederate Army, 1861–1865." PhD diss., Louisiana State University, 2005.

Young, Kevin. *Bunk: The Rise of Hoaxes, Humbug, Plagiarists, Phonies, Post-Facts, and Fake News*. Minneapolis: Graywolf, 2017.

Index